REA

ACPL ITE
DISCARD

ALLEN COUNTY PUBLIC LIBRARY
3 1833 03248 694

327. 73 T76d
Trubowitz, Peter.
Defining the national
  interest

AMERICAN POLITICS AND POLITICAL ECONOMY

A series edited by Benjamin I. Page

DEFINING THE

NATIONAL INTEREST

CONFLICT AND CHANGE IN AMERICAN FOREIGN POLICY

Peter Trubowitz

The University of Chicago Press / Chicago & London

Allen County Public Library
900 Webster Street
PO Box 2270
Fort Wayne, IN 46801-2270

PETER TRUBOWITZ is associate professor of government at the University of Texas, Austin.

The University of Chicago Press, Chicago 60637
The University of Chicago Press, Ltd., London
© 1998 by The University of Chicago
All rights reserved. Published 1998
Printed in the United States of America
06 05 04 03 02 01 00 99 98   1 2 3 4 5
ISBN: 0-226-81302-9 (cloth)
ISBN: 0-226-81303-7 (paper)

Library of Congress Cataloging-in-Publication Data

Trubowitz, Peter.
    Defining the national interest : conflict and change in American
foreign policy / Peter Trubowitz.
        p.   cm. —(American politics and political economy)
    Includes bibliographical references (p.   ) and index.
    ISBN 0-226-81302-9 (cloth : alk. paper). —ISBN 0-226-81303-7
(paper : alk. paper)
    1. United States—Foreign relations—Case studies.
2. Regionalism—United States—Case studies. 3. Geopolitics—United
States—Case studies. I. Title. II. Series.
E183.7.T84   1998
327.73—dc21   97-16316
                                                                      CIP

⊚ The paper used in this publication meets the minimum requirements of the American National Standard for Information Sciences—Permanence of Paper for Printed Library Materials, ANSI Z39.48-1992.

For Catherine, Joshua, and Alexander

Contents

Tables

Figures

Preface

The increasing openness and integration of the world economy is challenging old assumptions about the integrity and coherence of the nation-state. The growing international mobility of goods, capital, and technology is eroding the national unit and fracturing national identities. In the United States the accelerating pace of change has proven especially uneven and disruptive. Some occupations, industries, and cities have boomed and thrived in the new global economy while others suffer severely from foreign competition, the transnationalization of capital, and rapid technological diffusion. Because globalization creates winners and losers, it generates domestic conflicts of interest over foreign policy. Industries and interest groups that coalesced around Washington's efforts to build a liberal world order a half century ago are now sharply divided over how America should respond to the hardships and dislocations caused by global market forces. The country's political leaders are also divided. Foreign policies that enjoyed widespread political support only a few decades ago are now objects of fierce and often inconclusive debate.

This book analyzes domestic political fights over America's "national interest." It shows that the kinds of political divisions spawned by the recent era of globalization are not new. America's integration into the world economy has always been uneven, and this unevenness has always been a source of domestic political conflict over foreign policy. The phenomenon is not unique to the United States, but America's great regional spread and diversity ensures that regionalism is a potent force shaping fights over the national interest. America's three great regional formations—the Northeast, the South, and the West—have always occupied different positions in the national and international economies and have had their own economic trajectories and social imperatives. As a consequence, regions have distinctive and different stakes in how Washington responds to international change. I argue that these conflicts of interest—not the tension between our Jeffersonian and Hamiltonian traditions or the institutional framework of divided government—drive domestic debates over foreign policy. The uneven regional impact of international change also creates possibilities for political coalition and consensus. This helps to explain the programmatic shifts in the definition of the national interest that have punctuated American foreign policy in the twentieth century.

The analytic framework developed here relaxes basic assumptions of international relations theory: the distinctions between national and international forces, and between the economic and security dimensions of foreign policy. It becomes possible to shift the scale of analysis from the national to the regional. This is the geographer's move. Building on the work of political and economic geographers, I develop an analytic framework that reveals how patterns of regional competition and uneven growth have shaped American foreign policy over time. The framework is applied to three periods of transformation in the nation's foreign policy—the 1890s, 1930s, and 1980s. In each period, the country's strategic goals were redefined and programmatic policy change was achieved. In each case the redefinition of America's national interest grew out of deep conflicts set in motion by international developments. As old regional alliances and policy compromises collapsed, new opportunities for coalition-building emerged. The resulting policy shifts represented the victories of new political coalitions that united two of the country's great regions (the Northeast and West in the 1890s; the Northeast and South in the 1930s; and the South and West in the 1980s) at the expense of the third. Winners imposed their vision of "the national interest."

The link between geography and politics lies at the heart of this study. My interest in this topic was first sparked when I was an undergraduate at Clark University studying with Saul Cohen. It was rekindled as a doctoral student at MIT working with Walter Dean Burnham. My intellectual debts, however, extend beyond the classroom. I have learned a tremendous amount from the work of John Agnew and Richard Franklin Bensel, and from earlier generations of American geographers. Their work helped me to see the region as the bridge between the international and the domestic. Peter Gourevitch's analyses of the external sources of domestic politics helped me formulate my own arguments about the uneven consequences of international change. So has James Kurth's writings about American foreign policy and Thomas

Ferguson's work on party politics in the United States. The "revisionist" historiography of Walter LaFeber and Thomas J. McCormick forced me to think long and hard about the relationship between ideas and interests. By going to the regional level, I was able to connect the work of revisionists with that of "realist" scholars like Stephen Krasner, whose influential study of American foreign policy started me thinking about the national interest.

Many people helped improve this book. My thanks go first to Catherine Boone who encouraged me to pursue this project and has done more than anyone else to help me clarify and elaborate my arguments. She read and reread the manuscript and put her considerable editorial skills at my disposal. Whatever the book's shortcomings, her exacting standards improved it immeasurably. I am very grateful as well to John Agnew, Richard Bensel, Walter Dean Burnham, Lynn Eden, Lloyd Gardner, John Ikenberry, James Kurth, Farid Kahhat, Dong-Won Kim, José Morande, Benjamin Page, Edward Rhodes, Elizabeth Sanders, Robert Vitalis, and Harrison Wagner for reading part or all of the manuscript — their comments and criticisms helped me sharpen my arguments. Family, friends, and colleagues have also helped me greatly. My young and rambunctious sons, Joshua and Alexander, focused my attention on the future and reminded me of the political importance of the project. My parents, Shelley Trubowitz and Jacqueline Loeb, have provided moral support, as have my good friends Ivan Mimica and Bob Vitalis. Jim Fishkin and Brian Roberts have been valuable sources of professional support. Barbara Zuckerman has provided indispensable assistance in the last year. My students at the University of Texas at Austin have been an inspiration. There is nothing like an audience of three hundred students to focus one's thinking.

A number of people have contributed in various ways to making this book possible. Robert Keohane and Joseph Nye made it possible for me to spend a year in residence at Harvard's Center for International Affairs where I launched this project. A MacArthur fellowship granted by Princeton's Center of International Studies allowed me to work full time on the project the following year. Henry Bienen, the Center's Director, was very supportive and I benefited enormously from conversations with George Downs, Michael Doyle, Aaron Friedberg, Robert Gilpin, Atul Kohli, Charles Kupchan, and Ethan Nadelman. I have also enjoyed the support of three very capable assistants — Kendra Bartsch, George Bloch, and Erik Devereux — at various stages of the project. Ben

Page, the editor of this series, encouraged the entire enterprise. So did my editor, John Tryneski, who worked his considerable magic to bring the manuscript to fruition as a book. Leslie Keros and Bob Caceres, my copyeditor, played key roles in the final stages of the process. To all of these people I offer my thanks.

CHAPTER ONE

Regional Conflict and Coalitions in the Making of American Foreign Policy

The significance of the section in American history is that it is a faint image of a European nation and that we need to reexamine our history in light of this fact. Our politics and our society have been shaped by sectional complexity and interplay not unlike what goes on between European nations.

FREDERICK JACKSON TURNER, 1925

Introduction

The history of American foreign policy is punctuated by periods of fundamental change that qualitatively separate one era of foreign policy from the next. Eras such as the 1890s and 1930s were turning points in the nation's foreign policy, portending long-term consequences for the exercise of American power abroad and reshaping Americans' conceptions of the national interest. There is widespread agreement today that America's strategic interests are changing. The breakup of the Soviet Union and the opening of borders in Central Europe have resulted in growing pressure on American leaders to "reinvent" foreign policy. Concerns about the future of America's economic power have begun to overshadow more traditional fears about the political-military balance. With this, calls have been issued for the formulation of new strategies and policies that would enhance American competitiveness and economic power in relation to other countries, and prepare the nation to deal with the harsh realities of resurgent nationalisms in Europe and elsewhere. Once again, America's leaders face the task of articulating a vision of the national interest that commands respect abroad and inspires confidence at home.

The lesson of the past is that the latter may be harder than the former—building consensus at home may be harder than winning sup-

1

port abroad. While the 1890s and 1930s were decades of policy innovation and change, they were also years of intense debate and conflict over the nation's priorities. In each period, the conventional wisdom that politics in the United States "stops at the water's edge" was betrayed by protracted and divisive conflicts over how the country should respond to the breakdown of the old international order and the emergence of new strategic realities and economic challenges. Champions of "strategic adjustment" were challenged by defenders of the status quo. Deep fault lines surfaced, and debates over foreign policy took on strongly emotional and moral overtones. In each period, leaders experienced great difficulty in building a domestic political consensus over the national interest. It is no wonder that scholars and commentators who offer such different assessments of the strategic challenges facing the United States at the end of the twentieth century can nevertheless agree that the biggest obstacles to change lie in the domestic political arena.[1]

Why do American leaders find it so difficult to define the national interest? Why is the nation's foreign policy so conflict-prone? These are old questions: they have been asked in one form or another since Alexis de Tocqueville wrote *Democracy in America.* From Tocqueville to Lippmann to Kennan, observers have argued that the American foreign policy-making process is poorly suited to the needs of a great power.[2] In comparison with other industrialized nations, where leaders usually enjoy considerable latitude in setting strategic priorities, the American foreign policy-making process is highly politicized and notoriously inefficient, making it extremely difficult for the nation's leaders to mobilize and sustain broad-based political support. Questions of foreign policy often assume a prominent role in national politics and provoke intense and bitter debate. One consequence is that the nation's ability to act strategically in world affairs is compromised.[3] America, it is often said, has great difficulty in balancing the attributes that make for successful diplomacy: realism and imagination, continuity and flexibility, vigor and moderation.

Scholars explain domestic conflict over foreign policy in two general ways. Some locate the source of conflict in America's political culture. They argue that since the country's founding, Americans have held deeply divergent images of what their nation is, or what it should be, and that these differences invariably give rise to profound disagreements over the purposes of American power and the authority to exercise it.[4] Scholars have described this tension in Americans' understand-ings of their place in the world in various ways: as Hamiltonian versus Jeffersonian philosophies, realism versus idealism, power versus lib-erty, or pragmatism versus principle. From the view that emphasizes political culture, conflicts over foreign policy are essentially conflicts over America's identity. They surface during periods of international instability and crisis. It is then that the conflict between the imperatives of security (centralization, secrecy, and dispatch) and democracy (lib-erty, openness, accountability) is most conspicuous.

A second explanation is institutional. It focuses on the structure of the American state and identifies the nation's fragmented political system as an obstacle to coherent and purposeful statecraft.[5] The "weakness" of the American state, manifest in the sharing of foreign policy-making powers between the White House and Congress, is con-sidered to be, in Edwin Corwin's famous phrase, "an invitation to struggle" for control over the authority to make policy. The fact that presidents and members of Congress face different electorates—one national, the other local—compounds the problem by providing addi-tional incentives to disagree.[6] Presidents are held accountable for the broad effect of foreign policy choices; individual members of Congress generally are not. As a result, presidents must make decisions based on a national interest while members of Congress can respond to the needs of narrower, more particularistic interests. In short, the Constitu-tion invites conflict by dividing the authority to make foreign policy between the branches of government and by giving self-interested poli-ticians who occupy different positions in the national government rea-son to compete for control over foreign policy.

These explanations share three assumptions. First, like most work on American politics, neither attaches much analytic weight to the role of international or "external" forces in shaping the domestic playing field or in explaining domestic political conflict. In both the cultural and institutional models, politicians are compelled to respond to inter-national stimuli, but disagreements over how to act are rooted in Ameri-can values and institutions that persist in essentially unchanged form from one era to the next. Second, each assumes that societal interests play a minor role in struggles over foreign policy. The source of conflict may be ideational, or it may be institutional, but seemingly in contrast to what goes on in other nations, conflicts over foreign policy in the United States are not fights about the distribution of wealth and power in American society. Finally, both assume that the appropriate level of analysis is *national:* the focus is on national political traits or structures. While subnational structures and processes may influence the policies of other nations, these approaches all but rule out this possibility in the American case.

This book offers an alternative approach to the analysis of American foreign policy. It starts from the argument that it is necessary to shift the scale of analysis. In contrast to accounts that grant primacy to national ideologies or institutions, the book identifies America's *regional* diversity as the most important source of tension and conflict over foreign policy. I show that conflicts over the purposes of American power, as well as over the constitutional authority to exercise it, are fundamentally conflicts of interest. They are regional in nature, and they grow out of the uneven nature of the nation's economic development and integration into the world economy. Different parts of the country have different stakes in how the nation responds to international challenges and opportunities because of differences in what they produce, where they look for markets, their level of technological development, and more generally, their position in the international economy. Domestic conflict over how to define America's "national interest" is the result.

Domestic conflict in the United States is played out within the institutional structures of federalism and the two-party system. Institutions do matter—they structure the process and affect the outcome of political competition. But they are not themselves the source of conflict. Ideas matter, too. For politicians, ideas are political resources used to broker compromises, build support, and marginalize opponents. The role of institutions and ideas in shaping political outcomes can be assessed only against the backdrop of the larger socioeconomic context of politics. The argument here is that the very definition of the national interest is a product of politics. For all practical purposes, the United States does not have a unique "national interest" that only the smartest and most skillful politicians can realize. Rather, the national interest is defined by those societal interests who have the power to work within the political system (i.e., maneuver in federal institutions and the party system to build winning coalitions) to translate their preferences into policy. Thus, the national interest has a social base, which is defined in this book in geographic terms.

Summary of the Argument

This argument is developed by analyzing three periods of intense conflict over foreign policy: the 1890s, 1930s, and 1980s. In each period, debates over foreign policy divided the country along regional lines. The stakes in these struggles were high. The choices politicians faced over foreign policy were also choices about how to restore domestic prosperity and social stability. These choices entailed changes in the locus and scope of political authority at the federal level, and thus promised to alter the prevailing balance of power in the polity at large. More obviously, competing visions of the national interest carried with them different prescriptions for using the taxing, spending, and investment powers of the federal government. They implied choices about which overseas markets to pursue and secure, which sectors of the economy to subsidize and which to protect, and about whose blood and treasure should be invested in the pursuit of these ends. Who wins? Who pays? These were the fundamental questions that divided the nation in the foreign policy debates of the 1890s, 1930s, and 1980s.

During the 1890s, the debate between the "imperialists" and "anti-imperialists" on overseas expansion in Latin America and the Pacific Basin pitted the industrial Northeast against the agrarian South, with the West playing a decisive "swing" role. A quarter of a century later, politicians from the urban Northeast and the South found common ground in an "internationalist" foreign policy agenda and waged a fierce battle against their "nationalist" rivals in the rural West. At issue was whether the United States should assume a more assertive role in checking the spread of fascism in Europe and Asia and in promoting global economic recovery. Sectional conflicts divided the nation again in the 1980s, when intense debates over the rising domestic costs of American international leadership came to a head.[7] What many have defined as a struggle between "liberals" and "conservatives" is more usefully understood as a conflict between two broad coalitions of interest: one based in the declining "rustbelt" economies of the Northeast, the other centered in the growing "sunbelt" regions of the South and West.

Each of these periods was marked by acrimonious domestic struggles over policies that would promote the overseas expansion of American power and influence. Time and time again, attempts to redefine the nation's strategic objectives, commercial strategy, and military posture produced protracted fights that divided Americans along the fault lines of region. In the ensuing debates, the arguments were the familiar ones. On one side were those who stressed America's strategic interests and the need to establish a larger overseas presence to advance and protect those interests. Politicians who came from parts of the country that had the most to gain from an ambitious foreign policy agenda argued that the vigorous promotion of American power abroad was necessary to guarantee security and promote prosperity. Invariably, they were the ones who made the legal or constitutional case for a strong chief executive, insisting that in matters of foreign policy, the centralization of power in the hands of the president was necessary for success in a Hobbesian world of all against all. On the other side were politicians who came from regions that would bear a disproportionate share of the domestic costs of an expansionist foreign policy. They favored more restrained and cost-conscious approaches to foreign policy and stressed domestic priorities and needs. Those who opposed expansionism argued that efforts to promote American power overseas threatened republican ideals at home by concentrating political power in the executive branch and by wasting scarce economic resources in the pursuit of misguided foreign ventures.

This book argues that conflicts over American foreign policy must be viewed in the context of larger domestic struggles for regional economic advantage and political power. In debates over American expansionism in the 1890s, 1930s, and 1980s, regions defined "the national interest" in different ways because they faced different economic and political incentives, both at home and abroad. Conflict is grounded in the fact of uneven regional development—it grows out of the striking degree of regional economic specialization and differentiation that is an enduring feature of the development of the national economy. Economic differentiation is manifest in growth rates, production profiles, employment needs, spending and taxing preferences, market orientation, and the like. It produces regional competition over how federal resources should be spent and regional conflict over the federal policy agenda. Sectional fights over the country's *foreign* policy are part and parcel of this process. Regional antagonisms flare at times of economic restructuring or distress, at precisely those moments when the problem of "strategic adjustment" in the nation's foreign policy becomes most urgent and acute. Such was the case in the 1890s and 1930s, and it is true today. Issues of regional advantage and equity become powerful forces shaping the lines of both domestic and foreign policy debate.

The concept of regional economic differentiation is a structural one. Regional economic differences give rise to divergent interests that shape, constrain, and influence the behavior of politicians. Yet to analyze political struggles at the national level, structural features of the American economy must be linked to the choices and strategies of politicians. I establish this link by making a simple assumption about political behavior: politicians are political entrepreneurs who for electoral reasons seek to secure benefits for "constituents" (voters, producers, and investors) in the form of jobs, markets, and profits.[8] Their responses to international events and trends are shaped by their interests in promoting the fortunes of geographically defined constituencies. Their ability to secure such "goods," however, depends on their ability to compete against other claimants at the national level, and to do so within the institutional structures of a federal system dominated by two national political parties. This requires politics. Allies must be found and coalitions must be built. The geographic diversity of the American economy, and especially differences in how regions are linked to the larger world economy, makes possible some regional alliances over foreign policy. It makes others extremely unlikely. When it is time to build support and forge coalitions, political leaders try to capitalize on these regional disparities by using ideologies or visions of the national interest to mobilize larger regional constituencies for collective action. They also use the machinery and resources of the federal government to broker deals and cement alliances.

Those who favor cultural or institutional explanations claim that foreign policy struggles are grounded in the conflicting preferences for power or liberty. It is true that the relationship between the exercise of American power abroad and the preservation of republican ideals at home is an uneasy one. My argument is that where politicians stand on this question depends on the interests of those they represent and the interests of those they seek to mobilize. In the 1890s, 1930s, and 1980s, politicians who championed an expansionist foreign policy— call them the Hamiltonians, the realists, or the pragmatists—were those best-placed to exercise influence over and to benefit from the centralization of authority that would accompany such a foreign policy. Other politicians and ideologues who expressed fears about the excessive growth of executive power—the Jeffersonians, the principled idealists—were the ones who knew they would have little control over the strong state. Ideas were grounded in interests, and as interests changed over time, so too did regional political ideologies. Regions that favored greater governmental activism and executive power in one period opposed it in the next. These patterns make simple cultural explanations very difficult to sustain.

When regional interests changed, so did attitudes towards state power. Institutional conflict reflected these deeper and broader patterns of societal competition. Institutional explanations locate the source of conflict over foreign policy in America's divided constitutional order, but the most persistent and divisive conflicts were not drawn along stark institutional lines. The analysis here shows that in each of these periods, the Congress itself was deeply divided over foreign policy, and that these conflicts were structured along regional lines. Moreover, very often one or both of the national parties were themselves divided over foreign policy—and the parties were internally divided along sectional lines. Areas of the country that had a stake in the policies advocated by the president were willing to give the White House greater discretionary authority in the making of foreign policy. Politicians who came from regions that feared the distributional consequences of those same policies were the ones who advocated greater congressional oversight and participation in the making of foreign policy.

Sectional analysis thus produces an explanation of foreign policy conflict that directly challenges the theoretical interpretations that dominate the literature. Sectional analysis also makes it possible to reinterpret major shifts in the nation's external orientation, and to do so in a way that challenges deeply ingrained assumptions of international relations theory. In each of the periods examined here, domestic political conflict gave way to programmatic change, and the nation's foreign policy was fundamentally altered. In the 1890s, America shed its isolationist past and embraced a more ambitious, outward-looking foreign policy geared to opening new markets in Latin America and Asia and to spreading the ideology of American liberalism. America built a modern battleship navy, transformed the protective tariff into a bargaining tool to open foreign markets, and extended its strategic reach through the acquisition of foreign lands. In the 1930s, in the midst of depression and then world war, the United States "innovated" again. The private laissez-faire diplomacy of the Roaring Twenties was superseded by more direct government intervention on behalf of liberal-internationalist goals such as free trade, equal access, and collective security. The nation's foreign policy also underwent considerable change in the 1980s. After a decade of strategic retrenchment, the United States adopted a more assertive foreign policy. Stressing the virtues of military power, America's leaders modernized the nation's forces and established a more visible presence in regions of the world deemed strategically and economically vital.

What explains these programmatic shifts in American foreign policy? International relations theory offers two competing approaches to explaining foreign policy. The Realist approach looks to forces and circumstances arising in the international or "external" environment.[9] It argues that states conduct their foreign policy for strategic reasons of state survival in the international system, in response to international pulls and pressures. Realists do not deny that domestic politics influences foreign policy; indeed, they often attribute failed foreign policies to the intrusion of domestic pressures and impulses. Realists recognize that leaders' ability to succeed abroad depends in part on their ability to succeed at home. Elite support must be cultivated, mass opinion must be educated, and the nation's industrial and technological potential must be harnessed. The tendency remains, however, to treat domestic politics as an afterthought: a kind of residual category to explain untidy facts. For Realists the pressures of international competition in an anarchic Hobbesian world weigh more heavily in the formulation of a nation's foreign policy than do domestic forces.[10] From this vantage point, explaining programmatic change in American foreign policy requires looking at the United States from the "outside-in" and linking the state's foreign policies to shifts in the global balance of power, the rise of new foreign threats, and changes in its relative position in the international pecking order.

This view contrasts sharply with another branch of international relations that gives pride of place to domestic or "internal" forces. This school of thought grows out of early twentieth-century accounts of British imperialism and German *Weltpolitik*. It locates the roots of foreign policy in the social and economic structures of states.[11] States with similar domestic economic and political makeups pursue the same kinds of foreign policies when faced with similar international situations. The international system neither greatly constrains nor dictates foreign policy; it provides opportunities. In the American context, this approach is most closely associated with so-called revisionist historians who have reinterpreted the evolution of American foreign policy from the "inside-out." In contrast to Realist accounts of American foreign policy, those working in this genre attach great weight to the nation's socioeconomic structure and, in some cases, to the character of its domestic politics in explaining its international behavior.[12] In its strongest form, the imperatives of American capitalism drive American foreign policy: as the needs of capital change, so eventually does the nation's foreign policy.[13] More refined versions of this approach offer powerful analytic tools in distinguishing between different "sectors" of capital, allowing for political rivalry and conflict among capitalists, and/or assigning much greater weight to the "nuts and bolts" of politics: interest aggregation, coalition-building, logrolling, etc.[14] Sectoral analysis is necessary but not sufficient for understanding the politics of the national interest.

Despite their many and important differences, both approaches operate at the *national* scale of analysis.[15] They ignore what for geographers working on the United States is fundamental: regional difference. Realist accounts assume that the internal consequences of "external" forces are spatially uniform inside the country. This is not the case. America as a whole may face one external setting, with all its attendant pressures and opportunities, but its implications are not the same for all Americans. Just as regions' positions in the national economy differ, so too do their connections to the world economy. International changes can thus have fundamentally different consequences for people in various parts of the country. Industry and agriculture may depend on the stability of different international markets; fast-growing or technologically advanced regions may benefit from international competition while stagnant regions may be hurt by it; regional economies that are domestic market-oriented may be less affected by foreign crises than regions that depend on exports. These kinds of economic differentiation go far in explaining why regions so often collide over the national interest. Uneven regional growth and development affects American foreign policy in another way: it is itself a major force driving changes in America's position and role in world markets. As the work of John Agnew and other historical geographers suggest, shifts in the nature of American involvement in the world system are driven as much by the process of regional growth and decline as they are by the changes on the world stage.[16]

"Internal" explanations of American foreign policy suffer from other shortcomings. Their great strength lies in opening the "black box" of domestic politics and drawing attention to the fact that foreign policy is not solely a tool of international statecraft. It is also an instrument of domestic state-building and coalition-building. What they tend to forget is that in America, as in so many other countries, politics cannot be divorced from place.[17] All politics may not be local, but as V. O. Key pointed out long ago, in the United States regions are the "building blocs" of national coalitions.[18] Like E. E. Schattsneider before him, and Walter Dean Burnham after him, Key underscored the sectional dimension of party politics in the United States.[19] These scholars showed that each of America's great party realignments was also a sectional realignment, bringing with it a major shift in the underlying distribution of regional power at the national level. What is left out of existing accounts is the important role that foreign policy played in these "bloodless revolutions." As the analysis developed here will show, it is no accident that past periods of protracted struggle over the nation's foreign policy coincided with the erosion of existing regional alignments in the party system, and with acute political struggles between coalitions advancing conflicting regional agendas.

The implication of the sectional analysis developed in this book is that the distinction between the "external" and the "internal" that underlies both realist and "domestic structure" theories of foreign policy is an artificial one. My point is not that American foreign policy is the result of a combination of internal *and* external forces. This is obvious, even to those who subscribe to one school of thought or the other. Rather, the more fundamental point is that the two are so interwoven that drawing distinctions between them makes it impossible to explain foreign policy change. What is needed is a theoretical approach that transcends this false dichotomy between *Aussenpolitik* and *Innenpolitik,* between the "outside" and the "inside."

In this book, I offer such an approach by placing historic battles over the direction of American foreign policy in the context of broad changes—both at home and abroad—that have shaped the political economy and domestic politics of America in the twentieth century. I have made the *region,* lying at the intersection of international and domestic politics, the unit of analysis. This is the geographer's move. By changing the scale of analysis and moving to the subnational level, it is possible to explain patterns of conflict and consensus over the national interest, as well as the dynamic of stability and change in American foreign policy.

Theoretical Foundations

Most accounts of American foreign policy ignore sectionalism as a cause of domestic conflict.[20] At best it is seen as a contingency that accounts for specific policy conflicts at particular points in time. This reflects the widely accepted belief among foreign policy analysts that politics in the United States has become increasingly "nationalized" and divorced from place-specific interests. The regional nature of struggles that shaped the political debates in the nineteenth century over foreign trade, American involvement in European affairs, and continental expansion is generally assumed to have withered away in the twentieth century with the closing of the "national frontier," the steady urbanization of the American landscape, and the nation's integration into the world economy. Analysts now identify ideological and institutional cleavages at the national level as the source of political conflict, consensus, and stalemate over foreign policy. Sectionalism is viewed as a relic of America's past, a primitive impulse that has been displaced by the march of time.

Three claims about American foreign policy are developed in this book. The first is that place matters. When viewed over time and across a wide range of issues, sectional interests emerge as a powerful and consistent force shaping the nation's foreign policy. Foreign policy issues are debated in terms of their immediate and longer-range consequences for regional prosperity and social order. A second argument is that these sectional conflicts reflect the geographically uneven nature of American involvement in the world economy. The third claim follows from the first two: there is no single national interest. Analysts who assume that America has a discernible national interest whose defense should determine its relations with other nations are unable to explain the persistent failure to achieve domestic consensus on international objectives. A regional framework, which focuses on the competition among domestic coalitions for control of the foreign policy agenda, reveals how politically contingent the national interest actually is.

The book builds on a rich tradition of analysis in the field of geography that identifies regionally based political competition as one of the most distinctive and enduring features of American politics. Frederick Jackson Turner first identified the significance of sectionalism in the United States, declaring that "[t]here is no more enduring, no more influential force in our history than the formation and interplay of the different regions of the United States."[21] Drawing a parallel to European politics, Turner claimed that sections in the United States were comparable in scale to the nations that made up the European scene, and that the relations among them could be studied *as if* they were separate nations competing for political power and economic advantage. "The American section," he argued a few years after World War I, "may be likened to the shadowy image of the European nation, to the European state denatured of its toxic qualities."[22] For Turner, the section was one of the two great pivots of American politics (the other was "the frontier").[23]

In the wake of Turner's seminal work, a large literature has developed on the sources of regional strife over national political decisions. A common theme in this literature is that in the United States, regional political competition stems from conflicts of economic interest in general and from the geographically uneven nature of economic growth and development in particular.[24] The environmental determinism sometimes ascribed to Turner has been replaced by a more nuanced understanding of how regional interests form, and by a healthier appreciation of historical contingency. What remains however is a strong conviction that in America, sectional strife is, to use Richard Franklin Bensel's words, "grounded in economic competition."[25] In many other countries, regional strife is associated with ethnic or religious difference, even in cases where regions are economically differentiated. These political systems are typically studied within a center-periphery perspective, where regionalism manifests itself in the form of protest by culturally distinctive peripheries against political and economic exploitation by the center.[26] While ethnic and religious diversity is also an important feature of American politics, it is most conspicuous and salient at the "microregional" (neighborhood and city) level. At the "macroregional" level, the absence of the kinds of cultural cleavages present in other nations has meant that sectionalism is usually grounded in conflicts of economic interest.[27]

Uneven Growth and Foreign Policy

Since the nation's inception, the national economy has been marked by regional specialization and differentiation. Regions specialized in the production of goods for which they had a comparative advantage and "exported" to other regions, producing structural interdependencies among them. The circular and cumulative relationship between regional specialization and regional integration was a principal driving force in the rise of a nationally integrated set of regional economies by the beginning of the twentieth century.[28] Since then, and especially since World War II, the structure of regional specialization has undergone considerable change. Structural economic differences continue to be a profound discriminator among regions, however. Despite decades of regional convergence in the percentage of manufacturing jobs, improvements in transportation and communication, and heightened capital mobility, regional economic specialization remains an enduring fact of the nation's economic life.[29] The common identification of the Great Lakes with manufactures, the Southwest with raw materials, the Great Plains with agriculture, and so on, rests on firm empirical foundations.

Geographers stress a number of factors to explain the uneven nature of economic growth.[30] Some emphasize spatial variations in resources, markets, or the cost of factors of production.[31] Others focus on regional variation in technological innovation, or in the organization of labor and production.[32] In addition to analyzing factors internal to regions, geographers have also studied how growth trajectories are shaped by interaction between regions and by larger national processes. There is also a growing body of work on the international sources of regional growth and decline.[33] Geographers have devoted considerable attention to the role that the federal government plays in shaping patterns of investment and spending in the national economy and thus, possibilities for regional development.[34] Employing these approaches, geographers working on the United States have documented and analyzed sharp differences in regional economic structure. Their work has provided a foundation for analysts interested in explaining patterns of sectional conflict over national policy.

Differences in regional economic structure have political implications. Regional specialization gives rise to divergent interests which, in turn, can produce regional conflict. One reason for this is that regions differ in terms of their competitiveness, the composition of their labor force, and their vulnerability to fluctuations in demand. As a result, national policies that may promote growth in some regions may have the opposite effect in others. Regions tend to grow at different rates, due to differences in their international competitiveness, level of technological advancement, and social conditions of production (e.g., labor costs, unionization, tax structures, etc.). Such disparities have often led to regional conflict over federal policies that are perceived to propagate regional bias. Regional specialization can also lead to regional conflict when regions occupy sequential positions in the exchange process. The goods produced by one region may be inputs into the production of commodities in other regions, either in the form of raw materials, capital goods, or labor costs, leading to conflict over terms of trade. These sources of regional tension are well understood by geographers who study American domestic politics.

These sources of regional tension can also give rise to divergent sectional preferences when it comes to foreign policy. Three considerations are especially important in shaping regional attitudes. The first is export dependence.[35] Regions that specialize in sectors that are export dependent are likely to favor policies that promote liberal, open, or free trade, and to be more willing to permit the market to control their trade flows.[36] Regions that are heavily dependent on the home market or less well placed in global competition are more likely to support active government intervention to shelter or protect their markets from foreign competitors. The salience of this difference is most obvious in the area of trade policy, but as I will show, it also influences regional attitudes towards foreign policy more generally.

To see the political implications of regional differences in export dependence, one can start with a view widely held by students of international politics: international stability is a prerequisite for open trade, and such stability only arises in the presence of a "hegemonic power" willing and able to provide the collective goods of international economic predictability and international security.[37] As the world's dominant power, the hegemon has an incentive to cover the "overhead costs" of maintaining such a system: a powerful military, easy credit for foreigners, an open domestic market, and so on. This book grounds the conventional logic of "hegemonic stability" in a domestic political analysis by revealing the implications of the *regionally uneven* distribution of hegemony's costs and benefits. Hegemony may mean greater international "stability," but the benefits of such stability are not shared equally within the hegemonic country. Regions that are most export-dependent stand to reap most of the benefits of the exercise of hegemonic leadership and therefore have a far greater incentive to pay the necessary overhead costs. (If they can free-ride, as southern cotton exporters free-rode on British hegemony in the nineteenth century, so much the better.) This means that the willingness of elected officials to pay the "overhead charges" of hegemonic leadership (including the costs of defense spending, forward defense, and even military intervention) will vary, depending in large measure on their judgments about how such policies are likely to affect the fortunes of the parts of the country they represent. This was true in each of the cases examined in this book. Debates over security matters were symptomatic of deeper regional conflicts over the nation's commercial objectives.

A second consideration is particularly important in shaping regional attitudes toward foreign policy: federal foreign policy expenditures affect regional economies. In general, federal spending has a significant impact on regional growth and development, and military spending may be the most obvious case of this.[38] Military spending has clearly played a major role in shaping patterns of regional growth since World War II, when military spending consumed an ever-larger proportion of federal budgetary outlays. The same was true in the 1890s, when military expenditures also increased dramatically. Various locational factors (availability of skilled labor, industrial specialization, local tax structures, real estate prices, etc.) give some regions advantages as "sites" for military production, military bases, and military fortifications.[39] Regions that stand to reap the largest rewards (i.e., jobs, profits, growth) from military spending are more likely to favor such federal outlays than those which are less "ideal" as defense-production locations.[40] Parts of the country that pay the "overhead costs" of an expensive national defense while receiving a disproportionately small share of the rewards are likely to see costly foreign policies in "guns-versus-butter" terms. Indeed, in each of the cases examined here, the "relative gains" from defense spending emerged as a major source of political conflict among regions. The fights assumed a zero-sum character: a gain for one region was seen as a loss for another (at least by those representing the regional "loser"). In other words, defense spending was viewed as a transfer payment—it was seen in *redistributive terms.*

Studies that failed to uncover a "pork barrel" or "distributive politics" logic in U.S. defense spending missed the *re*distributive dimension of defense politics; thus they were mistaken when they concluded that "interests" have very little to do with where politicians stand on security matters.[41] It turns out that defense procurement decisions are not just about distributing pork. Politicians deserve more credit as political entrepreneurs than "pork barrel" models concede. The analysis presented in this book shows that who supports and who opposes military spending depends on politicians' judgments about the *net benefits* of those budgetary allocations for their constituencies.[42] Politicians face difficult trade-offs when thinking about defense policy. They weigh the economic benefits of federal military spending against opportunity costs. These "costs" are usually expressed in terms of inequitable tax burdens, increased local spending to cover social services (i.e., decreased *federal* spending on social services), or deteriorating terms of interregional trade. From a practical standpoint, the problem facing politicians is one of anticipating how federal priorities might affect the interests they represent in the medium- to long-run. These judgments are historically contingent: the case histories show that the trade-off facing the southern lawmaker in the 1890s was different from the one facing the northeastern politician in the 1980s. The constant is that both politicians were deeply concerned about the opportunity costs of defense expenditures for growth in the regions they represented.

A third consideration is how structural economic differences and interregional relationships can affect foreign policy preferences. Economic specialization means that regions occupy distinct positions in national and international markets (they can be competitive or non-competitive; export-dependent, import-dependent, and/or reliant on the home market), concentrate in the production of different commodities and goods (e.g., industry versus agriculture), and sell on different kinds of markets, both at home and abroad (e.g., industrialized countries as opposed to developing countries). These differences can in themselves give rise to divergent preferences over issues related to tariffs, export promotion, and defense expenditure. When regions' foreign policy preferences or needs are mutually exclusive, or when one region's gain is another's loss, conflict can arise. Tension and conflict is most likely when regions occupy sequential positions in the exchange process and when foreign policy decisions affect interregional terms of trade.

Conflict over foreign economic policy may arise between regions specializing in the production of raw materials and agriculture and regions that dominate the key circulation sectors of finance, commerce, and transportation. The classic example is the struggle between North and South over the strategic power that northern traders, bankers, and shippers held over southern cotton producers in the Atlantic trade arena, which contributed to southern secession and Civil War. In this case the struggle was exacerbated by conflicts between northern and southern producers—another form of exchange conflict—over the tariff and access to foreign markets.[43] The industrializing North relied on the agrarian South as a source of cheap raw materials and as a protected market for its high-priced industrial output, leading southern producers to search for alternative markets in Europe. In situations like these, regions that are disadvantaged may seek to alter foreign economic policies and tariff arrangements that give the dominant region strategic advantages in interregional trade. Political conflict is the predictable result. Arguments may take the form of debate over constitutional principle or strategic necessity, but the divergent preferences stem from conflicts of economic interest.

Sectionalism in American Politics

It is often said that America's political system is weak in the sense that power is fragmented and dispersed. Power is divided horizontally among the executive, legislative, and judicial branches, and vertically among federal, state, and local governments. To a greater extent than in other advanced industrialized nations, in the United States "policies require politics."[44] Federalism, separation of powers, and checks and balances make policy-making cumbersome and incremental. They have another effect as well: they accentuate regionalism as a force in the nation's political life. America's fragmented and dispersed institutional structure makes it necessary to develop regionally oriented political strategies to capture national power and shape policy. In the halls of Congress, in the party "war rooms," and out on the hustings, America's institutions give politicians reason to think "geopolitically."

The incentives and advantages in doing so are obvious. America's state may be weak, but it also commands great resources. In the foreign policy domain, federal control over major resources and "tools" of statecraft—military force, the tariff, and foreign aid—obviously provides incentives for regional interests to compete for influence and control in Washington. Meanwhile, many of the federal government's actions on the domestic front have very significant consequences at the regional level (even though it has rarely adopted policies that are explicitly designed to shape the regional distribution of economic activity).[45] This has become increasingly evident as the central state's powers and the resources available to it have increased. The state's growing role in determining the profitability of individual sectors of the economy, as well as its espousal of principles such as full employment and community preservation, make it a forum for regional interests seeking economic advantage and social redress.

As a result, influence within the state has become a primary objective of regional interests and groups, especially when the government's actions have distinctly uneven regional effects. Establishing control over strategic positions in the national government gives politicians and the voters and businessmen who "invest" in them considerable leverage in the battle for federal resources. In this competition, the central question is not whether an issue has to do with matters that lie inside or outside the nation's borders. The core issue is the redistributive consequences of the federal government's actions. When foreign policy strategies, doctrines, or expenditures are perceived to disproportionately benefit (or burden) one section of the country—as was the case during the 1890s, 1930s, and 1980s—regions react. Due to the fragmented structure of the federal government, regional interests have a large number of institutional channels or "access points" to levy claims on federal resources, initiate or obstruct policy change, and seek political protection from the vagaries of national and international competition.[46] In these struggles, institutional decentralization and the requirements of "majority rule" force politicians to pool their political power to be effective in a political setting that is, in Burnham's words, "dedicated to defeat."[47]

Building regionally oriented coalitions in Congress is a time-honored means of building voting blocs to advance common interests. This political strategy helps to ensure that sectional interests find expression at the national level. Sometimes regionally based congressional "blocs" assume quasi-institutional form. The Farm Bloc of the 1920s and, more recently, the Northeast-Midwest Coalition, are well-known examples. In other instances, the "ties that bind" regional representatives in Congress are more informal: examples include the urban-based Democratic Study Group, the largely western Rural Caucus, the New England Caucus, and the like.[48] Such blocs or groups are dominated by politicians from one part of the country, but their membership is often cross-regional. There is a good reason for this. The institutional imperative of majority rule forces congressional leaders hoping to influence national policy to seek extraregional support. A classic example is the Conservative Coalition—a loosely knit congressional bloc of southern Democrats and conservative Republicans, mostly from the Midwest—that sought to thwart Franklin Roosevelt's 1936 campaign promises for social reform.[49] Building regional coalitions around one set of issues often requires compromising on others: votes are traded, logrolls are brokered, and agreements to disagree are made.

The federal structure of the American political system heightens the role of territoriality in structuring national politics.[50] All societal interests are forced by the spatially decentralized nature of electoral politics to *organize geographically* to compete for political control over the central state. The national parties must do the same. As Archer and Taylor put it, "de jure spatial organization makes de facto sectional spatial organization a vital consideration."[51] One result is that sectionalism is a powerful force in national elections. Presidents, and their challengers, play sectional politics by using policy platforms to bridge regional differences within their party or to sow divisions within the opposition. Presidential politics can thus *heighten* sectional differences. More generally, party rivalry for control over the federal government can have the same effect. This process is well understood by analysts who study the regional bases of conflict over domestic policy matters.[52] This book shows that the same processes are played out in the domain of foreign policy. In fact, in the game of practical politics, sharp distinctions between "foreign" and "domestic" policy are rarely drawn.

The interplay of sectional interests at the national level and the role of electoral institutions in aggregating and mediating regional demands means that the political process itself plays a role in shaping regional interests. In foreign as well as domestic affairs, political parties are one mechanism for building regional coalitions and devising composite political responses to distinct regional interests.[53] Political ideologies (e.g., imperialism, internationalism, anticommunism) are another. Ideologies play a role in mobilizing regional interests, articulating regional concerns, binding cross-regional coalitions, and dividing the opposition.[54] So ideas do matter in politics: the issue is how, and under what conditions. In the foreign policy struggles of the 1890s, 1930s, and 1980s, they were at the service of powerful political interests. They provided the glue that cemented new geopolitical alliances—*domestic* geopolitical alliances around programmatic foreign policy change. The empirical chapters that follow show that parties and ideologies play an important role in determining how sectional conflicts that are grounded in patterns of uneven development are ultimately played out at the national level.

There is a large interdisciplinary literature on the ways in which regional politics has shaped the evolution of the American political system and the broad contours of national policy. Decisive periods of economic restructuring and political realignment—"turning points" in the nation's political life such as the 1890s, 1930s, and 1980s—have been interpreted as "geographic events" that spring from underlying shifts in the geography of economic activity and political power.[55] These transformations grow out of long-term stresses (e.g., industrial restructuring, new political divisions, mounting social conflict) in civil society that gradually accumulate and erode the existing regime for regulating economic and political life. The rupture of the old regime paves the way for changes that are clearly visible in the national political arena—the forging of new regional political bonds, new institutional networks for mediating political conflict, and new alignments of region and party.[56] The constellation of international and domestic forces that gives rise to these political upheavals varies. Obviously, the specific events and issues that finally trigger political realignment vary as well. Yet across cases, the net outcome is new configurations of regional power at the national level, the effects of which can be seen in the issues that make up the national policy agenda and the legislation enacted by the central state.

As this book shows, the geopolitics of American political development has a great deal to offer to the study of foreign policy. The historical canvas is wide; political economy considerations are prominent; politics has clear territorial dimensions; and the push-and-pull of electoral politics and policy-making is viewed against the broad backdrop of societally driven competition for power and advantage. Ideologies and institutional arrangements are important when analyzed within this broader context—they should not be seen as determinant because they are themselves outcomes of political competition. From this perspective, the government or state is an "arena" in which the struggles of place-specific interests are expressed and institutionalized. This is a decidedly society-centered view of the state: the national government is a "site" of competition and conflict for the resources and power the central state commands.[57] At this level, there is an affinity between sectional and class explanations of American politics in general and of American foreign policy in particular.[58] The distinction between the two is that for those who view American politics from a geographic perspective, economic interests are believed to find their clearest political expression as sectional or regional interests. As Turner put it, "[e]conomic interests are sectionalized" in the United States.[59]

This book analyzes the transformations in foreign policy that culminated in the 1890s, 1930s, and 1980s. "Strategic adjustment" in each of these eras coincided with fundamental shifts in the underlying structure of domestic political and economic power. Each of these key junctures in American history grew out of uneven patterns of regional economic growth and development, acute political conflict between regions driven by different economic and political imperatives, and partisan competition for advantage as new issues forced their way onto the national agenda. These upheavals produced new regional alliances and shifted the geographical bases of the national parties, thus altering the ability of regional interests to compete effectively for national power. As the case histories will show, the realignments were decisive in shaping possibilities for consolidating domestic consensus over the national interest.

Research Design and Methods

This study takes a comparative-historical approach to American foreign policy: support for the central argument is built by drawing comparisons between places, across issues, and over time. The basic unit of analysis is the region. This term refers to "a group of geographically contiguous areas which have certain common or complementary characteristics or which are tied by extensive interareal activity or flows."[60] In this study, I utilize the classic tripolar grouping that divides contemporary America's states into three "great regions," following roughly along the courses of the Mississippi and Ohio rivers: the Northeast, the South, and the West.[61] Imposing these categories on the "data" makes it possible to draw directly on the impressive body of literature on America's regional geography that is organized along comparable lines.[62] The "macroregional" level of analysis is supplemented as needed by more nuanced "microregional" analysis. Intraregional differences and urban-rural cleavages figure prominently in parts of the study. They too are part of America's political geography.

Foreign policy debate in each of the three historical periods involved bitter quarrels over America's ideals and the proper balance of constitutional power. All three eras have been scrutinized by scholars who attribute the divisiveness of the debates to either political culture or institutional structure. The periods selected thus provide "hard" tests for the argument that debates over the purposes of American power and the authority to exercise it can be best understood as conflicts of sectional interest. A comparative-historical approach makes it possible to show that as a region's position in the world economy varies, so too does its foreign policy preferences. This same approach makes it possible to rule out the rival explanations of foreign policy conflict.

In an analysis that is comparative and historical, one can "control for" political culture and its symbols (ideas, beliefs, values). Culture is relatively enduring; it cannot explain change (or reversals) in regional preferences from one generation to the next. By showing that sectional preferences toward the question that divided Hamilton and Jefferson—the question of America's mission—vary as sectional interests change, I effectively rule out America's "bipolar culture" as the fountainhead of conflicts over foreign policy.[63] "Testing" the relative explanatory power of institutional explanations and an interest-based, sectional account of foreign policy conflict is also straightforward. Institutionalist arguments take two forms. The standard one is that conflicts are grounded in a "fusion of functions and division of power" between the executive and legislative branches.[64] Call this the "strict" reading of the institutionalist's argument. A looser interpretation would move political parties to the forefront and explain foreign policy conflict this way: the party in power (i.e., the party occupying the White House) is opposed by the party out of power.[65] Fights over foreign affairs would thus be explained by the electoral rewards that party leaders can obtain by exploiting foreign policy matters to win votes, create patronage, and enhance the prestige of party leaders. If one adopts the strict reading, the hard "test" of the interest-based account is whether or not sectional cleavages in Congress structure fights over constitutional balance, and over how much power to concede to the White House. The analysis here shows that they do. In the case of the looser reading, the "test" is whether the parties speak with one voice on foreign policy matters, or split along lines that are consistent with a sectionally based explanation that places great weight on uneven development. A party-based explanation may provide a good "fit" in one of the periods. The comparative-historical approach used here reveals that it does not hold up over time. A sectionally grounded model does.

The book's central empirical task is to show that conflicts over American foreign policy have consistently divided the nation along sectional lines. In approaching this task, the study focuses on the House of Representatives.[66] Following other students of American politics, I treat the Congress as a "proxy" for the polity at large.[67] It is viewed as a "composite mirror" of the nation's politics—a reflection of the multitude of political forces, pressures, and contingencies that move the nation.[68] Members of Congress must take positions on most of the important foreign policy issues that the country faces. The positions they take, and the public explanations they offer, provide valuable information about how they see the world and about what they believe the implications of different policies to be. When viewed in conjunction with other data, such as their constituents' economic needs, their party affiliation, and their political power within the institutional structures of Congress, their choices (votes) and how they defend them reveal a great deal about motives. These sources of data also tell us much about what moves the parts of the nation they represent. This is because politicians who seek reelection must balance their own idiosyncratic impulses and ideological preferences against the practical reality of their constituents' interests and needs.

My methodological approach is both quantitative and qualitative. Many different types of quantitative data are used to describe regions' relative positions in the national and international economies, to track changes along these dimensions over time, and to analyze congressional voting alignments on foreign policy issues. The main measure of political alignments is congressional roll call votes. In each of the periods, votes were selected on three foreign policy issues that were identified by contemporary observers, as well as latter day historians, as bellwethers of the period. To facilitate comparison across time periods and to demonstrate the robustness of the sectional explanation, issues were selected across three broadly construed categories: foreign trade, defense spending, and foreign intervention.[69] The analysis shows that in a single time period, the same regional cleavages appear across all three issue areas.

The interpretation of congressional voting alignments is guided by an analysis of foreign policy debates in Congress. For most of the issues examined here, there is an impressive secondary literature produced largely by historians. Historians and other foreign policy analysts, however, make conflicting judgments about "what happened" and why. And because most adopt a national scale of analysis, they tend to ignore or downplay regional themes and variations in interests. Sectional conflict does appear prominently in primary sources such as the *Congressional Record,* which I rely on heavily as a record of public discourse over foreign policy. Yet one quickly learns that the *Record* does not speak for itself: analysts predisposed to cultural, institutional, or interest explanations will have no trouble finding prima facie evidence for their case. What is required is a method of "controlling" for plausible alternative interpretations. Here, the comparative-historical framework employed in this study provides great analytic leverage. By mapping-out the relationship between "rhetoric" and sectional interest, and comparing the two over time, I show that regions' foreign policy preferences change as their interests do.

Overview of the Analysis: Sectional Struggles over Foreign Policy in the 1890s, 1930s, and 1980s

Like so many of the fights over national policy during the late nineteenth century, the great debates over overseas expansion pitted the industrial Northeast against the agrarian South. The Republican Northeast was the region that had the most to gain from a strategy of imperial expansion, and thus its politicians backed a host of economic and military policies designed to open and secure new markets in Latin America and Asia in an era of great power rivalry and domestic upheaval. For the Democratic South, such a strategy offered few benefits and many costs. It also was fraught with risk: the threat of provoking British economic retaliation. The South favored a more laissez-faire foreign policy, a strategy that would involve continued reliance on British power to guarantee prosperity for the region's export-dependent growers and merchants. In this battle between North and the South, the key to success lay in political alliance with the "swing region," the West. Recognizing this, northern Republican leaders, who controlled the machinery of the national government, fashioned a foreign policy platform that enabled them to capture western support for their expansionist cause. In the process, they expanded their party's power in the trans-Mississippi West. America became a great power and the Republicans consolidated their control over the national political economy.

During the Great Depression, conflicting regional imperatives once again shaped debates over foreign policy. Lawmakers clashed over the causes of the depression and how the United States should respond to the international political upheavals it set in motion. The key question was whether or not America should assume an active role in promoting global economic recovery and preventing the emergence of closed spheres of influence in Europe and Asia. One side pressed the government to don the mantle of hegemony that Great Britain had long since given up (and which America once before, in the wake of World War I, had cast down). Politicians from parts of the country that had the

most to gain from an open, interdependent world economy—the urban Northeast and the agrarian South—generally favored policies designed to promote commercial liberalization, global monetary cooperation, and collective defense against Germany and the other Axis
powers. Opposed by a powerful "nationalist" movement based in the
West, internationalists in the Northeast's big urban-industrial metropolises joined political forces with the "small-town big men" who ruled
the South. Once again, the very policies that set American foreign relations on a new course helped to reshape America's own political landscape. Internationalism was one of the devices used by Roosevelt to
bridge that great fault line in American politics—the Mason-Dixon line.
The foreign policy nationalists, representing areas of the country that
depended on the home market for their prosperity, were forced on
the defensive, fighting rearguard battles against free trade, aiding the
Allies, and the 1930s military buildup. Westerners waged their fight
against internationalism by deploying the weapon of the weak, invoking Jefferson's admonitions against executive power. In the end, the
North-South internationalist coalition overwhelmed nationalist opposition and formed the foundation of the Cold War consensus to come.

By the 1980s, the battle lines had been redrawn once again. The
Northeast stood on one side, the South and West on the other. At issue were the uneven costs and benefits of policies associated with the
Pax Americana of the Cold War era. Once the fountainhead of Cold
War internationalism, the aging Northeast became a reservoir of neo-
isolationism, unwilling to pay the "overhead charges" of global stability
and economic openness: large defense budgets, low tariff barriers, and
extensive overseas commitments. Caught in the vise of "deindustrialization," political leaders in the largely Democratic Northeast backed a
policy of "strategic retrenchment." They combined appeals for defense
cutbacks with demands for increased protection from foreign imports
and greater congressional control over the nation's warmaking capacity. In the 1980s, it was the once-solid Democratic South and the Republican West—America's newest industrialized regions—that had the
most to gain from foreign policies that checked threats to international
stability and promoted the free movement of capital, goods, and currencies. By pushing a foreign policy agenda antithetical to the interests of
the declining Northeast, Republican leaders heightened North-South
tensions within the Democratic party and moved one step closer to
cementing the sectional coalition that had eluded agrarians nearly one

hundred years earlier: the southern-western alliance. In the foreign policy arena, this alliance successfully reversed a decade of foreign policy retrenchment and reasserted American "leadership" abroad.

In each of these periods, politicians from different parts of the country sought to equate regional interests with the national interest. Foreign policy issues were debated in terms of their immediate impact on regional prosperity and their longer-range consequences for the social and political arrangements that sustained regional economies. Elected officials approached foreign affairs in the same way they often think about domestic policies: in terms of who wins and who loses at home. The reason for this is straightforward. The domestic costs and benefits of decisions about the national interest are never distributed evenly across the country. The choices politicians made over foreign policy in the 1890s, 1930s, and 1980s reflected the fact that decisions over the nation's strategic objectives, market orientation, and military posture are not geographically neutral. There are regional winners and regional losers. Those who represented parts of the country that stood to benefit from foreign policies that would centralize power in the Executive Branch were the ones who espoused Hamilton's *raison d'état.* Competing visions of America's place in the world were grounded in sectional interests, and the institutional conflicts that arose between the executive and legislative branches reflected patterns of competition that were grounded in these broader societal conflicts over wealth and power.

It is impossible to explain the sectional nature of these conflicts without a mapping of the nation's economic geography. Functional position in the world and national economies alone, however, is too thin a reed to support a full account of shifts of such magnitude in the nation's foreign policy. In each period, the programmatic foreign policy agendas that ultimately triumphed promoted domestic political ends as well. The strategy of overseas expansion in the 1890s provided Republican leaders in the Northeast with a powerful weapon to divide western and southern agrarians and to strengthen their party's hold on the machinery of government. During the Great Depression, Franklin Roosevelt used internationalism both as a weapon to divide the once-dominant Republicans along East-West lines and to dampen the historic rivalry between North and South. The growing competitiveness of the urban Northeast created new "political space" for Democrats who had long tried to piece together a coalition encompassing northern elites and labor and the southern oligarchy. The New Deal coalition provided the underpinnings of America's postwar liberal-internationalist agenda: the exercise of American leadership after World War II was contingent upon it. When the coalition began to unravel along North-South lines in the 1970s, it opened new opportunities for Republican party leaders intent on building a "New Republican Majority" in the sunbelt states of the South and West. Domestic issues as well as foreign policy ones like the "Soviet threat" were used as "wedges" to divide regions, expand the Republican's electoral base in the South, and mobilize constituencies in the West. Here too, exigencies of domestic party politics help explain a major shift in the orientation of U.S. foreign policy. The masterminds and logicians of the 1980s "right turn" used foreign policy issues to promote domestic political ends. At the same time, the shift in domestic politics made possible the reassertion of American leadership abroad.

Politics is required to turn sectional interests into coalitions capable of realizing programmatic change in the nation's foreign policy. But the possibilities for party-building and state-building are not unlimited. They are constrained by economic realities. This is as true today as it was one hundred years ago. In the 1890s, hard-pressed western farmers, unlike southern cotton growers, saw advantages in an ambitious foreign policy aimed at opening markets in the underdeveloped regions of Latin America and Asia. This was a precondition for building an East-West alliance in favor of overseas expansionism. By the time of the 1929 Wall Street crash, the "structural conditions" that made this alliance possible had been transformed. The urban Northeast no longer benefited from the narrow imperialism of the 1890s. Big cities like New York, Chicago, and Detroit were now best served by policies aimed at maintaining an open world economy and stability on the European continent. This shift in the urban Northeast's interests is what made alliance with the free-trade, European-oriented South possible. For big business and their political representatives, the collapse of the world economy and the looming war in Europe made such an alliance imperative. One "structural condition" underpinning the internationalist alliance was the urban Northeast's competitiveness in the world economy. This was undercut by the erosion of the America's position in the world economy in the 1970s, the economic and social consequences of which were concentrated in the Northeast. As the costs of internationalism in the manufacturing belt began to outstrip the benefits, elected officials in the region saw less virtue in the exercise of hegemonic leadership on the world scene. By contrast, politicians from the growing economies of the sunbelt had less to lose, and much to gain, from an expansionist foreign policy. There was a second "structural condition" underpinning the internationalist alliance between the Northeast and the South, but this one was not economic. Keeping matters of race off the national agenda was a precondition of the North-South condominium. The civil rights movement in the 1960s that divided the Democrats and pushed apart North and South thus played a strategic part in the demise of the internationalist bloc.

Moments of transition and flux in American foreign policy like the 1890s, 1930s, and 1980s reveal a truth that is often blurred in times of stability: "the national interest" has a geographic dimension. When viewed from the bottom up, that is, from the *subnational* level, one sees that the geopolitical imperatives facing one part of the country often differ radically from those facing another. During periods of consensus, like the one that followed World War II, what recedes from view are the domestic political circumstances that make "the national interest" appear as though it were somehow suspended above politics and interest. When support for policy initiatives is sufficiently broad, and when the policy-making process works with enough regularity, it is easy to forget the domestic political circumstances that give political leaders "autonomy" and make the national interest appear "objective." In times of strategic adjustment at home and abroad, this comfortable illusion about the foreign policy-making process dissolves; the inherently political nature of the national interest is revealed in stark form. Old compromises unravel, policy prescriptions diverge, and economic logics are laid bare. We see the regional imperatives and alignments that make consensus over foreign policy possible in some periods, but not in others.

The book thus stands realism on its head. It views the politics inside America as realists view politics among nations: as a fight for power, wealth, and hegemony. This is the implication of Frederick Jackson Turner's observation that politics in America bears a "shadowy image" of European power politics. A geographic approach provides a powerful lens for reinterpreting large "chunks" of America's history as a great power. It also offers new perspective on the shape of things to come. As the United States approaches the end of the twentieth century, it faces challenges abroad that raise profound questions about how it will make foreign policy at home. Will America maintain a commitment to the liberal international economic order it began to build over a half-century ago? Are Americans likely to turn to nationalistic alternatives, as they have in the past? How will the United States find the means to pursue ends which are so ill-defined? Answers to these questions cannot be "read off" the external environment. They lie in Turner's version of realpolitik: the game of sections.

Sectional Conflict and the Great Debates
of the 1890s

Introduction

Few eras in American history had a more profound impact on the nation's foreign policy, or have enjoyed more attention by American diplomatic historians, than the 1890s. Having created a continental empire in the nineteenth century, the United States set its sights on more distant frontiers. Every textbook on American diplomatic history states that in the 1890s, the United States became a great power, breaking with its long-standing tradition of self-isolation and adopting a more assertive, outward-oriented diplomacy. In the space of just ten years, the country's political leaders set a course that would carry America forward into the twentieth century as a global power of enormous influence underwritten by investment capital, advanced technology, and abundant resources. A majority of the country's sixty-plus million citizens came to associate their own prosperity with the overseas extension of American commercial interests, military power, and political influence.

Americans were hardly strangers to overseas trade and investment. Many industrialists, bankers, and farmers had foreign business interests in the years that followed the Civil War, and many of the nation's business magazines and newspapers espoused the virtues of foreign trade and investment. Yet when it came to diplomacy and foreign relations, America's dealings in the 1870s and 1880s "were composed of incidents, not policies—a number of distinct events, not sequences that moved from a source toward a conclusion."[1] Before the 1890s, it was largely private initiatives, rather than public policies, that shaped America's dealings with the rest of the world. Little in the outside world seemed relevant to Washington's principal concerns, which were *continental* expansion and development. Even the occasional secretary of state who thought that government should do more was constrained by the limited means at his disposal. Little money was set aside for foreign affairs, and few politicians were prepared to make the case for more.

A major change of the 1890s occurred at the level of policy: for the first time, the American state began to actively promote economic activity overseas. Government bureaus were created to encourage foreign trade and investment, and new policy tools were devised to give leaders more military and diplomatic leverage in their dealings with foreign countries. America modernized its navy, transformed the tariff from a passive instrument of protection into a bargaining tool for opening foreign markets, and seized foreign lands to extend the nation's strategic reach. These policy initiatives were supplemented by others: the decision to rebuild the merchant marine, efforts to reform the spoils-based diplomatic corps, and later, the creation of a larger, more professional army. Never before had the American government acted so strategically or systematically in foreign affairs. Anyone who cared (and many in public and private life did) could see that the nation's priorities were changing.

This shift in priorities is often viewed as the inevitable result of America's rise as a world power. Such interpretations begin with the obvious: the country was growing at a spectacular rate. Between the end of the Civil War in 1865 and the beginning of the Spanish-American War in 1898, the population of the United States more than doubled, and the gross national product (measured in constant dollars) nearly trebled. As a result, per capita income increased from $531 to more than $933, enabling Americans to purchase more.[2] Production of staple crops, raw materials, and basic manufactures soared: wheat output shot up by 256 percent over the period, corn by 222 percent, refined sugar by 460 percent, coal by 800 percent, and steel rails by 523 percent.[3] Long a world leader in agricultural output, the United States by the turn of the century had surpassed Germany, France, and even Great Britain, the original "workshop of the world," in steel and coal production, as well as total manufacturing output. A decade later, America alone accounted for fully one-third of the world's industrial production.

As the national economy expanded, so did Americans' commercial interests overseas. Between 1865 and 1898, exports expanded from $281 million to roughly $1,231 million, making America the third greatest exporter in the world behind Britain and Germany. While most of this increase was due to the steady expansion of agricultural production, by the late 1890s iron and steel had moved far enough up the export ladder to compete with the country's traditional export sectors—cotton and wheat. In 1870, roughly 67 percent of all American exports were made up of crude materials and foodstuffs.[4] Thirty years later, agriculture was still the dominant export sector, accounting for just over 40 percent of the country's exports, but manufactures were rapidly closing the gap with 35 percent of the export trade. Even more important, most of these exports were in metals, machinery, and transport equipment—the fastest growing areas of the world's manufactured trade and sectors in which many of America's big corporations were trend-setters in modern production and marketing techniques.

Foreign investments, though much less important than commercial contracts, increased as well. Once highly dependent on foreign capital to finance both industry and agriculture, America's leading banks and corporations increasingly looked overseas for investment opportunities. Some of this money went for the purchase of foreign government bonds or foreign-owned corporations, but most of it was invested directly in the development of foreign subsidiaries and branch plants. Investment strategies varied.[5] In Latin America, investors looked mostly to transportation and raw materials. Investors won concessions from foreign governments to build railroads, develop mines, and establish plantations. In Europe, Canada, and Asia, the big investors were manufacturers like General Electric, American Tobacco, and Westinghouse who built foreign assembly plants to avoid being shut out by tariffs and to reduce the costs of shipping to market.

There is little question that these economic contacts led many Americans to think differently about foreign affairs and the role of government. The more business Americans did abroad, and the more dependent they became on foreign markets, the more they looked to the government at home for help in promoting their interests. Investors sought greater protection from unscrupulous foreign leaders as well as from the danger of civil unrest, especially in the underdeveloped countries of Latin America and Asia. Traders sought wider and easier access to foreign consumers and formed powerful "lobby groups" like the National Association of Manufacturers to press their case in Washington and elsewhere. There were many things, big and small, government could do. Collecting statistical information about international market conditions and opportunities was one. Building a canal in Central America to shorten the distance from the great port cities of Boston, New York, and Philadelphia to the fabled China market was another.

Creating a large, powerful navy to keep foreign rivals in check and to protect American property and lives in some troublespot was yet one more.

Americans' interest in overseas expansion intensified when good times turned bad. Severe depressions in the 1870s and 1890s, and a somewhat milder contraction in the 1880s, contributed to the perception that foreign markets were essential to American well-being. Overproduction was seen as the cause of these crises, and each one sent more and more farmers and manufacturers in search of new markets to sell their surplus goods.[6] The discontent and turmoil engendered by these economic downturns had no less an impact on America's lawmakers. They eyed foreign markets the way an earlier generation of politicians had looked to the national frontier: as a "safety valve" for economic and social problems. There was a growing conviction in the 1890s that continental expansion had reached an end, and this only underscored the sense of urgency that many felt about the "export solution." Many on Capitol Hill concluded that unless surplus manufactures and foodstuffs could be sold abroad, it would be impossible to break the cycle of "boom and bust" that had already produced so much economic hardship and social unrest.

It is clear that as the country's stake in the world economy expanded, so too did the government's foreign policy powers. What the main accounts of U.S. expansion in the 1890s ignore or unduly minimize is the equally obvious fact that this change in the government's role was the outcome of a protracted and divisive process. From the start, expansionist policies generated intense domestic political conflict. If most Americans favored the goal of commercial expansion, plenty of them objected to the strategies or means used by successive administrations to create a new "commercial frontier." Their objections are telling. The problem was not only that many Americans were leery of "entanglements" with the "foreign world." The more pressing concern was the uneven distribution of the costs and benefits associated with the adoption of a more activist, expansionist foreign policy. "Who would benefit" was the core issue dividing Americans and their elected representatives in the 1890s.

Like the great battles over foreign policy both before and since, the conflict in the 1890s polarized the nation along sectional lines. On one side was the industrial Northeast, and on the other, the agrarian South. In between lay the West. Of the three regions, the Northeast had the most to gain, politically and economically, from government policies designed to assist private firms interested in overseas expansion. Support for a policy of territorial expansion in the Caribbean and Pacific regions emanated from the nation's big, heavily Republican industrial and commercial-seaport cities. For its own political and economic reasons, the South rejected the preachings of the neomercantilists to the North. The planters, farmers, and merchants who dominated southern economic life favored a more liberal laissez-faire approach to overseas expansion. So did the old-line Democrats who dominated southern politics. Their motto was clear, if no less self-serving: free and open trade, yes; militarism and colonialism, no.

This chapter focuses on three issues that figured prominently in this conflict: the battleship navy, territorial expansion, and tariff reciprocity. Each played a key role in America's rise as a great power. At the same time, all were part of a larger power struggle between the Republican-dominated Northeast and Democratic South for control over the national political economy. The stakes in the foreign policy debates of the 1890s were high. Politicians fought for control over the federal purse, over how and where to open foreign markets, and for political dominance at the national level.

In the analysis that follows, I use the case of the naval buildup to show how the Northeast's changing position in the international economy affected its foreign policy interests and to highlight the spending and revenue implications of the foreign policy decisions of the 1890s. The discussion of colonial expansion is used to underscore the political consequences of the Northeast's and South's differing stakes in world markets. As in the case of the Navy, America's uneven integration into the larger world economy becomes a critical source of political strife between the industrial Northeast and the agrarian South. This analysis also shows how politicians on both sides of the Mason-Dixon line used foreign policy issues shrewdly in advancing their own domestic political purposes. The last case, tariff reciprocity, is used to highlight the relationship between party politics, sectional interest, and foreign policy innovation in late nineteenth-century America.

Each policy is discussed in turn. In every case, the political lineup was the same, with the industrial Northeast supporting the naval buildup, the acquisition of overseas colonies and territories, and the bargaining tariff, and the agrarian South opposing all three. Northern Republicans controlled the machinery and patronage powers of government. For them, an expansionist foreign policy that placed a premium on naval power offered new ways to create industrial jobs and subsidize big business. Such a policy would also help dispose of the politically embarrassing fiscal "surpluses" generated by the high tariffs that Republican Congresses regularly imposed on foreign manufactures. In this regard, the naval modernization program was similar to the infamous military-pension system which southern Democrats also opposed unsuccessfully. Both were used by Republican politicians to redistribute government receipts generated by the tariff from the southern "periphery" to the northern "core" and to strengthen the party's long-standing political ties to key constituencies: industrial elites, urban workers, and Union veterans.[7]

Once constructed, a more powerful Navy would serve as a key instrument of overseas commercial expansion, and in this capacity it would serve the commercial interests of the Northeast. Seeking outlets for its surplus manufactures and capital, the industrial core supported policies that would make the underdeveloped markets of Latin America and East Asia more accessible. Establishing a strategic presence in places like Hawaii, Cuba, and the Philippines was one way to promote and protect American access to these markets. Logic and circumstance led the plantation South and its elected representatives to view the issue differently. Costly policies aimed at opening new markets in Latin America and Asia were not appealing to southern producers, who specialized in raw materials, especially cotton. The South looked to industrial markets in Europe for outlets for its goods and was therefore leery of policies or actions that might invite retaliation by other industrial powers. Still chafing from the legacy of northern Reconstruction, most southerners also almost automatically opposed policies—domestic or foreign—that would require a larger military establishment and expand the coercive power of the central government and, by implication, the northern Republican core.

For northern Republicans, an expansionist foreign policy also promised to solve the one problem that actually threatened their political dominance at the national level: agrarian populism. Republican party leaders split the agrarians' ranks by offering hard-pressed western farmers foreign markets as an alternative to the sweeping economic reforms demanded by the Populists. The bargaining tariff opened up new markets in Latin America for U.S. manufactures and foodstuffs, while continuing to protect the home market against competitive European imports. In doing so, it promoted the interests of northern industrialists *and* western farmers at the expense of southern planters, growers, and merchants. For southerners, the Republican tariff strategy was a disaster. Not only did it continue to force the South to consume high-priced protected northern goods, but it also risked foreign retaliation by threatening to erode Europe's special trading arrangements in the Western Hemisphere. Fearful of foreign retaliation, having little stake in expanded trade with nonindustrial countries, and resentful of their own colonial status within the national political economy, southerners advocated free trade.

The Blue-Water Navy: Fights over Markets and the Federal Purse

The development of the modern Navy was arguably the most important strategic change initiated by American leaders in the 1890s. In a way that few actions could, the decision to begin building a battleship navy in 1890 signalled the nation's willingness to assume a more vigorous role in world affairs. In the quarter-century that followed the Civil War, the Navy had disintegrated into what historian Walter LaFeber described as a "flotilla of deathtraps and defenseless antiques."[8] Most politicians in the 1870s had been preoccupied with other matters and had seen little need for anything other than light-draft gunboats and seagoing raiders. Even in the 1880s, when attitudes toward the Navy began to change and when Congress started to replace the nation's obsolete ironclad and wooden-ship fleet with new steel-hulled, steam-powered cruisers, there was little change in the Navy's primary missions: defending the coastline and protecting American commerce. The result was that at the end of the 1880s, the American Navy was still a third-rate power, slow in speed and short on firepower. It lagged far behind the great navies of Europe.

America did not begin to produce a world-class navy until 1890.[9] In that year, Congress broke new ground by authorizing the construction of the first three in a new fleet of battleships, equal in size and power to the best in the world, at the unprecedented cost of more than $3 million apiece. Secretary of the Navy Benjamin Franklin Tracy had set the stage for this departure in naval policy the year before. He deplored the nation's long-standing tradition of relying on light cruisers as the first line of defense, and insisted that only a fleet of heavily armored battleships capable of interdicting and destroying an enemy fleet of capital ships at sea could safeguard the nation's wealthy port cities and expanding overseas trade.[10] Echoing the views of a growing number of naval strategists, Secretary Tracy argued that the navy's traditional missions were no longer sufficient to guarantee the nation's security. In the future, the best defense would be a good offense. What was needed were two new battleship fleets—one stationed in the Atlantic, the other based in the Pacific.[11]

A vigorous proponent of expansion, Secretary Tracy set the navy on a new course. The program to rebuild the Navy gained tremendous momentum during the 1890s. Over the course of the decade the Navy's share of the federal budget more than doubled, rising from $22 million in 1890 to $56 million, with Congress authorizing on average at least one battleship per year (fig. 2.1). By 1905, it had doubled again. The shift toward a battleship navy was reflected in the Department of the Navy's budget: a growing share went for investment and capitalization, spurring demand for the output of America's shipyards and steel mills.[12] The results were dramatic. In 1890, the American Navy ranked twelfth among the navies of the world, behind Turkey and China. By the turn of the century, the United States had become a major naval power. It was now fourth in battleship strength and sixth in overall fleet size. America had developed a navy worthy of Secretary Tracy's ambitions: "The sea will be the future seat of empire. And we shall rule it as certainly as the sun doth rise."[13]

The Rhetoric of Reform

America had never pursued a military program of this magnitude in peacetime. Such a break with tradition would not have been possible without the backing of many naval enthusiasts in Congress. While Republican and Democratic administrations alike favored developing a battleship navy, the program encountered very tough resistance. In the face of untiring opposition, those in favor of naval buildup found it necessary to compromise to win sufficient backing for naval appropriations. One strategy was to push the radical agenda under the banner of "reform." At first, this meant presenting the case for capital ships in ways that resonated with the Navy's traditional mission of coastal defense. The first three battleships authorized by Congress in 1890, designated the *Oregon, Indiana,* and *Massachusetts* to please a wide audience, were thus referred to as "sea-going, *coastline* battleships."[14] Naval expansionists like Charles A. Boutelle (R-ME), the Chairman of the powerful House Naval Affairs Committee, insisted that the new battleships would be purely defensive in nature, policing areas of vital interest in close proximity to American seaboards.[15] Henry Cabot Lodge, then a member of the Massachusetts delegation, adopted

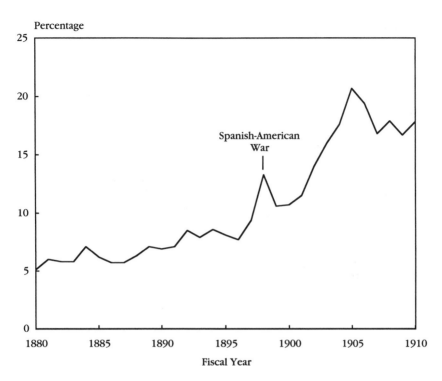

Figure 2.1 Naval Share of Federal Budget, 1880–1910

Source: Bureau of the Census, *Historical Statistics of the United States, Colonial Times to 1970,* 2 vols. (Washington, D.C., 1975), Series Y 457-465, p. 1115.

roughly the same line, depicting the Navy bill as a modest extension of traditional naval legislation.[16]

As a result, the debate over the new Navy was initially limited to issues concerning the vulnerability of America's coastal cities. Those who championed the cause of the battleship argued that the nation's ports were vulnerable to enemy blockade and could no longer be protected by a small fleet of light cruisers and gunboats.[17] The growing power of Britain, France, Germany, Italy, and Japan made it essential, both politically and militarily, to improve the nation's capacity to rapidly concentrate and project military power at sea. Such arguments were dismissed by opponents who claimed that the country's geopolitical position made a large battleship navy superfluous: "The condition of this country, its isolation and great internal resources, exempts it from any complications which create the necessity for a navy which

surround other nations. Nations are most usually governed by their interests, and it is not to the interest of any nation in the world to go to
war with the United States."[18] A small navy consisting of light cruisers
and backed-up by coastal fortifications, they insisted, would be more
than adequate to guarantee American security for the foreseeable future.

The scope of the debate over naval expansion was soon broadened.
Arguments about the threat facing America's seaports were subsumed
by the more fundamental and pressing issue of commercial expansion.[19] Naval expansionists began to argue that sea power was the sine
qua non for commercial expansion. To develop the case, they cited
Captain Alfred Thayer Mahan, whose influential book, *The Influence
of Sea Power upon History,* pointed to a future marked by increasing
rivalry among the Great Powers for overseas markets.[20] Successful competition in the struggle for commercial supremacy would require a
strong merchant marine which, in turn, would require adequate protection from foreign predators. Only a fleet of capital ships, they argued, could provide such protection for American ports and shipping.
The key to all was, in Mahan's words, "command of the seas." Without
control of the sea lanes in broad areas contiguous to the United States,
American shipping would be at the mercy of the great powers. One member of Congress captured the essence of the argument: "Our future
growth lies in the success of our commerce, and no great commerce
has ever been built up without the assistance of a navy to protect the
merchant marine and enforce the rights of merchants and traders."[21]

Those who believed that the American government should play an
active role in opening foreign markets found the logic of the argument
irrefutable. In 1892 Congress responded by authorizing a new man-of-
war, the *Iowa,* and one armored cruiser. After suffering a setback in
1894, naval advocates pushed ahead the following year, getting Congress at the height of the economic depression that began in 1893 to
authorize the construction of two additional 11,000-ton battleships,
christened the *Kearsarge* and *Kentucky,* as well as six torpedo boats
and eight small craft of various types. Many lawmakers had come to
see the $10,000,000 bill as a small price to pay to put Americans back
to work. One year later, the Cleveland administration urged Congress
to authorize another round of battleships and torpedo boats. The House
and Senate agreed after much maneuvering to authorize three more
capital ships, the *Alabama, Illinois,* and *Wisconsin,* and ten additional
torpedo boats. The war with Spain resulted in even more shipbuilding.

In 1898 Congress funded a long list of new ships, including three first-class battleships, the *Maine, Missouri,* and *Ohio,* and sixteen destroyers.[22] Following America's victory at Manila Bay, the pressure to build was almost irresistible: five additional battleships were called for over the next two years, along with a number of armored cruisers and smaller vessels.[23]

Each move to enlarge the Navy was controversial. Not everyone agreed that naval supremacy was the key to American commercial expansion. Many claimed that the relationship was a spurious one: Commercial advantage flowed to those who produced goods that were in demand. Why, opponents charged, should the United States rely on a navy to accomplish what could be achieved at much less expense to the taxpayer by a strategy of free and open trade? Foreign nations, they argued, were so dependent on trade with the United States that they had little incentive to harass American commerce or blockade the nation's ports. In a fiery speech on the House floor, the populist "Sockless" Jerry Simpson of Kansas mocked the navalists' arguments about a British blockade: "Every interest of Great Britain," Simpson declared, "puts her under bonds to keep the peace with us. Why, sir, if Great Britain should throw her shells into any of our great cities—Boston, New York, or Philadelphia—she would in all human possibility destroy more property belonging to British subjects than to American subjects."[24] The real threat facing America was not foreign aggression but rather misguided government policies. A large and expensive steel-hulled navy might feather the nests of shipbuilders and steel producers, but it would do little to address the nation's most pressing economic and social problems: idleness, poverty, and hunger. Worse yet, a big naval establishment raised the spectre of European despotism:

> I predict, sir, that if you allow this extraordinary scheme now presented, this unexampled increase of the Navy, to be carried out, the enlargement of your Army, now recommended, will follow, and this Republican Government, in imitation of the European powers, will stand before the world, not great in the strength of a happy and prosperous people, but in the strength of its military establishment, its imposing standing Army, and its great Navy, a splendid Government in imitation of the low ambition of European powers. England impoverishes her people by maintaining a great navy to overawe her people at home and domineer over her vast outlying possessions. Have we

any motive for imitating her wretched and despotic policy? Have we any outlying possessions to impoverish and oppress, or is this great navy we are to maintain to overawe our own people?[25]

Navalists invariably dismissed such arguments as misleading, and worse, short-sighted. Most followed Secretary Benjamin Tracy's lead, arguing that security knows no price: "The cost of building a navy casts no perceptible burden upon a country of our vast resources. It is the premium paid by the United States for the insurance of its acquired wealth and its growing industries. It is a cheap price to pay for safety."[26] Even in the midst of the depression years of the mid-1890s, naval expansionists saw little need to revise their judgment about the economic benefits of naval spending. Speaking for many others in the House and Senate, Senator Orville Platt of Connecticut reminded the Navy's detractors that "[c]ompared with other nations we are richer than any. Our national debt is less in proportion to our ability to pay it than that of any other nation. Our opportunity to raise money without seriously taxing the people is greater than the opportunity of any other Government. We would do well not to forget that the United States is rich and able to build such a navy as it requires."[27] As for the notion that a large navy was incompatible with the nation's republican ideals, naval advocates were quick to respond that security is the handmaiden of liberty.

It is possible to interpret the political debate over American naval expansion in terms of competing judgments about what was strategically necessary and politically acceptable for the nation as a whole.[28] At what point would the need to establish an American presence on the high seas conflict with the nation's interest in avoiding foreign entanglements? Did America's growing interest in overseas commerce require, ipso facto, the development of a battleship navy? Alternatively, it is possible to see the debate as revolving around philosophical questions of institutional power and constitutional authority. Would the creation of a large peacetime naval establishment subvert America's constitutional order? Would military expansion create an "imperial presidency" and sap the power of the Congress? These themes did run through the discourse over the new Navy, but the point of the analysis that follows is that there was a far simpler text. As always, concrete interests were not far from the surface. These are what defined the main battle lines of debate and ultimately determined where politicians stood on the issue. Like so many issues in late nineteenth-century America, naval expansion divided the country along industrial-agrarian lines. On vote after vote in Congress, politicians from the Northeast and South clashed over a wide array of issues linked directly and indirectly to the issue of naval expansion.

Sectional Bases of the Conflict

Figure 2.2 summarizes the pattern of voting in Congress on naval expansion. The vast majority of the roll call votes on the Navy during the decade dealt directly with appropriations for naval buildup.[29] Those concerning the price of battleship armor-plating spoke to the issue of naval expansion while raising Populist concerns about "price-fixing" and, more broadly, the power of the Eastern "trusts." Support for the new Navy was strongest in the Northeast throughout the decade, especially among congressmen from the New England and Middle Atlantic states. This bloc of urban and coastal interests was opposed by one that was centered in the South.[30] The pattern of voting in the West is more mixed. Much of the region aligned with the Northeast in the fight for naval expansion. Western support for naval build-up was strongest along the Pacific Coast and in the upper Great Plains. Representatives from the lower Great Plains (Kansas, Missouri, Nebraska) and the Mountain West (Colorado, Idaho, Montana) were more likely to align with southern lawmakers. Together, these westerners and the southerners waged a rearguard battle against the new Navy, constantly searching for ways to slow the pace of warship construction.

The Northeast

An ambitious naval shipbuilding program served the interests of America's industrial heartland in three important ways. First, a modern seagoing navy served the interests of industrialists and bankers who sought greater access to and control over markets in Latin America and Asia. These parts of the world were the focal points for America's growing trade in manufactured goods and direct overseas investment, as well as a focal point for northern politicians looking for concrete ways to signal their commitment to solving the problem of "overproduction" by opening new markets. Second, such a program promised high-wage jobs for the Northeast's workers, lucrative federal contracts for its shipyards, steel mills, and gun foundries, and business for many of its ancillary industries. Finally, naval expansionism proved to be enormously popular among the leaders of the Republican party. Republicans used

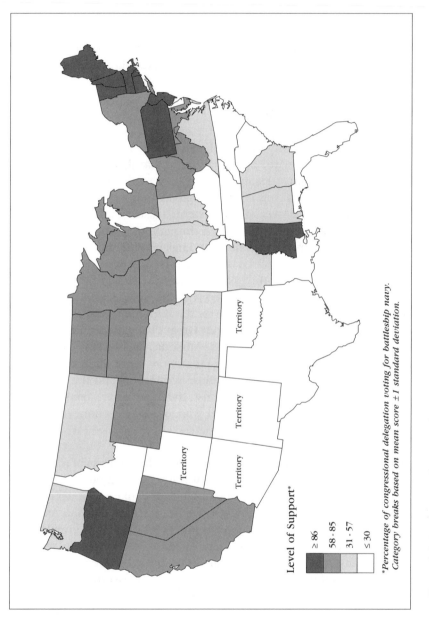

Level of Support*

≥ 86
58 - 85
31 - 57
≤ 30

*Percentage of congressional delegation voting for battleship navy.
Category breaks based on mean score ±1 standard deviation.*

Figure 2.2 Congressional Support for Naval Buildup, 1890–1901

the Navy to create patronage, expand the party's political base in the western states, and siphon off politically embarrassing budgetary surpluses generated by the protective tariff.

It is clear that a larger, more powerful navy served the commercial interests of the Northeast. The late nineteenth century was an era of rapid growth in American exports, especially in manufactures. A growing share of this trade was with Latin America and Asia.[31] Investment follows trade, and by the 1890s a large proportion of U.S. overseas investment was in raw materials extraction and agriculture in the Caribbean Basin.[32] The parts of the country with the most substantial and rapidly growing interests in Latin America and Asia were precisely those with "significant manufacturing interests."[33] The need for a powerful navy (and deployable ground troops) was abundantly clear to those who believed that government action was necessary to promote access to such markets, protect shipping lanes from foreign rivals, and deter local leaders from seizing American property.

One does not have to attribute the naval buildup to the dominance of "big business" to recognize that shipbuilders and steel producers, among others, also had a considerable stake in the modernization of the Navy, and to see that these producers generally acted in ways that were consistent with their interests.[34] Shipyards clearly profited by the demand for a strong navy. Economists at the time went even further and gave the government credit for almost single-handedly creating the steel shipbuilding industry.[35] Steel producers also enjoyed handsome profits, and before the 1890s many were already "active lobbyists and propagandists for naval expansion."[36] At a time when rail and structural steel markets were poor, there was much to be said for a long-term, federally financed program involving large sums of money and little risk, even if it did involve some degree of government regulation.[37] Congress insisted that only domestic steel, which was more expensive than European steel, be used in the construction of American warships, and this fact only made the program more appealing to an industry that had massive capital requirements, and that therefore looked for ways to stabilize markets and allow for orderly debt amortization.

The geographic distribution of these industries all but guaranteed the Northeast the lion's share of the Navy's procurement budget. Fifty-seven percent of all naval contracts to shipbuilders during the decade went to northeastern shipyards—almost three times the share that went to either southern or western shipbuilders (fig. 2.3). Similarly

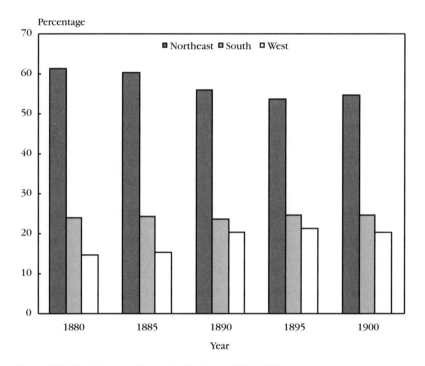

Figure 2.3 Naval Expenditures by Region, 1880–1900
Source: Annual Report of the Secretary of the Navy, selected years.
Note: Based on federal outlays to Navy yards and docks.

northeastern steel producers won the bulk of the contracts for armor plating, gun forging, steel projectiles and other accoutrements of warship production.[38] The Middle Atlantic and Great Lakes regions accounted for over four-fifths of the nation's iron and steel output, with major concentrations in Pittsburgh, Youngstown, Buffalo, Cleveland, Detroit, and Chicago. Even though one of the nation's newest and most prolific centers of steel production was located in Birmingham, Alabama, the South as a whole accounted for less than one-fifth of the nation's pig iron.

Northern politicians also had their own political reasons to push for a bigger navy. By increasing America's relative power in the international system, they would also be expanding their own power here at home. For starters, more federal money for shipbuilding meant more opportunities for patronage. Despite repeated calls to reform and clean up the navy yards located along the East and West coasts, the federal government's shipyards continued to function as patronage machines.[39] A reliable source of votes in good times, naval contracts were especially valuable during difficult years. As the naval historian Benjamin Franklin Cooling puts it, the new navy "was really a vast public works project designed to further stimulate the business community."[40] Such considerations were clearly at work during the depression-racked Cleveland years. Although he initially opposed Republican-style "pump priming," Cleveland relented in the face of mounting pressure, calling on Congress to fund the construction of three new battleships and twelve additional torpedo boats.[41] Meanwhile, naval appropriations could be tailored to serve the goals of coalition-building, especially with the West.

The West

Navy contracts were one of many devices used by political leaders to weaken resistance in Congress, and to broaden the geographic bases of support for overseas expansion in the process. California, Oregon, and Washington were clearly the biggest beneficiaries of these efforts, and the Harrison administration's decision in 1890 to push for the development of two battleship fleets—one stationed in the Atlantic, the other based in the Pacific—was as political as it was strategic. Elected officials from these western states had their own reasons for favoring naval buildup. Even before the 1890s, the Pacific Coast states had reaped the largest share of the Navy's budget on a per capita basis.[42] Union Iron Works of California was one of the nation's largest shipbuilders, and there were many smaller ones stretching from San Pedro to Seattle.[43] Moreover, there was large carrying trade, and Latin America and Asia were areas of special interest to western manufacturers and merchants.[44] In the final analysis, that the Pacific Coast states aligned with the Northeast on the naval question is not surprising. By most measures of economic development, the far western states had more in common with the Northeast than they did with the rest of the West.[45]

Naval expansion served even broader coalition-building strategies for northern Republican leaders. The intertwined issues of naval reform, commercial expansion, and the bargaining tariff provided them with the basis for an electoral alliance with politicians from the agrarian West. As I will argue in the section of this chapter dealing with the bargaining tariff, northern Republicans sought to shore up their party's position in the agrarian West by putting together a foreign policy package that would address the "overproduction crisis" in agriculture. This strategy, designed to undercut the appeal of the Populist movement, was based on the argument that commercial expansion in Latin America and Asia was the remedy for the West's economic problems. Commercial expansion, in turn, required a more powerful Navy. The two, northern Republicans argued, were different sides of the same coin:

> Not only respect for us depends upon the Navy, but commercial supremacy depends upon a proper and adequate naval force, a force proportioned to the magnitude of the country, to its resources, to its aims, to its purposes. No nation that does not maintain a navy can obtain commercial supremacy. Foreign trade flourishes where there is an adequate and proper navy to defend and protect it, or languishes where the navy is insufficient to protect and defend it. We of this country desire commercial supremacy.[46]

Despite opposition, the Republican's strategy worked in Congress. Many lawmakers representing hard-pressed farmers in the trans-Mississippi West found the promise of new markets in Latin America and Asia hard to resist. Whatever suspicions western farmers had about eastern Republicans, they also held "deep misgivings" about their vulnerability to British commodity traders, and they viewed the growing competition from other wheat exporters, most notably Russia, with alarm.[47] British efforts to reduce dependence on American wheat only seemed to confirm their worst fears about the future of the European market. As a result, by the mid-1880s western farmers were already agitating for new markets in other parts of the world, particularly Latin America and Asia. Sensing the West's vulnerability on this issue, Republican leaders seized the opportunity to call for more aggressive commercial strategies and a powerful navy to back them up. They succeeded, splitting the agrarian populists' ranks and winning crucial support for naval appropriations.

The South

Logic and circumstance led the plantation South, and its elected representatives, to view the issue of naval reform differently. Part of the explanation lies in the distribution of proposed naval expenditures. While the Northeast could hope to realize gains from greater federal spending on the Navy, most of the agrarian South could not, and in fact did not. In large part, of course, the regional bias in naval contracting was unavoidable: most defense-related sectors were located in the Northeast and the Pacific Coast. Compounding matters was the fact that southern influence on the House and Senate Committees of Naval Affairs was quite limited.[48] On average, southerners held one-third of the seats on the House and Senate Committees.[49] This means that few southern congressmen could expect to "bring home the bacon" by winning navy contracts; only committee members and those who represented southern constituencies around the Navy yards in Norfolk and Pensacola (and perhaps the steel mills in Birmingham) could be optimistic in this regard. For most members from the southern periphery, there were few political rewards in supporting naval shipbuilding, regardless of which party occupied the White House or headed the Navy Department. If naval spending were warranted (and few were prepared to concede the point), then for southern representatives it made political sense to try to limit the amount invested. One way to justify such limits was to stress the continuing viability of the more traditional and less costly naval missions of coastal defense and commerce protection.

Although it struggled to restrain the naval buildup, the periphery maintained a sizable stake in foreign trade. Like their northern colleagues, southern politicians were very keen on overseas commercial expansion. For the South, however, there was a key difference. Unlike the industrial core, the agrarian South produced raw materials (e.g., cotton, metals, lumber). The South's share of national manufacturing production had increased since the Civil War, but raw materials, especially cotton, were still the region's most important class of exports. And markets for raw materials were not to be found in Latin America or Asia. On the whole, raw materials producers sought industrial markets either in the United States or Europe.[50] A large, offensive U.S. navy might be useful in promoting trade in American manufactured goods (and perhaps foodstuffs) with nonindustrialized countries, but it held little promise for securing buyers for cotton. Those markets already existed, and European demand for southern raw materials was strong. The South already enjoyed a privileged position on European markets, supplying almost 80 percent of Europe's cotton imports at the time.

A large and powerful American navy was not required to guarantee access to overseas markets for the South. Expanded world trade may have required a militarily powerful hegemon to open markets, but as far as the South was concerned, the British navy was still doing an adequate job. Indeed, it was not uncommon for southern politicians to defend the status quo by pointing to the dependability of the two traditional guarantors of American security and access to the world economy—the Atlantic ocean and the British navy. Given this logic, most southern lawmakers were unmoved by arguments about the commercial value of a new U.S. blue-water navy. One analyst puts the point this way: "While the Southerners were as interested in commercial expansion as other Congressmen, they doubted the need for a large naval establishment to implement commercial policy. Like Mahan, Southern Congressmen believed that commerce was the 'civilizing' factor that enabled the prosperous nations to help the unfortunate peoples of the world; unlike him, however, they were satisfied that commerce could perform this mission without the help of a new navy."[51] For southerners, what was to be avoided were policies that might provoke or exacerbate tensions among industrial nations and thereby threaten American access to European markets. When southern politicians stressed the dangers of a naval arms race, it was not because they valued peace over trade. On the contrary, they were quite sensitive to the commercial issues at stake. For the South, an American policy of free trade was the best way to promote regional prosperity.

There was, however, a more immediate reason for agrarian opposition to the development of a blue-water navy. Increased federal spending on the Navy would help to justify high tariff barriers, and this was clearly damaging to southern interests. The relationship between the Navy and the tariff was not lost on southern politicians, many of whom viewed a vote for naval spending as a vote for high tariffs. The relationship between the naval expenditures and customs duties is not difficult to understand. Each year since the end of the Civil War, revenue generated by the tariff (the single largest source of federal revenue at the time) exceeded government expenditures.[52] One of the continuing issues before Congress was how to deal with the surplus. One option was to reduce it by cutting taxes—i.e., by lowering trade barriers to foreign goods. Southerners favored this option because it would lower the costs of goods that they consumed. Another was to maintain tariff barriers and increase federal spending. This option was much more attractive to northern congressmen for all the reasons already discussed.

The trade-offs were clear to political representatives from the periphery. William Oates of Alabama concluded that it was hard to view the naval program as anything other than "a well devised scheme to take advantage of that unsubstantial and transitory popular idea in favor of building a navy, to make a permanent disposition of the surplus revenue, and thereby dispense with the necessity of revising the tariff and reducing taxation."[53] He was not alone. Most of his southern colleagues saw naval appropriations as a clever method for disposing of customs duties and redistributing wealth from the agrarian periphery to the industrial core. In this regard, the naval build-up program was not considered much different than the military pension, which also recycled revenues generated by the tariff.[54] Like the military pension plan, the naval buildup disproportionately favored the Northeast. Disposing of government revenue by investing in the Navy was perhaps a more indirect and subtle means of redistributing wealth, but from the South's vantage point the underlying purpose was the same. The industrial core would prosper at the expense of the agrarian periphery.

Politicians from the Northeast vigorously denied any such motive. All parts of the country, they claimed, stood to benefit from efforts to improve the nation's ability to protect its coastlines and project power abroad. How, they asked, could farmers and sharecroppers expect to sell their cotton and wheat overseas if America could not even protect its coastlines? Responding to criticisms from congressmen from agrarian states, William G. McAdoo (R-NJ), the future assistant secretary of the Navy, observed: "One month of blockade of our ports on the seacoast and you would burn more corn in Kansas than you now do. . . . One of the vessels thundering from her iron sides is defending the humblest homes out on the prairies in Indiana, the great cities in the Mississippi Valley, and the miners upon the Pacific Coast just as much as she is the cities upon the Atlantic."[55]

Naval enthusiasts warned that playing to divisive regional interests might be good politics, but it was damaging to the national interest. Sensing the danger and leaving nothing to chance, navalists called on their colleagues to take the high road and refrain from playing the sectional card. Paraphrasing Daniel Webster, Henry Cabot Lodge, the ardent expansionist from Massachusetts, urged members to remember that in matters of state "all sectionalism ought to cease at the water's edge."[56] Such appeals may have struck a responsive chord in some quarters, but for those who opposed the naval buildup, they were nothing more than self-serving rhetoric:

It is well to remember, that the sums of money Congress is called upon to appropriate for these purposes will be drawn from our people by excessive and exhaustive taxation, taxation not necessary for the national defense, and will be expended in a limited section of our country, a section said to be prosperous, drowning in the fruits of the labor of other sections of the Union for the local benefit of the favored section, and this, while the industries of the greater portion of our country, the great agricultural interests, are fearfully depressed.[57]

The Debate over Colonialism: The Drive for Markets and Domestic Political Advantage

In debates over foreign policy in the late nineteenth century, the northern core's gain was often viewed in the periphery as the South's loss. More often than not, it was. One of the striking lessons of the decade-long debate between the "imperialists" and "anti-imperialists" over the acquisition of foreign colonies and protectorates is that even issues that involved matters of great principle were not immune to sectional conflict. "The Great Debate" is often interpreted in symbolic terms, as an epic struggle between Americans who welcomed the nation's emergence as a modern industrial power and those who looked back toward a simpler, less threatening agrarian past. Closer inspection reveals that the fights over empire-building and colonialism had less to do with clashing views about America's identity as a nation than they did with conflicts of interest.[58] Politics, not principle, was at the bottom of the debate over the new American empire.

Contemporaries viewed the question of expansion as a momentous one. Everyone knew that a policy of colonial expansion would usher in a new and unprecedented era in the nation's foreign relations. In the past, American leaders had shunned European-style colonialism and the large military establishments that colonial rule required. Preoccupied with internal matters and free of any significant foreign dangers, the country accepted the advice of George Washington's legendary Farewell Address, avoiding the "entanglements" of power politics. For the most part, political leaders limited their territorial ambitions to the large, unpopulated lands that were contiguous to the United States, or as in the case of the Alaskan Purchase of 1867, lands that were located on the North American landmass. There were exceptions. Franklin

Pierce, for example, attempted to acquire Cuba in the 1850s and Ulysses S. Grant tried to do the same with Santo Domingo two decades later. Such actions were rare, lying well outside the boundaries of what most Americans considered legal, proper, or necessary.

In view of this history, it is not difficult to see why the debate over imperialism is so often interpreted as a struggle over the nation's identity. A policy of colonial expansion violated one of America's oldest republican traditions—its repudiation of empire and colonial hegemony. It also raised thorny legal questions: Did the Constitution give the federal government the power to acquire overseas possessions? If so, did the constitution follow the flag? Or, was it possible to annex foreign lands without granting indigenous peoples all the rights and privileges accorded American citizens under the Constitution? Nor is it hard to see why some analysts have emphasized the institutional dimensions of the conflict over imperialism.[59] After decades of congressional dominance over foreign policy, the Supreme Court's 1890 decision on inherent presidential powers (in the *Neagle* case) opened the door to presidents seeking greater discretionary power in making international agreements, deploying military forces, and seizing foreign territories.[60] Capitalizing on the Court's expansively worded dicta proved difficult, however, because many in Congress opposed such an expansive reading of the president's constitutional authority. The result was a great deal of rancorous legislative-executive conflict.

What cultural and institutional accounts cannot adequately explain is why the issue of colonial expansion split the country along regional lines. Time and time again, the imperialism issue and all that it implied about the scope of presidential power inflamed sectional strife. The political line-up in Congress was the same on all five key territorial issues of the 1890s—Cuba, Hawaii, the Philippines, Puerto Rico, and the Isthmian Canal (table 2.1). In every instance, support for empire-building was centered in the industrial Northeast, with strong pockets of political backing coming from the western states. Anti-imperialist sentiment, while not exclusively a southern phenomenon, was dominant in the South.[61] The majority of southern newspapers opposed imperialism, and southerners made up the single largest block of imperial naysayers in Congress.[62] No matter what form of tutelage was under consideration, the southern response to northern expansionism was always the same: no.

Why did the issue of imperialism divide the country so deeply? And why did efforts to extend American rule to foreign peoples divide the

Table 2.1 Regional Support for Imperialist Policies (percentage)

Region[1]	Intervention in Cuba[2]	Annexation of Hawaii[3]	Isthmian Canal[4]	Control of Philippines[5]	Puerto Rican Tariff[6]
Northeast					
New England	95.8	95.7	91.3	85.7	82.6
Middle Atlantic	87.8	92.9	63.9	66.7	61.4
Great Lakes	73.7	91.3	77.1	73.9	70.4
South					
Southeast	20.3	32.8	36.5	14.3	14.7
Southwest	4.0	4.5	15.8	4.5	0
West					
Great Plains	54.2	73.3	61.0	67.4	59.6
Mountain West	0	50.0	33.3	25.0	16.7
Pacific Coast	45.5	90.0	88.9	88.9	90.9

Source: Computations from House roll call data.

[1] The Northeast includes New England, the Middle Atlantic, and the Great Lakes:

New England: Connecticut, Maine, Massachusetts, New Hampshire, Rhode Island, Vermont

Middle Atlantic: Delaware, Maryland, New Jersey, New York, Pennsylvania

Great Lakes: Illinois, Indiana, Michigan, Ohio, Wisconsin

The South includes the Southeast and Southwest:

Southeast: Alabama, Florida, Georgia, Kentucky, Mississippi, North Carolina, South Carolina, Tennessee, Virginia, West Virginia

Southwest: Arkansas, Louisiana, Oklahoma, Texas.

The West includes the Great Plains, Mountain West, and Pacific Coast:

Great Plains: Iowa, Kansas, Minnesota, Missouri, Nebraska, North Dakota, South Dakota

Mountain West: Arizona, Colorado, Idaho, Montana, Nevada, New Mexico, Utah, Wyoming

Pacific Coast: California, Oregon, Washington

Territories that were not incorporated as states by 1890 are not included.

[2] Vote on Dinsmore (D-AR) Amendment recognizing Cuba as an independent nation. A vote against the amendment is a vote for imperialism. April 13, 1898.

[3] Final vote on Newlands (D-NV) Resolution to annex the Hawaiian islands. A vote for the resolution is a vote for imperialism. June 15, 1898.

[4] Vote on Hepburn (R-IA) Amendment providing for the construction of an American canal in Nicaragua with military fortifications. A vote for the amendment is a vote for imperialism. May 2, 1900.

[5] Vote on so-called Spooner Amendment granting president power to govern the Philippines in peacetime. A vote for the amendment is a vote for imperialism. March 1, 1901.

[6] Final vote on bill to reduce tariffs on goods from Puerto Rico. A vote for the bill is a vote for imperialism. April 11, 1900.

country along *sectional* lines? The answer is not self-evident. After all, most elected officials, irrespective of party or geography, favored commercial expansion.[63] Even the South's most outspoken critics of empire—men like Augustus Bacon of Georgia, James McCreary of Kentucky, and Hugh Dinsmore of Arkansas—agreed with their counterparts to the North that expanded trade was necessary to help combat the problems caused by overproduction. Arguments focused almost entirely on the *means* by which commercial expansion should be achieved.[64] Would overseas empire facilitate the expansion of trade, or could America's foreign trade expand without political and military burdens? Should new economic opportunities be sought in underdeveloped or advanced regions, in South America and Asia, or Europe? On these questions of means, consensus gave way to conflict, and debate polarized along sectional lines.

To understand why this was so, one must go beyond the rhetoric of empire and consider the political imperatives facing northern and southern lawmakers. The place to begin is the economy. The northern and southern economies differed enormously, and the differences help explain why northern and southern elites could agree on the need for expanding trade and yet disagree so vigorously over the best approach for promoting it. Despite the development of a *national* economy after the Civil War, the United States in the 1890s remained in many ways a single nation-state with two distinct *regional* economies: one specializing in manufacturing, the other in agriculture. This meant that these regions had very different things to sell on the world market. And as the debate over naval buildup revealed, it also meant that their elected officials had quite different ideas about *where* America should cultivate commercial ties. Seeking outlets for its surplus manufactures, the industrial Northeast looked primarily to nonindustrialized areas of the globe, particularly South America and Asia. By contrast, the plantation South was highly dependent on industrial markets for selling its raw materials. It looked to Europe for expanded trade.

Where to expand was one thing; *how* to expand was yet another. For northern Republicans who were looking for ways to justify the naval buildup, empire-building had distinct advantages. If a modern blue-water navy was needed to open markets in underdeveloped countries, then this navy would require overseas fueling and repair stations. Those bases, in turn, needed protection from potential enemies. The dual strategy of military build-up and imperialism appealed to core congressmen who were looking for ways to signal their commitment to hard-pressed workers while reaching out to the powerful industrial and financial concerns interested in overseas commerce and investment. If empire made "good" politics above the Mason-Dixon line, anti-imperialism did no less below it. Facing the most serious challenge to their rule in decades from reform-minded agrarians, anti-imperialism was a "safe" issue for old-line southern Democrats. Under the guise of the great Jeffersonian principles of "liberty" and "self-rule," they could evoke the glory of the "Lost Cause" while exploiting deep-seated fears about northern militarism and coercion. At the same time, by stressing the advantages of laissez-faire liberalism, they could attend to the needs of their political base: the planters, farmers, and merchants who dominated southern economic life.

What follows is an analysis of one key chapter in the debate over empire: the fight over Hawaii. Arguably the country's most important overseas acquisition in the 1890s, the efforts to annex the Pacific archipelago generated debate that continued almost uninterrupted for five years. The fight between annexationists and anti-annexationists began in the winter of 1893 and climaxed with the annexationists' ultimate triumph in May of 1898. Northern and southern officials alike recognized that the outcome would establish a powerful precedent for future expansion in the Pacific and Caribbean. As they anticipated, the debate over Hawaiian annexation in many ways presaged the ensuing controversies over Cuba, Puerto Rico, and the Philippines. Some of the faces changed, but in all cases the arguments and interests that drove the fights remained the same. Hawaii was a harbinger of things to come.

The Hawaiian Question

America had close ties with Hawaii long before the annexation of the islands in the 1890s. Links first forged by American merchants en route to China in the late eighteenth century were strengthened by the arrival of New England whalers and missionaries in the early nineteenth century.[65] Gradually, as Americans secured the best sugar and planting lands on the islands and became politically powerful, ties between the United States and Hawaii diversified. By the 1840s the relationship was considered important enough in Washington that President John Tyler extended the Monroe Doctrine to include the island kingdom, turning aside British and French claims and signing a treaty that assured Hawaii's future independence. A decade later, the United States went a step further, announcing its intention to annex the archipelago. This move was blocked by the British and by the growing conflict in Congress over the issues of slavery and colonial expansion. A commercial reciprocity treaty negotiated by the Grant administration in 1867, which was viewed by many in Congress as the first step toward annexation, suffered the same fate.

Things began to change in the 1870s. In January 1875, American officials negotiated another reciprocity treaty with the Hawaiian government. Under the terms of the treaty, Hawaiian sugar—the kingdom's chief export—was allowed to enter the huge American market duty-free in exchange for the reduction or abolition of import duties on American goods entering the islands. Concern about British and French intentions in the region led the Senate to tack on an amendment that gave the United States de facto control over the island's key strategic inlet—Pearl Harbor. This strategic arrangement was made even clearer in another reciprocity treaty signed by the Cleveland administration in 1885. By granting the United States exclusive rights to use Pearl Harbor as a coaling and repair station for its ships, the treaty turned the island into a valuable strategic asset in the American search for overseas markets. In President Cleveland's words, Hawaii was now "the stepping-stone to the growing trade of the Pacific."[66]

The 1875 treaty linking the American and Hawaiian economies was a huge success. Sugar production in Hawaii boomed and exports to America quadrupled over its first ten years.[67] By 1890 nearly 99 percent of Hawaii's exports were shipped to the United States, and over 75 percent of its imports came from the American mainland. But the lopsided nature of the relationship created its own problems. The Hawaiian economy was very vulnerable to political shifts in the United States.[68] This became painfully clear in 1890 when Congress passed the McKinley Tariff. By allowing all sugar to enter the United States duty-free, the new law wiped-out the huge advantage enjoyed by Hawaii.[69] The consequences were literally revolutionary. The Hawaiian economy collapsed and anti-Americanism flared on the island. Fearing that their property might be confiscated by the Hawaiian monarch, Queen Liliuokalani, sugar planters of American descent and merchants took matters into their own hands in January 1893. With the aid of American naval detachments under orders from John L. Stevens, the U.S. Minister to Hawaii, the wealthy foreign minority overthrew the monarchy.

The revolutionary government quickly sent word to Washington that it sought a treaty of annexation. Seizing the opportunity, President Harrison authorized his secretary of state, John W. Foster, to draft and sign such a treaty. The document was rushed to the Senate with a message from the White House urging prompt and favorable action. The president hoped to have the treaty ratified before president-elect Grover Cleveland took over in March.[70] The Senate Committee on Foreign Relations quickly approved the treaty, but it immediately ran into trouble among southern Democrats on the Senate floor. Seeking to avoid a major confrontation, Harrison left office with Senate action on the Hawaiian treaty still pending.[71]

A week after he was inaugurated, Grover Cleveland withdrew the treaty for reexamination. Two days later, he appointed James Henderson Blount, a former Georgia congressman and chairman of the House Committee on Foreign Affairs, as a special commissioner to Hawaii. Shortly after arriving in Hawaii, Blount caused a political stir by ordering that the American flags flying over government buildings be lowered. The Blount mission soon became a subject of great controversy. As many Republicans had feared, the final report submitted in July 1893 blamed the former Minister Stevens and implicitly, the Harrison administration, for aiding the revolution. Endorsing Blount's findings, Secretary of State Walter Q. Gresham recommended that the Queen be restored to her throne. Cleveland agreed, but he found it impossible to forge an arrangement acceptable to the Queen and the island's new leader, Sanford B. Dole. Frustrated, the president announced plans to abandon Harrison's annexation treaty and called on Congress to devise an alternative plan for Hawaii.

An angry partisan debate ensued. Neither party was willing to accept responsibility for the Hawaiian fiasco. Democrats depicted Republican support for the Hawaiian *coup d'état* as morally loathsome; Republicans excoriated the Democrats for hauling down the American flag on Hawaiian soil and restoring a monarch to power. Beneath the partisan bickering were more serious issues. Indeed, many of the questions concerning overseas expansion which became so familiar to Americans later in the decade were raised in debates over the Hawaii question, often at considerable length. Some congressmen stressed the strategic and commercial value of the islands; others expressed deep concerns about the legal and moral implications of annexing territory so far from America's shores. Did the country need Hawaii to guarantee wider and easier access to the markets of Asia and to prevent the European powers from gaining yet another naval base on America's "flanks"? Should the United States break with its tradition of self-imposed isolation and containment and pursue a policy of imperial expansion like the great European powers?

The answer at this stage was clearly no. Each chamber of Congress passed resolutions against annexation.[72] In the House, the critical vote was a February 1894 decision on a resolution introduced by Henry W. Blair of New Hampshire. The amendment urging the recognition and eventual annexation of Hawaii was crushed by a vote of 164 to 90.

Southern opposition was massive: only one southerner broke ranks to vote in favor of the measure. Roughly two-thirds of the ninety votes in favor were cast by northern lawmakers. The rest came from the West. The vote clearly represented a defeat for the annexationist forces in Congress.

For the next few years the United States assumed a hands-off policy toward Hawaii. Several incidents kept the issue alive in American politics, however.[73] Most important was an attempt by Britain in 1894 to secure one of the smaller uninhabited Hawaiian islands for use as a cable landing.[74] Seeing no reason to oppose the British request, Cleveland asked Congress in early January 1895 to modify the treaty with Hawaii so as to enable Britain to build its cable station. The request caused great alarm. It fueled intense speculation about British intentions in the Pacific, and also led many in Congress to charge that it was further proof of Cleveland's excessively pro-British inclinations. Cleveland also advocated low tariffs and the gold standard, and only a month earlier, he had proposed withdrawing from the Samoan Islands, leaving Britain and Germany in control.[75] Now it appeared that he was willing to let the British encroach on the Hawaiian islands and give them free reign in the Pacific—or so expansionists like Henry Cabot Lodge of Massachusetts believed.

Sensing that Cleveland was politically vulnerable, expansionists killed his request in committee and moved to turn the situation to their advantage. In February 1895, the Senate approved a $500,000 subsidy for laying an underwater telegraphic cable from California to Hawaii. In an impassioned speech on the Senate floor, Lodge had urged his colleagues to back the cable plan, calling it "the most important thing involved in any appropriation bill before Congress."[76] The House did not share the Senate's sentiments, and the lower-chamber soundly rejected the Republican-hatched plan. Once again, southerners were at the forefront of the opposition, with over 90 percent of the southern delegation voting against building the Pacific cable. Expansionists had to accept their partial victory. They had foiled British plans to build a cable station on Hawaiian soil, but they could not win enough support to construct an American cable to the archipelago and more importantly, to establish a precedent for annexing the islands sometime in the near future. Southerners continued to pose a serious obstacle to those bent on empire.

In 1897 the Hawaiian issue surfaced again in American politics. Cleveland's successor, William McKinley, submitted a new treaty of annexation to the Senate. This treaty had been negotiated quickly with the Hawaiian government; it comprised practically the same features as the 1893 pact. And like the earlier treaty, McKinley's annexation pact encountered stiff resistance in Congress. Although those favoring annexation in the Senate lobbied hard over the ensuing months, they prudently avoided a showdown on the Senate floor. They recognized that solid southern opposition on the matter meant that they would not have the two-thirds majority needed to ratify the treaty. Abandoning the ratification process as hopeless, expansionists opted for the tactic that was used a half-century before to bring Texas into the Union: a joint resolution. Unlike a treaty, a joint resolution required only a simple majority in both chambers.

The turning point came on May 4, 1898—just three days after America's victory over Spain at Manila Bay. Representative Francis G. Newlands (I-NV) introduced a joint resolution for Hawaiian annexation. This resolution made it to the House floor, where it filled page after page of the *Congressional Record* with impassioned oratory. Opponents were on the defensive: Commodore Dewey's thrilling defeat of the Spanish fleet gave those in favor of the treaty a decided edge in the fight for the public mind. By opting for a joint resolution to secure annexation, expansionists also gained a significant tactical edge in the legislative battle. What probably guaranteed victory was the Republican landslide of 1896, which gave the Republicans control over both the White House and Congress. By the time the final roll was taken, the issue was no longer whether the Hawaiian islands would be annexed, but rather how large the expansionists' margin of victory would be.

After five years of debate over Hawaii, the expansionists finally carried the day (fig. 2.4). The House voted in favor of the amendment by a margin of 209 to 92, with the Northeast accounting for over two-thirds of the affirmative votes. Nearly three-quarters of the nay votes were cast by southerners. In the end, the northern expansionists' triumph proved to be every bit the "entering wedge" that southern leaders had feared. Within *seven months* of annexing Hawaii, the United States acquired Guam, the Philippines, Puerto Rico, and Wake Island. Cuba followed shortly thereafter. In each case, arguments followed lines laid down in the Hawaii debates.

From the initial clash over Harrison's attempt to annex the Hawaiian islands in 1893, to the fierce battle precipitated by Cleveland's proposal to let the British build a cable station on the islands, to the climac-

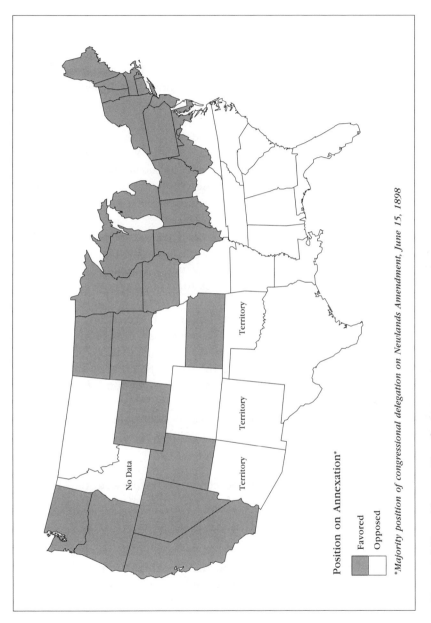

Position on Annexation*

Favored

Opposed

*Majority position of congressional delegation on Newlands Amendment, June 15, 1898

Figure 2.4 House Vote on Hawaiian Annexation

tic battle over the joint resolution for Hawaiian annexation, both sides professed adherence to high ideals and to general principles of republican democracy. Each side claimed that its position best served the national interest and was the most consistent with the Constitution and legal precedent. While these were not idle claims, they should be taken with more than a grain of salt, for they were tailored to advance more concrete sectional interests. In the politics of American overseas expansion, what matters most in explaining the divisions on Capitol Hill are issues that have to do with sectional advantage. Which parts of the country stood to gain the most from policies aimed at opening markets in Asia and South America? This was the core issue.

The "Great Debate"

In the Great Debate over expansion in the 1890s, there was no shortage of appeals to America's destiny as a great power or to the calling of Anglo-Saxon peoples to civilize the backward, benighted savages of the Pacific. Northerners indulged the rhetoric of American exceptionalism. Americans, they argued, were a chosen people who could assume the responsibilities of overseas empire while avoiding the evils of tyranny and despotism that plagued other, less enlightened imperial powers. Yet behind the high-minded arguments that politicians advanced for and against empire were their own political interests — as well as the interests of the districts, states, and regions they hailed from. In the end, the arguments that really told were the ones that dealt with the hard realities of the world economy in the late nineteenth century.

The World Economy

For most of the century, the world economy revolved around Great Britain. The world's banker, workshop, and policeman, England used its power to establish an international economic order which, at its peak, emphasized principles of free trade, nondiscrimination, and equal treatment.[77] By the mid-nineteenth century, colonialism as a strategy of overseas economic expansion had declined in importance as Britain came to rely on its commercial and financial power to exploit the world's markets and riches. At the same time, British naval supremacy enabled her to constrain her continental European rivals and deny them overseas colonies. It goes without saying that Britain was the primary beneficiary of this system, but by mid-century other European nations began to benefit as well. As trade barriers fell, international trade and productivity increased, first on the continent, then elsewhere. Buoyed by growth, more and more nations began to accept the concept of comparative advantage, which promised greater aggregate wealth if countries specialized in what they could produce most cheaply.

In the 1870s this system started to fall apart. After about twenty years of boom, prices slumped, profits plummeted, and Europe fell onto hard times. As the crisis sparked by the Panic of 1873 spread across the continent, more and more countries began to revert to more traditional mercantile strategies.[78] One after another, the major European states abandoned the liberal trading order epitomized by the Cobden-Chevalier Treaty of 1860.[79] Germany was the first to break ranks, raising tariffs to shelter agriculture and its nascent manufacturing industries. France and Sweden soon followed, imposing stiff taxes on foreign foodstuffs and manufactures. On the other side of the Atlantic, the United States turned away from roughly fifteen years of liberal trade. Of all the industrial nations, only Britain held fast to the doctrine of free trade.

Even more striking was the thrust outward—the scramble for empire. As British economic power declined, pressure mounted in countries like Germany, France, and Japan to secure access to cheap sources of raw materials. Asia, Africa, and to a lesser extent Latin America became sites of imperial expansion and great power rivalry. In the four decades before World War I, about one-quarter of the world's surface was distributed or redistributed as colonies among a half-dozen nations.[80] Britain and France each increased their imperial holdings by some three to four million square miles. Germany, Belgium, and Italy each acquired about one million new square miles, and Russia, Japan, and others followed suit. As the era of uncontested British hegemony in the world economy ended, there was little to prevent other governments from using mercantilism and imperialism to revive their slumping economies and pacify domestic discontent. Even the United Kingdom, the paragon of laissez-faire liberalism, joined other great powers in safeguarding and enlarging its imperial markets in Africa, Asia, and elsewhere.

Northern Interests

As the case of Hawaii suggests, America was not immune to these forces. Fears of overproduction and colonial encirclement led a growing number of politicians from the Northeast to call for acquisition of the Pacific archipelago. Following Captain Alfred Thayer Mahan's arguments, northern politicians stressed the island's strategic and commercial importance.[81] Hawaii was pivotal, they said; it occupied a central position in the Pacific, the center of a circle whose radius touched San Francisco, the Samoan Islands, and the Gilbert and Society Islands. "The main thing," William F. Draper (R-MA) explained, "is that those islands lie there in the heart of the Pacific, the controlling point in the commerce of that great ocean."[82] Whoever controlled Hawaii, and its strategic asset Pearl Harbor, would control not only the northern Pacific but as Mahan and other military strategists argued, the prospective isthmian canal route to the Orient.[83] Just as control of the Suez canal depended largely on command of Malta and Gibraltar, so too was control of the yet to be completed Panama Canal contingent upon control of Hawaii.[84] Better that America gain control over the "Gibraltar of the Pacific" than some other country.

Of the potential rivals, Britain was considered the most formidable challenge. It fielded the best navy in the world, and its possessions in the Atlantic and in Canada already insured it flanking positions along the Atlantic Coast. In the Pacific, Britain's positions out-numbered those of all the other powers: Japan, Germany, France, Russia, and Spain. According to expansionists like Draper and Lodge, Britain lacked only one position to establish hegemony in the Pacific and complete its encirclement of the United States: Hawaii.[85] No one believed that England desired war with America. The concerns voiced by northern Republicans were more subtle. By establishing a commanding military position in the Pacific, they warned, Britain would be in a more powerful bargaining position vis-à-vis commercial rivals like the United States. Should Congress fail to act, the message would be only too clear: America lacked the political will needed to promote its interests. Northern politicians argued that the consequences of American inaction on Hawaii would be enormous.

America's stake in foreign trade was sizable, and it was growing. Many of the factories and mills that lined the manufacturing belt looked abroad for critical raw materials, and many northern industrialists looked to foreign markets to make up for shortfalls in domestic demand.[86] What was critical from a geopolitical standpoint was the changing geographical pattern of America's export trade (see fig. 2.5 and table 2.2).[87] Before the Civil War, the bulk of America's exports went to Europe, particularly to Great Britain, which was the largest importer of American cotton and wheat. Although Europe continued to be the

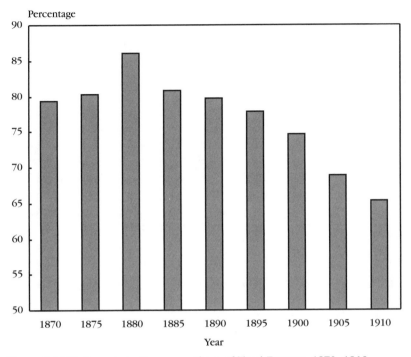

Figure 2.5 U.S. Exports to Europe as Share of Total Exports, 1870–1910

Sources: Ratios were estimated from data in Emory R. Johnson et al., *History of Domestic and Foreign Commerce of the United States* (New York: Burt Franklin, 1915), 2:75, table 58; David E. Novack and Matthew Simon, "Some Dimensions of the American Commercial Invasion of Europe, 1871–1914: An Introductory Essay," *Journal of Economic History* 24 (December 1964): 594–95, table 1.

biggest export market for the United States in the post–Civil War period, as America industrialized it sold an increasing proportion of its exports in North America, Asia, South America, and other non-European regions.[88] By the turn of the century, these regions were taking roughly 35 percent of all American exports.

The key fact is that *manufactures,* led by the sale of finished goods, accounted for the bulk of this trade with *less developed nations.* Raw materials continued to make up the single largest class of exports to the Old World.[89] By the 1890s it was clear that the real "commercial struggle between Europe and the United States centered not in the European market, but in the underdeveloped markets throughout the remainder of the world."[90] This was obvious to many congressional

Table 2.2 Europe's Share of American Exports, 1871–1910 (percentage)

Year	Crude Foodstuffs	Raw Materials	Manufactured Foodstuffs	Semi-Manufactures	Finished Manufactures
1871	68.3	91.6	76.7	71.4	59.0
1875	87.1	98.1	70.6	50.7	54.4
1880	94.3	99.7	81.8	57.7	51.4
1885	94.1	98.9	74.6	63.6	46.3
1890	88.8	94.9	79.8	63.3	43.8
1895	91.3	90.7	80.4	78.6	43.5
1900	90.7	85.9	82.8	82.5	44.0
1905	81.6	85.4	78.7	70.4	33.8
1910	73.1	85.9	73.6	71.0	33.8

Source: Mathew Simon and David E. Novack, "Some Dimensions of the American Commercial Invasion of Europe, 1871–1914: An Introductory Essay," *Journal of Economic History* 24 (December 1964): 598, table 3.

delegations from the Northeast, and they saw the acquisition of Hawaii as a significant first step in winning this struggle. Hawaii itself was not the prize. It was seen as a "stepping stone" to larger and better markets in the Pacific, and as a test of the American government's resolve to open the markets of the developing world. Here was where America's great advantage lay. Any New Yorker—even a Democrat like William Sulzer (D-NY)—could see the truth in that:

> We know today that we can not successfully compete with England, France, and Germany in the manufacture of many goods that are sold in Europe. They have the markets there, and they hold the markets there. They are great manufacturing countries, and they can manufacture materials just as cheap if not cheaper than we can. They pay, as a general thing, less wages than we do, and their workmen and artisans labor more hours a day. We, too, are a great manufacturing country. We must find a market for our surplus goods. What we can not sell in Europe we must find a market for in Central and South America, in Asia and Africa, in the East Indies and the South Seas. Here is a new outlet and a great market. There is no doubt our merchants are aware of it and alive to its great advantages and rich opportunities. On account of time, distance, and the cheapness of transportation, the advantages are all with us for profitable trade and commerce in the Pacific.[91]

In retrospect it is clear that Sulzer and others overestimated America's need for markets in Asia and Latin America, but this fact is irrelevant here. In the 1890s, the belief that the country would be running a permanent industrial surplus, well in excess of effective domestic purchasing power, was widespread in the northern core. So was the notion that America's best trading partners were nations less developed than the United States. If America did not move on these markets, other industrial powers would. The irrepressible Jonathan Dolliver (R-IA) spoke for many: "[T]he United States is a great manufacturing nation" which "must find new markets" in areas that are "fast passing under the control of other nations. . . . [O]ur history is filled with unaccepted opportunities. How much longer shall we hesitate?"[92] Islands like Hawaii, Dolliver and others charged, were needed to deny other powers access to land and sea zones vital to American security and commerce.

Arguments for territorial expansion closely paralleled some of the most important arguments advanced in favor of the building of a blue-water Navy. Indeed, in the minds of most northern congressmen, the two were inseparable. Naval power was needed to promote the spread of American commerce overseas; territory for naval bases and coaling stations was needed to enhance the Navy's ability to project power in a timely fashion.[93]

The case for annexing Hawaii was thus both economic and strategic. And it was more, for in arguing for annexation, northern Republicans were also advancing their partisan interests. Empire-building was a way of addressing the needs of hard-pressed workers during the country's worst economic crisis. The modernization of the Navy meant jobs for northern workers, which in turn meant votes for northern politicians. A strategy of territorial expansion also no doubt helped Republican leaders to shore-up and consolidate political support among industrialists, bankers, and merchants who were interested in expanded foreign trade and investment. Meanwhile, support for policies that promised to open markets in Latin America had pay-offs in the West, where such policies helped Republicans to counter the populist challenge. Finally, northern Republican leaders used the issue of expansionism for the most narrow of partisan purposes, using jingo nationalism as a "bloody shirt" to mobilize partisans and silence discontents.[94] It certainly was not the first time in American history that elected leaders played politics with the national interest.

In the politics of overseas expansion, constitutional arguments proved to be vehicles for advancing sectional interests. Many northern congressmen argued that the Constitution did not speak directly to the question of overseas expansion. Others argued that the Constitution was outdated. The Founding Fathers, they claimed, could not have anticipated how strategically valuable islands like Hawaii would eventually be. In either case, the only relevant consideration was whether acquiring Hawaii was in the national interest. Over and over again, northerners argued that this was the key question. To make sure the point was not lost on their southern colleagues, they pointed to Thomas Jefferson's own admission that the Constitution did not give him the authority to acquire land through the Louisiana Purchase. If Jefferson could set the Constitution aside when it came to foreign policy, why should contemporary issues of great national import be treated any differently?

Southern Anti-Imperialism

That northern politicians equated their section's interests with the nation's interests was no accident. Such rhetorical transpositions are commonplace in foreign policy debates, but rarely do they go unchallenged. From the outset of the debate over Hawaii, southerners objected. The acquisition of Hawaii, they argued, would mark a dangerous departure from one of America's oldest republican traditions—its repudiation of what John Quincy Adams once called "the murky radiance of dominion and power." Their point was this: America could not maintain its diplomatic independence from the entanglements of power politics if it wasted its strength by imitating the colonial aspirations of European nations. Instead, they warned, America would be transformed from a peaceful republic into a militant empire, burdened with the high costs of a standing army and powerful navy to defend colonies and put down internal dissent far from her shores. America would end up like the great imperial powers of the past: overextended, drained, and ultimately defeated.

> We hear much of "manifest destiny." That is a charming phrase. It tickles the ears of men; it panders to human vanity; it feeds the lurid flames of our ambition; it whets the sword of conquest; it is an anodyne for the troubled conscience, but it lureth to destruction. At the last it biteth like a serpent and stingeth like an adder. It is, however, no new doctrine. It is as old as the hills, "rock-ribbed and ancient as the sun." . . . Oh yes!

Manifest destiny is a seductive thing. It is the beautiful, the irresistible, the wicked Circe beckoning us on to our undoing. The entire pathway of man since the day when Adam was driven from Eden with flaming swords is black with the wrecks of nations who harkened to the siren song of "manifest destiny," and the epitaph upon whose tombstones is: "They were, but they are not."[95]

Southerners argued that America's security needs were different than those facing other nations. Flanked by two oceans and bordered by states too weak to pose a danger, the United States did not face the same imperatives that most other nations confronted. Even if one were to concede that America needed to protect itself from foreign powers, they argued, the acquisition of Hawaii would be counterproductive. The islands would present a vulnerable point to potential enemies, and require the maintenance of strong armed forces for their defense. It was more "cost effective," they suggested, to fortify defenses along the Pacific Coast to deter an attack on the United States than to invest resources some 2,000 miles from the nation's shores. More fundamentally, southern lawmakers discounted the "threat" posed by the leading Pacific powers, Britain and Japan. They noted that both powers had disclaimed any designs on Hawaiian sovereignty, and argued that neither had any incentive to provoke the United States. In the end, annexation would only involve the United States in great power rivalries and intrigues that were far better to avoid for both strategic and political reasons.

For every northern lawmaker who claimed that America's imperial destiny was calling, there was a southerner who warned of the danger of concentrated power. Like other republics that had indulged "the lust for empire," the United States would have to arm against other predatory colonial rivals. The net result would be a burgeoning state apparatus that would dispense patronage and control a powerful military establishment—the very evils that Jefferson, Madison, and others had labored so hard to prevent. James Richardson of Tennessee spoke for the vast majority of his southern brethren when he charged that a policy of territorial expansion in Hawaii would lead to "the magnifying of the National Government and national power, as against local and State authority. It is centralization itself."[96] The problem was not Hawaii. Southerners easily conceded that acquiring it was not, in itself, going to lead to tyranny. Like northerners, they were mostly concerned about precedent. But where northerners warned about the consequences of failing to annex Hawaii, southern lawmakers stressed the problems that annexation would bring. Annexation, opponents argued, would signal the impending decline of basic American principles: limited government, individual liberty, and "self-rule" for foreign peoples.

Such concerns and worries were almost always framed in legalistic language. Southerners said that colonialism contradicted the Declaration of Independence's emphasis on natural rights. The Constitution, they continued, only gave the federal government the authority to expand into territory that was contiguous to the United States, or at least situated on the North American continent. Acquisition of Hawaii was thus expressly forbidden by the "sacred text." Moreover, the government could only acquire territories with the express intention of admitting them to full statehood within a "reasonable" time frame, a possibility that even the most ardent imperialists were reluctant to consider. In contrast to their northern colleagues, southern representatives took the position that the Constitution must follow the flag.[97]

Why did southern lawmakers so fiercely oppose the acquisition of Hawaii, and imperialism more generally? Three reasons stand out: the southern economy, the populist movement, and southern racism.[98] By any measure, the South had a sizable stake in overseas trade. In fact, the region was more dependent on foreign markets than either the Northeast or the West. Between 1870 and 1910, the South's exports averaged between 15 and 20 percent of its regional output. By contrast, the Northeast's ratio of exports to regional output was much closer to the national average of exports-to-GNP of between 5 and 6 percent (see table 2.3). Even the West, which specialized in the production of exportable foodstuffs such as wheat and cattle, was sending less than 10 percent of the regional gross product abroad by the 1890s.[99]

Considering the South's heavy dependence on international markets, it is not surprising that southern politicians were among the most vocal proponents of expanded trade. Yet unlike the northern core, the southern periphery was first and foremost a producer and exporter of raw materials. Raw materials, especially cotton, were still the region's most important class of exports, accounting for more than 80 percent of its foreign sales in the late nineteenth century (table 2.4).[100] And as we have seen, markets for raw materials were not to be found in Asia or Latin America. Unlike the industrial Northeast or the agricultural West, the plantation South required industrial markets, either in the United States or Europe. The acquisition of islands like Hawaii might

Table 2.3 Regional Export Dependence, 1870–1910

Region	Ratio of Regional Exports to Regional Output				
	1870	1880	1890	1900	1910
East	.017	.039	.023	.021	.024
Midwest	.029	.122	.036	.062	.034
South	.192	.264	.206	.146	.109
West	.166	.184	.059	.059	.032
United States	.049	.075	.049	.062	.039

Sources: Ratios were estimated from data in William K. Hutchinson, "Regional Exports to Foreign Countries: United States, 1870–1914," in *Research in Economic History,* ed. Paul Uselding (Greenwich, Conn.: JAI Press, 1982), 7:133–237. In the case of *Regional Exports,* estimates are based on those indicated in Hutchinson, 145, table 1. *Regional Output* was calculated from Gross Regional Product Estimates of Hutchinson (200, table B.6), converting these from nominal to real terms using the GNP deflated index in Robert E. Lipsey, *Price and Quantity Trends in the Foreign Trade of the United States* (Princeton: Princeton University Press, 1963), 422–23, app. G, table G-8. Hutchinson's regional classification scheme differs from the one used here. In Hutchinson, states from the Great Lakes and Great Plains make up a separate category. In the table above this category of states is referred to as Midwest. The "East" refers to the New England and Middle Atlantic regions.

be useful for promoting expanded trade with nonindustrialized countries that could import northern manufactures and even western foodstuffs, but it held little promise for securing foreign buyers for southern cotton, tobacco, and other raw materials. Those markets already existed in Europe.

The southern experience thus contradicted the notion that "trade follows the flag." Overseas possessions were not required to guarantee wider access to foreign markets for the South.[101] For this reason, many southern lawmakers found arguments about the commercial value of islands like Hawaii to be unpersuasive. William M. Howard (D-GA), a member of the House Foreign Affairs Committee, hit the nail on the head when he stated, "I am in favor of the extension of commerce, but I do not regard commercial extension of our commerce as synonymous with territorial aggrandizement."[102] What southerners feared was policies like naval buildup or colonialism that might inadvertently exacerbate tensions among industrial nations and thereby threaten American access to the great industrial markets of Europe. For the South as a whole, the economic rewards of imperialism were minimal, and the political risks—both abroad and at home—were unacceptable.

Southern lawmakers were risk averse: they were more sensitive to possible losses than potential gains. The "prophets of the New South"—newspapermen like Henry Grady of the Atlanta *Constitution,*

Table 2.4 Regional Exports by Commodity Type, 1870–1910 (percentage)

		Exports				
Region	Class[1]	1870	1880	1890	1900	1910
East	Materials	8.7	8.9	8.5	9.8	17.3
	Food	30.4	53.2	56.4	11.1	0.8
	Manufactures	60.9	37.9	35.2	79.2	79.9
Midwest	Materials	5.0	2.2	4.1	1.2	2.2
	Food	80.9	92.1	83.3	98.0	81.5
	Manufactures	14.2	5.6	12.6	0.9	16.4
South	Materials	98.5	86.4	89.8	81.5	85.6
	Food	1.0	11.9	9.2	15.1	9.0
	Manufactures	1.1	1.7	0.9	4.3	5.3
West	Materials	—	1.0	0.1	1.2	3.8
	Food	93.3	96.7	82.1	89.3	25.4
	Manufactures	6.7	3.7	17.8	10.1	70.7

Source: Based on data in William K. Hutchinson, "Regional Exports of the United States to Foreign Countries: A Structural Analysis," in *Research in Economic History,* ed. Paul Uselding (Greenwich, Conn.: JAI Press, 1986), 10:131–54, 140, table 3. For each region and year the columns add up to 100 percent except for rounding error. Hutchinson's regional classification scheme differs from the one used here. In Hutchinson, states from the Great Lakes and Great Plains make up a separate category. In the table above this category of states is referred to as Midwest. The "East" refers to the New England and Middle Atlantic regions.

[1]The five standard commodity classes were organized as follows: materials (raw materials); food (crude and manufactured foods); manufactures (semi- and finished manufactures).

Daniel Augustus Tompkins of the Charlotte *Observer,* and Henry Watterson of the Louisville *Courier-Journal*—may have believed that aggressive commercial and territorial expansion in South America and Asia provided a key to curing the South's depressed, colonial condition. They, however, were a distinct minority in the South, and few of the region's representatives in Washington were prepared to argue their position.[103] Most politicians saw whatever gains southern industry could hope to reap through expanded trade in the Pacific Basin as vastly outweighed by the needs of southern agriculture. Old-line Democrats' attitudes toward empire-building in Hawaii and elsewhere reflected this essential fact. Twenty-five years after the end of the Civil War, more than two-thirds of the southern labor force was still involved in agriculture, and most of these were engaged in the cultivation of cotton. Here lay the Democrats' core constituency, not in the new urban, professional "business class" sprouting up in cities like Atlanta,

Birmingham, and Charlotte.[104] Few southern Democrats were prepared to compromise agriculture in the name of industrial progress, especially when such temporizing could open them to attack from southern populists. They had every reason to worry.

The Populists posed a formidable electoral challenge, the likes of which the Democratic party had not faced since the 1850s. Populism was a descendant of earlier independent or third-party movements, and it spread throughout the South in the 1880s. By the beginning of the 1890s over a million rural southerners were members of the region's leading agrarian organization, the Southern Alliance. Promising economic relief for dispossessed farmers, the Alliance seized control of the Alabama and Florida legislatures and won a majority of the congressional seats in Georgia, Virginia, Kentucky, and North Carolina. The Alliance was superseded by the new People's party in the 1892 three-way presidential contest between Cleveland, Harrison, and the Populists' candidate, General James B. Weaver. The Populists demonstrated surprising strength in the rural South, and by 1894 they had made deep inroads into the Democracy's base in North Carolina, Alabama, and Georgia. Populists would never again demonstrate such political strength, but they had managed to shake the foundations of the southern political establishment. Democratic leaders found themselves scrambling for their political lives. Their response was predictable. Conservative Democrats tried to bury the Populists' main issue—economic justice—by invoking the issue of race. They resorted to what C. Vann Woodward called "the implacable dogmas of racism, white solidarity, white supremacy, and the bloody shirt."[105]

For the Old South, the imperialism debate was ready-made for rallying poor marginal whites back to the Democrats' fold. Southern Democrats seized the anti-imperialist cause in part because it allowed them to present themselves as defenders of white society against the twin dangers of immigrant onslaught and populist egalitarianism. Having openly appealed for black votes on the promise of political equality for all, the populists faced daily barrages of racist slurs. Meanwhile, the old Democrats argued that the annexation of "tropical lands" like Hawaii would mean the unrestricted immigration of "inferior races" to the United States. They stressed the dangers that "cheap coolie labor" in the Pacific would pose to southern agriculture, knowing full well what a chilling effect this would have on poor whites. The South's old leaders also warned of the perils of miscegenation, leprosy, and the breakdown of the social order. The country had enough problems with race. Why, they asked, compound them? Southern conservatives thus lumped together populists and imperialists, painting both as threats to white society. In the 1890s, the political survival instincts of the old southern elite help to explain their apparent obsession with the racial purity of America's "national identity" and their virulence and enthusiasm in denouncing the imperialists.

To be sure, such racist concerns were not a uniquely southern phenomenon. Neither side in the Great Debate over empire was liberal in the contemporary sense of the word.[106] Northern imperialists and southern anti-imperialists shared the prevailing view in white America that Anglo-Saxons were superior to other peoples. But as the debates over Hawaii make clear, the most strident nativist arguments against acquiring overseas possessions came from the South. Democrats used issues like Hawaii to obfuscate and otherwise distract the southern electorate from more pressing and less tractable realities like the falling price of cotton on the world market. The point is not that imperialism was a decisive issue in the war between southern conservatives and populists. It was not: southern Populists were as opposed to imperial expansion as southern Democrats, and thus could not be easily outmaneuvered on this issue. The point is that for southern Democratic leaders, anti-imperialism proved to be a safe and convenient political issue. While never losing sight of the commercial interests of the planter class, the old elite was able to give the farmers one more reason not to turn their backs on the Democracy—the party of white supremacy—by voting Populist.

Preaching the doctrine of "white supremacy" was one way to appeal to southern farmers. Playing on long-standing fears of Republican militarism and political domination was another time-honored tactic. There was, of course, more here than mere electioneering. Just as northern leaders viewed southern resistance to overseas expansion as parochial, sentimental, and backward, southern representatives equated an expansionist foreign policy with the Republicans' traditional policy of bigger, more centralized, and more intrusive national government. The recent experience with the 1890 "Force Bill"—a move to give federal courts power to supervise elections in congressional districts, which was championed by the same Henry Cabot Lodge who led the crusade to annex Hawaii—only made southern whites more apprehensive about policies that would extend the power of the central government.[107] What assurances were there that the large military establishment needed to suppress political resistance in foreign colonies would not someday be used to coerce underdeveloped areas within the nation's borders? As in everything else in American politics, the Civil War cast its long shadow on the debate over imperialism.

If appeals for "self-reliance" and "self-determination" for foreign peoples were very popular in the South, then this is partly because they were as much anti-Republican as anti-imperialist. In the minds of most southerners, fighting imperialism was a proxy in the war against Republicanism, Wall Street, and the Eastern Establishment. The question that must be asked is this: Why was anti-imperialism not as politically salient in the West?

In fact, on all of the key issues—Cuba, Hawaii, the Philippines, Puerto Rico, and Isthmian Canal—western states tended to align with northeastern ones in Congress (see table 2.1). Given the region's economic profile and political make-up, one might have anticipated more opposition to Republican expansionism. Like the South, the West was heavily agricultural. The West was also a "colony" of the Northeastern "metropole." If the southern variant of populism was the most potent, the western "wing" of the People's party was nevertheless a force to be reckoned with. How then were northeastern leaders able to win the support of western politicians? An analysis of the fight over the tariff, and its relationship to overseas expansion, sheds a great deal of light on the matter.

The Bargaining Tariff: Winning the West to the Expansionist Cause

The drive to open foreign markets also led American leaders to search for ways to turn the tariff into an instrument of commercial expansion. Before the 1890s, the United States used the tariff the way most developing countries do today: to protect industry and produce revenue. Various ideas for expanding the tariff's role circulated in Washington in the 1880s, but each ran up against the resistance of congressional pork-barrelers, log-rollers, and deal-brokers who defended parochial interests vested in existing tariff legislation. Harrison's administration was the first to successfully merge the tariff with broader foreign policy concerns. In the summer of 1890, as legislators debated the McKinley Tariff, Benjamin Harrison's secretary of state, James G. Blaine, pressed Congress to surrender part of its prerogative over trade. He asked lawmakers to give the president authority to use the tariff as a lever to pry open markets in South America for American producers. After much maneuvering, Congress attached a key provision to the bill known as the "reciprocity clause," which granted the White House the power to raise duties on imports from countries that denied American producers access to their markets. That action started a contentious process of reform. This process moved in fits and starts, gradually transforming the tariff into an instrument of statecraft and commercial expansion.

With the possible exception of the "silver question," no political issue provoked more heated debate in the 1890s than the tariff and attempts to reform it. Political representatives from the northern industrial core and the southern agrarian periphery clashed repeatedly over the issue on the House and Senate floors. This was no ordinary fight: parliamentary tradition and decorum often gave way to personal innuendo and insult. Support for reciprocity was strongest in the Northeast. Many western politicians also came to see wisdom in using the tariff as a bargaining instrument to open new trading outlets for farmers, millers, and ranchers. Southern congressmen strongly opposed these institutional reforms, arguing that they were inconsistent with the nation's laissez-faire liberal heritage. The alternatives they offered advanced a competing set of political and economic interests. Every major piece of tariff legislation during the period divided the country along these sectional lines.[108]

Analyses of America's "inexorable drive" toward overseas expansion ignore the protracted debates that advanced and stalled tariff reform. The divisiveness of the issue requires explanation. Why did tariff reciprocity provoke such bitter controversy? Why did powerful interests oppose the bargaining tariff with such vigor, making tariff revision so much more incremental than it might have been? After all, most Americans were convinced that overseas markets were needed to avoid overproduction and to maintain domestic prosperity and social harmony.[109] Indeed, industrialists and agrarians were of one mind on this essential point. And the use of reciprocity to stimulate trade was hardly a radical idea: other nations routinely used "bargaining tariffs" as levers to open foreign markets.[110]

In the American case, the bargaining tariff proved to be so divisive because it would inevitably serve the interests of some parts of the country at the expense of others. Like the naval buildup, tariff reciprocity disproportionately benefited the northern core. For this reason, rather than for cultural or constitutional ones, the southern periphery vehemently opposed northern plans for turning the tariff into an instrument of export expansion. As noted by John Sherman, the venerable senator from Ohio, "The real struggle in tariff legislation is one of *sections.*"[111] A large part of the story of overseas expansion in the 1890s lies in explaining how the Northeast was able to prevail by mobilizing western support for its cause. In the politics of coalition-building, the tariff proved to be a critical instrument in the hands of northern politicians.

Reciprocity and Protection

To understand the 1890s debate over tariff reform, one must put contemporary notions of reciprocity aside. When the term is used today, it connotes open or liberal trade.[112] Reciprocity is seen as a method for promoting the free flow of goods across national boundaries. One hundred years ago, reciprocity meant something quite different and served much more limited ends. Neither an instrument of free trade nor a tool of pure protection, it was something in between. In the words of historian Thomas McCormick, reciprocity was an "eat-your-cake-and-have-it-too" commercial stratagem designed to protect the domestic market from foreign competitors while opening foreign markets to American producers.[113] In short, reciprocity was seen as the status quo plus: it held open the promise of new markets for some of America's producers while offering protection for those who depended on the home market. Champ Clark, congressman from Missouri, expressed many ardent free traders' negative view of reciprocity when he called it a "deceptive scheme"—"nothing but free trade in spots or protection with free trade on the side."[114]

What Secretary Blaine and others asked Congress to do in 1890 was give the president the authority to raise or lower tariffs on specific goods. The president could use this power to pressure nations that exported to the United States to "reciprocate" by giving special or preferential treatment to American products.[115] From the very beginning, the notion of reciprocity embodied in the bargaining tariff was aimed at nations that were less developed than the United States, particularly those located in South America.[116] Some form of pressure to open these markets was deemed necessary because American producers faced stiff competition from British exporters, whose share of the regional market dwarfed America's (see fig. 2.6). In the battle for South American markets, American officials held one card they could play: South American reliance on the United States as a consumer of its raw materials.[117] American imports from these countries far exceeded American

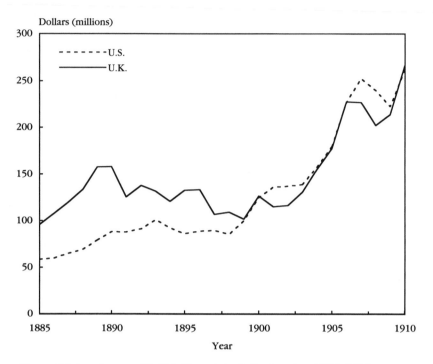

Figure 2.6 American and British Exports to Latin America, 1885–1910

Sources: Estimates for British exports based on data contained in Custom and Excise Department, *Annual Statement of the Trade and Navigation of the United Kingdom with Foreign Countries and British Possessions,* selected years. Estimates for American exports based on data in *Statistical Abstract of the United States,* selected years. British exports (£) were converted to dollars using exchange rate figures in B. R. Mitchell, *British Historical Statistics* (Cambridge: Cambridge University Press, 1988), 702.

exports to the region, and U.S. officials recognized that this gave the United States considerable leverage (fig. 2.7). The basic idea was simple enough: force South America to pay for the privilege of exporting to North America.

Instituting a bargaining tariff required giving the president unprecedented tariff-making powers. This is not what vexed many congressmen, though opponents of reciprocity did resort to constitutional principle—such arguments seemed *de rigueur* when debating tariff legislation.[118] And no one seemed particularly upset about using strong-arm tactics to pry concessions from South American leaders. Ideals were not really the issue; interests were. What generated controversy

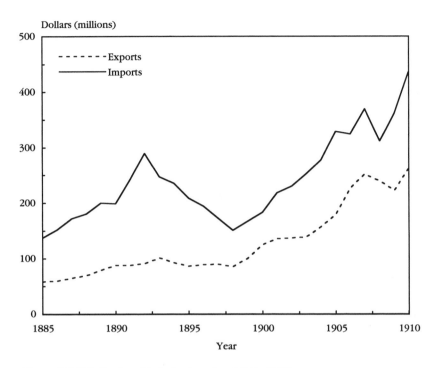

Figure 2.7 U.S. Trade with Latin America, 1885–1910
Source: Compiled from *Statistical Abstract of the United States,* selected years.

was the fact that some parts of the country would benefit much more from trade with South America (and expanded presidential power) than others. Reciprocity was good news for the American manufacturer, as well as for merchants and bankers who had a stake in freer commercial relations in the hemisphere. The countries of South America were importers of manufactured goods; their economies might also make good markets for American foodstuffs. Reciprocity, however, had little to offer other raw materials producers. Because South American economies were essentially extractive, specializing in the production of one or two raw materials or specialty items like sugar or coffee, they made poor markets for parts of the United States that produced commodities like cotton. Meanwhile, for cotton and other raw materials producers who depended on Europe to sell their surpluses, heavy-handed bargaining tactics to displace the British in South

America carried the same risks as naval build-up and territorial acquisition: such tactics ran the unnecessary risk of triggering a trade war.

These controversies plagued each attempt to rewrite the country's tariff laws in the 1890s. The McKinley Tariff, named after William McKinley (R-OH), the Chairman of the House Ways and Means Committee, was passed over the vehement protests of free traders. This legislation, with its so-called bargaining tariff, raised the average duty on imports to 48.4 percent from the average 45.1 level set in 1883 (fig. 2.8). More importantly, the new law moved five "tropical" commodities imported in large volume from South America (sugar, molasses, coffee, tea, and hides) to the "free list" of goods that entered the United States without paying duty.[119] Responding to Secretary Blaine's persistent calls to give the president more discretion in setting tariff policy, the House and Senate granted the White House the power to reimpose duties on any "tropical list" commodity if the exporting nation charged duties on American goods that the president deemed "to be reciprocally unequal and unreasonable." In addition, Congress gave the president the authority to negotiate bilateral reciprocity treaties with exporting nations to bind the specified commodities on the free list.

None of these actions by the president required approval by the Congress. Yet even the Senate, whose members jealously guarded their power to ratify treaties, found this arrangement acceptable. Over the next two years the Harrison administration signed reciprocity treaties with ten countries, seven of which were independent nations or colonial possessions in South America: Brazil, Guatemala, Honduras, Nicaragua, Salvador, Santo Domingo, Spain (for Cuba and Puerto Rico), and Britain for its Caribbean possessions (Barbados, Jamaica, Leeward Islands, Trinidad, Windward Islands, and British Guiana).[120] Tariff concessions were made by foreign nations on a range of goods including livestock, meat products, grains, railway cars, structural steel and iron, and machinery. In exchange, the United States allowed "noncompeting goods"—items not produced (or not produced in large quantities) by American producers—onto the domestic market. Agreements concerning meat products were also reached with two European nations: Germany and Portugal. And in three cases, the Harrison administration actually retaliated by reimposing duties on exporters who refused to cooperate with the United States: Venezuela, Colombia, and Haiti.

Reciprocity was temporarily shelved in 1894, when Congress passed the Wilson-Gorman Tariff Act, which lowered tariff rates and relied less on strong-arm strategies. The bill was designed to balance

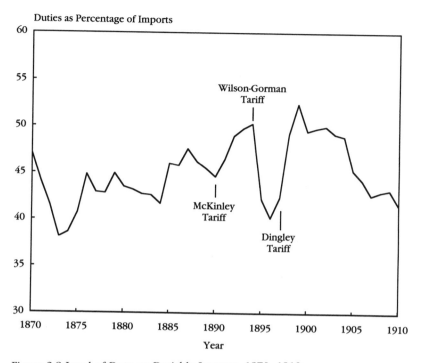

Figure 2.8 Level of Duty on Dutiable Imports, 1870–1910

Source: Bureau of the Census, *Historical Statistics of the United States, Colonial Times to 1970,* 2 vols. (Washington, D.C., 1975), Series U 207-212, p. 888.

sectional interests within the Democratic party by offering New England lower duties on raw materials and the South lower duties on manufactured goods. After quickly passing the House 204 to 140, the bill ran into trouble in the Senate. Northern interests were not satisfied. Senator Arthur Pue Gorman of Maryland, leading a group of Democrats, joined Republicans in "gutting" the bill, amending it some 634 times.[121] The final outcome, passed into law without President Cleveland's signature, was a law that seemed to please no one.

The bargaining tariff reemerged in 1897 with the signing of the Dingley Tariff Act. Shortly after assuming power, President McKinley asked for "especial attention" to the "reenactment and extension" of reciprocity in making a new tariff. McKinley claimed that the success of the 1890 tariff law "amply justified a further experiment and additional discretionary power in the making of commercial treaties."[122] Working closely with his friend Nelson Dingley, Jr. (R-ME), the new Chairman of the Ways and Means Committee, the president's aides fashioned a bill that sailed through the Republican-controlled House after only two weeks of debate. It encountered tougher going in the Senate, but in the end the Senate passed a version of the bill that closely resembled the House's measure. The result was a sharp increase in the nation's tariff rates. The average rate on dutiable imports rose to 47.6 percent, compared with the 41.2 percent under the 1894 Wilson-Gorman Act and the 48.4 percent under the McKinley Tariff. No one could say that the Republican party—"the party of protection"—had failed to meet its commitment to shelter the home market from foreign goods.

Like the McKinley Act, the Dingley Tariff sought to balance high tariffs with reciprocity. In a limited version of the "reciprocity clause," the executive branch was allowed to threaten penalties on coffee and tea to win trade benefits from countries in Latin America and Asia. The president was also allowed to offer some concessions in an effort to win French support for international bimetallism.[123] Most significantly, Congress granted the president authority to negotiate reciprocity treaties that could lower U.S. duties up to 20 percent in exchange for similar reductions on American goods by other nations.[124] Those who were alarmed by this delegation of tariff-making power to the president could take comfort from the various conditions that Congress imposed on the treaty-making process. Every treaty had to be completed within two years, could only be in force for five, and required consent of both the Senate and House.

McKinley had hoped for wider powers, but he made the most of what Congress gave him. Over the next two years, the administration negotiated thirteen treaties, including major ones with France, Argentina, Ecuador, and Jamaica (by Great Britain).[125] The treaties were submitted to Congress in late 1899. There they languished and ultimately died a quiet death. Free traders saw little reason to support treaties that did little to bring down America's high tariff walls. Legislators who did support the dual strategy of protection and reciprocity saw less urgency in the latter as the economy began to recover from the severe downturn of the mid-1890s. Remaining hopes for the treaties were dashed in September 1901 when McKinley was struck down by an assassin's bullet. A day before, in his last speech, the president proclaimed that America's "period of exclusiveness is past" and that reciprocity was "the natural outgrowth" of the nation's industrial devel-

Table 2.5 Regional Support for Bargaining Tariff (percentage)

Region	1890[1]	1894[2]	1897[3]
Northeast			
New England	87.5	76.9	96.2
Middle Atlantic	65.3	61.6	89.6
Great Lakes	67.1	43.6	78.2
South			
Southeast	18.1	6.3	21.3
Southwest	0	16.0	25.0
West			
Great Plains	75.0	50.0	65.8
Mountain West	100.0	50.0	0
Pacific Coast	75.0	72.7	55.6

Source: Computations from House roll call data.

Note: Territories that were not incorporated as states by 1890 are not included. See table 2.1 for regional groupings.

[1] Final vote on the McKinley Tariff. A vote for the bill is a vote for protectionism plus reciprocity. May 21, 1890.

[2] Final vote on the Wilson-Gorman Tariff. A vote against the bill is a vote for protectionism plus reciprocity. February 1, 1894.

[3] Final vote on the Dingley Tariff. A vote for the bill is a vote for protectionism plus reciprocity. March 31, 1897.

opment.[126] It was only a matter of time before others took up where the fallen president left off.

The Politics of Reciprocity

Final votes on each bill provide a barometer of political support for reciprocity. A vote for the McKinley and Dingley bills was a vote for reciprocity plus protection; a vote for the Wilson-Gorman bill was a vote against this tariff strategy. As table 2.5 indicates, support for a commercial strategy combining protection and reciprocity was strongest in the Northeast, especially in New England, and the West. Elected officials from both regions generally favored the McKinley and Dingley bills and opposed the Wilson bill. By contrast, congressmen from the South generally favored free trade; they consistently opposed tariff revisions that relied only on the bargaining tariff. Southern support for the Wilson bill was revealing. Not only did southern lawmakers favor lowering duties on imported raw materials and manufactures, they also favored an alternative scheme for generating federal revenues—a graduated income tax on personal and corporate wealth which would fall disproportionately on the Northeast.

The Northeast

Any explanation of the Northeast's interest in reciprocity must start with business, which was the source of pressure on the government to promote trade with South America. Seriously concerned about the problems of surplus production and idle capital, leading industrialists like Andrew Carnegie favored expanding the nation's export trade and believed that reciprocity was "the best step" for penetrating markets where the United States was at some disadvantage.[127] Theodore C. Search, the president of the National Association of Manufacturers, a vocal trade association representing small-to-medium-sized corporations, agreed. Looking back on the McKinley Tariff, Search argued that the use of reciprocity in 1890 "opened a new era in our international commerce and provided the means for an enormous expansion of the foreign markets for our products."[128] One historian argues that for industrialists like Search, "the term reciprocity took on an almost mythological cast;" it was a "new god" uniting and transcending "the lesser deities of protection and free trade."[129] In more secular terms, the bargaining tariff was seen as a way to break Britain's hold on the South American market. This in turn meant new vents for expanding American production and a remedy for chronic industrial depression.

If industrialists worshipped reciprocity, northern politicians were only slightly less enthusiastic. Once deeply committed to the notion that the American market was big enough to guarantee stable growth, more and more politicians now believed that economic growth was dependent on foreign trade. Albert J. Hopkins, the powerful Illinoisan, spoke for many northern House members: "We have reached a point in our industrial and agricultural development where, in order to further the continued success and prosperity of our people, we must have our full share of the foreign trade of all the great countries, not only in Europe, but in Central and South America." This can only be achieved, Hopkins went on, "under the principles of reciprocity."[130] Hopkins was not alone in believing that domestic overproduction was the source of America's economic woes, or that the national government would have to play a more active role in finding new markets for domestic producers. Politicians from the Northeast quickly learned that this argument was a powerful one on the hustings and employed it regularly. By 1896, the Republicans christened reciprocity one of the "twin measures of American policy" in the party platform. The other, not surprisingly, was protection.

For years northern congressmen had manipulated the industrial tariff. They placed heavy duties on European manufactures to keep import prices high. Like everyone else, northeasterners had to pay higher prices for imported and domestic manufactured goods. However, unlike other parts of the country, the northern industrial core recaptured the taxes it paid in the form of federal expenditures in the Northeast. As the early twentieth-century economist Alvin S. Johnson explained it, the protective tariff system that was erected after the Civil War channelled capital "from all other classes in society to the capitalist manufacturer."[131] At a time when the tariff was the major source of national revenue (accounting on average for 50 percent of total federal revenue between the 1880 and 1910), it was the Northeast, and especially the Middle Atlantic and Great Lakes regions, that reaped the lion's share of federal expenditures (fig. 2.9, table 2.6).[132] This system paid handsome political dividends for core congressmen. They had an obvious stake in preserving what was basically a forced transfer payment from the agrarian periphery to the industrial core. The system not only protected northern profits and jobs from European imports, but it also produced huge revenues that could be used for political patronage and coalition-building. Elaborate schemes were devised to turn customs duties into political capital. The most notorious was the expansion of the veterans' pension program: it disproportionately favored Union veterans and their survivors.[133] The naval buildup of the 1890s worked in a similar way. It is clear why northern congressmen so strongly opposed southern free-trade proposals that would bring down the tariff walls.

Above the Mason-Dixon line, one of the great attractions of tariff reciprocity is that it made it possible to lower *some* tariffs without threatening this system. Little would be sacrificed and much could be gained, provided that reciprocity was aimed only at nations exporting goods that did not compete with American industry. This proviso was crucial, and its importance was hardly lost on Secretary Blaine. In an effort to reassure those who feared that reciprocity might actually be "free trade in spots," Blaine explained in the pages of the *New York Tribune* and the *Chicago Tribune* that the bargaining tariff "was not in conflict with a protective tariff, but supplementary thereto" because "the enactment of reciprocity is the safeguard of protection."[134] Proponents of reciprocal trade who followed the secretary's lead in seeking to exchange South American raw materials for North American manufactures could expect the support of most reelection-minded congress-

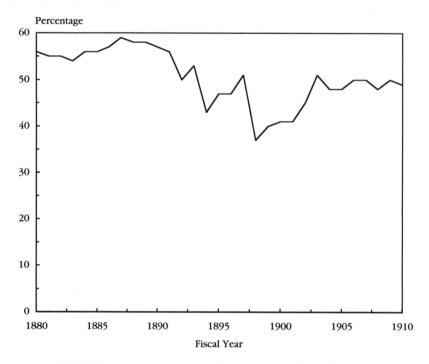

Figure 2.9 Tariff Revenue as Share of Federal Income, 1880–1910

Sources: Based on Richard Franklin Bensel, *Sectionalism and American Political Development, 1880–1980* (Madison: University of Wisconsin Press, 1984), 69. Recalculated from Bureau of the *Census, Historical Statistics of the United States, Colonial Times to 1970*, 2 vols. (Washington, D.C., 1975), Series Y 352-357, p. 1106.

men in the manufacturing states. In many instances, they could even expect the support of those representing districts with highly protectionist industries like textiles, iron, and steel. Yet this would not be enough to guarantee success. Leaders like Harrison and McKinley understood that industrial interests needed allies. In America in the 1890s, the West was the key to success.

The West

The intertwined issues of naval reform, commercial expansion, and the bargaining tariff provided Republican leaders with the basis for an electoral alliance with politicians from the agrarian West. This was a clever strategy. Not only did it deal with the immediate problem of winning support for the Northeast's foreign policy agenda, but it provided a

Table 2.6 Percentage of Federal Expenditures by Region, 1880–1900

Year	Northeast	South	West
1880	67.2	21.1	11.4
1885	51.6	35.1	14.2
1890	49.0	31.3	19.9
1895	43.7	36.6	20.5
1900	54.2	27.7	17.9

Sources: Percentages were estimated from data in Lance E. Davis and John Legler, "The Government in the American Economy, 1815–1902: A Quantitative Study," *Journal of Economic History* 26 (December 1966): 514–52, table 1. Per capita data was recalculated using state population figures for appropriate years. Population data is from Bureau of the Census, *Historical Statistics of the United States, Colonial Times to 1970* (Washington, D.C., 1975), 1:24–37. For each year the columns add up to 100 percent except for rounding error. In Davis and Legler, Delaware and Maryland are treated as southern states.

means to counter the powerful and seductive appeal of agrarian populism.[135] The populist insurgency posed a serious challenge to the Republican party's dominance in the Great Plains and parts of the Mountain West. The fear was not so much that the newly founded Populist party would replace the Republican party, but rather that the Democrats would be the beneficiaries of any three-way competition, picking up House and Senate seats. Republican leaders were looking for ways to forestall further party losses.

Aware that wheat growers and millers were suffering from weak markets and looking for new outlets, they seized the opportunity. Starting from the premise that low farm prices, one of the farmers' chief causes for complaint, stemmed from overproduction (rather than manipulation by powerful trusts), Blaine and others argued that tariff reform was the remedy for the West's problems. By manipulating tariff rates on "tropical goods" like sugar and coffee, the monocrop nations of South America could be pressured to open their markets to western farmers as well as to northeastern manufacturers. A more powerful navy would help guarantee new markets.

Many populists believed that the Republicans were up to no good. Some accused them of trying to divert the attention of the masses from the real problems—usurious interest rates, exorbitant prices for farm equipment, and greedy transportation rates. Others contended that the party of Lincoln was more interested in their votes than their well-being. Despite opposition, the Republicans' strategy worked in Congress.[136] Hard-pressed farmers seized the promise of new overseas markets. As one House member noted, "Blaine's plan has run like a prairie fire all over my district."[137] In Washington, politicians from the rural West embraced Blaine's tariff strategy—perhaps because they thought it would work, but certainly because it allowed them to show constituents that their elected officials were working hard to solve the agrarian crisis.

Western farmers have sometimes been depicted as ignorant or naive for choosing the Republicans in this contest, for in the end Latin American markets did not hold much promise for American grain producers. One problem with this argument is that it underplays the tremendous sway of the "overproduction thesis" in the 1890s and the hope that producers in many economic sectors (not just small farmers) placed on overseas solutions.[138] There is another problem with the view of farmers as ignorant and manipulated: it views their political calculus in very restricted terms.[139] Many farmers and lawmakers from the trans-Mississippi West found Republicans' promises of economic relief hard to resist, for whatever did happen on Latin American markets, the dominant party in Washington could find many ways to reward western support on foreign policy issues. Republicans were in a position to address many immediate issues of pressing concern to western farmers—inflationary money legislation, railroad regulation, monopoly control, etc. If the cost to the West was support for reciprocity legislation that offered uncertain benefits, then so be it. The fact that reciprocity posed no real *threat* to western farmers' interests made the choice even easier.

For the Northeast, this coalition-building strategy produced gains that may have exceeded what even Secretary Blaine thought possible. For the rest of the decade, on all of the key tariff votes in the House (and most Navy votes), most western congressmen sided with their colleagues from the Northeast. The politics of tariff reform grew more complex with the rise of the "silver question" as a national issue, but the Northeast's strategy remained the same: co-opt the West.[140] The Republicans succeeded in dividing the Populists' ranks and fatally weakening the movement.

On the foreign policy front, it was a brilliant maneuver that the Democrats were not able to match. What made the Republican strategy so shrewd is that it split the agrarians along sectional lines. Western agrarians joined the reciprocity movement; southern agrarians were left behind.

The South

There was never much chance that the South would support reciprocity. The kind of tariff reform that Harrison, Blaine, and McKinley advocated might be useful in selling steel and wheat to nonindustrialized nations in South America, but it held little promise for southern producers who depended on industrialized markets in the United States and Europe (especially Britain) for the sale of their raw materials, especially "King Cotton." Roger Q. Mills (D-TX), former head of Ways and Means and long-time champion of free trade, underscored the regional bias inherent in the reciprocity measures pushed by Blaine and his supporters. The fact that reciprocity was designed to serve the interests of the industrial Northeast was obvious, he argued, given that it was aimed at South America, not Europe. Meanwhile, Mills sought to undercut the northeastern-western alliance in support of the bargaining tariff:

> If its advocates are sincere in wanting to find larger markets for agricultural products, why do they not move for reciprocity with Europe instead of with South America? Europe takes from us more than $600,000,000 in agricultural products yearly, which is sixty times as much as the southern countries takes. If reciprocity with South America would increase our exports 50 percent—and it probably would—it would open a market for $5,000,000 more of farm products, and similar results, following from reciprocity with Europe, would increase our exports of farm products by $300,000,000. Now, if the farmer is the person to be benefited, we must look eastward, not southward, for markets. . . . It is not to the 50,000,000 shepherds and farmers to the south of us, but to the 300,000,000 shopkeepers to the east of us, that we must look to consume our surplus farm products.[141]

For all that has been written about the rise of the "New South" at the turn of the century, with its nascent textile and steel industries, the region remained a prisoner of its long-standing position in the world economy.[142] The South was more dependent on international markets than any other region in the country, and free trade was overwhelmingly its strategy of choice.[143] As we have seen, southern politicians had no interest in commercial strategies like reciprocity that might antagonize the British. Some southerners expressed concerns that Britain would respond to America's bargaining tactics in South America by turning to Indian or Egyptian suppliers of cotton.[144] Challenging British dominance in South America might be in the Northeast's interests, but such a strategy could backfire on the South. For the South, a strategy of free trade made geopolitical sense.

Southerners also had good domestic reasons for opposing reciprocity. Reciprocity would maintain the pernicious effects of a tariff system that imposed what Richard Bensel calls a "twofold tax" on the region: southern wealth was transferred to the northern core directly, in the form of higher prices for manufactures, and indirectly, in the form of tariff revenues.[145] Most southerners categorically rejected northern arguments about the need for a bargaining tariff that would protect northern industry. They scoffed at the notion that American industry could not compete against the Europeans. If industries feared European producers so much, they asked, then why not simply cut production costs to make them more competitive? One way to do this was to allow raw materials like iron, coal, and wool to enter the country duty-free.[146] They also ridiculed claims that the tariff was in the interest of workers and farmers. In a speech that received prolonged applause on the House floor, Charles F. Crisp (D-GA), future Speaker of the House, captured the prevailing view: "No amount of juggling, no amount of sophistry, no amount of theory will prevent them from understanding really what this protective system is; that its effect is to take from one class to give to another, to take from the masses to give to a class."[147] Southerners also had a response to the argument that protective tariffs were needed to generate federal revenue. If money were truly needed to meet the federal government's obligations (which they doubted because government revenues usually exceeded federal expenditures), then why not tax the wealthy to make-up for the shortfall? Was it not fair to ask those who benefited the most from protection to pay more to help government serve the people?

Just as northerners used reciprocity as a political weapon, southerners used free trade as a political stratagem. Their arguments were clearly designed to divide-and-conquer the forces lining up behind the bargaining tariff. In an effort to sow divisions between industrialists and their workers, southerners appealed to the latter as consumers rather than as producers, offering them the advantages of lower prices on manufactured items. Calls for lower tariffs on raw materials were similarly aimed at playing on New England industry's fear of competitors in the Midwest.[148] Merchants, traders, and bankers from the great port cities of Boston, Philadelphia, and especially New York were potential coalition-partners for southerners—they too had a stake in freer trade and in avoiding gambits that could antagonize European interests. Efforts to couple tariff reductions with a graduated income tax were politically motivated as well. Such proposals were always popular in the low-income South, and the idea of taxing the wealthy was a compelling one in the Great Plains where it resonated with populist ideals.[149] Industrial workers have been known to support such ideas as well.

Southern efforts to block the bargaining tariff and dismantle protective tariffs ultimately proved to be less than successful, but it was not for lack of trying. Southern politicians were as relentless as their counterparts from the northern core, but they faced obstacles that made success unlikely. One problem was that the trade strategies associated with the bargaining tariff eroded support for free trade in the West. If the Democratic party as a whole had chosen to "market" free trade as a way to improve the farmer's lot, it might have been able to preempt western support for tariff reciprocity.[150] This was the very strategy Roger Mills had used in his attacks on reciprocity. Failure to exploit this option points to the more fundamental problem facing agrarian Democrats. The party was controlled by its northern wing—the "Cleveland" Democrats in the 1890s. Politicians who represented the "old South" were "radical" proponents of free trade; they could not agree with those who championed the cause of the "New South," let alone their colleagues to the North. Lacking control over party machinery, southern Democrats were largely consigned to fighting rearguard battles against Republicans and the commercial stratagem designed to promote and defend the interests of the industrial core.

Conclusion

America's emergence as a great power was forged in the crucible of domestic political struggle. Often depicted as a contest between competing visions of America's purpose in the world, the conflicts over expansionism in the 1890s were bred on conflicts of interests. The stakes were high. The foreign policy choices that politicians faced at the end of the nineteenth century were also choices about how to restore domestic prosperity and maintain social stability in the midst of what was then considered America's worst depression. The choices entailed changes in the institutional configuration of state power, for a more activist state would necessarily be a more centralized one. More power would flow into the hands of those who already controlled the center. More obviously, competing visions of what would best serve "the national interest" in the 1890s had very different implications for how federal revenues would be generated and spent, for who would pay and who would gain. Those who stood to gain the most faced the challenge of mobilizing a domestic political coalition broad and stable enough to overcome the resistance of their opponents. These were the fights that divided the nation at the end of the nineteenth century.

The debate over expansionism was part of a larger struggle over whether the federal government should play a more active role in promoting American commercial interests overseas. There was no consensus over the need to build a "promotional state." The problem was not only that many Americans remained wedded to laissez-faire liberalism, or that many feared a more active foreign policy would mean a more powerful presidency. The more pressing concern was who would benefit from the adoption of a more vigorous, expansionist foreign policy. The answer to this question did not turn simply on who won the most naval contracts, received the biggest tariff subsidies, or could distribute the most political patronage. In the 1890s, as during other periods of the nation's history, politicians viewed foreign policy issues against a larger political canvas. The issues of naval spending, territorial expansion, and tariff reform were debated in terms of their impact on each region's overseas commercial interests and on post-bellum political arrangements that continued to make the agrarian South a "colony" of the industrial Northeast.

This approach to explaining American foreign policy and the problem of consensus-building contrasts sharply with cultural and institutional explanations. Those who favor such explanations must explain away the fact that where politicians stand on questions of foreign policy is shaped by interests—their own, as well as those of the constituencies they represent. This is plainly evident in the case at hand. Politicians who championed the battleship navy, the acquisition of foreign territories, and the bargaining tariff came from parts of the country that had the most to gain from the centralization of power that would accompany an ambitious, outward-oriented foreign policy. Those who remained wedded to the liberal or Jeffersonian ideals of free trade and a small brown-water navy, and who expressed fears about the "excessive growth of the state," were the ones who knew they would have little control over, and derive little benefit from, the strong state. Ideas were grounded in interests, and institutional conflict between the executive and legislative branches (and the Republican and Democratic parties) reflected patterns of competition that were grounded in deeper and broader societal conflicts.

The analysis of America foreign policy-making at the end of the nineteenth century also tells us something about the limits of more traditional geopolitical explanations of foreign policy change. Those accounts give pride of place to the "external" environment in explaining foreign policy change. They argue that America did not so much seek empire as have empire thrust on it.[151] For much of its history, the United States had lived in "splendid isolation." America, wrote James Bryce, "sails upon a summer sea," free of internal discord and unfettered by the miseries of European strife.[152] But by the late nineteenth century the geopolitical conditions that assured American safety in the past—geographical isolation, British naval power, and the balance of power in Europe—were rapidly disappearing. "The era which had seen the new world fattening on the follies of the old," writes British historian John A. S. Grenville, "was coming to an end; soon the follies of the old world impinged on the peace and prosperity of the new."[153] In the traditional geopolitical account, the United States, no longer able to assume the safety of the Western Hemisphere, was forced to respond by developing new means to deal with the new external realities. America adapted, reluctantly and with periodic lapses, but it adapted all the same.

Such accounts remind us of the importance of the international environment in explaining foreign policy change. They are limited, however, in two important ways. In the 1890s, as in other eras, uneven growth meant that the implications of external developments varied internally in the United States. One region's strategic imperative was another's economic albatross. By viewing America in the 1890s as a single entity, analysts who think about foreign policy from the "outside-in" ignore the fact that different parts of the country occupied fundamentally different positions in the world economy, and thus had different views about how the national government should respond to the shifting distribution of power among nations. For the South, the erosion of British power and the rise of imperial rivalry threatened an already weakened liberal trading order that the South was vitally dependent on. Given England's commitment to free trade, to say nothing of its huge purchases of southern cotton, a strong Britain with the power to enforce international order was in the South's interests. For the industrial Northeast, the situation was more complex. The decline of British hegemony opened up new opportunities for American industry to expand overseas. But the resulting power vacuums, and the rush by other powers to fill them, would also make the international environment more fluid and dangerous. From this perspective, Captain Alfred Thayer Mahan's great contribution lay in devising a grand strategy that could allow the northern industrial core to seize the opportunities while holding other great industrial powers in check.

The second limitation of the geopolitical perspective is its inability to explain how changes in the international system are translated into U.S. foreign policy. The external environment matters, but its effects on policy are mediated by internal politics. In the final analysis it was the realities of power in the United States, not the distribution of power in the international system, that determined the outcome of the Great Debate. It was northerners' ability to prevail in Washington that produced a mighty blue-water navy—without this Mahan's ideas might well have gathered dust on the shelves. The agrarian South faced overwhelming odds in the fight over expansion. Politicians from the northern core dominated the corridors of power in Congress and enjoyed the backing of powerful industrial and commercial interests, as well as "open lines of communication" with powerful executive agencies, especially the State Department and Department of the Navy. When political allies were needed, the advocates of imperial expansion had at their disposal the means to build winning coalitions. They could use the lure of naval expenditures to win support from politicians representing port cities, a tactic that worked best along the Pacific coast with its natural harbors and skilled labor force. In the rural West, the bargaining tariff could be used to appeal to hard-pressed western farmers who hoped that Latin America would become an outlet for their surplus foodstuffs. By coupling the issues of naval reform and territorial acquisition to commercial expansion in the underdeveloped world, the Northeast made the West an offer that was hard to refuse.

The Northeast's strategy had a hard edge as well. Republican leaders were able to use foreign policy as a powerful weapon in their battle against the Populists. Overseas expansion was a "wedge issue:" northern Republicans used it to split the western and southern branches of the radical agrarian movement and consolidate their control over the national government. The Republican's foreign policy agenda is thus best seen as part of a larger electoral strategy in the 1890s that was designed to exploit sectional differences in the agrarian periphery and to prevent an alliance against the industrial core.[154] Foreign policy was not only a tool for state-building, it was also an instrument of party-building. Expanding the capacity of the federal government to project power abroad helped to expand the Republican party's electoral base at home. Southern elites, well practiced in the art of sectional politics, were wise to the game. Being able to do something about it another matter. In politics, as in war, there are objective realities, and in the late 1890s the possibilities for a southern-western alliance over foreign policy were remote.

Several forces worked against possibilities for an alliance between the South and West. First, the economic needs of the agrarian South and agrarian West differed in important ways. The South depended on European markets to sell its raw materials far more than the West did. Western farmers' principal market was at home, rather than abroad. Policies that challenged British dominance in the southern half of the Western Hemisphere raised potential risks for the South, while for western agrarians and the politicians who represented them, there seemed to be real advantages to opening underdeveloped markets in Latin America and Asia. Second, because the West was not as dependent on overseas markets as the South, it could use its votes in Congress on issues important to the Northeast—naval spending, foreign bases, the bargaining tariff—for logrolling purposes. Western lawmakers could exchange their support on foreign policy issues for northeastern concessions on matters that were of great political import in the trans-Mississippi West—currency reform, railroad regulation, monopoly control, etc. The export-dependent South simply could not afford this option. Third, although the West fancied high tariffs less than the Northeast, it was more threatened by foreign imports than the South. It thus found southern doctrines of free trade and "tariff-for-revenue-only" less attractive than a strategy combining tariffs at home with market expansion abroad.

So it was that the West threw its weight behind the northern core's foreign policy agenda, creating the domestic political base and momentum needed to redefine America's national interest in the 1890s. These changes made it possible to build the "promotional state" that would propel America's rise as a great power in the twentieth century.

CHAPTER THREE

North-South Alliance and the Triumph of Internationalism in the 1930s

Introduction

In early December 1940, while vacationing aboard the *U.S.S. Tusca-loosa* in the Caribbean, President Roosevelt received an urgent message from Winston Churchill warning that England was in desperate shape. The Prime Minister informed the president that Britain could not hold out indefinitely without American aid. German submarines were taking a heavy toll on British shipping, and Churchill's government was running perilously low on dollars and gold to pay for the ships, planes, artillery, tanks, and guns that were needed in ever greater numbers to defend the British Isles and to turn the tide against the Axis powers. The time, Churchill declared, was rapidly approaching when England would "no longer be able to pay cash" for goods ordered from the other side of the Atlantic.[1] Promising that Britain would "suffer and sacrifice to the utmost for the Cause," the Prime Minister expressed confidence that the recently re-elected Roosevelt would find "ways and means" to assure the continuing flow of supplies to support England's fight against tyranny and fascism.

Churchill's plea did not go unanswered. Roosevelt moved swiftly to step up American aid to the British. In one of his most memorable speeches, the president urged the American people to dispel the "notion of 'business as usual.'"[2] "We must be the great arsenal of democracy." Britain's fight was now America's fight. "If Great Britain goes down," he cautioned, "the Axis powers will control the continents of Europe, Asia, Africa, Australia, and the high seas," and "all of us, in all the Americas, would be living at the point of a gun." Admitting that his plan to aid the British was not without risk, he went on to insist that it was the best means available to defend the Western Hemisphere and to avoid sending American boys into another foreign war. The president told his listeners, "There is far less chance of the United States getting into war, if we do all we can now to support the nations defending themselves against attack by the Axis than if we acquiesce in their defeat, submit tamely to an Axis victory, and wait our turn to be the object of attack in another war later on."

The public response to the president's speech was encouraging. A Gallup poll found that 61 percent of those who heard or read it agreed with the president's position.[3] Letters and telegrams to the White House were also overwhelmingly positive. Believing that he had a mandate for expanded American aid, Roosevelt called on Congress to grant him full authority to help England.[4] As he explained to House and Senate leaders in early January, he wanted a bill that would limit neither the amount nor the kind of aid he could send.

Roosevelt would have his way, but not before the country endured one of the most bitter fights over foreign policy in its history. Although the president received plaudits for his speech, there was no consensus on policy. The American people were deeply divided on international matters. Aid to the Allies won high marks throughout the South and in the urban Northeast, but in the West, especially in the more rural areas, it was roundly condemned.[5] When Congress took up the so-called Lend-Lease bill in early 1941, sectional politics defined the main battle lines of debate.

For nearly three months, the country debated the need, merits, and dangers of the president's proposal. All of the old arguments about the ends and means of foreign policy were replayed. Those in favor of aid to Britain made the case on strategic grounds, calling it a matter of national self-defense. Secretary of War Henry Stimson, founding father and patron saint of the Eastern Establishment, spoke for many like-minded internationalists: "We are really seeking to purchase her aid in our defense. We are buying—not lending."[6] Secretary of State Cordell Hull, the former congressman from Memphis, Tennessee was even more direct. England, he argued, was America's first line of defense.[7] He told the House Foreign Affairs Committee that without British sea-power, the Atlantic Ocean offered little security for the Western Hemisphere. On the other side were those like Senator Gerald Nye of North Dakota, a leading agrarian isolationist and head of the widely publicized Senate inquiry into the role of big business in dragging the United States into World War I. Nye and other isolationists attacked Lend-Lease on legal as well as strategic grounds. Again and again, the senator charged that the bill would give the president dictatorial powers and be a major step down the road toward direct American involvement in another costly war. Lend-Lease, he warned, was not about self-defense; it was about the proper balance between the executive and legislative branches. "Fear and hate have obsessed us, blinded us, fooled us," he told his Senate colleagues. The real danger facing America was not German or Japanese expansionism but rather "the encroachments upon our constitutional status, and the impairment of the regular process of our government by the forces within the Government itself."[8]

The Lend-Lease debate was the climax of a decade-long struggle over how to define America's national interest. The collapse of the world economy in the early 1930s had unleashed powerful centrifugal forces in the international system.[9] Each of the core industrial nations sought to save itself through autarkic measures of planned production at home and managed trade abroad and, in the cases of Germany and Japan, through military intimidation and war. As the decade wore on, the force of external events polarized American opinion, destroying the uneasy balance that the Republican administrations of Harding, Coolidge, and Hoover had struck between internationally oriented and domestically oriented interests in the 1920s. From Japan's seizure of Manchuria in 1931 to Mussolini's invasion of Ethiopia in 1935 to the Nazi occupation of France in 1940, America's leaders were unable to agree over how to respond to the downward spiral of international conflict. The same tensions that had prevented compromise over the Versailles Treaty and membership in the League of Nations in 1919 resurfaced and intensified. Policy differences became less tractable and debates over how the nation should respond to international events became hopelessly embroiled in fights over means. Were new governmental mechanisms needed to restore the international economy and safeguard against another breakdown? Should the United States assume a more assertive role in deterring expansionism and punishing aggression? And who should have the power to decide matters of such gravity—the president or Congress?

The stakes in the fight over the authority to make foreign policy in Washington were high, for they also had direct implications for the distribution of wealth and power at home. During the 1930s, as in the 1890s, disputes over constitutional prerogative were inextricably linked to domestic conflicts of interest. So were debates over "entangling" the United States in foreign rivalries. Arguments for and against an assertive American foreign policy echoed those of the 1890s. What changed, and dramatically so, was *who* lined up on each side of this great debate. This time, it was the rural West, not the agrarian South, that led the fight against foreign entanglements and expanded presidential powers—a battle that it, like the South in the 1890s, would lose. In the 1930s, the South favored a vigorous assertion of American leadership in world affairs, a position it ironically now shared with the urban Northeast. Once deeply divided over how the United States should define "the national interest," northern and southern leaders found common cause in the 1930s fight against economic nationalism, military intimidation, and imperial expansion. A tacit agreement emerged: however much they might disagree on the rights of Negroes and labor, politics would stop at the water's edge. This agreement paved the way for sweeping changes in the conduct of American foreign policy.

The benchmark for assessing the scope of these changes must be the laissez-fairism of the preceding decade. During the 1920s, laissez-faire was America's credo in foreign as well as domestic policy. For the most part, the United States maintained a low political and military profile overseas. Although Washington continued to promote overseas expansion (as it had since the 1890s) and did not completely abandon gunboat diplomacy and interventionism, the Republican administrations of Harding, Coolidge, and Hoover downsized the military, kept their distance from the League of Nations, and backed disarmament treaties.[10] The disengagement of the 1920s did not exactly constitute isolationism, however. Most Republican leaders, especially those from the East who continued to dominate the party, shared Woodrow Wilson's vision of a more liberal international order, even if they rejected collective security as a means to that end and were more concerned about securing equal access to foreign markets than lowering tariff barriers. But fears of excessive government involvement in international affairs, and the demands of coalition-building within an increasingly regionally divided Republican party, led American officials in the 1920s to rely on limited means in pursuit of expansionist ends. They turned to what historian Herbert Feis called the "diplomacy of the dollar"—private means were used to advance a public agenda in foreign policy.[11] American businessmen were encouraged to assume a leading role in stabilizing the war-ravaged European economies through bank loans and private investment and to create the conditions in which American influence could spread. What emerged was a kind of semi-internationalism, an "independent internationalism" based on private initiative rather than government activism.

In March 1933, when Franklin Roosevelt was inaugurated, twelve years of Republican-dominated foreign policy came to an end. Laissez-fairism gave way to what would prove to be an era of unprecedented government activism in foreign affairs. In the decades that followed, the nation's leaders gradually created what historian Emily Rosenberg has called an "international regulatory state" equipped with a panoply of new governmental mechanisms and agencies to guide the development of an open and integrated world economy in which American influence could spread.[12] Though it would not emerge full-blown until the Cold War era, the basic features of this new regulatory state were hammered into place during the 1930s. Functions once performed by private business, such as granting loans to foreign countries, were increasingly undertaken by the public sector. Institutions for regulating international currencies were created, as were agencies for stimulating foreign trade. The tariff was transformed once again, this time into a tool of executive diplomacy. By the time the United States entered World War II, the president had acquired extraordinary powers.[13] Some were obtained by executive fiat under existing statutes, but most of Roosevelt's new powers—such as those in the areas of trade reform, Lend-Lease, and the military draft—had been granted to the president by Congress. They had been won on the House and Senate floors over the strident objections of isolationists. It took the combined political power of the urban Northeast and agrarian South to carry the day.

What explains the rise of a new foreign policy coalition that crossed the once impenetrable Mason-Dixon line? Why did the once-powerful alliance between the Northeast and West break down? Though many factors contributed to this realignment over foreign policy, much is explained by a single development: By the late 1920s, the Northeast was far more deeply enmeshed in, and deeply dependent on, the world economy than it had been in 1890s. The story of America's emergence as a mature industrial and financial power in the 1920s is largely the story of this region. World War I had transformed the United States into the world's leading economic power. The sources of this rapid ascendancy—and its fruits—were concentrated heavily in the Northeast, the site of the country's largest financial institutions and most productive industries. As a result of this growing economic power and international interdependence, the Northeast's leaders in Congress came to associate domestic security and prosperity with international stability and openness. They were prepared to grant the president the means necessary to pursue these ends.

Unlike northern industrialists and bankers, western farmers and ranchers had become more dependent on the *home* market since 1900.

They had little incentive to support government efforts to liberalize and stabilize the international system. Westerners saw greater advantages in protecting domestic markets from foreign producers. As the interests of the Northeast and West diverged, their political representatives in Washington found it harder to achieve consensus. Sectional tensions between East and West resurfaced in Congress, and the politics of coalition-building over foreign policy grew more disorderly and uncertain. Economic crises and party politics in the 1920s and 1930s compounded matters. The disastrous "farm crisis" of the 1920s, the failure of successive Republican administrations to find a solution to the farmer's plight that was also acceptable to their party's powerful backers in the business world, and the Great Depression itself fueled anti-Eastern resentment in the West. Antiparty sentiment spread through the Great Plains and Mountain West. The turn of much of the northeastern Republican establishment toward internationalism deepened the crisis within the party. Antipartyism meant that Republican losses in the region did not automatically translate into Democratic gain. By the mid-1930s, partisan loyalty was at best issue-specific. On matters of domestic recovery and reform, western congressmen often backed Roosevelt. The president was not so fortunate when it came to foreign policy.

The changing position of the Northeast in the world economy pushed East and West apart. The same forces had the opposite effect on the two sides of the Mason-Dixon line. The Northeast's deepening integration into the world economy pulled North and South together. In the past, northern protectionism had been one of the two great obstacles to cooperation. (The other, of course, was race.) As northern industry and finance matured, and support for internationalist tenets of free trade and equal access increased in the region, so too did opportunities for greater cooperation on foreign policy with southern agrarian interests. Southern elites had their own reasons for backing Roosevelt's internationalist agenda. One was party loyalty and the benefits that accrued from it, though there were real limits to this. More significant was the South's continued reliance on foreign markets. Although the agrarian South, like the rural West, reaped few of the rewards of America's expanding foreign investments and manufacturing trade, it nevertheless remained heavily dependent on access to international markets to sell raw materials, still the mainstay of the southern economy. In this respect, little had changed in the South since the late nineteenth century. What changed was the international political situation. The rise of economic nationalism in Europe and Asia, and the very real possibility that the United States could be pushed down a similar path, posed a clear and present danger to the southern oligarchy and the "southern way of life." Under these conditions, constitutional matters—the South's fear of a strong executive—took a back seat to economic concerns. North and South closed ranks behind the internationalist cause.

Sectional conflict over foreign policy in the 1930s crystallized around three concrete issues: neutrality, free trade, and military preparedness. The sources of regional conflict and the resulting political fights over these issues are analyzed in this chapter. Of the three, the fight over neutrality was the most divisive. The central issue was this: Should the president be given the discretionary authority to embargo war supplies to belligerents, or not? Lawmakers from the South and urban Northeast generally favored strengthening the president's control over trade; representatives from the rural West were almost always opposed. The issue was joined as early as 1933 when the Roosevelt administration, convinced that the best way to prevent German and Japanese aggression was to signal America's willingness to impose punitive economic sanctions, sought to win from Congress the authority to do so. Congress refused. Instead of expanding the president's discretionary power over commerce, it passed a series of so-called neutrality acts designed to guarantee American noninvolvement in any future war by prohibiting the sale of arms to nations at war. The country was forced through a bruising and bitter debate. In the end, the administration was able to put together a coalition in Congress that was strong enough to roll back the neutrality laws. Congress allowed Britain and France to obtain arms from the United States, first on a cash-and-carry basis, then through lend-lease, and the president was given the authority to apply economic sanctions against Japan and Germany.

Like the fight over neutrality, the question of trade liberalization raised divisive economic and political issues. Here too the administration sought to greatly expand the Executive's discretionary power in parcelling out economic rewards and punishments. Roosevelt wanted broad, advance authority from Congress to negotiate reciprocal tariff-cutting agreements with other nations without further congressional action—tariff negotiations would become a more direct tool of economic diplomacy. Under the proposed Reciprocal Trade Agreement Act (RTAA), tariffs would be lowered against the products of nations that granted American goods reciprocal concessions. Because the United States now adhered to the most-favored-nation principle, reductions given to one nation would then extend to all except those that continued to discriminate against American commerce. The president had never demanded so much discretionary power to bargain with foreign nations. This carrot and stick approach to foreign trade proved to be very appealing in the South and Northeast, for both stood to benefit enormously from the restoration and liberalization of world trade. The rural West firmly opposed this initiative. It saw in reciprocal trade little but an economic threat in the form of import competition. Congressional passage of the RTAA in 1934 was a hard-won victory for the internationalists.

Trade and defense were related. Administration officials believed that military as well as economic means were needed to halt the drift toward war and to restore international order. The extensive rearmament program launched by the administration in 1938 was part of a larger strategy designed to deter German and Japanese aggression and to prevent the further collapse of the world economy into closed spheres of influence. Roosevelt's efforts to build up the nation's military capabilities provoked resistance, which was centered in the rural West. Legislative battles over military preparedness reflected how much the internal "geopolitics" of American foreign policy had changed since the 1890s. Now positions were reversed: While western lawmakers now worried about the redistributive costs of defense spending, southern congressmen stressed the strategic value of a strong U.S. military. The flip-flop could be seen in western lawmakers' hostile references to predatory eastern "trusts" and in the almost unanimous support that military spending proposals received from southern lawmakers on the House and Senate floors. For the South, the road to stability and prosperity now required a powerful American military presence overseas. The threat to its markets in Europe explains the change in southern attitudes towards the centralization of power that military rearmament and preparedness implied.

By tracing debates over neutrality, trade, and rearmament, this chapter shows how sectional division and alliance structured the politics of foreign policy-making in the 1930s. The analysis is divided into three main parts that focus on the interests and strategies of the three great regions: the Northeast, South, and West. The Northeast is discussed first. Most accounts of how America redefined its national interest in the 1930s overgeneralize from the experience of the urban Northeast, assuming that what was true for the nation's big urban-industrial centers was true for the country as whole. This was not the

case. Sharp sectional disparities are critical to explaining the acrimonious fights that actually determined the course of foreign policy-making.
The second part of the chapter deals with the agrarian South. This history is less well known and less understood, which is ironic given that
the South was the most internationalist section of the country. Roosevelt's dependence on the South on international matters gave southern
leaders considerable leverage over his domestic policies. The worse
the world situation grew, and the more crucial southern congressional
support became to the Roosevelt administration, the less likely it was
that northerners would challenge the southern oligarchy on domestic
matters critical to southern elites, most notably race. So it was that in
the 1930s, progress on civil rights at home was sacrificed to building
a domestic political coalition to underwrite American internationalism.
The last part of the chapter deals with the West. Contrary to the legends
of the era, the West's isolationism was not born of ignorance or backwardness. It reflected the harsh realities of uneven development and
America's uneven integration into the world economy. Forced to protect their interests, western agrarians waged a rearguard battle against
liberal internationalism and against what would become an "imperial
presidency."

The Internationalization of the Northeast

In a chronicle of Henry Stimson's life, Godfrey Hodgson tells the story
of American diplomacy in the twentieth century.[14] Born less than three
years after Lincoln was assassinated, Stimson lived through the entire
period of America's "rise to globalism": from the rapid growth of the
western frontier after the Civil War, to the heady expansionism of the
1890s, to the apex of American power at the end of World War II. For
almost half a century, "the Colonel," as he liked to be called, was near
the center of power, moving back and forth between his Wall Street
law firm and high-ranking positions in Washington. He was a friend and
confidant of Theodore Roosevelt; he also served as Franklin Roosevelt's
secretary of war. In between, he was secretary of war in the Taft administration, the governor general of the Philippines under Calvin Coolidge, and Herbert Hoover's secretary of state. During this time, few
individuals left as large an imprint on the nation's foreign policy as
Stimson. Although a conservative Republican, Stimson's decision to put
partisanship aside and join Franklin Roosevelt's administration in 1940

set a precedent that internationalists would continue to follow long after the Colonel left government for the last time in 1945. Many of the younger men who would shape the nation's foreign policy after World War II were strongly influenced by his views about America's place in the world.

Stimson was the link that connects the foreign policy of the 1890s to the foreign policy of the 1930s; he was, to paraphrase Hodgson, the link between imperialism and internationalism.[15] Stimson was once a fervent proponent of colonial expansion. By the 1930s he had turned away from the raw, assertive nationalism of Theodore Roosevelt, having concluded that free trade was more cost-effective for the United States than imperialist strategies aimed at establishing restrictive spheres of influence. His views about the purposes of American power also evolved over time. Prior to 1915, Stimson, like most northern expansionists at the time, viewed America's "responsibilities" in regional as opposed to global terms. He worried more about how to improve America's access to and influence over Latin America and the Pacific Basin, the country's traditional spheres of ambition, than about how to promote international stability and openness. Yet it was the latter goals that would preoccupy him as Hoover's secretary of state and Roosevelt's secretary of war. Stimson came to believe that the collapse of European leadership after World War I left a vacuum at the heart of the international system that the United States could ignore only at its peril. Although he accepted the need for American global leadership, the Colonel never embraced the idealism and pacifism that became associated with Woodrow Wilson's goal of an interdependent world order. Stimson was a realist: he favored a world kept peaceful by collective security, guaranteed by American military power. In Stimson's vision, the United States would be the world's workshop, banker, and policeman, all rolled into one.

Stimson's vision was widely shared by the Eastern Establishment and, more generally, in the urban Northeast. As the Colonel turned away from the narrow nationalism of the McKinley era, so too did mass and elite opinion in the big urban-industrial metropolises that dominated the nation's economic and political life. Spheres of interest and protective tariffs, once cherished in the urban Northeast, were now considered harmful to the national interest. So was imperialism, at least in its expansionist colonial form. Indeed, with the exception of southern lawmakers, no group of elected officials was more internationalist in outlook by the 1930s than those who hailed from the nation's largest and oldest industrialized cities: Baltimore, Boston, Chicago, Cleveland, Detroit, Philadelphia, Pittsburgh, and New York.[16] In the urban Northeast, Republicans as well as Democrats backed free trade, aid to the Allies, and military rearmament. Most shared the Colonel's fears about the spread of nationalism and fascism overseas. In ever larger numbers, urban northerners shared Stimson's conviction that the United States had to stop the Axis powers, even at the risk of American involvement in a European war. Isolationist sentiment was strong in upper New England and the rural Midwest in the 1930s, but in big urban centers along the East Coast and Great Lakes, traditional reservations about American entanglement in European affairs had given way to an assertive internationalism.

The Northeast in the World Economy

Why did the urban Northeast, whose political leaders in the 1890s stressed the virtues of American "self-sufficiency" and spheres of influence, now embrace the principles of free trade and international openness? Why did they now associate the nation's security and welfare with European stability? A large part of the answer lies in the emergence after 1900 of America's manufacturing belt as the core region of the world economy, eclipsing the great "iron triangle" in Europe running from Stuttgart to Antwerp to Paris.

Although the United States was already one of the world's largest producers of manufactures before 1890, it was still very much a nation on the periphery of the global trading system, providing raw materials and investment opportunities for the core European economies. In the 1890s, America exported mostly primary goods (agricultural commodities) and most of these went to Europe. Industrial exports grew, but as of 1900 finished manufactures still made up less than one-quarter of the country's total exports, and most of these were still being sold within the Western Hemisphere.[17] For the most part, America's overseas financial dealings were also confined to the hemisphere. The country's investments overseas did grow considerably after 1890, stimulated by industry's increasing reliance on foreign sources of raw materials.[18] As important as this activity was, it did not make America the dominant player in the international economic system. The United States remained a leading international borrower and host of foreign direct investment.

In the years between 1900 and 1914, the United States surpassed Great Britain as the world's leading industrial producer and also became the world's fastest growing exporter.[19] America's exports doubled in value from $1.2 billion in 1899 to $2.3 billion in 1914.[20] Most significant was the extraordinary rise in the nation's *industrial* exports. Semi-finished and finished manufactures grew nearly 300 percent, from $381 million in 1899 to $1.1 billion in 1914, and by World War I finished manufactures alone accounted for nearly one-third of all U.S. exports. Even more telling was the European reaction: Europeans spoke of an American "invasion" as American manufactured goods flooded onto their markets. Under pressure from domestic groups, European capitals retaliated, increasing tariff barriers and attempting to form customs unions.[21] The invasion of Europe was only part of a "worldwide onslaught by American manufactures."[22] The United States was rapidly winning market share in the so-called third markets of Latin America and Asia. By World War I it was truly one of the world's leading commercial powers. Yet Great Britain, the world's banker, continued to hold a decisive edge.

World War I transformed the world economy and America's place in it. As a result of the war-inflated economic boom, the national trade surplus climbed to over $3.5 billion in 1917, with manufactured goods accounting for over 60 percent of total exports.[23] Desperately in need of war supplies but lacking the funds to pay for them, the Allies borrowed heavily from American banks and, once the United States entered the war, from the American government. American holdings of foreign bonds soared. Foreign direct investment also grew rapidly. American corporations took advantage of the war to expand into areas long dominated by Europeans, most notably Latin America. The flow of American capital overseas was so great that the nation's international financial position was quickly reversed. In just five years, the United States moved from being a debtor nation with net liabilities of $3.7 billion (1914) to being a creditor nation with a balance of over $3.5 billion in assets.[24] In addition, foreign governments owed the American government over $10 billion as a result of Allied war debt obligations. Great Britain, the world's greatest lender at the beginning of the war, was now deeply in debt to the United States. Thus, by the beginning of the Roaring Twenties, the United States was not only the most productive nation in the world, but also its leading source of capital.

This trend in American investment accelerated through the postwar years. The nations of Europe needed foreign capital to fund their recovery and development programs; American investors needed foreign outlets to dispose of surplus capital. Between 1919 and 1927

America's net holdings of foreign securities increased in all years except 1923.[25] Initially, the Allies received the lion's share of the loans, but over time American lending shifted toward other borrowers, including Germany, Canada, Italy, Mexico, Argentina, and Brazil.[26] By the end of the 1920s, America's holdings in foreigners' promissory notes had more than doubled. United States investors now held portfolio investments of over $7.8 billion, of which a significant amount represented the obligations of foreign governments.[27]

America's largest corporations kept pace with the nation's big Wall Street banks. Foreign direct investment nearly doubled, rising from $3.9 billion in 1919 to $7.6 billion in 1929. By the end of the 1920s, American overseas investments totaled $15.4 billion. Latin America continued to take the largest share, followed by Europe and Canada. Once relatively insignificant in the American economy, the nation's overseas assets had become equal to over one-fifth of total national income by the time of the 1929 Wall Street crash. That level would not be reached again until the early 1980s.[28]

Though less dramatic, the growth of America's overseas trade was also important. Exports increased from $1.4 billion in 1900 to over $5.1 in 1929.[29] More significantly, the composition of this trade changed radically. In the past, the United States had been chiefly an exporter of primary goods to Europe. On average, raw materials accounted for 48 percent of all American exports in the 1890s.[30] Cotton and wheat alone accounted for 36 percent of the total. This began to change in the early 1900s.[31] Exports of raw materials declined in relative importance while finished manufactures increased as a proportion to the total (fig. 3.1). Cotton remained the leading export commodity, but exports of automobiles, machinery, iron and steel, and petroleum and its products grew rapidly, even after the war-induced boom tapered off. The value of automobile exports increased more than 1,500 percent between 1914 and 1929; foreign sales of machinery expanded 260 percent; exports of petroleum grew by over 247 percent; iron and steel exports rose 120 percent.[32] By the 1920s each of these sectors had a considerable stake in foreign markets, exporting on average between 5 and 10 percent of its total output.[33] Overall, Europe remained America's single most important overseas market, but exports of manufactured goods to non-European nations were growing at a much faster pace.

As the country's position in the world economy changed, America's leaders reassessed the nation's role in international affairs. Incentives to do so were especially strong in the Northeast, where most of

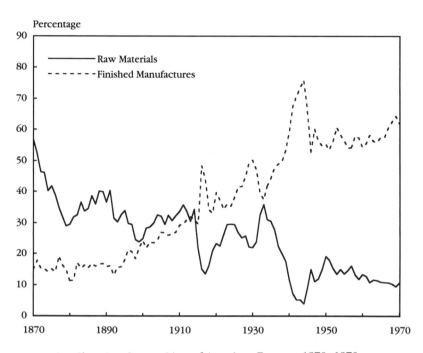

Figure 3.1 Changing Composition of American Exports, 1870–1970

Source: Bureau of the Census, *Historical Statistics of the United States, Colonial Times to 1970,* 2 vols. (Washington, D.C., 1975), Series U 213-224, p. 889.

the wealth and prosperity generated by the rapid economic growth in the country's overseas trade, investment, and lending was concentrated. Despite the expansion of industry and finance in other parts of the nation (especially the Far West), the Northeast remained the core of the national economy. The region's commercial and investment banks continued to control most of the nation's bank deposits and most of its financial dealings with the outside world. Its industrial dominance remained unrivalled. With roughly half of the national population, the region stretching from southern New England to the Potomac and west to the Mississippi continued to produce over two-thirds of all manufacturing jobs in the country.[34] The Northeast also accounted for nearly 60 percent of the jobs in related service sectors such as transportation, commerce, and finance (table 3.1). More impressive still was the region's productivity. Seventy-five percent of the total value-added in manufacturing came from the manufacturing belt.

The fact that proved to be decisive in shaping the politics of the

Table 3.1 Regional Distribution of U.S. Labor Force by Sector, 1930 (percentage)

Region	Manufacturing	Resource	Service	Total
Northeast	66.4	29.4	57.6	52.3
South	18.5	34.9	21.6	27.9
West	15.1	35.7	20.8	19.9

Source: Based on data in Harvey S. Perloff et al., *Regions, Resources, and Economic Growth* (Baltimore: Johns Hopkins University Press, 1960), tables 90, 101, 102, and 107.
Note: May not add up to 100 percent due to rounding. Due to differences in regional classification schemes, Arizona and New Mexico are included as southern states here. See table 2.1 for regional groupings.

Northeast—and Roosevelt's ability to forge an internationalist foreign policy coalition—was the growing economic strength and political clout of the region's urban-industrial metropolises. The manufacturing belt was not one continuous industrial complex; it had always comprised a number of distinct urban-industrial systems. Each was organized around a single metropolitan center that both provided crucial financial and commercial services and acted as a "gateway" to the larger world economy.[35] In the 1800s, these industrial systems were located exclusively along the East Coast. In time, they spread westward, spurred by population growth, improved transportation and communication, and the lure of new sources of raw materials, especially coal deposits and iron ore. By the beginning of the twentieth century, the largest and most important of these industrial systems were centered around the "Big Eight": Baltimore, Boston, Chicago, Cleveland, Detroit, Philadelphia, Pittsburgh, and New York. Separately, they enjoyed levels of manufacturing activity and trade with the outside world that were much higher than the national average. In combination, their economic might was truly impressive. With 22 percent of the nation's population in 1929, the Big Eight cities accounted for 33 percent of the nation's industrial workforce and 37 percent of all value-added in manufacturing.[36]

This means that America's deepening integration into the world economy was led by the Northeast, and that within this region, direct stakes in the world economy were very heavily concentrated in a few great metropolitan centers. Nearly two-thirds of the nation's foreign trade passed through the ports of the Northeast's biggest cities. The region's big investment banks were now major players in international financial markets. And the country's most export-dependent industrial sectors—petroleum, motor vehicles, machinery, rubber, nonferrous metals, and forest products—were highly concentrated here as well.

Table 3.2 Regional Location of U.S. Industry by Sector, 1929

Sectors[1]	Wage Labor Force (percentage)		
	Northeast	South	West
Food and beverages	52.4	9.4	38.2
Textiles	63.6	34.9	1.6
Forest products	69.8	20.0	10.2
Paper and printing	71.8	13.2	15.0
Chemicals	70.1	21.1	8.7
Petroleum	38.9	43.3	17.7
Rubber	91.2	2.8	6.0
Leather	82.2	6.7	11.1
Stone, clay, and glass	68.3	20.9	10.9
Iron and steel	83.7	10.5	5.9
Nonferrous metals	91.5	3.3	5.2
Machinery	87.7	4.4	8.0
Vehicles	90.1	4.3	5.6

Source: Data on wage jobs (i.e., regional shares of average number of wage earners employed) are from Bureau of the Census, *Location of Manufactures, 1899-1929* (Washington, D.C., 1933), tables 6, 8, 26. On the designation of export dependent sectors see David A. Lake, *Power, Protection, and Free Trade: International Sources of U.S. Commercial Strategy, 1887-1939* (Ithaca: Cornell University Press, 1988), table 2.2.

Note: See table 2.1 for regional groupings.

[1] Sectors in italics export more than 5 percent of output.

With the exception of petroleum, the Northeast held no less than 70 percent of the jobs in these export-dependent sectors (table 3.2), and within the Northeast, the biggest eight metropolises accounted for a very significant share: 49 percent of jobs in automobile plants, 36 percent in machinery, 36 percent in nonferrous metals production, and 33 percent in processing forest products.[37] Because the most export-dependent industries also tended to be America's most important foreign investors, the urban Northeast's growing stakes in foreign trade and investment were mutually reinforcing.[38]

Many accounts of America's rise as a world economic power in the early twentieth century bury the domestic political story of this era by suggesting that what was true for the urban Northeast was true for the country as a whole. Such accounts overgeneralize: even within the Northeast, concentration of internationally oriented economic activity in the leading cities meant that most of the region remained on the margins of the global economy. For places like upstate New York, Vermont, and rural Michigan, neither position in the world economy nor foreign policy preferences had changed much since the 1890s. The feeling that Europe was peripheral to American security and prosperity was alive and well in the Northeast in the 1930s. This polarized the politics of the region and strengthened the hand of the isolationists. Rather than overgeneralizing the case of the urban Northeast, other versions of 1930s history suggest that the interests of the Eastern Establishment were sufficient in themselves to produce major foreign policy shifts.[39] The problem here lies in explaining how the needs of Wall Street and big business were translated into a national political coalition strong enough to overcome resistance mounted by nationalists. To do so, it is necessary to look beyond big business.

Liberal internationalism met with resistance stiff enough to contribute to the partisan realignment of the 1930s, alter profoundly Roosevelt's hopes for the New Deal, and constrain America's ability to respond to the mounting crisis in Europe. In understanding the nationalist-internationalist struggles of this decade, the polarization of the Northeast along the urban/nonurban divide turns out to be critically important. Without allies in the nonurban Northeast, western isolationists would have lacked the political ballast needed to sustain the acrimonious fight against the internationalists throughout the 1930s. Meanwhile, had Roosevelt not been able to split the Republicans to forge a liberal-internationalist alliance grounded in the Democratic party, he would not have been able to build the foreign policy consensus that underwrote America's rise to international political greatness.

The Shift toward Free Trade
The urban Northeast was at the vanguard of support for liberal-internationalism in the 1930s. This is most obvious in the area of tariff policy — the standard barometer of political attitudes toward the liberal-internationalist agenda. Table 3.3 summarizes northeastern support in Congress for freer trade during the period running from the protectionist "Mongrel Tariff" of 1883 to the 1945 extension of the Reciprocal Trade Agreements Act.[40] The data show that support for freer trade in the urban Northeast is considerably stronger in the 1930s than it was in the 1890s, and that the liberalization of the urban Northeast occurred in stages.[41] In the late nineteenth century, New York and Baltimore were the only major cities in the region that consistently supported freer trade. With the passage of the Underwood Tariff of 1913, they were joined by Chicago and Cleveland. By the mid-1930s, Boston was alone among the "big eight" in opposing freer trade. In the rest of the Northeast, by contrast, little had changed. Protectionist sentiment con-

Table 3.3 Trade Preferences of Major Northeastern Urban Delegations

	Tariff Revision												
	1883	1890	1894	1897	1909	1913	1922	1930	1934	1937	1940	1943	1945
Boston	P	P	FT	P	FT	FT	P	P	P	P	P	FT	P
Baltimore	FT	FT	FT	P	FT	FT	FT	FT	FT	FT	FT	FT	FT
Chicago	P	P	FT	P	P	FT	P	FT	FT	FT	FT	FT	FT
Cleveland	P	P	FT	P	—	FT	FT	FT	FT	FT	FT	FT	FT
Detroit	P	FT	FT	P	P	FT	P	P	FT	FT	FT	FT	FT
New York	FT	FT	FT	P	FT	FT	P	FT	FT	FT	FT	FT	FT
Philadelphia	P	P	P	P	P	P	P	P	P	FT	FT	FT	FT
Pittsburgh	FT	P	P	P	P	P	P	P	FT	FT	FT	FT	FT
Other	P	P	P	P	P	FT	P	P	P	FT	P	FT	P

Source: Computations from House roll call data.
Note: "FT" indicates that a majority of the urban delegation supported a "free trade" position; "P" indicates that majority supported protectionism.

tinued to hold sway in the region's secondary cities, small towns, and rural hamlets.

The growing gap between the urban and rural Northeast over the tariff was accompanied by broader changes in the region's political make-up. Once a Republican citadel, the urban Northeast was gradually transformed into a Democratic stronghold.[42] Figure 3.2 charts the Democrats' growing share of congressional seats in the big cities between the 1890s and the 1930s. The cities remained predominantly Republican until the 1920s, when the Democrats' base in the urban Northeast expanded substantially. The cities sent more and more Democrats to Congress and exercised ever-greater influence in national Democratic politics. The nomination of Alfred E. Smith of New York, the spokesman of "urban Democracy," as presidential candidate in 1928 underscored the growing power of the cities. By the 1930s a majority of the urban Northeast's votes were going to Democratic presidential candidates.[43]

In the rural Northeast, by contrast, Republicans continued to win the lion's share of House seats and the presidential vote. In some years Democrats managed to win a majority of rural congressional seats, but the advantage was always shortlived. Even during the Great Depression, when Democrats tightened their grip on the cities, they were unable to register lasting gains in the rural areas. The 1932 election that put Franklin Roosevelt in the White House gave the Democrats over 50 percent of the Northeast's rural House seats—their largest

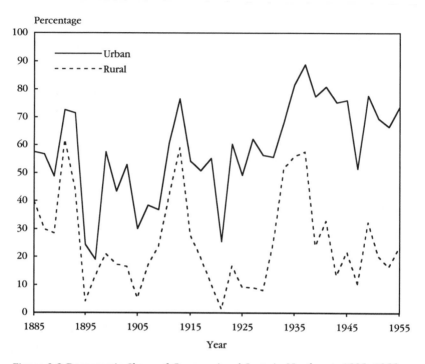

Figure 3.2 Democratic Share of Congressional Seats in Northeast, 1885–1955
Source: Computations from House roll call data.

share since Woodrow Wilson's victory over Theodore Roosevelt and
William Taft in 1912. The Democrats held and even increased their
edge in the 1934 midterm election, and again in the 1936 presidential
contest. Then came the correction of 1938. The Democrats' share of
rural House seats plummeted, falling back to below 30 percent, just
about the share they had averaged since the 1880s.[44] The Republicans,
having lost control of the big cities, quickly rebounded in the Northeast
by reestablishing control over the rural areas.

The gap between the urban and rural Northeast in the 1930s was
thus fueled by economic and political changes. The two were related.
Support for freer trade was stronger in the parts of the manufacturing
belt that benefited most from the country's trade in manufactures (i.e.,
the urban-industrial areas). In general, the more competitive the nation's biggest industrial-commercial cities became internationally, the
less attached they became to the protective tariff *and* the more re-

ceptive they were to the Democratic party and its free trade stance. It is true that the rise of the "urban Democracy" was not a simple byproduct of the urban centers' growing competitiveness. As political scientist V. O. Key observed, it was the combined (and interrelated) forces of industrialization, urbanization, and immigration that created the huge pool of potential Democrats.[45] The flood of immigrants into the cities earlier in the century paid big dividends for the Democrats in the 1930s.[46] As time went by, more and more Irish, Italians, Jews, and Poles voted Democratic. For them, as for Negroes, pulling the Democratic lever became even easier once the sectionally divisive issues of the Ku Klux Klan and religious fundamentalism passed from the scene in the 1920s. The despair caused by the Great Depression accelerated the urbanization of the Democratic party.

The internationalization of the urban Northeast had created new political possibilities. In the past, Democratic politicians faced an uphill battle in the staunchly protectionist and Republican Northeast. Only in New York and Baltimore could Democratic candidates safetly run as free traders, and even here they hedged, running on a "free raw materials" only platform. By the 1930s free trade was no longer anathema in the cities. On the contrary, as FDR came to realize, trade liberalization could be used to broaden the Democrats base in the Northeast and to weaken the Republican party by exacerbating sectional rivalry within it. The protective tariff, once a Republican elixir, now divided the party. The Eastern Establishment, still heavily Republican, advocated freer trade. Western Republicans, reluctant allies of the protectionists in the 1890s, had become the tariff's staunchest supporters.

The Democrats found themselves well positioned in the 1930s to reap the rewards of internecine struggles within the Republican party over free trade. Roosevelt found new allies in powerful members of the Eastern Establishment like Colonel Stimson, who backed the Democrat's reciprocal trade program and who urged fellow Republicans to do the same. The message was that when it came to foreign economic policy, the stakes were too high to let partisanship stand in the way. Influential organizations like the Council on Foreign Relations, the Foreign Policy Association, and the Carnegie Endowment for International Peace endorsed the idea of reducing the tariff through reciprocal bargaining with other countries.[47] So did prominent business leaders like Thomas A. Lamont, a senior partner at J. P. Morgan, and Thomas J. Watson, president of IBM. For Roosevelt, the political advantages in moving decisively toward freer trade soon became clear.[48] The administration proved to be willing to sacrifice the rural West and rural Northeast, where both Democrats and Republicans opposed free trade, in order to adopt commercial policies that disproportionately benefited the urban Northeast and agrarian South.

This process paved the way for the party realignment of the 1930s that would deliver Democratic majorities to Roosevelt and ultimately provide the domestic political foundation for a more activist foreign policy. Angered by the Republican party's commitment to high tariffs, many "business internationalists" left the Grand Old Party in the 1936 election.[49] On the electoral front, the internationalization of the urban Northeast economy opened the doors to major Democratic gains in the region. The alliance between southern internationalists and urban northeasterners, institutionalized in the Democratic party, gave FDR the political foundation he needed not only to move the liberal-internationalist agenda forward, but also to sideline his one-time backers in the rural West. One political price to be paid was Republican gains in the West. Another was the jettisoning of much of the domestic reform agenda that had propelled Roosevelt's own rise to power.

On the trade issue, "business internationalists" and their allies argued that the American political economy depended on overseas commercial expansion and that the nation's export trade could only be expanded by reversing the international trend toward higher tariffs and managed trade.[50] What this meant in concrete terms was that America would have to make it easier for other nations to export their goods to the United States. "To sell," insisted Alfred P. Sloan, the Chairman of General Motors, "we must buy."[51] To purchase American manufactures, other countries needed dollars, which they could only obtain through loans or (preferably) through exports to the United States. That, business internationalists argued, was the "true" lesson of the 1920s. Internationalists like Stimson argued against economic nationalists like Senator Gerald Nye and historian Charles Beard, who claimed that the Great Depression was rooted in America's excessive dependence on foreign trade and investment. For Stimson and his allies, the roots of the depression lay in America's political failings: rather than assuming the "responsibilities" that accompany great power, America had pursued narrow, short-sighted policies on tariffs, war debts, and foreign lending in the 1920s.[52] In the absence of American leadership, foreign governments had found it difficult to resist political pressure to pursue autarkic strategies in their domestic economies and overseas empires. International fragmentation and rivalry was the result.

The implication was clear: American prosperity depended on not only open world markets, but also forceful U.S. leadership to keep things that way.

Lawmakers from the urban Northeast generally found these arguments persuasive. Most recognized the importance of free trade to their districts, and the depression's impact on foreign trade drove home the lesson. Between 1929 and 1933, world trade dropped 30 percent in volume. America suffered disproportionately: U.S. exports fell over 50 percent in quantity.[53] Rural America bore the initial brunt of the contraction in international trade, but by the early 1930s the effects had spread to the manufacturing belt. Exports of automobiles fell 83 percent; machinery exports declined some 78 percent; iron and steel dropped nearly 62 percent.[54] If the United States was going to regain its manufacturing trade, it would have to exercise leadership in opening international markets. "Does it not seem obvious," asked Thomas H. Cullen, a member of the House Ways and Means Committee from New York City, "that if we do not buy from other countries we cannot sell to other countries?"[55]

Tariff reform would have to begin at home. New means were needed to negotiate down international trading barriers. This, in turn, would require institutional changes. Congress would have to give up some of its tariff-making authority to the president. Free traders argued that this was unavoidable, for Congress—plagued by indecisiveness, narrow-mindedness, and pork-barrel politics—was poorly equipped to deal with the challenge of tariff reform:

> This is not a matter which can be satisfactorily disposed of in Congress. . . . It is a matter for slow and careful consideration. It must be gone into cautiously, step by step, with the idea of a general plan. Congress cannot do this, for in this country the tariff is to each Member of Congress a local issue. The tariff has always been a logrolling issue. Such an issue can have no general plan, and without a general plan the issue can never be settled. We must have a national tariff policy. At the present time we can have it in no other way except by giving the authority to formulate it to the President.[56]

The administration approached Congress with its trade reform package in March of 1934. Congress passed the Reciprocal Trade Agreement Act three months later. The new law authorized the president to negotiate trade agreements which could reduce U.S. tariffs by as much as 50 percent of 1930 levels without further congressional action. Under the RTAA, tariff concessions made to one country would extend automatically to all nations possessing most-favored-nation (equal access) commercial agreements with the United States.[57] This legislation represented a significant break with past practices. The doctrines of free trade and equal access, both strongly favored by business internationalists, were merged for the first time. And in giving the president such broad authority to raise or lower tariff duties, Congress relinquished much of its traditional tariff-making power.[58] No tariff law had ever given the chief executive so much discretionary power to bargain with other nations, or committed the country so firmly to the twin ideas of liberal trade and equal treatment.

Over the next five years the United States signed over two dozen trade agreements.[59] Although their effect on international trade ultimately proved far less formidable than the State Department had predicted, they did have a significant impact on U.S. exports, especially in manufactures.[60] Between 1933 and 1939, overseas sales of American goods roughly doubled: well short of the 1929 level but a sizable gain nonetheless.[61] Most of this increase was attributable to trade agreements negotiated under the RTAA. Roosevelt gave top priority to trade agreements with countries in the Western Hemisphere (especially Canada); these countries absorbed one-third of all American exports, most of which were manufactured goods.[62] The United States also reached trade agreements with a number of European countries. The most important by far was the so-called Anglo-American agreement of 1938, which covered a broad range of agricultural as well manufactured products. In part, this deal reflected the administration's deepening concerns about events in Europe. As the political situation worsened, U.S. officials began to view trade in strategic as well as economic terms, seeing it as a means for developing a counterweight to Germany's growing power.

Responding to the Nazi Threat

The administration had been searching for an "answer" to Adolf Hitler for some time.[63] Initially, the State Department entertained the idea of withholding commercial and financial support in an attempt to provoke a popular uprising against the new German leader. The idea was that without American loans and credits, Hitler might not be able to deliver on his promise of economic prosperity for working class Germans. Once it became clear that Hitler and the Nazis were firmly in control, the State Department changed course. It began trying to appease Germany, offering it equal access to American and other markets in hopes it would abandon discriminatory trade practices and dismantle its powerful military machine. This approach was also short-lived. Finding Hitler unreceptive to such overtures, the administration adopted a more assertive strategy: the White House began to push for an extensive rearmament program. At the same time, the State Department launched a drive to increase the president's power to impose sanctions against expansionist nations and to aid their victims. In contemporary strategic parlance, the administration favored a strategy of "deterrence plus reassurance." It sought to dissuade Germany from making aggressive moves against its neighbors while reassuring Britain and France of American support in the event that deterrence failed. The cornerstone of this effort was the State Department's campaign to repeal the neutrality laws.[64]

The first of the neutrality laws had been enacted in August 1935, shortly after Italy attacked Ethiopia. By prohibiting the export of arms and munitions to warring nations, the legislation was designed to limit the president's ability to pick sides in foreign military conflicts, thereby reducing the chances that the American people would be drawn into another European war.[65] In February 1936 isolationists went a step further: in addition to extending the arms embargo, they prohibited Americans from issuing loans to belligerents. Like the arms embargo, the ban on loans was ostensibly aimed at avoiding the "mistakes" of the last war.[66] Isolationists argued that by restricting the nation's financial involvement in a foreign war and limiting its dependence on wartime profits, America's leaders would face less pressure to intervene from powerful business interests. An even more comprehensive law was adopted the next year—the so-called permanent Neutrality Act of 1937. Passed in the midst of the Spanish Civil War, it extended the main features of the earlier laws to foreign *civil* wars. More importantly, it prohibited American merchant ships from carrying arms or munitions to belligerents. Roosevelt could authorize cash sales of nonmilitary goods to warring nations, but those goods had to be paid for in advance by foreign countries and shipped out of the United States in foreign bottoms.

These laws had real bite. They made it virtually impossible for the president to make the kinds of commitments that might deter German aggression.[67] Though frustrated by Congress's actions, Roosevelt felt he had little choice but to sign each of the neutrality bills into law.

Wanting the support of many western isolationists to pass his New Deal legislation, the president studiously avoided a test of strength with Congress on neutrality matters.

It was not until 1939, and only after the Nazis invaded Poland, that the White House launched its campaign to convince Congress to repeal the arms embargo. Even then the White House found it politically necessary to disguise its true objectives. Denying that it had any intention of amending the neutrality laws in order to aid Britain and France, the administration claimed that its sole purpose was to keep the United States out of war. The best way to avoid American involvement, it insisted, was to give the president the authority to help the Allies fight Germany. On September 21, three weeks after war broke out, the president called Congress into special session to reconsider the neutrality question. A colossal battle ensued. *Time* called it the "greatest legislative battle since the 1919 Senate fight over . . . the League of Nations."[68] After four weeks of fierce debate in the Senate and three days of the same in the House, Congress repealed the arms embargo. The repeal was passed by the Senate in late October by a vote of 63 to 30, the House followed suit a week later with a decisive 243–181 vote. American exporters were now free to sell arms and ammunition.[69]

The administration's victory was a turning point in the struggle between the internationalists and isolationists. Roosevelt was gradually wrenching greater control over foreign policy from Congress. By the end of November 1941, the White House had the authority to do almost anything short of military intervention to aid the Allies against Germany. It could supply lend-lease aid to Germany's enemies; it could use armed American merchant ships to transport goods all the way to England; and it could use U.S. warships to "patrol" the western Atlantic. During this period many in Congress continued to resist the expansion of executive authority. The administration's victories were attributable in large measure to the support of congressmen from the Northeast. As on other foreign policy issues, northeastern support for expanding the president's powers was strongest in the big cities. Lawmakers from the big cities were much more likely to vote with the administration on the question of neutrality than those from other parts of the Northeast (see table 3.4).

Why was the urban Northeast concerned about the Nazi threat? Answers lie in economics and politics. Support for repeal of the neutrality laws was in large part a reflection of this region's position in the world economy: for the industrial-urban Northeast, prosperity at home

Table 3.4 Northeastern Support for Neutrality Revision (percentage)

Area	Year		
	1937[1]	1939[2]	1941[3]
Urban	89.2	57.8	76.5
Other	51.9	17.7	41.8

Source: Computations from House roll call data.

Note: See table 3.3 for cities classified as urban.

[1]Vote on Fish (R-NY) Amendment to 1937 Neutrality Act. A vote against the amendment is a vote for greater presidential authority. March 18, 1937.

[2]Vote on Vorys (R-OH) Amendment to 1939 Neutrality Act. A vote against the amendment is a vote for greater presidential authority. June 30, 1939.

[3]Vote on Tinkham (R-MA) motion to recommit bill amending the 1939 Neutrality Act. A vote against the motion is a vote for greater presidential authority. October 17, 1941.

and stability in Europe were inseparable. For most lawmakers from the big cities, support for free trade and willingness to take sides in the European conflict were complementary positions. They feared that if Germany went unchecked, Hitler and his Axis partners would partition the world economy into exclusive spheres of influence and harm American interests. They worried that a victorious Germany would not only close the doors of Europe to American manufactures, but also that it would use its economic leverage to draw countries in the Western Hemisphere, especially Latin America, into its economic orbit. This concern was extremely salient for Northeast industrialists, whose chief export markets in the 1930s lay in Latin America, not Europe.

America's international bankers and portfolio investors had obvious, direct stakes in the stability and financial solvency of European governments and big business. As the next part of this chapter will show, this provided firm grounds for common cause between northern financiers and southern cotton exporters, who also depended on European clients and European markets. For northeastern industry in the 1930s, the stake in Europe was no less important; it was, however, more indirect and therefore less obvious. In the 1890s, American industry had exported to Latin America, but it had found Europe largely irrelevant to its interests. Forty years later, developments in Europe had become critical enough to northeastern manufacturers to make them largely immune to isolationists' appeals for bilateral, Western Hemisphere–centered solutions to the international crisis.

In the 1880s, the complementary nature of the American and Latin American economies had facilitated and simplified commercial rela-

tions between the two. Latin America produced tropical goods like coffee, sugar, and bananas that it sold in the United States to earn foreign
exchange to purchase American semi-manufactures and finished goods.
By the 1900s, things had become more complicated. The countries located in the temperate parts of South America had become major producers of commodities like cotton, wheat, and meat. The problem was
that these goods were also produced in great abundance in the United
States. The Western Hemisphere could not consume all of the food and
fiber it produced. This meant that by the early 1900s, the ability of
Latin American nations to purchase American manufactures increasingly came to rest on their capacity to obtain foreign exchange through
their agricultural exports to metropolitan *Europe.*

As long as Europe remained free, Latin America's dependence on
the Old World's markets did not pose a problem for American producers and exporters. Europe would continue to import Latin American
foods and fibers, and Latin America would use the foreign exchange
it earned to import high-quality American manufactures. Should the
Nazis establish control over Europe and its 300 million consumers,
however, all bets were off. Simple arithmetic helps explain why. Under
normal conditions, the United States took about one-third of Latin
America's exports, while Europe imported more than half.[70] A victorious Germany's bargaining position would thus be considerably
stronger than America's. The Nazis could use their economic advantage
to compel individual Latin American countries to spend the proceeds
from their exports on German manufactures. Having relied heavily on
bilateral barter arrangements to consolidate their economic hold on
Mittleuropa, there was every reason to believe that Germany would
adopt a similar strategy toward Latin America. This logic suggested that
unless Washington took preventative steps, the country would find itself sooner or later at the receiving end of a German economic blitz-
krieg:

> I think the world agrees that this European war is basically an
> economic one and that there is nothing that the Hitler Govern-
> ment wants more than to gain economic footholds throughout
> the world, and particularly in our Western Hemisphere. If a
> disaster should occur to Great Britain, it is my belief that the
> first form of an indemnity demand of the German Government
> would be the delivery of the shares of stock contracts, or agree-
> ments representing British ownership of railroads and indus-

tries in the nations of South and Central America. Possessed of the evidences of ownership, Hitler would have won a war in the Western Hemisphere without firing a shot, and free labor and industry of our western republics will have as their bedfellows the robotlike workmen in the profitless factories which is the goal of the totalitarian state.[71]

These fears were widely shared by the Northeast's business editors and corporate executives. Most were openly pro-British and strongly opposed Congress's mandatory arms embargo. Most also opposed the restrictions on foreign loans and domestic shipping.

Isolationists rejected this vision of economic interdependence and the disaster scenarios it spawned. They believed that the United States, with its huge continent-spanning common market and the protection offered by the Atlantic Ocean, had little to fear from a Nazi victory in the Old World.[72] In response to northeastern industry and exporters, they argued that bilateral trade agreements and political alliances within the Western Hemisphere would suffice to guarantee American interests. This vision did appeal to some prominent corporate chiefs, like Henry Ford, Jay Hormel, and Robert Wood, chairman of the board at Sears, Roebuck and Company, who actively participated in the isolationist *America First* movement.

By the 1930s, however, most of the corporate world patently rejected "Fortress America" thinking.[73] Business executives and editors readily conceded that Nazi Germany did not represent a direct military threat to the United States. The hemisphere contained an ample supply of strategic minerals and an adequate security perimeter. The real threat, they contended, was economic. The problem was that the New World contained two vast agricultural areas, but only one industrial center. The agricultural goods produced by the southern half of the hemisphere competed with those produced in the northern half. No matter how militarily secure the Western Hemisphere was, it would not be able to function successfully as a self-sufficient commercial unit, at least not without extensive federal control of commercial transactions beyond the water's edge.

Thus, for most of corporate America, the issue was not whether the United States had a stake in European stability. The real question was how to respond to the Nazi challenge or, more to the point, how much foreign policy-making authority to place in the president's hands. Many business executives distrusted Roosevelt and the band of liberal

New Dealers who occupied key posts in his administration. Still, seeing little alternative, big business generally favored giving the president a freer hand in dealing with the Axis powers. What the White House learned time and again was that business's support could not be taken for granted. As long as the expansion of the president's foreign policy-making powers did not jeopardize corporate autonomy, the White House could expect support for its foreign policies, especially among industrial sectors that had a sizable stake in foreign trade and investment. This is a major reason why the State Department's efforts to roll back Smoot-Hawley, and to repeal the arms embargo, enjoyed so much support in the business community. Both actions were compatible with the interests of internationally oriented business, and neither seriously threatened corporate discretion over all-important production decisions. Corporate America's jealous guarding of its own autonomy also helps explain why Roosevelt moved as cautiously as he did in building up the nation's military forces. For when it came to military preparedness, Congress was not the problem. The main challenge the White House faced was getting business on board.

The rural-urban cleavage that divided northeastern politicians over the tariff and neutrality disappeared on matters of national defense (table 3.5). With the exception of lawmakers from the rural West, most congressmen backed the president's requests for increased defense spending. Between 1934 and 1940, military appropriations nearly tripled. To be sure, most of the increase came after the outbreak of war in Europe. Yet even before the Nazi blitz on Poland, military spending was on the rise. From a low point in 1934, military spending grew annually and quite dramatically for the rest of the decade, with increases ranging between 10 and 40 percent per year.[74] Investment in national defense rose from less than 7 percent of all federal expenditures in 1934 to more than 10 percent by 1937. By 1940, the military accounted for over 17 percent of the federal government's budget. Even when overall government spending declined, as it did during the recession of 1938, Congress approved increases in the defense budget. Whatever misgivings Congress had about making the kinds of diplomatic commitments that might have prevented war, it was less hesitant to follow the president's lead when it came to expanding the nation's military capabilities. Congress not only approved Roosevelt's requests for larger defense appropriations—often it went beyond them.

Big business was a different matter. Their immediate concern was the New Deal and their fears of government regulation and planning.[75]

Table 3.5 Northeastern Support for Military Preparedness (percentage)

Area	Year			
	1935[1]	1937[2]	1939[3]	1941[4]
Urban	100.0	95.2	90.0	96.4
Other	100.0	97.6	91.4	100.0

Source: Computations from House roll call data.
Note: See table 3.3 for cities classified as urban.
[1] Vote to recommit H.R. 5730, a bill enabling United States to expand Navy. A vote against the motion is a vote for internationalism. June 12, 1935.
[2] Final passage of H.R. 9218, a bill authorizing increased naval spending. A vote for the bill is a vote for internationalism. March 21, 1938.
[3] Sutphin (D-NJ) Amendment to increase fortification of Guam. A vote for the amendment is a vote for internationalism. February 22, 1939.
[4] Final passage of H.J. Res. 222, an amendment to the Selective Training and Service Act of 1940, extending the term of military service. A vote for the amendment is a vote for internationalism. August 12, 1941.

Convinced that reformist New Dealers were intent on using military preparedness as an instrument to expand public authority over private business decisions, big business lobbied hard against military mobilization.[76] Even after war broke out on the European continent and after the president declared a "limited" national emergency, the business community resisted. The problem was not military spending per se. What concerned corporate America was the process of mobilization. Business demanded assurances that military mobilization would not interfere with civilian production, impose rigid limitations on profits, or force it to adhere to New Deal social and labor legislation. Corporate executives also wanted assurances from Roosevelt that any "War Industries Board" or other government agency responsible for military procurement would protect their management prerogatives from interference by New Dealers and organized labor. As one analyst puts it, corporate executives "wanted an administrative process that maximized their discretionary authority, and minimized the development of independent governmental authority."[77]

Roosevelt could not afford to ignore these demands. Corporate leaders' cooperation would be essential to any war effort. "The job," writes Bruce Catton, a participant in the mobilization effort, "couldn't be done without them, but their fears and suspicions—which, where Franklin Roosevelt was concerned, were deep and beyond number—had to be allayed."[78] Meanwhile, business leaders had forged a powerful alliance with top military brass, who had their own reasons for wanting to limit the influence of New Dealers on military procurement matters.

In the end, the president had little choice but to bow to business preferences. Concessions were offered to elicit corporate participation in the
mobilization effort. Other assurances came in the form of personnel
changes. The most important was Roosevelt's decision to make Henry
Stimson secretary of war in June 1940. Beyond the obvious political
advantages of picking a Republican of such stature to head the War
Department in an election year, Stimson's selection represented a setback for New Dealers and organized labor and for the New Deal itself.
Stimson was corporate America's man. He understood big business and
its fears of big government. He also understood the bottom line. As he
noted in his diary: "If you are going to try to go to war, or to prepare
for war, in a capitalist country, you have got to let business make
money out of the process or business won't work."[79] If America had
to prepare for war, certainly no one was better placed to bring big
business on board than the Colonel.

The Paradox of Southern Internationalism

By any measure, the South was more committed to a vigorous assertion
of American leadership overseas than any other part of the country.
Opinion polls consistently showed southerners to be more internationalist and interventionist than nonsoutherners.[80] The vast majority of the
region's newspaper editors endorsed Roosevelt's foreign policies, even
though many took exception to his domestic policies. Southerners
even led the country in volunteer enlistment in the armed services.[81]
These sentiments were widely shared by the region's elected representatives in Washington. All but a small minority spoke out in favor of
reciprocal trade, collective security, and military preparedness. On issues of momentous importance, their votes made the difference between victory and defeat for the White House: proposals to repeal the
arms embargo, lower tariff barriers, offer lend-lease aid, and institute
a military draft all turned on southern support. As Paul Seabury writes,
"The South's legislative role was not only marginally decisive; it fur-
nished the bedrock of support without which United States policy
might well have been paralyzed in the European crises, or at least far
more irresolute than it was."[82]

The southern case is an intriguing one. Conventional explanations
of the isolationist impulse in twentieth-century America attribute this
foreign policy stance to ignorance, backwardness, or parochialism. If

this were the case, we would expect the isolationist sentiment in Dixie to be very strong. Certainly no section of the country was more economically underdeveloped, had a higher proportion of illiterates and poorly educated people, or was more isolated and cut off from the American mainstream (let alone the rest of the world) than the South.[83] If cosmopolitanism was a "correlate" of internationalism, then by all rights southerners should have been at the vanguard of the isolationist movement. The South's commitment to New Deal internationalism seems paradoxical in another way, for it was ipso facto a commitment to a larger, more powerful presidency. When contrasted with southern lawmakers' opposition to the centralization of foreign policy-making powers in the 1890s, their willingness to delegate vast amounts of legislative power to the executive branch in the 1930s is striking. It seemed to represent a dramatic shift in southern attitudes toward executive privilege and power. Southern attitudes are often cited as the classic case of culturally driven policy preference, but in the debates over foreign policy in the 1930s, southern politics flew in the face of culturalist explanations.

What explains the curious case of southern internationalism? Why did the South, whose political leaders spoke so eloquently about the dangers of an "imperial presidency" in the nineteenth century, now so readily accommodate the consolidation of presidential power? Analyses that focus on party politics tell part of the story, but do not ultimately answer these questions. Roosevelt was remarkably popular among southern voters, and he swept the South by huge margins in each of his runs for the presidency. Seasoned southern leaders in Washington understood that their power was inextricably linked to the new president's. Having endured twelve long years in the minority, Democrats desired to retain power as the majority party. Yet party loyalty, and Roosevelt's personal charm, cannot explain southern policy choices. In spite of the president's popularity in the region, there was strong grassroots opposition to his administration's domestic agenda. Elites, for their part, were not ready to acquiesce on matters of vital interest just to ensure the president's success. Southern lawmakers sought to expand the Democratic administration's *foreign* policy-making powers, but they also sought to circumscribe severely the federal government's *domestic* powers.

The answer to the "paradox" of southern internationalism does not lie in party politics. The southern commitment to internationalism was ultimately about the preservation of an established social order. The collapse of the world economy, the unfolding crisis in Europe, and the reformist impulses of the New Deal all threatened the power of the conservative oligarchy that ruled most of the region. The rise of economic nationalism on the European continent risked closing-off vital foreign markets to southern agriculture. On the home front, this could only reinforce the economic nationalism and "social reform" tendencies of the early New Deal. Both jeopardized the "southern way of life" and could upset the underlying racial caste system. Thus, for southern politicians and for the planter and business classes with whom they were so closely aligned, internationalism provided an "external" solution to the "internal" problem of maintaining their own power and political hegemony in the South. Internationalism was a means to an end—it held out the promise of regional economic recovery, which would help stave off extensive outside (i.e., federal) intervention in state and local affairs. Faced with a choice between executive dominance over foreign or domestic policy, southern elites readily opted for the former.

The European Crisis and the South

In February 1933, Roosevelt tapped a southerner, Cordell Hull, to be his secretary of state. The president's announcement was warmly received in the South.[84] An apostle of economic internationalism, Hull had crusaded tirelessly against the protective tariff—"the king of evils" he once called it—during his twenty-three years as a congressman and senator from Tennessee. Though few southern leaders were as fanatical on the subject of international trade as "Judge" Hull, most shared his basic views.[85] Like the new secretary of state, they believed that the liberalization of international trade was the key to domestic recovery. They too saw it as the best way to overcome the problem of "surplus production" that plagued southern farmers (as well as northern businessmen) without resorting to the excessive central planning and regulation that liberal New Dealers advocated. They shared Hull's view that the Smoot-Hawley tariff passed by Congress in 1930 was an abomination, bearing much responsibility for the sharp decline of world commerce that followed. Many also agreed with Hull when he claimed that the revival of world trade would also reduce international tensions by lowering the "economic barriers [that] lie at the root of the world's major ills."[86] "The truth is universally recognized," proclaimed the secretary in testimony before Congress, "that trade between nations is the greatest peacemaker and civilizer within human experience."[87]

Delighted by the selection of "one of their own" to fill such a prestigious cabinet position, southerners hoped the president's choice meant that his administration would work hard to liberalize world trade and restore traditional markets for American exporters. Their optimism about the president's intentions was soon tempered, for although Roosevelt was predisposed toward internationalism, initially he found it politically expedient to avoid making a clear choice between nationalist and internationalist policies.[88] Roosevelt tried to cultivate support from both groups, appointing prominent internationalists like Cordell Hull as well as ultranationalists like George N. Peek, who was made head of the Agricultural Adjustment Administration and special adviser on foreign trade. The president moved decisively toward the internationalist pole over time, but only after Hull had suffered some serious setbacks and after early New Deal domestic programs had been put in place. Roosevelt's decision to send Hull's plan for promoting freer trade to Capitol Hill in March of 1934 was one sign of the shift. His decision to accept Peek's resignation the following year was another. For Secretary Hull, the president's actions were a personal victory. For the South, they were a political one. In Hull, the South had a strong advocate of its traditional point of view in a position of power close to the president's ear.

The situation in Europe represented a real and immediate threat to southern economic interests. Shortly after Hitler became chancellor in January 1933, Nazi officials instituted a system of bilateral barter designed to induce other nations to buy as much as they sold when trading with Germany. Offering an array of commercial incentives, the Nazis were able to extract special trade privileges from various nations, particularly in *Mittleuropa* and the Balkans.[89] What made Germany's actions so ominous was the parallel track the Nazis were following on security matters. In October 1933, Hitler abruptly withdrew Germany from the World Disarmament Conference in Geneva and from the League of Nations. A few months later, Hitler stunned his European neighbors by announcing that Germany had secretly built an air force and would reinstate universal conscription, directly violating the Versailles Treaty. While Hitler repeatedly claimed that his intentions were peaceful, many in Washington feared that the rapid arms buildup meant that Germany would ultimately attempt to redraw the boundary lines in Europe. The remilitarization of the Rhineland in March 1936, and Hitler's decision later that year to sign pacts with the fascist leaders of Italy and Japan, only lent credulity to the arguments of those in the administration who warned that the United States had to become more engaged in events on the European continent.

No region of the country more avidly supported a "get tough" strategy toward the Nazis than the South.[90] Placing little stock in Hitler's rhetoric and convinced that preventing German dominance on the continent was vital to their interests, southerners agreed with administration officials like Hull who wanted to expand the president's power to punish aggression. Even before the Nazi invasion of Poland in 1939, two-thirds of the South believed that America's future depended on a British victory. By the spring of 1941 almost 90 percent of all southerners surveyed were of this opinion. Whenever respondents were asked whether the United States should do more to aid the Allies, southerners invariably replied more favorably than other regional groups. The same was true when it came to the question of military spending and conscription. Alfred Hero, the leading scholar of southern opinion on foreign policy, writes that "[d]uring the pre–Pearl Harbor period Southerners were more willing to go further, to take greater risks of United States involvement in the war, and to make more sacrifices for the opponents of the Axis than were residents of any other region, including the Northeast."[91] The South's one-time opposition to an assertive American foreign policy was now ancient history.

Southern votes on key foreign policy legislation in Congress point to the same conclusion. Figures 3.3 through 3.5 compare the South against the rest of the country on indices measuring support for the three issues examined in this chapter: neutrality revision (interventionism), military rearmament, and reciprocal trade. Each of these should be interpreted as a measure of support for greater executive power in foreign policy and as a measure of support for internationalism. All three were opposed by isolationists on the grounds that they would greatly expand the president's freedom to maneuver in foreign affairs, and in the case of neutrality revision and military rearmament, increase the likelihood of costly and unnecessary American military involvement in Europe or Asia. On each policy initiative, support is much higher in the South than it is outside the region. Moreover, there is much less variation in the voting behavior of the southern delegation as a whole than there is among congressmen from the Northeast or the West. The southern "block" in the House was more cohesive than its regional counterparts.

The president could not have turned back the isolationist tide in Congress without solid southern backing. As the situation in Europe

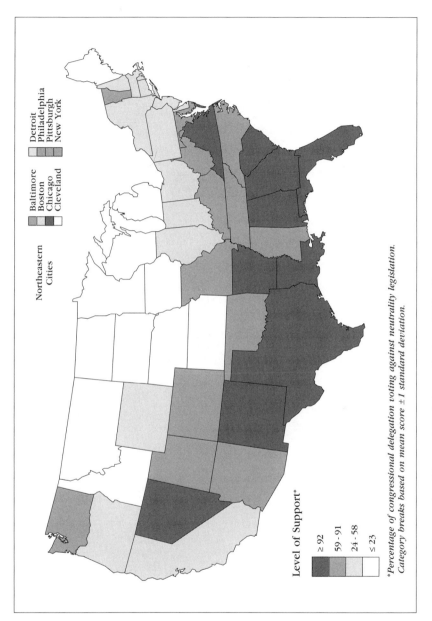

Northeastern
Cities

Baltimore
Boston
Chicago
Cleveland

Detroit
Philadelphia
Pittsburgh
New York

Level of Support*

≥ 92
59 - 91
24 - 58
≤ 23

*Percentage of congressional delegation voting against neutrality legislation.
Category breaks based on mean score ± 1 standard deviation.

Figure 3.3 Congressional Support for Interventionism, 1933–41

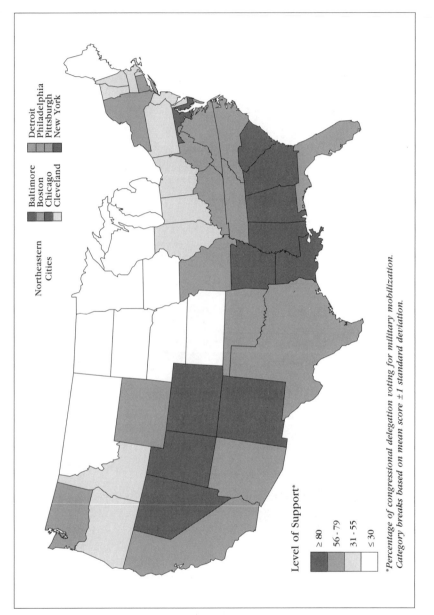

Level of Support*

≥ 80
56 - 79
31 - 55
≤ 30

Northeastern
Cities

Baltimore
Boston
Chicago
Cleveland

Detroit
Philadelphia
Pittsburgh
New York

*Percentage of congressional delegation voting for military mobilization.
Category breaks based on mean score ± 1 standard deviation.

Figure 3.4 Congressional Support for Military Preparedness, 1933–41

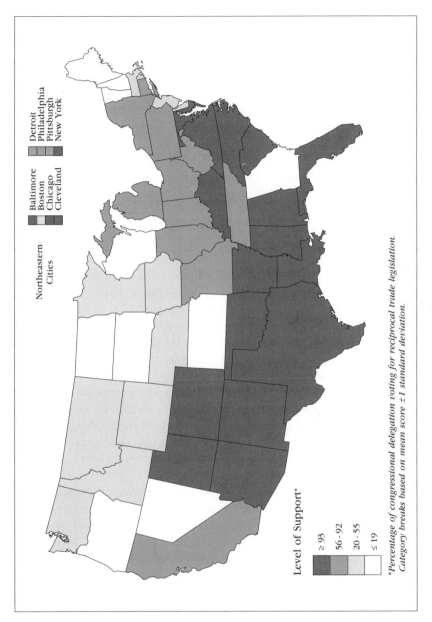

Level of Support*

≥ 93
56 - 92
20 - 55
≤ 19

Northeastern Cities

Baltimore
Boston
Chicago
Cleveland

Detroit
Philadelphia
Pittsburgh
New York

*Percentage of congressional delegation voting for reciprocal trade legislation. Category breaks based on mean score ±1 standard deviation.

Figure 3.5 Congressional Support for Free Trade, 1933–41

deteriorated, the administration became even more dependent on southern congressmen. This is because there were heavy Democratic losses in the 1938 mid-term election. Coming on the heels of a sharp downturn in the economy, a rash of labor strikes, and an upsurge in nativism, the Republicans were able to pick up eighty-one seats in the House, the majority of which were from isolationist states in the West. The Republicans won another eight seats in the Senate, and thirteen new governorships.[92] In the face of these setbacks, Roosevelt needed the solidly Democratic South more than ever. Most accounts of internationalism's rise focus on the interests of Wall Street bankers and northern industry, but it is overwhelmingly clear that northeastern big business could not have carried the day without solid southern support.

Southern support for a more ambitious and decisive foreign policy sprang from multiple sources. The region's long-standing "cultural and blood ties" to Great Britain may have played some role. One can also factor in the South's interest in federal military outlays, especially once the nation moved decisively toward a strategy of military preparedness in 1938. Well before the attack on Pearl Harbor, southern business and political leaders could see "opportunities for profit and prosperity" in the expanding military budget, and they sought to guarantee that should war come, the South would receive its "fair share" of defense contracts and military bases.[93]

Yet in the final analysis, there can be little question that the South's interests were determined by its position in the international economy. Historian Wayne Cole puts it succinctly: "Hitler's barter system and Japan's drive for a Greater East Asia Co-Prosperity Sphere promised nothing good for a South which was dependent upon foreign markets for an important part of its economic well-being."[94] Indeed, the South was more vulnerable to the loss of overseas markets than other sections of the country. On the eve of the Great Depression, southern exports made up 30 percent of all American exports and accounted for roughly 20 to 25 percent of the South's total economic production.[95] By comparison, the nation as a whole was exporting only 5.3 percent of total GNP.[96] Raw materials made up the bulk of southern exports to its principal markets in Europe and Asia. It is estimated that exports of raw cotton and tobacco leaf alone comprised two-thirds of all southern exports in the late 1920s (table 3.6). Cotton exports averaged about 58 percent of average annual production; roughly 40 percent of the tobacco crop was exported. All totaled, the value of southern exports was equal to about 40 percent of gross farm income and cash farm

Table 3.6 Southern Exports by Major Commodity, 1926-39

Commodity	1926-29[1]		1936-39	
	Share of Exports	Share of Output	Share of Exports	Share of Output
Raw cotton	56.4	57.8	41.2	38.2
Unmanufactured tobacco	9.8	39.7	17.3	28.5
Petroleum products	21.6	15.4	29.0	13.4
Wood and wood products	4.3	—	3.6	—
Naval stores	2.2	49.4	2.3	42.0
Sulfur	1.0	33.5	1.5	29.3
Other[2]	4.7	—	5.1	—

Source: Adapted from B. U. Ratchford, "The South's Stake in International Trade—Past, Present, and Prospective," *Southern Economic Journal* 14 (April 1948): 365, table 2.
[1] Average.
[2] Includes semi- and manufactured cotton and manufactured tobacco.

receipts in the region. "It was no exaggeration to say that the South at the time had to export or die."[97]

The collapse of the international economy in the 1930s dealt the region a severe blow. While the impact was felt throughout the American economy, the South was hit hardest by the loss of overseas markets. Before 1930, southern exports were valued at approximately $1.4 billion per year. A decade later, they had declined by half.[98] (Nonsouthern exports fell by one-third.) Cotton suffered the most: exports declined by more than 60 percent in value, from some $830 million in the late 1920s to about $300 million before World War II.[99] During the 1930s, tobacco exports also fell, as did sales of most of the region's other main export commodities. For those involved in cotton production, the impact was brutal. Cotton exports provided a livelihood for some 6.6 million southern workers and their dependents.[100] Of the eleven million persons in the South who depended directly on King Cotton, approximately 60 percent depended on exports to Europe and the Far East.

Few southern leaders needed to be reminded of the value of the European market. Most were old enough to remember August 1914, when cotton lost one-half its value in only two months and the world cotton market virtually disappeared.[101] When southerners contemplated the possibility of a British naval blockade of Europe in the Fall of 1914, fear and panic spread through the region. Everything turned topsy-turvy: normally pro-British members of Congress spouted anti-British rhetoric on the House and Senate floors. "So powerful was the demand for retaliation," explained Mississippi Senator John Sharp Williams in a letter to Woodrow Wilson, "that every politician in the South had to be anti-British."[102] The British, worried that southern lawmakers might forge a powerful anti-British alliance with pacifists and isolationists in Congress, began to artificially support the price of cotton through purchases on the open market. This was sufficient to turn the tide of southern opinion. The episode revealed how "price sensitive" southern Anglophilia really was. It also dramatized the South's vulnerability to political events in Europe.

Once the "cotton crisis" was resolved, the South moved decisively behind the Allied cause.[103] Southern lawmakers overwhelmingly backed Wilson's calls for military preparedness and emergency war powers.[104] So did most southern newspaper editors.[105] To be sure, there were southerners who took exception to Wilson's wartime policies. In Congress, a small group of southern agrarian-progressives waged a determined if losing battle against the administration's pro-British policies and preparedness program. Led by Claude Kitchin, the Democratic majority leader from North Carolina, this group was centered in parts of the South—North Carolina, Oklahoma, Texas—wherein radical agrarian sentiment remained a powerful force. For them, the real threat to southern society was not Germany but the rapid expansion of federal power that Wilson's wartime policies would produce. Most white southerners shared their concerns about states' rights on the Negro question but not when it came to the war in Europe.[106] They could not afford to. Southerners overwhelmingly rejected anti-militarism and anti-interventionism.

The South was a region that depended heavily on exporting commodities to world markets, and in this regard little changed in the years between the two great wars. Europe continued to take the bulk of its raw materials. From 1932 to 1935, the European powers purchased 57 percent of southern cotton.[107] Roughly 67 percent of all exported southern tobacco leaf found its way to the British Isles or Continental Europe. Markets in Asia consumed most of the balance.[108] It is easy to see why most southerners viewed the spread of nationalism in the 1920s and 1930s with alarm. For them, the collapse of the liberal European-oriented world system presented a fundamental threat. "However else the crisis of that world might have been viewed by others," writes Seabury, "the articulate South saw Nazi aggression as a dagger thrust at the heart of this system."[109] If Germany defeated Britain, Hitler and his Axis partners would establish economic hegemony over the European continent and divide the world into exclusive spheres of influence. If Hitler were not stopped, he would close the doors of Europe to American exports and move against U.S. commercial interests elsewhere. The South had little confidence in the carrot of economic appeasement. Southern leaders were ready to rely on the stick of military intimidation:

> There is nothing in the history of Hitler to justify anybody believing that his plans for world domination can be thwarted otherwise by force or by the recognized ability to use force. A career of broken promises, of cruel aggression, and of inhuman oppression of peaceful people suggests no hope for the plans of those who would pat the beast on the head and offer no aid to those who are his present prey, expecting that when he has devoured them his appetite will be sated.[110]

The South and the New Deal

If the rise of economic nationalism overseas was a nightmare for the South, so too was the possibility of its spread here at home. The two were not unrelated in the minds of southern economic and political elites. Cordell Hull's fear about the domestic consequences of trade blocs was theirs: if Germany and Japan succeeded in carving up the world into exclusive trade zones, severely reducing America's access to international markets, then the federal government would be forced to intervene in the economy to create an internal balance between domestic production and home consumption. The presence of so many "planners" in Roosevelt's administration, plus the fact that the president had initially moved in this general direction, only made such a threat more palpable in the South.[111] The nationalist road to recovery— with its tariff barriers, production controls, and quota systems—would have posed severe, but perhaps not insurmountable problems of economic readjustment in the more industrialized and agriculturally diversified regions of the country. For the southern oligarchy and its constituents, such a "solution" would have meant the end of a "way of life."

The South of the 1930s was still very much a closed society. The plantation remained at the center of southern society, shaping not only its economy but its social and political structure as well. Industry was still relatively weak, and the merchants, bankers, and lawyers who made up the southern middle class continued to align with the "planter class" that dominated politics and society in the South. The progressive movement after World War I strengthened the hand of commercial and industrial interests, but the region's economic future continued to hinge on the fortunes of the planters. In this sense, the promise of the New South movement of the 1920s remained unfulfilled.[112] Per capita income was still far below the national average. While the region's largest cities now had more people working in industry than commerce, the urban South's economy remained largely commercial.[113] Rapid expansion of the urban South had not materially altered the region's status as a primary producer, or its dependent and tributary position in the national economy.[114] In 1929, only 25 percent of the South's income came from manufacturing. By the early 1930s, no more than 5 percent of the most important southern corporations were headquartered in the South.[115]

Even more striking was the tenacity of the county and small-town elites who had dominated the region's politics for so long. Historian Dewey Grantham writes that "the years between World War I and the onset of the Great Depression represented a period of consolidation in the evolving pattern of state politics in the South." The role of urban-industrial interests expanded, as did the functions of state and local government, but the "basic features of the one-party system were as solidly established in custom and law as ever."[116] Fashioned in response to the Populist challenge of the 1890s, the southern party system concentrated power in the hands of affluent planters and their business allies in commerce and industry. From that point onward, political competition in the region revolved around the Democratic primary—the de facto election in the one-party South. Safeguarded by an array of restrictive registration and voting laws, most notably the infamous literacy tests and poll taxes, the system disenfranchised millions of poor blacks and whites and thus precluded the reemergence of effective, class-based opposition. The South's one-party system was designed to ensure that after the 1890s, the poor and dispossessed would never again threaten the wealthy's political power and economic domination.

Southern state legislatures and party conventions were regularly controlled by local elites from small towns and rural hamlets. These state and local officials almost always shared the wealthy's interest in insulating the region from national political and market forces. And southern elites were nothing if not creative in responding to reformist winds from the North. A case in point is the southern response to "progressivism's" attempt to regulate business, reform the workplace, and improve public education in the 1920s.[117] Reforms that were heralded by some as "a revolution in southern life" proved to be impossible to implement without the assent of powerful small-town and county-seat elites. Would-be reformers found it necessary to soft-pedal business regulation and social reform and to concentrate instead on building roads, protecting low wages, and luring northern capital. Ironically, many of the reforms backfired by "widening disparities between the South's 'haves' and 'have nots.'"[118]

The region's leaders in Washington responded to the reformist winds of the 1930s in much the same way. Southern congressmen shared Roosevelt's desire for economic recovery, but not his administration's commitment to social reform. Historian Frank Freidel writes that "most of the leaders of Southern democracy developed, in time, an embarrasing ambivalence toward Roosevelt and the New Deal."[119] In battles over FDR's proposals to liberalize the Supreme Court, nationalize labor standards, and revise relief programs, the president learned that southern support was conditional, not automatic.[120] In Congress, the administration could count on southern backing as long as its policies did not threaten the "twin pillars" of the established order: low wages and white supremacy. Many southerners who voted with Roosevelt during the administration's first one hundred days became disenchanted as the New Deal became more "liberal," and more "northern."

For the conservative South, the New Deal promised needed economic relief, but at a cost to regional autonomy.[121] As far as southern leaders were concerned, the issue was not "big government" per se, or an unwavering attachment to "state's rights." They may have been conservative, but they were not foolish enough to become hostages of their own shopworn rhetoric. The real problem was that the New Deal challenged the social power structure in the region:

> The general effect of the New Deal was the erosion of the authority of the county-seat elites, the "small town big men," whose control of labor, credit, and municipal government guaranteed their power. Relief interposed federal officials between the laboring people and the local bosses. Labor standards eliminated the low wages that forced entire families to work in one man's textile mill. Government credit skirted bankers.[122]

Even though Roosevelt himself never openly challenged white supremacy, many of his administration's programs—from crop limitations, to codes and labor standards, to worker relief—mitigated the effects of racial discrimination and threatened the South's hierarchical social structure.

As economic depression racked the South, regional elites thus faced a dilemma: they desired federal assistance, but they feared and resented federal intervention. So apprehensive were they that many likened the New Deal to a second Reconstruction. Southern congressmen had to walk a fine line. They were drawn to solutions, like those contained in the Agricultural Act of 1933, that delivered federal fiscal support while delegating most administrative control and prerogative to states or localities.[123] For southern officials, the advantages of federal-state arrangements that localized policy control were equally obvious: they could claim credit for bringing economic relief to the region while blunting the impact of federal "forays against the established order."[124] The problem was that it was not always possible to assure local control over federal policy, or to limit executive fiat to a specific time-table as had been done in the case of the Works Progress Administration (WPA). In cases like the Wage and Hour Bill, Wagner's antilynching proposal, and federal housing legislation, southern leaders found themselves on the defensive, forced to fight rearguard battles. Skillful parliamentarians, and occupying positions of power in both chambers, they turned to traditional devices of obstruction and strategic control: procedural maneuvers in the House Rules Committee, filibuster on the Senate floor, and the powers of committees and committee chairmen.[125]

The guardians of conservative rule in the South represented a formidable challenge to the New Deal. They feared that if domestic economic recovery were not assured through an opening of international markets—a solution that required putting a stop to the Nazis—the New Deal would assume a life of its own. Closure of the international trading system would not only close off their vital markets, but also would inevitably force the American government into ever-intensifying regulation and control of the domestic economy. For the southern oligarchy, loss of overseas commodities markets, coupled with loss of economic and political autonomy on the state and local level, would spell the demise of the social order that underpinned both power and privilege.

On domestic matters, southerners found it increasingly necessary to align with conservative Republicans.[126] This fact provides sufficient grounds for moving beyond the "party loyalty" explanation of southern politics during the New Deal. Meanwhile, explanations that focus on the South's traditional adherence to constitutional principles and states' rights also fall short. Southern stands on foreign policy in the 1930s show that when strengthening presidential control over policy did *not* threaten the southern oligarchy, or was perceived as the best way of ensuring its longevity, southern leaders did not hesitate to favor the centralization of control over policy-making and implementation. When it served their interests, southerners where prepared to qualify, if not altogether abandon, the cherished doctrine of states' rights and constitutional principles of limited government.

State Power and States' Rights

On international matters, most southern members of Congress were quick to grant the executive branch wide discretionary power over policy.[127] Southerners, in fact, were Roosevelt's strongest allies in committee and on the House floor. In debate, they proved remarkably flexible, deploying the very *raison d'état* arguments that an earlier generation of southerners had so vehemently opposed in the 1890s. Often expressed in the language of constitutional law, southerners' positions on domestic matters and foreign policy regularly conflicted, leaving them open to ridicule and attack. It is easy to see why their colleagues across the aisle derided them: In the 1930s it became altogether too obvious that southern lawmakers' commitment to the great Jeffersonian principle of limited government was contingent. They were Jeffersonian when it served their interests.

Southerners were willing to overturn Congress's neutrality laws to increase the White House's power to impose economic sanctions against belligerents in Europe and Asia. This was an indication of how far they were prepared to go in strengthening the president's hand in foreign affairs. One need not believe that Roosevelt was looking for "legal ways to circumvent the Constitution" to recognize that he did want legislation that would give him great autonomy and freedom to maneuver.

Another sign of southern "flexibility" when it came to constitutional questions was their support for the Export-Import Bank, Lend-Lease, and the general principle of government-sponsored foreign lending. During the 1920s, private loans to foreign countries had underwritten much of the nation's foreign trade. The Export-Import Bank reversed these policies by relying on tax-supported dollars to finance the sale of U.S. goods. First approved by Congress as a tool to promote foreign trade in 1935, Roosevelt quickly turned the bank into a diplomatic instrument and eventually into a weapon for the kind of economic warfare that Congress, through its neutrality legislation, was trying to avoid.[128] After the fall of France in July 1940, the State Department moved to secure congressional approval for providing vast amounts of war materials to Great Britain, and subsequently all of America's allies. This was the initiative popularly known as Lend-Lease. The enabling legislation gave the president extraordinary powers, and as a result it provoked heated debate on Capitol Hill over its constitutional implications. Once again, the southern heirs of Jefferson voted overwhelmingly in favor when the final roll was called.

Southern support for expanding the president's foreign policy-making powers was not a belated response to the deteriorating situation in Europe. As early as March 1934, when Secretary Hull's beloved reciprocal trade package was submitted to Congress, the South's willingness to grant broader foreign policy powers to the White House was evident. Ninety-seven percent of southern congressmen voted for the new trade law. In 1937, 94 percent voted to renew the administration's negotiating authority.[129] Compelled to explain the shift in their attitude toward executive power, southern lawmakers followed Secretary Hull's lead, stressing the gravity of the crisis that faced the nation, at home and abroad.[130] To the RTAA's opponents, this was eyewash. Speaker after speaker on the House floor pointed out that the country confronted the same crisis when southerners were called on to vote Smoot-Hawley up or down. They pointed out that like the RTAA, Smoot-Hawley granted considerable powers to the president under its "flexible-tariff" provision.[131] Back then, when Republicans occupied the White House, southern leaders in the House would have no part of a bill that reduced Congress's tariff-making power. No less an authority than Judge Hull called the flexible-tariff "subversive of the plain functions of Congress" and an "unjustifiable arrogance of power and authority to the president." It is no wonder that James Beck of Pennsylvania, one of the few Republicans who had spoken out against Smoot-Hawley, derided his southern colleagues in 1934 for leaving him "like a deserted and forlorn bride on the church steps." For Beck, one of the House's leading voices on legal matters, the attitudes of the southern delegation toward the RTAA were an unfortunate reminder of how self-serving constitutional arguments were:

> I do not doubt that many Members of this House do take what is an academic and sentimental interest in the Constitution as it came from the master architects of our Government, but, as

far as affecting a single vote is concerned, I have yet to discover that any effort of mine or any effort of any other Member of the House has ever changed a vote in respect to a question, where the doubt was purely that of constitutional power. In this connection I am reminded of the facility with which changes of opinion can take place in matters of constitutional powers, although they concern the oath that we all take when we come into this House to defend and protect the Constitution of the United States.[132]

Few southern lawmakers could concede Beck's point—at least not directly.

It is clear that the South's support for reciprocal trade reflected the region's stake in international trade. "Sixty percent of our cotton moves abroad," noted one southern lawmaker. "Unless we are to develop our foreign markets, have we not of necessity to give that trade up?"[133] The point was well taken: since most of the cotton crop was sold to British, German, Japanese, French, and Italian textile makers, the well-being of the southern states was dependent on the ability of these countries to obtain dollar exchange through trade. Meanwhile, there can be little doubt that southern support for tariff reform was intensified by the desire to right what Peter Molyneaux, editor of *The Texas Weekly,* called an "ancient wrong."[134] "To say that the national welfare requires the maintenance of a high-tariff policy," wrote the Texas pundit, "is equivalent to saying that the national welfare requires the irreparable submersion, economically and socially of the greater part of the population of a whole region [i.e., the South] of the country." Although few southern congressmen made the "colonial" argument the centerpiece of their case for tariff reform, most were sensitive to this view. The tariff was an old sore. Even the administration's reformist *Report on Economic Conditions of the South* acknowledged the tariff's political import when it concluded that high tariffs and freight rates, that other southern hobby-horse, were powerful vices that "squeezed" the South and "kept it from moving along with the main stream of American economic life."[135]

The issue was not just one of short-term profits or righting old wrongs. Southerners' larger concern was the alternative—economic nationalism. Echoing the views of southern elites, Molyneaux defined the situation this way: "The outlook for the cotton states will be determined very largely by whether the United States follows a policy of international economic cooperation, on the one hand, or a policy of narrow economic nationalism on the other."[136] What made the RTAA so attractive is that it pointed in the right direction. For commercial farmers who never reconciled to crop restrictions, price pegging, or government operations in the marketplace, Secretary Hull's market-oriented brand of New Dealism had its advantages.[137] Although it could not guarantee prosperity in the short-run, it did offer commercial farmers hope. More importantly, it did nothing to jeopardize (and promised to sustain) the power and privilege of the "small town big men" who controlled southern society. By contrast, the alternative stirred up deep fears of federal regimentation of the economy and social conflict. In a speech that received thunderous applause on the House floor, A. Willis Robertson of Virginia laid out the choice in stark terms: "Let us frankly face the fact that to be self-contained we must strictly regiment not only the cotton growers . . . but likewise the wheat growers, the tobacco growers, the apple growers, the hog growers—in fact everything that is now produced on the farm. If we are to be self-contained, let us frankly face the fact that there will come inevitably conflict between the 30 millions now directly dependent for a livelihood upon agriculture and those who labor in our mills and factories."[138]

To most southern leaders the choice was clear. Theirs was not an internationalism rooted in abstract legal principles or in an unwavering devotion to party and president. Their commitment to internationalism was grounded in the fears and interests shared by conservative southern elites. For southern politicians looking for ways to preserve the southern social order, Secretary Hull's brand of New Dealism was tailor-made. Hull's interest in promoting an "open door" abroad dovetailed with their interest in protecting a "closed society" at home. If protecting the "southern way of life" required delegating vast amounts of foreign policy-making power to the executive branch, then so be it.

Having Judge Hull in a position of power certainly helped make such a choice easier for the faint of heart. They had to know that those charging them with hypocrisy were not wrong. At the level of legal or constitutional discourse, southerners were inconsistent. Southern officials played both sides of legal arguments, arguing for and against "executive privilege" as situations warranted. At the level of politics, there was nothing inconsistent about trying to limit the federal government's domestic powers while expanding the chief executive's international authority. The power of the conservative southern oligarchy depended on federal noninterference in local affairs *and* on an open

international order. This explains the paradox of southern internationalism.

The Agrarian Roots of Isolationism

If internationalism was the credo of the South, isolationism was the
ideology of the West. The same polls that ranked southerners as Roosevelt's strongest supporters on foreign affairs showed westerners to be
his toughest critics. Westerners were generally more skeptical than
other Americans about the virtues of foreign trade, collective security,
and military preparedness; they were more reluctant to give the chief
executive greater discretionary authority in making foreign policy; and
they were less willing to spend American blood or treasure to check
Germany's or Japan's drive for hegemony in Europe and Asia.[139] Even
after war broke out in Europe in September 1939, and after a majority
of the nation's citizens had concluded that the United States had to
aid the Allies, support for American interventionism was noticeably
weaker in the West. Isolationism reigned supreme in the 1930s in the
rural areas of the "trans-Mississippi West," that is, in the Great Plains
and Mountain West. Western isolationists, steeped in the region's agrarian traditions, looked above the Mason-Dixon line and found allies in
other parts of rural America. At the height of its influence before Pearl
Harbor, the rural western credo penetrated as far east as the Ohio Valley and as far west as the Columbia Plateau, creating what has been
called "the region of isolationism."[140] The depth and constancy of its
isolationism is what distinguished the West from the rest.

Western views were well represented on Capitol Hill. No elected
officials defended isolationism more passionately than those from the
trans-Mississippi West, and none embodied the movement's agrarian
impulses more perfectly than Senator Gerald P. Nye, the Republican
Progressive from North Dakota. As the head of the sensational Senate
investigation into the influence of munitions makers and international
bankers on foreign policy, the senator established his position as a leading figure in the isolationists' campaign against eastern big business
and New Deal internationalism.[141] Nye was convinced that American
intervention in World War I was a mistake, a result of powerful business
pressure and weak political leadership. He lobbied hard for legislation
that would limit the president's ability to pursue an expansionist (i.e.,
internationalist) foreign policy, and for legislation that would make

America more "self-sufficient" and less economically vulnerable to political developments on the European continent. In what would prove to be a losing battle, Nye and other isolationists tried to prevent American involvement in another foreign war by limiting the president's freedom to maneuver in foreign affairs. Every time the Roosevelt administration approached Congress for greater discretionary authority in responding to the mounting crises in Europe and Asia, isolationists mobilized in attempts to rein in the president and to prevent American entanglement in overseas conflicts.

For years the dominant explanation of western isolationism was a cultural one. The region's isolationism, it was argued, reflected its demographic make-up. With large numbers of Americans of German and Irish descent, the West was pulled toward isolationism: German Americans disapproved of policies that might harm Germany; Irish Americans opposed the same policies because they aided the British. First introduced by Samuel Lubell, a prominent political analyst in the 1950s, this "ethnic hypothesis" was severely criticized at the time.[142] Studies revealed that the theory did not fit the facts.[143] Americans of German and Irish descent were no more isolationist in outlook than any others. Members of Congress who represented districts with large German or Irish constituencies were no more inclined than other congressmen to vote for isolationist legislation. Opinion polls did show westerners to be more isolationist than southerners and easterners. What was off the mark was the conclusion that Lubell and others drew from this fact—that westerners were more "emotional" or "irrational" in dealing with the outside world. However misguided isolationist policies like neutrality may have been, the last thing westerners were was irrational.

Westerners opposed internationalism for concrete reasons. Imperatives rooted in the West's position in the world economy were the most important. Unlike the agrarian South, the rural West looked primarily to the domestic market for its prosperity and thus had little incentive to back the RTAA. Having less at stake in Europe than southerners, westerners also felt comparatively little urgency in aiding the Allies or expanding the nation's capacity to project military power overseas. By the 1930s, the looming "threat" of foreign imports of grains, livestock, and minerals caused more apprehension than the possibility of "losing" markets in Europe or Latin America. Opposition to internationalism was fueled by the West's traditions of agrarian radicalism and antipartyism, which were expressed in part in long-standing antipathy toward Wall Street and Great Britain. Political traditions thus colored the issues of neutrality, reciprocal trade, and rearmament with emotional and symbolic overtones. Imperatives of pure, practical politics solidified the West's commitment to isolationism. Western progressives in Congress favored domestic solutions to the nation's economic problems. By limiting the president's freedom to pursue an ambitious foreign policy, they hoped to check the drift toward internationalist solutions to the economic crisis in the 1930s.[144] Westerners rightly feared the redistributive costs of Roosevelt's internationalist foreign policy agenda.

The West in the World Economy

The early twentieth-century West was a study in contrasts. On the one hand, the region grew at a spectacular rate, outpacing the South and even the Northeast on some measures of regional growth. On the other hand, the West's pattern of economic development was very uneven and its prosperity was highly concentrated. Growth occurred mainly in cities and large urban areas, especially in California and along the Pacific Coast. Manufacturing and service industries boomed in Los Angeles, San Francisco, Portland, and Seattle, attracting millions of Americans to the West in search of a better life. Despite the impressive growth of industry and finance in these areas, the West remained predominantly a raw materials-producing region in the 1930s. With roughly 20 percent of the national workforce in 1930, about one-third of western labor still worked in agriculture. The West's share of manufacturing jobs was below the national average (table 3.7). Agriculture and mining dominated the sparsely populated areas in the Great Plains and the Rocky Mountain states. In these parts of the West, the story was not one of continuous growth, expanding markets, and steadily rising incomes. Farmers, ranchers, and miners who were the backbone of these economies experienced great hardship and instability after World War I. Living on the edge, many were heavily indebted and extremely vulnerable to fluctuations in international commodity prices and to the vicissitudes of politics in Washington.[145]

This unevenness is the key to understanding western attitudes towards foreign policy. The more rural the western state, the more likely its representatives in Washington were to oppose Cordell Hull's brand of internationalism. There is little mystery in this. In contrast to the agrarian South, which still relied heavily on access to industrial markets in Europe to sell its cotton, the rural West's crops were primarily sold

Table 3.7 Western Labor Force by Sector, 1930 (percentage)[1]

Area[2]	Agriculture	Resources[3]	Manufacturing	Services[4]
Great Plains	33.6	.1	21.0	44.0
Mountain	30.1	.7	18.0	45.4
Pacific Coast	14.1	.3	26.0	56.3
United States	21.4	.3	28.9	47.1

Source: Computed by author from data in Harvey S. Perloff et al., *Regions, Resources, and Economic Growth* (Baltimore: Johns Hopkins University Press, 1960), app., tables A1–A7.
Note: May not add up to 100 percent due to rounding.
[1] Figures in italics are above the national average.
[2] Great Plains includes Iowa, Kansas, Minnesota, Missouri, Nebraska, North Dakota, South Dakota. Mountain states include Arizona, Colorado, Idaho, Montana, Nevada, New Mexico, Wyoming. California, Oregon, and Washington make up the Pacific Coast.
[3] Includes mining, forestry, and fisheries.
[4] Includes transport and communications, trade and finance, professional services, and personal and domestic services.

on the domestic market. Wheat, the region's leading farm export, illustrates the point. In the 1920s the West threshed close to 70 percent of the country's wheat, most of it grown and harvested in the Great Plains. Less than 20 percent of this crop was sold abroad each year— about the same proportion as in the late nineteenth century (fig. 3.6).[146] The South, by comparison, was exporting roughly 60 percent of its annual cotton output in the 1920s. Producers of other leading crops in the West were even less dependent on overseas markets than wheat farmers were. Corn was the nation's leading crop from the standpoint of value and acreage, and exports of this product still averaged less than five percent of the annual harvest.[147] Oats were another big crop in the region; only about 1 percent of total output was exported.[148]

The rural West had long looked to the home market for its prosperity, and this dependence increased after the turn of the century. One reason was increased foreign competition. The rise of Canada, Argentina, and Australia (among others) as major farm exporters, as well as the spread of American fertilizing and breeding methods to the continent, reduced opportunities for expanded trade with Europe, which was still the main market for American grains and meats.[149] World War I temporarily reversed this trend. European imports of American foodstuffs surged between 1915 and 1918 when transportation problems interrupted the flow of farm goods from competitor nations. Once normal trade routes were reestablished, America's advantage quickly

Percentage of Annual Output Exported

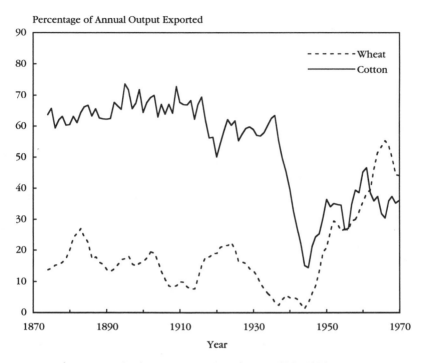

Figure 3.6 Cotton and Wheat Export Dependence, 1870–1970
Source: Bureau of the Census, *Historical Statistics of the United States, Colonial Times to 1970*, 2 vols. (Washington, D.C., 1971), Series U 274-294, pp. 897–98.
Note: Five-year moving average.

evaporated.[150] Exports of crude foodstuffs fell from $673 million in 1921 to $257 million in 1923. They amounted to only $421 in 1927, the post-1921 peak year in the decade.[151] Washington only compounded the problem by reimposing high tariffs on foreign goods in the early twenties, making it hard for European countries to earn the foreign exchange needed to purchase American foodstuffs. Lacking funds to purchase American products, European nations responded by encouraging domestic production and by strengthening commercial ties with newer agricultural nations and with their colonies. Loans and credits from the United States enabled the Europeans to continue purchasing farm goods for a while after the war, but as soon as the loans stopped, European purchases of American products, especially agricultural commodities, came to a halt. Most of the money American investors had loaned the Europeans in the 1920s was spent on U.S. manufactures, and this had further weakened the farmers' already tenuous ties to the Old World.

The agrarian South had to export or die in the 1930s; the rural West faced no such imperative. In fact, western farmers were far more concerned about protecting the home market than they were about winning back foreign markets. There were structural reasons for this. Once chiefly an importer of finished manufacturers, the United States had become one of the world's leading importers of primary goods. Between 1900 and 1930, purchases of foreign crude foodstuffs increased 74 percent.[152] Imports of raw materials rose by 72 percent. The scope of this shift was evident by the early 1920s, when the United States began running what Gabriel Kolko has called "a vast, permanent raw materials deficit."[153] Roughly one-half of America's imports came in the form of raw materials and crude foodstuffs, mostly from Latin America, Asia, and Africa. Agrarian leaders argued that many of these commodities competed directly with the products of American farms. Foreign producers enjoyed decided advantages: cheaper labor, stronger agricultural organizations, protective tariffs, and lower costs of production in general. A representative of the American Farm Bureau Federation, a leading farm organization in the 1920s, explained that if farmers were to hold onto the home market, they would need a great deal of help from the federal government:

> Formerly before the United States developed into a great consumer and creditor nation, competition from abroad was not a factor relative to agriculture and when we were sending much larger amounts of farm crops across the seas than is now the case free trade was not so depressing. . . . It is the realization on the part of agriculture that our exports are coming to be less and less agricultural in nature, and our imports more and more of agricultural commodities that causes farmers to view with the greatest disturbance any letting down of barriers between them and their low-cost producers abroad.[154]

This view was dominant in the rural West after World War I. The leading farm organizations endorsed the Fordney-McCumber and Smoot-Hawley Tariffs. So did most of the region's representatives in Washington. The rural West's position on tariff matters did not change markedly in the 1930s. Many farmers were willing, albeit reluctantly, to give Roosevelt's RTAA a chance in 1934 because they were unsure about the administration's intentions. They were also unsure about the connection between reciprocal trade and New Deal programs that were popular in the West, such as the Agricultural Assistance Administration. Western misgivings about the RTAA turned into outright hostility a year later, when Washington did exactly what some farm leaders had feared from the beginning: sign a trade agreement with Canada, a major producer of foodstuffs, offering to reduce tariff duties on a long list of competitive farm products in return for tariff concessions on a wide range of American industrial products. Support for reciprocal trade in the rural areas evaporated.

When western lawmakers made the case for "self-sufficiency" and "self-reliance," they had good reason to believe that protectionism was in the best interests of the local economies they represented. This did not mean that they envisioned an America cut off, ostrich-like, from the rest of the world. Economic nationalists like Senator Nye considered such a course to be neither feasible nor desirable. In an article for the *New York Times Magazine,* the senator outlined his case for "self-sufficiency."[155] He and other isolationists did not want "to cut off commercial intercourse with other nations or to be entirely indifferent to the political, moral and social problems of other nations." Isolationists, he argued, were "first of all realists" who believed that the nation's foreign policy should be based "on an honest estimate of our national physical strength, on an honest weighing of the gains and losses to us and to other peoples of each practical measure suggested." Since the nation's power was limited, priorities had to be set. "Our power is not evenly distributed over the earth but localized sharply in this hemisphere, where there is a job big enough for us to do." If America had to be vigilant about anything, the senator wrote, it was the temptation to "make itself the guardian of international virtue." This was the hard lesson of America intervention in the last war. Responding to those urging greater American involvement in the current European crisis, the senator asked "What, may I ask, is there in it for America? Economic advantage? Did the last war bring us that? It brought, if I am not entirely blind, a depression which we are still wrestling."

Nye's views were widely shared by other lawmakers from the Great Plains and Rocky Mountains. They did not want to sever trade and credit relations with other nations. And as Wayne Cole cautions, most westerners were not pro-Nazi, pro-fascist, or pro-Axis. Very few were pacifists, though they were not above manipulating pacifist sentiment in the region.[156] In this sense, the term "isolationist" can be misleading.

What western congressmen favored was a more narrowly prescribed definition of the country's interests—one that squared with the needs and interests of the farmers, country bankers, and small businessmen who lived in their districts. For them, the issue was not so much whether America had overseas interests but rather where and how vulnerable these interests were. Some were persuaded that America had important commercial interests in Latin America, even though few believed those interests were at any risk, militarily or economically. To the extent that manufacturers and farmers needed access to Latin America to dispose of surpluses, that could be negotiated out country by country, or even commodity by commodity. Few argued that a German victory would be in America's self-interest, but most did not believe that German control of the European continent, or for that matter Japanese dominance in Asia, would change the underlying realities of the global market. As historian Justus Doenecke writes:

> Wall Street financiers and large numbers of eastern corporation leaders might link the American national interest to the preservation of English and French hegemony, and often to the survival of an independent Nationalist China. The isolationists almost took pride in seeing the national interest in more narrow terms. The continent—the Hemisphere—contained such an abundance of riches that the United States could avoid foreign commitments.[157]

The West wanted no part in Europe's wars. Western lawmakers remembered the "false prosperity" that World War I had produced at home. It was true that "our American people had enjoyed a little temporary prosperity at the beginning of the World War 25 years ago," argued Representative Dewey Short of Missouri, "but afterward came the deluge, and all that we have received for our efforts has been 10 years of depression, 10,000,000 men out of work, $13,000,000,000 of bad war debts which we will never collect, and 4 cemeteries in France."[158] No westerner forgot what had happened to the small farmer. In the 1910s, farmers were lured into increased production and land speculation by high prices, inflation, and patriotic appeals by Washington to "Plow to the Fence for National Defense." Many did not survive the sharp drop in world prices that followed the armistice. Bankruptcies skyrocketed, farm values fell, and the farmer's purchasing power fell below prewar levels. Westerners remembered how farm income, which had reached a high of nearly $17 billion in 1919, had fallen to less than $9 billion by 1921. Income had only risen to $12 billion by the end of the decade, still well short of the wartime peak, or even the level achieved before 1914.[159] Above all, they remembered the pain, suffering, and grief that had followed the peace. "In the place of the boom psychology that had accompanied and succeeded the war, the whole agricultural population suffered from an atmosphere surcharged with gloom."[160]

The collapse of prices in 1920, and the recession that followed, affected industry as well. Agriculture was hit hardest, however, and unlike industry it was unable to make a relatively quick comeback. Agriculture languished in the 1920s.[161] As one observer put it, "Agricultural prices fell first, fell fastest, and fell farthest."[162] The wheat and corn belts suffered the most.[163] Between 1919 and 1921 the price of wheat dropped by one-half, from $2.16 to $1.03 a bushel. Corn fell from $1.51 to .52 cents a bushel.[164] Livestock prices also declined sharply. The price of cattle dropped by more than half between 1918 and 1922.[165] Hog prices, which averaged over $18 per hundredweight in 1919, were only a little over $8 by 1921.[166] As food prices plummeted, so did land values. Thousands of farmers and cattlemen who had bought new farm land and grazing pastures during the prosperous war years were suddenly faced with mortgage foreclosure. Many went into bankruptcy.[167] Others were forced to sell their land and equipment to pay off their debts. The lucky ones were those who managed to hold onto their land and who watched helplessly as their land values fell to alarmingly low levels.[168]

The farm crisis of the 1920s weighed heavily on western politics. The spreading malady of low prices, foreclosures, and bankruptcies fueled agrarian discontent. Economic troubles spawned political action. Farmers organized to seek relief from Washington, and their representatives formed a "farm bloc." Various farm relief measures were proposed. All had one thing in common: government intervention. Each called for more direct federal action to protect the American farmer from the depressing effects of low world market prices. The most elaborate initiative was the so-called McNary-Haugen plan, proposed by George N. Peek and Hugh S. Johnson of the Moline Plow Company in Illinois.[169] The plan was introduced in Congress in early 1924 by Senator Charles L. McNary of Oregon and Representative Gilbert N. Haugen of Iowa. The basic idea was simple enough: the tariff could do for the western farmer what it had done for the eastern industrialist in the

1890s. Stripped down to its essentials, the plan called for the establishment of a two-price system for American produce: one a tariff-protected price for the domestic market, and the other, the international price for the foreign market. A federal marketing agency, financed by participating farmers, would purchase surpluses at the American price and "dump" them abroad at the world price, thereby stabilizing commodity prices in the United States.

No issue provoked more bitterness in Congress in the 1920s than this one. Votes on the floor of the House were intensely sectional, pitting West against East, with the South playing the crucial swing role.[170] The bill was voted down twice—in 1924 and 1926—by an alliance between the cotton South and industrial East. Twice it was vetoed by Republican presidents; first by Coolidge in 1927 and then in 1928 by Hoover. Yet McNary-Haugenism remained a powerful symbol. It signalled that farm leaders were no longer content with the old Populist nostrums of cheap money and monopoly control, or with the lure of overseas markets. Farm leaders of the 1920s wanted direct federal aid in the form of price supports and tariff protection.[171] At the same time, the battle over McNary-Haugenism rekindled old western grievances against the East. Farmers were caught between rapidly falling farm values and fairly rigid industrial prices, and many saw the plan as a device for redressing what they considered to be an imbalance of economic power within the nation. The redistributive implications of the plan were certainly not lost on big business or urban labor. As Richard Bensel writes: "Under any guise, the McNary-Haugen proposal ran into 'wild' opposition on Wall Street and hostility from industrial labor. Business condemned the legislation as 'socialism,' while to workers whose employment was already protected by the tariff the mechanism implied an intolerable rise in the cost of living."[172]

Antipartyism and Neutrality

The anti-eastern thrust of western politics was nothing new. The Grangers' fight against the railroads in the 1870s, the Populists' battle for "cheap money" and "free silver" in the 1890s, and the McNary-Haugenites campaign for a "farmer's tariff" in the 1920s were variations on a common theme in the sectional politics of the West: what historian Paul Kleppner and others have called "anticolonialism."[173] "Westerners," writes Kleppner, "saw their states and territories as colonies of a not-very-benevolent eastern imperium, controlled by and exploited for the benefit of that region's dominant economic interests."[174] Although less radical than the Populists of the late nineteenth century, western progressives of the 1920s and 1930s remained deeply suspicious and resentful of the East. Anticolonialism remained a powerful political sentiment, especially in states in the Great Plains and Mountain West that were in acute distress in the twenties.[175] The "anticolonial thrust" of late nineteenth-century populism "did not expire with the failure of Bryan's crusade in 1896. The battles during the following decades against the railroads, the banks, and corporations generally were examples of anticolonialism turned loose in politics. Westerners attacked these institutions both for their practices and for what they symbolized, and their control by outsiders—usually easterners—was a critical facet of that symbolism."[176]

This symbolism was grounded in economic realities. The persistence of anti-eastern sentiment in the West partly reflected the fact that the West was forced to rely heavily on eastern capital in financing its development. It also reflected mounting frustration over agriculture's deteriorating position in the national economy and the concurrent shift in power from the farm to the city. But politics also played a role. Weak partisan norms and antipartyism reinforced western resentment toward the East. More so than other Americans, western voters tended to pick and choose among candidates rather than follow party cues. The national parties were held in low repute by large numbers of voters, many of whom viewed the parties as instruments of powerful eastern interests. Split-ticket voting was thus much more frequent in the West than elsewhere, and western voters were far more prone to switch parties from one election to another. Many did not hesitate to vote for third-party candidates. As a result, the political parties were relatively weak institutions in most western states, incapable of sustaining broad and consistent support and usually unable to mobilize western voters for collective action. Historically, the Republican party carried the region in presidential contests. But rarely was it able to translate western support at the national level into Republican power at the regional level. The party never exercised the kind of hegemony in the West that it did in the Northeast.[177]

Since western voters did not attach great weight to party labels, political candidates had an incentive to run as self-styled political independents. "Candidates did not tend to run as part of a team, but as independent operators creating their own campaign organizations, stressing their own qualifications and claims to office, and building their own electoral coalitions."[178] Although many were nominally Republicans or Democrats, once elected to Congress they behaved as independent entrepreneurs, often bucking the party hierarchy in Washington. Thus, for western politicians eager to demonstrate their independence, the parties were tempting targets of attack. "Electorates that did not value parties in the first place quite naturally responded to public attacks on the baleful influences of party."[179] For the same reasons, western politicians found the East an irresistible target of attack. Lashing out against the great symbols of eastern power and control—the railroads, Wall Street, and New York—appealed to a sense of regional self-interest and identity, especially in areas hit hard by the agricultural depression of the twenties. These symbols were the "hot buttons" of western politics. Voters rewarded politicians who could articulate their concerns and fears about agriculture's future in a rapidly industrializing society.

Western voters also rewarded politicians who were able to secure federal moneys. The two issues—eastern dominance and federal funds—were in fact closely related. Unlike southern congressmen, who sought to limit federal activity in their region, western lawmakers sought to promote it. Washington provided the only real alternative to private eastern capital in financing western economic development, and the region's congressmen and senators worked hard, often trading away votes on major national issues, to secure federal expenditures for western roads, irrigation, reclamation, and power projects. A politician's ability to "bring home the bacon" was a measure not only of his political clout in Washington but also of his commitment to breaking the shackles of eastern finance and industry.[180] During the 1930s, westerners looked to Washington for solutions to their problems, and they did not hesitate to cross party lines to reward those who made good on promises to secure federal aid. In the West, perhaps more so than in any region, a politician's fate turned on his ability to secure federal resources.[181]

The issue of neutrality emerged against this political backdrop. Like the battle over McNary-Haugenism in the rural West, the fight over American neutrality stirred deep resentment against the East. This was no accident: from the start, western lawmakers played the sectional card.[182] Arguing by analogy, they blamed Wall Street, the "enemy of agriculture," for dragging the United States into an ill-considered war in 1917. "You cannot deny the fact," argued Democrat James O'Connor of Montana, "that it was through investments made by the international bankers of the city of New York that caused, ultimately, the American boys to die on foreign soil."[183] "Why not be frank and honest," claimed a Republican lawmaker from the wheat belt during the 1939 debate over repeal, "and say that the reason for the repeal of the embargo is to enable us to sell munitions and implements of war for the money we can make out of it, for the profit we can wring from the desperate and unhappy people at war?"[184] Pages of the *Congressional Record* are filled with vitriolic speeches denouncing the Morgans, du Ponts, and Rockefellers for their role in the last war and warning America that it was on the verge of being "sucked in" to another war by munitions makers, arms merchants, and investment bankers. To those who claimed that repealing the arms embargo would be good for the American economy, there was this:

> Dream all you want to of the pot of gold that lies beyond the war zone, but do not place us in a position where we must again go through the horrors of another great war in the pursuit of war profits. No amount of war trade can ever repay us for the tremendous loss we sustained. Sure, the doors of trade were wide open. Our exports were greater than they had ever been. We made profits unheard of before. We made new millionaires by leaps and bounds. We were reveling in wealth. We owned over half the gold in the world, and we became the richest nation on earth. We were worshipping at the shrine of the "Golden Calf." But there was not blessing in those ill-gotten gains. It was blood money garnered in the game by the merchants of death. The mad dance was merry as long as it lasted. But oh, the awakening after the *delerium tremens* came to an end! What a headache there was the morning after the night before.[185]

From an indictment of Wall Street it was but a short step to attack the entire industrial and financial metropolis bounding both sides of the North Atlantic. The British were singled out: imperialism was as bad as fascism; British propagandists had lured an idealistic America into the last war; they had welched on their war debts.[186] The lesson for America was plain: it should steer clear of the "historic hatreds," "entrenched greed," and "rank animosities" that had fueled conflict in Europe for hundreds of years. "[N]ever, never more must we be misled by the mirage of war profits. Never, never more must we lend our ears to the siren song of the emissaries from abroad to join them in the dance of death."[187]

On Capitol Hill, the arguments of the rural West's representatives tapped a wellspring of anxiety, resentment, and bitterness in the region. The vast majority of the region's farmers held Wall Street in low repute, and the City of London's standing in the region was not much higher. Few westerners attached much credence to the notion that American and British security interests were interdependent, or to the idea that the British Navy and the French Army were America's "first line of defense." In western eyes, such strategic rationales were nothing more than self-serving British propaganda and Ivy League sophistry. Calls for greater military spending and a military draft were greeted with the same skepticism. Many farmers still blamed American participation in the last European war for the region's economic difficulties and its deteriorating terms of trade with the East. Why should they think that American involvement in another world war would improve their personal circumstances? As one student of the period puts it: "The farmer feared that he would once more become an 'economic goat' as a result of intervention. Suspicious of the industrial-commercial East, he frequently protested against huge 'defense' spending at the sacrifice of aid to agriculture."[188]

If the United States was to avoid being drawn into another war by British propagandists and their allies in this country, steps had to be taken to make "the siren song of the emissaries" less enticing to American business. For western lawmakers, neutrality laws prohibiting arms shipments and foreign loans seemed an obvious first step. Arms restrictions would make Americans less susceptible to war hysteria that might be sparked by the sinking of an American cargo ship at sea, and thus leave their elected representatives less vulnerable to public pressure. Prohibiting loans to Britain or France also made sense. There was little question about how the Nazis would view American loans to their enemies. Nor was there much doubt in the minds of isolationists that such loans would increase America's dependence on war trade. Loans and arms shipments, they believed, would also make it harder for average citizens to resist Washington's appeals to patriotism.[189] Eastern industrialists and bankers would pay the price of neutrality laws that restricted their freedom of action; for the farmer, the material and symbolic gains appeared immediate and concrete. Isolationists like Senator Nye were careful to insure that all of the self-denying provisions in the neutrality laws applied primarily to the more urbanized and industrialized segments of the economy.

Westerners were far more likely to vote for neutrality legislation than congressmen from the Northeast or South (see fig. 3.3). Even as growing numbers of congressmen from other parts of the country closed ranks behind the president in the late 1930s and early 1940s, congressmen from the West held firm. As on other foreign policy issues, western support for legislation restricting the president's discretionary powers was strongest in heavily agrarian parts of the West—that is, in the Great Plains and Mountain West.

Guns versus Butter

Suspicions of England and Wall Street aside, westerners had local reasons for backing neutrality. Of all regions in the country, the West was hit hardest by the Great Depression.[190] Real income declined more than the national average: twelve of the twenty states that posted the sharpest declines in income were in the West, including seven of the top ten.[191] In North Dakota, Senator Nye's home state, average per capita income during the depression fell to $145, less than half the national average. "Low prices for farm products, an almost nonexistent market for minerals, the worst drought in the region's history—all of these worked a greater hardship on the West than on other sections of country."[192] By 1932 farmers' incomes in the trans-Mississippi West had declined to almost one-half of their already low 1929 levels. Extractive industries suffered as well: thousands of miners and lumbermen were thrown out of work. With few opportunities for profit or employment, the flow of capital and people from the East slowed to a trickle.

If western states were most affected by the Great Depression, then they were also the New Deal's biggest beneficiaries. On a per capita basis, the West led all other sections in federal relief and loans.[193] Between 1933 and 1939, the Rocky Mountain states received $716 per capita from the federal government, the Pacific Coast states $536, and the Great Plains states $424. By comparison, the highest-ranking region outside the West was the Great Lakes region, with $380 per capita. The South, which Roosevelt called the "Nation's Number One Economic Problem," received less that half the West's allocations on a per capita basis. Expenditures in Montana, for example, were $710 per capita while they amounted to only $143 in North Carolina. Overall, western states received three times as much as the national average of annual

Table 3.8 Flow of Federal Dollars by Region, 1933-39[1]

| Region | Federal Expenditures to Tax Revenues (per capita) | | | | |
	Mean	Std. Dev.	Minimum	Maximum	States
Northeast	1.97	1.70	0.24	7.35	16
South	8.38	12.09	0.36	42.72	14
West	15.38	15.00	1.87	50.90	18
United States	8.87	12.46	0.24	50.90	48

Sources: Calculated by author. Expenditure data come from Don C. Reading, "New Deal Activity and the States, 1933 to 1939," *Journal of Economic History* 33 (December 1973): 808, app., table 1. Revenue data from U.S. Department of Commerce, *Statistical Abstract of the United States* (Washington, D.C.: GPO), selected years.
Note: See table 2.1 for regional groupings.
[1] Nondefense expenditures only.

federal expenditures.[194] More importantly, they received far more in grants and loans from Washington than they were sending back in tax revenue (table 3.8). This partly reflected the region's relative poverty. Federal agencies generally spent more in areas hit hardest by the depression. It seems that politics also played a role. Unlike the South, which was securely in the Democratic camp, the West's electoral behavior could not be taken for granted by either party. More than one analyst has suggested that Roosevelt was trying to buy votes.[195]

The western bias in New Deal spending gave the region a huge stake in domestic recovery programs and federal expenditures. This helps explain why many western congressmen harped on the potentially ruinous domestic consequences of American involvement in a European war. "The only thing we could get out of another conflict," argued one western congressman, "would be deeper debts, longer depressions, higher taxes, and more graveyards. We burned our hands once; should we be so silly as to rush back into the fire?"[196] In the debates over neutrality, Lend-Lease, and military rearmament, the rural West was not only fighting against the industrialized East, it was also fighting over the nation's fiscal priorities. In contrast to the agrarian South, whose dependence on European markets made it easy for southern lawmakers to grant the president greater discretionary authority to advance American interests abroad, the rural West had no interest in international trade to offset its distrust of Washington. For western politicians, it all boiled down to a choice between guns and butter. Westerners' great fear was that involvement in a foreign war would shatter the New Deal and deprive the region of much-needed federal moneys.

The fact that western lawmakers were more apt to vote against Roosevelt's requests for larger defense budgets than southern or northeastern representatives was testimony to this. In the end, "the big government, big military, federal regulation, large government expenditures, and huge deficits that came with American participation in World War II were as much a defeat for the western progressive domestic programs as they were a defeat for their programs in foreign affairs."[197]

The fight against internationalism was waged as part of a larger struggle to defend and advance western interests. When western lawmakers tried to restrict the president's power in applying sanctions against foreign belligerents, they argued not only in sectional terms but also in terms of constitutional principle and institutional politics. They argued that concentration of foreign policy-making power in the president's hands was unconstitutional, and there is little doubt that many were genuinely concerned about the growing power of the executive branch. Yet as their support for early New Deal legislation revealed, westerners were quite flexible on the issue of executive power. At first, when the New Deal "seemed largely a southern-western movement which was imaginatively attacking the problems of these regions," western politicians backed Roosevelt's initiatives.[198] Western lawmakers may have grumbled occasionally about excessive bureaucracy, but their distrust of "bigness" and centralized power did not prevent them from backing big centralized federal programs like the Agriculture Adjustment Act (AAA) and the Civilian Conservation Corps (CCC). Those programs were popular in the region; whatever the reservations of their representatives in Washington, they kept them to themselves. It was not until after Roosevelt's smashing victory in the 1936 election, when the administration began moving from "economic recovery" toward "social reform," that western attitudes towards the New Deal began to change. Increasingly, westerners came to regard the Roosevelt administration "as an eastern, urban, and indeed somewhat alien operation."[199]

Much as it had in the South, enthusiasm for the early New Deal in the West gave way to grudging acceptance and then to suspicion. To a large extent these suspicions reflected practical political realities. The social base of the Democratic party *was* shifting—organized labor had become a key element in Democratic party affairs, and most urban workers now saw it as "their party." And many of those who staffed federal agencies were from eastern corporate and educational institutions. Westerners, argues historian James Patterson, came to believe that the New Deal had "shifted from its southern-western base of 1932 to an eastern and midwestern movement increasingly influenced by spokesman for low income groups in the cities."[200] "Westerners," Patterson continues, "could appreciate early measures such as the AAA and CCC, and they welcomed federal money pouring in for irrigation, highways, and conservation. But the Wagner act, the minimum wage law, and the heavy relief spending in eastern cities proved less popular."[201] Western opposition to "federal intervention" and "executive power" was thus largely pragmatic. The more it appeared that Roosevelt's administration was falling under the influence of eastern interests, the less tolerable western progressives found policies that infringed on states rights' and responsibilities, the principle of home rule, and congressional prerogative. The point is that where western lawmakers stood on the question of constitutional power depended on how—or more precisely, in whose behalf—that power would be exercised. This was true in foreign as well as domestic policy.

Western appeals to the Constitution in the neutrality debates can best be understood in this context. For the rural West, constitutional argument made good institutional sense. If westerners were to have any control over matters of war and peace, the power to make those decisions had to remain in Congress.[202] While most were reluctant to say it publicly, they believed that the State Department, given half a chance, would use any discretionary authority granted by Congress to strengthen the nation's commitment to collective security, which for all practical purposes meant siding with the British and French. The results could be disastrous for the country as a whole and for the West in particular. Westerners realized that as the country grew more "entangled" in European affairs, and as American intervention became an ever-greater possibility, the nation's fiscal priorities would dramatically change. Aiding the allies and raising an army would necessarily take precedence. The parts of the country that looked to the federal government as source of a regional investment would be the big losers. In the face of the administration's call for the power to choose sides in foreign wars, the rural West's negative response was logical.

Western reservations about executive power were not limited to the issue of neutrality. Similar concerns were raised by western lawmakers in the battle against reciprocal trade.[203] Here too, the struggle against internationalism that was often waged on the high ground of democratic principle was driven by local priorities. Opponents charged that the tariff program was an unconstitutional delegation of congressional power. More often than not these arguments were representative of the same kind of "oratorical camouflage" that congressmen employed during the neutrality debates.[204] Harold Knutson, a Republican from Minnesota and a member of the House Ways and Means Committee, conceded as much in the Committee's hearings on Secretary Hull's trade proposal. Asked by a colleague across the aisle to explain why he opposed expanding Roosevelt's tariff-making powers when just a few years before he backed Hoover's request for similar authority, Knutson did not mince words: "Frankly, I know the purpose of this legislation is to lower rates. If I thought for a minute that it was proposed to raise rates to meet the present conditions, I would vote for this legislation and be glad of the opportunity to do so."[205] Knutson may have been more candid than some of his colleagues, but they too were more concerned with the local and regional impact of Judge Hull's proposals than with abstract principles of good government. As historian Arthur Schatz observes, "western opposition to reciprocity had a strong sectional flavor."[206] A vote for reciprocal trade was seen in much of the rural West as a vote for eastern industry, lower farm prices, and expanding bureaucratic control.

The same fears found expression in the "eleventh hour" battle over Lend-Lease. By this point there was little doubt in minds of western lawmakers that their region's interests were being sacrificed by Roosevelt in an effort to win support for his foreign policies. Ever since the 1936 election, when Roosevelt won overwhelmingly and with impressive urban strength, he had felt less obliged to attend to the wishes of western progressives than he had during his first term.[207] As Roosevelt's electoral base in the Northeast expanded, his dependence on the West decreased. Fortunately for the South, Roosevelt could not have his with way in foreign affairs without them. Knowing that internationalist policies could not pass in Congress without the support of conservative southerners, Roosevelt was forced to make concessions to the South. The president's dilemma, explained Rexford Tugwell, a member of Roosevelt's "Brain Trust" was this: western congressmen would support an interventionist domestic agenda but not an assertive foreign policy; southern lawmakers would support an active foreign policy agenda but not economic and social reform.[208] As the situation in Europe worsened, and as *domestic* pressure for a more decisive American commitment to the democracies mounted, Roosevelt's support for social reform necessarily waned. The interests of western progressives were a casualty of this shift. Little wonder that old progressives like Gerald Nye viewed matters of foreign policy in sectional terms.

Conclusion

American efforts to rationalize the international environment and to bring it under greater control began in the 1930s. An even greater surge of American expansionism occurred after World War II. From the late 1940s onward, American policy makers sought to refashion Europe in the image of American liberal capitalism.[209] They also worked to ameliorate Europe's chronic geopolitical troubles by encouraging economic integration, interdependence, and growth. The Marshall Plan, the General Agreement on Tariffs and Trade (GATT), and the North Atlantic Treaty Organization (NATO) were all part of a larger effort aimed at liberalizing the world economy and preventing the kind of breakdown experienced after 1929. Under American leadership, new governmental mechanisms were created to regulate the world economy; new institutions and agencies were established to disperse American economic relief; and new military means were developed to strengthen the nation's presence overseas and to deter other nations, most conspicuously the Soviet Union and then China, from taking advantage of political instability on the Eurasian landmass. In contrast to the decade following World War I, when America's leaders relied mostly on private means to pursue public goals, the years following the Second World War were marked by direct government involvement in world affairs. Internationalism was in; isolationism was out.

Students of world politics offer two explanations for the shift in America's foreign policy from the narrow nationalism of the post-World War I years to the enlightened internationalism of the post World War II era. One explanation stresses changes in American industrial structure, and especially in the interests of some of the country's leading industrial and financial groups.[210] It argues that America's turn to internationalism was driven by the emergence of an internationally oriented cluster of industrialists and bankers who favored greater government activism on the international front. Frustrated with the narrow nationalism of the Republican party, big business turned toward the Democratic party in the 1930s, seeing it as the best hope for stabilizing the world economy in the wake of the Great Depression and for implementing internationalist doctrines of free trade, equal access, and currency convertibility. Coalescing behind Franklin Delano Roosevelt, this "historic bloc" of capital-intensive, globally competitive industries and their financial allies on Wall Street made the decisive move when they walked away from the Republican party. Together with Roosevelt, they imposed their will on a reluctant country.

This account is an important one. It highlights the critical role of northeastern business in America's turn to internationalism, and it underscores the role of the Republican split in transforming national politics and making internationalist victories possible. In the last analysis, however, this explanation casts an analytic net that is too narrow. The changing attitudes of big business played a critical part in the shifts in American diplomacy during the interwar years, but alas, Wall Street's tale is only part of a larger story. Northeastern big business, even as a united front, could not have pulled it off alone. What these accounts ignore is the vital role that agrarian interests played in internationalism's victory. The southern dimension is left out of the story. This is not just a historical footnote, for the triumph of internationalism—like its later demise—cannot be explained without understanding the South's internationalist orientation and the power that its representatives in Washington wielded over foreign policy. In the 1930s, big business may have enjoyed great influence in Cordell Hull's State Department and Henry Stimson's War Department, but in Congress, where isolationists like Gerald Nye enjoyed considerable power, Roosevelt could not have carried the day without the support of powerful southern lawmakers like Robert Doughton (D-NC) of Ways and Means, Texas' Luther Johnson on Foreign Affairs, and Carl Vinson (D-GA) of Naval Affairs. If Roosevelt did not fully appreciate this fact when he entered office, by the late 1930s he had come to understand how crucial to his foreign policy southern political support actually was.

It is therefore correct to argue that before the United States assumed the mantle of global leadership, American politics had to be transformed. But the decisive change on the *political* landscape of the 1930s was sectional, not partisan, in nature.[211] The momentous shift involved the creation of an internationalist alliance that spanned the Great Divide in American politics: the division between North and South. Three things made this possible: the internationalization of the urban northeastern economy, the rise of the Nazi threat to northeastern *and* southern interests, and Roosevelt's decision to keep civil rights off the national agenda. This alliance lasted for over a quarter of a century. At its apogee in the late 1940s, it assured that America would not once again "win the war but lose the peace." It provided the political grounding for the Marshall Plan, NATO, Point Four, and other internationalist initiatives. No parts of the country lined-up more solidly behind liberal internationalism than the urban Northeast and the Solid South. Without this backing, postwar American foreign policy would not have achieved the level of stability, coherence, and consistency that it did—regardless of big business interests. The point is that the Cold War consensus was not so much a bipartisan coalition of northeastern business elites as it was a broad-based cross-sectional alliance that united two very different parts of America. It is ironic that the rise of the activist internationalist state depended on the support of the segments of society most closely associated in American historiography with laissez-fairism and antistatism: Wall Street and the South. Economic interest and political need counted for more than constitutional principle.

A sectional analysis also improves on more traditional accounts of America's turn toward internationalism. For years, scholars in the realist tradition have been puzzled by American foreign policy during the interwar years. The United States emerged from World War I with the industrial, financial, and military capacity to impose its will on Europe, but it declined to act.[212] Instead of offering bold leadership to a world that desperately needed it, America retrenched. It rejected Wilsonianism, refused to join the League of Nations, and adopted narrow nationalist policies on tariffs, war debts, and foreign lending. The one country capable of pulling the world economy away from fragmentation and toward a more interdependent and stable order failed to assert its will. In the 1920s, the United States suffered from what might be called "imperial understretch." Power outstripped policy; America's *capacity* to lead the international community toward a more secure and prosperous future exceeded its *willingness* to do so. America equivocated, pursuing contradictory and inconsistent policies: "[t]he same administration encouraged foreign lending and trade protection against the goods of borrowers, worked for international monetary cooperation and sought to sabotage it, struggled to reinforce European reconstruction and impeded it at critical junctures."[213] There is irony here too, for in the 1980s many worried that America was suffering from the reverse problem: "imperial overstretch."[214] The desire of the United States to lead other nations outstripped its capacity to do so. In both cases, realists have a hard time explaining the imbalance between will and capacity, the mismatch between ends and means.

In an effort to account for the awkward anomaly of the 1920s, realists depart from "externally driven" explanations and fall back on domestic political culture and institutions.[215] America's obsolete institutions and archaic traditions are blamed for preventing the country from assuming the mantle of leadership placed by destiny at its doorstep. State building was impeded by America's "cult of antistatism"; the state's weakness, in turn, impeded programmatic action. As a result, important national decisions were subordinated to local interests and international considerations were subsumed by domestic politics. In the end, writes historian Charles Kindleberger, "the one country capable of leadership [i.e., the United States] was bemused by domestic concerns and stood aside."[216] The United States, behaving as though it were an ordinary country in ordinary times, failed to build the kind of administrative apparatus that was needed to design and implement an integrated and consistent foreign policy in the 1920s. In the 1930s, Americans reaped the bitter fruits of their failure to act decisively, first in the Great Depression, and then in another world war. It was only after suffering the harsh consequences of its failed diplomacy that Americans began to truly appreciate the importance of American leadership in a world prone to instability, anarchy, and war.

An analysis of the regional bases of competition over American foreign policy during the interwar years leads to a different conclusion. America's dominant position after World War I may have provided the nation's leaders an opportunity to shape the international system, but the failure to do so was not due to ignorance, culture, or institutional weakness. The policy contradictions of the 1920s were grounded in politics and conflicts of interest, and especially in the sectional divisions that made it nearly impossible to build stable coalitions within the then-dominant-Republican party. Badly split along East-West lines, party leaders tried to finesse issues like tariff reform, European reconstruction, and debt cancellation. Their efforts only exacerbated tensions within the party. Continuing integration of the urban Northeast into the international economy contributed to the political earthquake of 1932. The depth and breadth of the Democrat's victory in the Northeast created new possibilities for a sectional alliance spanning the Mason-Dixon line. Developments in the Republican party—again, driven by power and interest, not bemused distractedness—reinforced this movement. In defeat, the center of gravity in the Republican party moved westward, further alienating the eastern wing of the party and driving it toward bipartisan alliance with the Democrats.

A sectional approach thus generates an explanation of American foreign policy during the interwar years that is far more consistent than the realist account. The evolution and interplay of sectional interests explains the policy vacillations of the 1920s; these same forces also explain the turn around of the 1930s. As early as the 1934 House vote on the RTAA, the broad outlines of the new foreign policy coalition embracing the urban Northeast and agrarian South could be seen. The once-dominant bloc that bridged the Northeast and West had collapsed. This new alliance would shape the nation's foreign policy for decades to come.

CHAPTER FOUR

The Rise of the Sunbelt: America Resurgent in the 1980s

Introduction

Foreign policy was a gut issue in the 1980 presidential campaign. A string of international setbacks the previous year left the American people angry about the apparent loss of control over foreign affairs. More than 80 percent of the public believed that the country had sunk into "deep and serious trouble."[1] The Republican candidate, Ronald Reagan, echoed these fears, repeatedly invoking the image of a weakening America in a world dangerously out of control, a world where Americans could be taken hostage by hostile radical groups and where the nation's economic lifeline was increasingly vulnerable to blackmail. Starting from the premise that the erosion of American power was the result of misguided policies, the former California governor and Hollywood actor blasted Jimmy Carter, blaming the Democrats for letting America's position in the world decline—for weakness and vacillation and for allowing the Soviet military power to surpass that of the United States. America, Reagan and the Republicans insisted, now faced "the most serious challenge to its survival in the two centuries of its existence."[2] If the nation was to meet the challenge, it would have to move swiftly to restore its military strength. New priorities would have to be set and Washington politics as usual would have to end.

The Republicans won big in the November election. Although Reagan received only 51 percent of the popular vote, he won overwhelmingly in the electoral college. Moreover, the Republicans captured control of the Senate for the first time since the Eisenhower years. They also made substantial gains in the House and at the state level.[3] Exit polls showed that the economy, racked by double-digit inflation and rising unemployment, was the decisive issue, but the Republicans also gained a distinct electoral edge from foreign policy issues.[4] The size of Reagan's electoral college victory and Republican gains in the Senate gave the president-elect an opportunity to redefine the nation's priorities and make good on his campaign promise to "Make America Great Again." Liberal observers who tried to console themselves by recalling that another Cold Warrior, Richard Nixon, had moved toward "the center" once in office, found little comfort in the new president's rhetoric or actions. Unwilling, some say unable, to distinguish the Oval Office from the campaign trail, Reagan continued to denounce the Soviet Union as an outlaw empire prepared "to commit any crime, to lie, to cheat," in order to achieve its goals.[5] Détente, arms control, and trilateralism, the dogmas of the 1970s, were out; anticommunism, military spending, and unilateralism were in. After a decade of strategic retrenchment, the United States went on the "geostrategic offensive."[6]

Nothing symbolized the shift in America's priorities more than the "Reagan buildup." The largest military buildup since the Korean War, Reagan's program was the linchpin in the Republican's strategy to reassert American leadership abroad. Between 1981 and 1986, Reagan spent well over $1 trillion on national defense, a sum nearly equal to the total spent by Nixon, Ford, and Carter during the previous twelve years.[7] Military spending authority doubled in just five years, with much of the increase going to research and development of new high-tech weapons systems. The rapid expansion of American military capabilities occurred in the context of expanding commitments. During the 1970s, the country's leaders had sought to narrow the nation's overseas interests and commitments. Despite important differences in emphasis and style, the Nixon, Ford, and Carter administrations all adopted strategies and policies that sought to minimize the costs of American leadership. Sharper distinctions were drawn between "vital" and "peripheral" interests in the Third World. Various devices, ranging from Nixon and Kissinger's opening to China to Carter's "three percent solution" (i.e., 3 percent of GNP) for NATO members, were used to shift some of the burden of collective defense (i.e., containment of the Soviet Union) to other countries (China, Germany, and Iran). Meanwhile, efforts were made to reduce tensions with the Soviet Union by pursuing areas of limited mutual interest, especially arms control. Reagan and his advisors rejected this course, equating it to Britain's appeasement of Nazi Germany. Old commitments to allies and friends, neglected or downplayed in the 1970s, were renewed and strengthened. At the same time, the new administration sought to reassure both foreign and domestic audiences about American resolve in the post-Vietnam era by signaling its commitment to check unrest in regions deemed vital (the Persian Gulf, Central America, and Southern Africa) and to make America's presence overseas more visible through offshore naval deployments, large-scale military maneuvers, and the funding of military proxies like the Nicaraguan *contras,* the Afghan rebels, and UNITA in Angola.

National security was the cornerstone of Reagan's foreign policy agenda. But the administration's strategy for restoring American power also called for a new approach to economics. Shortly after taking office, Reagan unveiled a comprehensive economic plan to "put the nation on a fundamentally different course."[8] Major shifts in federal budgetary, regulatory, and tax policy were advanced, while many of the domestic responsibilities that the federal government had assumed over the past several decades were eliminated, reduced, or transferred to state and local governments and to the private sector. Personal and corporate taxes were slashed, federal regulations on industry were rolled back, and federal spending on New Deal-style welfare programs was cut. Dubbed "Reaganomics" by its critics, the administration's "Program for Economic Recovery" drew few distinctions between domestic and international economic policy. The latter was an extension of the former, especially in the area of trade. Trade restrictions put into place in the 1970s were rolled back. Exporters long dependent on financing from the federal government were encouraged to turn to the private sector. And workers whose jobs were threatened by foreign competitors were given notice: they could no longer count on Washington for financial relief. Such programs, they were told, sapped America's strength.

The magnitude of the changes initiated by Reagan sparked heated debate. Political commentators were sharply divided over the merits of the policy changes. Some stressed the benefits of putting the Soviets on the strategic defensive; others worried about the high costs of Reagan's program, which seemed to put the nation at risk of financial insolvency. Scholars continue to debate the impact of Reagan's foreign policy.[9] Did the Soviet Union collapse because of or in spite of the administration's foreign policies? Was the Reagan administration's blend of "military Keynesianism" and "supply-side" economics responsible for disequilibrating international trade and monetary relations? When viewed from the perspective of domestic "geopolitics," the significance of the 1980 election and the Reagan Revolution is clear. For the first time in this century, "the national interest" was not defined in terms of those of the urban Northeast. In the 1980s, the foreign policies advanced by Reagan and his successor, George Bush, reflected the political imperatives of America's newest industrializing regions— the South and West.

Reagan's victory signaled the death of the coalition that had shaped the country's foreign policy since the 1930s. For nearly three decades, the nation's foreign policy had been based on an alliance that spanned the Mason-Dixon line—Franklin Roosevelt's New Deal coalition. Forged in the shadows of depression and war, this liberal-internationalist alliance embraced the interests of big business, northern labor, and the "small town big men" who dominated southern society. The urban Northeast and the agrarian South were the domestic bases of political support for the *Pax Americana* that America's leaders erected after the World War II.[10] These parts of the country were the earliest and largest beneficiaries of the policies of foreign aid, forward defense, and liberal trade that were aimed at promoting an open, interdependent world economy, and at the Cold War isolation or "containment" of nations that threatened it. Because this coalition was rooted in the regional power base of the Democratic party and the powerful eastern wing of the Republican party, it provided the institutional framework for the bipartisan foreign policies of the Truman, Eisenhower, and Kennedy administrations. Politics did not stop at the water's edge during the Cold War years; rather, shared interests kept political divisiveness in check.

The bipartisan coalition lasted until the 1970s, when it began to fall apart under the combined weight of three developments: mounting social tensions triggered by the civil rights movement and the Vietnam War; the economic decline of the industrial Northeast and the rise of what political strategist Kevin Phillips called the "sunbelt" states of the South and West; and the shift in the Republican party's center of gravity to west of the Mississippi.[11] The first two drove North and South apart. The third created new opportunities for coalition-building between West and South. As the Republican party aligned itself with the rapidly growing West, it searched for allies in the country's other late developer, the South. "Structural conditions" made such an alliance possible; Republican political stratagems made it a reality. Republicans from the West aggressively pushed a foreign policy agenda that was now antithetical to the interests of the declining northern core. The party's long-standing commitment to anticommunism was grafted onto a "new" Republican foreign policy agenda that favored less government regulation, a strong national defense, and "bolder, more assertive" leadership. By playing on these and other issues (such as race), Republicans wrought havoc in the Democratic party. Southerners left the party in droves. The Democrats' stronghold narrowed to the aging Northeast. No longer restrained by the demands of coalition-building, the Democratic leadership adopted a foreign policy strategy that played well in the northern "rustbelt": retrenchment. While most Democratic leaders continued to favor continued American participation in international institutions, they urged greater restraint in the use of military force, a smaller defense establishment, and a larger role for Congress in the foreign policy-making process.

As the domestic underpinnings of Cold War internationalism gave way, a new axis of regional competition over foreign policy emerged. Sectional competition within the United States found expression in conflicts between the rustbelt and the sunbelt.[12] Democrats held on to their base in the industrial heartland; Republicans consolidated their hold on the West and established a powerful presence in the South. By the late 1970s, this process had undermined the institutional and political bases of the internationalist house that Roosevelt built. In its place arose a new coalition, albeit an unsteady and not-fully-tested one, dedicated to the resurgence of American power in the international system. Much of the significance of the 1980 election lies here, in the changing relationship between section, party, and the world economy.

What happened in 1980 was not a classic power shift in which one clearly articulated coalition replaces another. In contrast to what happened in the 1890s and 1930s, when new hegemonic blocs arose out of struggles set in motion by uneven growth, in the 1980s the sectional conflicts of the preceding decade simply intensified. Issues like defense spending, military intervention, and foreign aid continued to divide the country. Meanwhile, the "new sectionalism" that arose in the 1970s was sharpened over the course of the 1980s by the growing vulnerability of the manufacturing belt to international competition and by the vigor and single-mindedness with which Reagan pursued his foreign policy agenda. Whatever promise the administration's foreign policy held as "grand strategy," its mix of military Keynesianism and laissez-faire economics threatened the interests of the Northeast's so-called sunset industries and aging metropolises, and—needless to say—the power bases and influence of the politicians who represented these constituencies. For Republicans in the 1980s, foreign policy was a political weapon. It was an instrument for redistributing wealth from the northeastern "core" to the southern and western "periphery," and for expanding the Republican party's electoral base in what was once the solidly Democratic South. Forced onto the political defensive, northern Democrats waged a rearguard battle, employing time-honored stratagems of obstruction and delay.

Seen in this light, the fights between Republican and Democrats over what America should do about Nicaragua's "Marxist" regime, Russia's "heavy missiles," or Japan's trade practices take on new meaning. They were battles in a larger, sectionally based political war for control of the federal government and its vast resources. Sometimes these sectional interests were laid out starkly; more often they were expressed in the lofty discourse of the Founding Fathers. The Republicans' foreign policy agenda, blending Hamiltonian realpolitik and Jeffersonian laissez-faire, was the sunbelt's agenda. It was a far cry from the isolationism of western Republicans in the 1930s. The liberal Democrats who now set the party's agenda were the guardians of the rustbelt. They too invoked the Founders. But in contrast to the Roosevelt years, Democrats now warned of the risks and costs of foreign crusades and centralized power—of concentrating too much political power in the executive branch and wasting resources sorely needed at home. America's role, they argued, should be to act as a model for—not a guarantor of—other peoples' quest for freedom from tyranny and repression.

In the 1980s, as in the 1890s and 1930s, politicians from different parts of the country held fundamentally different views about how America should define its role in the world. They also held conflicting views about *who* should define it: the president or Congress. Yet in contrast to the 1890s, when the Northeast dominated the Executive, now southern and western interests had cornered the powers of the Presidency, while the Northeast controlled most of the levers of congressional power. The result was regional deadlock: conflicts of regional interest were institutionalized as fights between two branches of government that were controlled by bitterly opposed political parties. Under such conditions, the political tensions rooted in uneven growth and development proved more difficult to manage and resolve.

This helps explain why Reagan, despite his personal popularity, was unable to forge a consensus over foreign policy, and why in some cases (Nicaragua) the White House resorted to secrecy while reversing course in others (arms control and human rights).[13] It also explains why George Bush, whose support in the South and West was never as solid as Reagan's, found it politically prudent to use the occasion of his Inaugural Address to call for a "new engagement" between the executive and the Congress, a new spirit of bipartisanship.[14] Bush's peace offering was not, as some scholars would have it, just a natural swing of the pendulum between separate but equal powers. Nor can the rise of party conflict over foreign policy in the 1980s be understood in strictly ideological terms. Ideas cannot be so easily divorced from interests. In the 1980s, foreign policies that were deemed strategically imperative by "conservatives" were those that spoke to the interests in the rapidly growing sunbelt: to its high-tech firms, export-oriented businesses, and military-industrial metropolises. "Liberals" who branded Republican policies reckless and destabilizing, and who called for more butter and fewer guns, were voicing the apprehensions and needs of the region suffering the brunt of foreign competition and what some even described as deindustrialization—the Northeast.

This chapter analyzes sectional conflict over foreign policy in the 1980s. The narrative structure differs from that employed in chapter 2 (organized around policy issue) and chapter 3 (organized by region). Here, three main arguments about sectional politics and American foreign policy—the three dominant themes of this book—are brought together to provide a framework for analysis of the 1980s. I use these theoretical tools to solve three "puzzles" that have engaged international relations scholars in the 1980s and 1990s.

The first part of the chapter drives home the argument that place matters. Sectionalism remains a fundamental feature of American politics, and the politics of foreign policy is no exception. Like other periods in American history when ideological conflicts over foreign policy were shaped by deeper conflicts of interests, foreign policy conflicts between liberals and conservatives in the 1980s had a geographic dimension. Herein lies the key to solving the puzzle of foreign policy stalemate in the 1980s. Partisan and ideological disputes of the 1980s proved to be so intractable because they were rooted in a deeper, regionally based struggle over foreign policy that pitted the rising sunbelt against the declining rustbelt.

The second section of the chapter takes up the argument that conflicts of sectional interest are grounded in America's uneven integration into the world economy, and are the wellspring of domestic conflict over foreign policy. I show that conflict over trade policy during the Reagan years divided the nation along sectional lines, and that the declining international position of the northeastern rustbelt and the ascendance of the southern and western sunbelt goes far in resolving the "paradox" of declining American hegemony—that is, America's continuing support for the liberal trading order constructed in the early postwar era, despite its declining economic fortunes in the world economy.

The last section develops the argument that politicians view foreign policy in redistributive terms. It shows that conflict over the national interest in the 1980s was part and parcel of a larger regionally based struggle for control over the federal government's resources that arose in the early 1970s. I argue that these conflicts intensified in the late 1970s and early 1980s as economic disparities between the rustbelt and sunbelt widened, and as the political parties saw greater advantage in exploiting this sectional cleavage. This helps explain the puzzle of politicians' preferences when it comes to voting on defense policies in the 1980s. Although the influence of "the military industrial complex" may be hard to see in the Congress's voting record, it is nevertheless clear that politicians vote the interests of their sectional constituents when it comes to defense. The argument is developed through an analysis of the struggle over the Reagan buildup.

The "New Sectionalism" and the End of Bipartisanship

American leaders were able to mobilize broad domestic support for their foreign policies during the quarter-century that followed World War II. While the conventional wisdom that "politics stopped at the water's edge" was at best a half-truth, the fact remains that presidents enjoyed considerable latitude, if not deference, on matters of foreign policy—certainly far more than they did on domestic policy issues.[15] By the end of the Cold War those days seemed light-years away. The 1980s were not years of consensus. Divisions over foreign policy that first surfaced in the 1970s intensified during the Reagan presidency, which was marked by pitched battles between the White House and Congress on issue after issue: foreign aid, defense spending, arms control, war powers, foreign trade, covert operations, and others. Each new understanding between the president and Congress proved to be but a prelude to the next clash. Third parties eventually appealed for a cease-fire. Writing in the wake of the Iran-Contra imbroglio, two former Secretaries of State, Henry Kissinger and Cyrus Vance, themselves of different parties, called for greater bipartisan cooperation between the branches.[16] Unless the national purpose was "fixed" at some point, the

Secretaries warned, the United States risked "becoming a factor of inconstancy in the world" and doomed to "growing irrelevancy."

Their concerns about the future of American foreign policy were widely shared. To be sure, some observers cautioned that bipartisan cooperation was no substitute for wisdom. (The ill-fated Tonkin Gulf Resolution, which gave Lyndon Johnson a "blank check" to prosecute an undeclared war in Southeast Asia, enjoyed bipartisan backing.) Still, most agreed that the constitutional pendulum had swung too far in Congress's favor and believed that reforms were badly needed. Exactly what needed reforming depended on where one thought the source of trouble lay.

Analysts in the 1980s and 1990s have devoted a great deal of attention to the puzzle of foreign policy stalemate. In the opinion of many, the "breakdown of ideological consensus" between the nation's great parties is the root cause.[17] They argue that, in contrast to the early postwar era when Republicans and Democrats agreed on the purposes of American power and which branch of government should exercise it, the parties in the 1980s and 1990s have been sharply divided on matters of substance and procedure. Democrats, the party of Congress, have been prone to neo-isolationism. Republicans, the party of the White House, have espoused a militant internationalism. Ideological disputes are transformed into partisan rivalries and, in turn, into institutional warfare between members of the executive and legislative branches. Irresolution and inaction has often been the result.

As a description of the stalemate of the 1980s and much of the 1990s, this analysis has considerable merit. The problem is that it simply begs the question at hand: *Why* did consensus erode? *Why* have the parties been at loggerheads? After all, things were not always so.

This book has argued that conflict and consensus in American foreign policy grow out of the impact of changes in the international economy on regional interests, and the ways in which these interests are aggregated into coalitions through political parties. The balances of power that emerge produce consensus, conflict, or stalemate. This chapter applies this argument to the case of the 1980s. I show that partisan conflicts over foreign policy during the Reagan years were rooted in a larger regionally based struggle that pitted the manufacturing belt against the sunbelt. Support for the expansive and expensive Cold War foreign policy agenda was strongest in the West and South — regions of the country that were becoming increasingly Republican. In the Northeast, now the Democratic party's electoral base, politicians favored a more restrained and cost-conscious approach to foreign policy. The polarization of the party system along this rustbelt-sunbelt divide intensified these sectionally based conflicts over foreign policy and ensured that they would find institutional expression as party conflicts. The source of conflict between the White House and Congress in the 1980s can thus be found in the changing sectional bases of the Democratic and Republican parties.

American Globalism and the Cold War

From the late 1940s to the mid-1960s, American foreign policy rested on a broad base of domestic support for Cold War internationalism. This was a grand strategy driven first and foremost by geopolitical realities and economic interests. American political, economic, and military means were devoted to rearranging the global chessboard to construct an international order that would guarantee the peace and promote American prosperity. It was a strategic vision that, in the words of historian Melvyn Leffler, gave "primacy to geopolitical configurations of power and to warmaking capabilities."[18] The central geopolitical goal had been defined by Nicholas Spykman in 1941: it was the preservation of a balance of power in Eurasia to prevent any state (or coalition of states) from establishing control over the Eurasian landmass, "where alone lay the resources and population levels which, if ever amalgamated, might overwhelm American might."[19] As Leffler argues, the international balance of *economic* power was crucial in this geopolitical vision, for policymakers believed that America's might resided ultimately in its economic and technological superiority. Adversaries could threaten American security only if they could undermine the American economy or develop comparable or superior industrial warmaking capabilities.[20] This meant that in America's grand strategy for postwar foreign policy, security and economic dimensions would be inseparable and mutually reinforcing.

While initially focused on Europe and Japan, the strategic vision that was laid out in the late 1940s and early 1950s was quickly extended to other parts of the world. What emerged is what James Kurth calls a "national project of international expansion"—the rise of a *Pax Americana* that rested on an interlocking network of international economic, political, and military institutions that were led and dominated by the United States.[21] Its cornerstones were the International Monetary Fund, the World Bank, the General Agreement on Tariffs and Trade (the

"Bretton Woods system"), and the North Atlantic Treaty Organization (NATO), whose main purpose was to promote the development of an open international economy and contain the Soviet threat.

U.S. economic and security policies in the late 1940s and 1950s were part of a grand design to promote economic recovery in Europe and Japan, limit or contain the political impact of communism on the European continent and in East Asia, and integrate these regions into an American-led international economic order. In essence, *Pax Americana* was organized around two axes: a so-called Atlantic axis binding North America and Western Europe, and a Pacific axis tying Japan to Southeast Asia and the United States.[22] Economic, political, and military means were used to weld together the American-led alliances. The sheer power of the United States in the international system in the late 1940s and 1950s gave American officials considerable influence over the West Europeans and the Japanese. The West Europeans and Japanese also saw advantages in this arrangement, and this helps explain how the United States won their backing.

A domestic political consensus over Cold War internationalism provided the context within which Eisenhower, Kennedy, and Johnson built on the overall approach advanced by Truman in the late 1940s. In so doing, they expanded the geographic scope of the *Pax Americana*. As the situation in Western Europe and Japan stabilized, American policy-makers began to focus much more of their attention on the underdeveloped regions of the world, seeing political upheaval in these areas as the most dangerous threat to global stability and prosperity.[23] Indeed, in retrospect, what was perhaps the most important feature of American foreign policy during the 1950s and 1960s was the weight that American officials attached to incorporating large parts of the Third World into an open, increasingly interdependent, American-led world economy.

The domestic political viability of this strategy depended on the alliance between Northeastern and Southern interests that had been forged by President Roosevelt in the 1930s.[24] Foreign aid, military alliances, and military rearmament were all key elements in promoting and stabilizing markets for American industry, which was heavily concentrated in the Northeast. The southern periphery's long-standing commitment to industrial markets outside the northern core for its primary goods—and the rapid development of America's military infrastructure in this region during World War II—gave political representatives from the South a major stake in supporting Cold War liberalism.

In Congress, this alliance found institutional expression in the development of a strong committee system that gave control over the agenda in key policy domains to powerful committee chairmen from the Northeast and the South. These arrangements worked to mute the expression of potentially divisive conflicts between the Northeast and South and to marginalize opponents from the Great Plains and Mountain West.[25] The North-South coalition was strong and stable through the mid-1960s, affording American leaders considerable latitude in managing the nation's foreign policy. Then, around the late 1960s, the sectional bases of Cold War internationalism began to crumble. This process was driven in part by changes in the international system.

The rebuilding of the international economy after the war produced the longest boom in the history of capitalism. The boom was marked in the 1960s by the revival of Germany and Japan—the "economic miracles" of the Cold War era—as economic competitors to the United States, increased capital mobility and transnational investment, and the beginnings of the economic troubles that were to dog the United States through the 1980s: declining industrial productivity and balance of payments deficits. Cracks in American economic hegemony in the 1960s developed along with cracks in the nation's strategic power. The Soviets rapidly closed the nuclear gap and by the end of the decade had achieved a position of rough nuclear parity or equality with the United States. The end of American nuclear supremacy coincided with the rise of political divisions with our military allies in Europe. This was also the era of growing commitment of American power and prestige to an area of the world few Americans knew anything about: Southeast Asia. The Vietnam War would produce social turmoil at home and distort the national economy. It destroyed Johnson's presidency, raised doubts around the world about the wisdom of America's leaders, and raised fundamental questions at home about the efficacy and morality of America's role as the world's policeman.

By the early 1970s the American economy was deep in recession, and the growing economic power of West Germany and Japan raised new questions about the capacity of the United States to maintain its privileged position in the world economy. And while the United States was bogged down in an increasingly unpopular and perhaps even unwinnable war in Vietnam, more questions were raised about the credibility of America's nuclear guarantees. As Thomas McCormick put it, the United States—still indisputably the most powerful nation in the world—showed clear evidence of relative decline.[26] The age of *Pax*

Americana, only a quarter-century old, already seemed to be winding down.

Inside the United States, this process produced uneven regional effects. It would soon give rise to a new round of foreign policy conflict, this one every bit as divisive as the conflicts of the 1890s and 1930s. While many Americans continued to attach great weight to anticommunism, many others began to suspect that American leaders had exaggerated the threat of Soviet and Chinese expansionism, questioning the legitimacy of containment as an instrument of foreign policy. Policies aimed at maintaining high levels of defense expenditure and at extending containment from Western Europe and Northeast Asia to parts of the Third World no longer enjoyed widespread support. Support for a continued American presence in Western Europe and East Asia and for a liberal world trading order remained strong, but beginning in the early 1970s even these fundamental tenets of Cold War internationalism were open to challenge. Even more critical was the fight over the authority to make foreign policy.[27] As the disaster in Southeast Asia deepened, the generally accepted notion that only a strong chief executive could make responsible foreign policy was called into question. Congress dramatically reasserted it right to participate in nearly all areas of foreign policy.

In the 1970s, anticommunist consensus gave way to a split between "hawks" and "doves"—conservatives and liberals—who advanced competing strategic visions of America's place in the world.[28] So-called doves called for an immediate end to the Vietnam war, reductions in defense spending, improved East-West relations, and a greater emphasis on human rights and political reform in dealings with pro-American governments in the Third World. At the core of the liberal critique was a sense that the United States had miscalculated—that in its zeal to check communist expansion, America had neglected its responsibilities at home. For liberals, the answer was clear: America had to retrench. The country's extensive overseas commitments had to be scaled back and a runaway "military-industrial complex" had to be restrained. The United States, they argued, could no longer afford the hidden costs of Cold War internationalism: wasteful and inefficient defense spending, a trading relationship with Japan that was "unfair" to American workers, and the "free ride" enjoyed by America's military allies.

Hawks saw little value in such prescriptions. For them, America was suffering from a failure of will, not a shortage of power. That, according to conservatives, was the real lesson of the debacle in Southeast Asia. Where liberals called for a rapid withdrawal from Vietnam and unilateral reductions in defense spending, hawks stressed the need to prevent a communist victory in Southeast Asia and dismissed talk of a trade-off between guns and butter as "pop" economics. Similarly, many saw arms control as a chimera—a liberal fantasy that only played into the Kremlin's hands. Where doves sought to scale back America's overseas commitments, hawks continued to support a policy of containment toward the Soviet Union, whose human rights abuses, they argued, were worse than those of pro-American authoritarian regimes in places like the Philippines, South Korea, Iran, and South Africa. As liberals distanced themselves from the internationalist nostrums of the Cold War, conservatives embraced them with renewed passion and a crusading spirit.

In the 1980s, this split deepened and fights over the nation's priorities intensified. Huge military outlays, massive trade deficits, and a ballooning federal debt fueled the debate.[29] Liberals charged that Reagan's geopolitical offensive against the Soviets was both unnecessary and ill-advised. For a country already living beyond its means, the price of rearmament and "roll back" was too high. The long-term threats facing America were economic, they argued. The rise of new industrial competitors and the loss of dominant positions in energy, technology, and agriculture were eroding American self-sufficiency. Unless checked, these processes would force the United States to make drastic changes in its foreign policy. Republican loyalists in Congress fought back. Liberal remedies—arms control, the nuclear freeze, and military reform—were dismissed as misguided and even dangerous. Soviet adventurism, conservatives argued, was an inescapable fact of life. This made the decline of American military capabilities in the early 1970s the real threat to American security. Liberal solutions to the country's economic problems—domestic content laws, bilateral trade, industrial policy—were also rebuffed. To conservatives the "twin deficits," the trade and budget deficits, were symptoms rather than causes of the nation's economic ills. The root cause was a declining rate of profit in domestic industry that discouraged new investment. By removing the obstacles to investment—costly business regulations, hefty corporate taxes, and high labor costs—the nation's commitments could be kept in balance with resources.

These fights are often depicted as the product of irreconcilable ideological conflict born of American failures in Vietnam. Ideological conflict split Congress into two warring camps, the Democrats and the Republicans. The analysis that follows shows that in fact, the bases of the conflict were sectional, not ideological. Most of the so-called doves were liberal Democrats and Republicans from the traditional manufacturing belt. While Cold War internationalism continued to strike a responsive chord in the South, it had lost much of its appeal in the Northeast. The Northeast was no longer willing to pay the price—in foreign economic aid, liberal trade policies, and a global military presence— necessary to maintain the world order built under the aegis of American hegemony after World War II. The hawks were a group made up of conservative Democrats from the South and Republicans from the West. This sectional alliance anchored the so-called Reagan right's foreign policy agenda, which favored increased trade and investment overseas, the "rollback" of purported Soviet advances in the Third World, and greater federal spending targeted at defense industries.

The quantitative analysis reveals the regional character of Cold War internationalism's domestic bases of political support and shows that the conflicts that emerged and deepened in the 1970s and 1980s were, in fact, regional ones. The pattern of ideological conflict that surfaced in the 1970s grew out of secular changes in the nation's regional geography that brought into conflict a declining northern "core" and a rising southern and western "periphery."

Sources of the Breakdown of Bipartisanship

Changing relationships between section, party, and foreign policy since World War II are evident in trends in House voting on the economic and strategic policies that promoted Cold War internationalism. To test the competing argument that foreign policy debates became more partisan due to ideological polarization in the 1980s, an index measuring support for "Cold War internationalism" was created using roll call votes on the House floor.[30] This concept is defined here as support for international policies and programs and domestic institutional arrangements designed to promote an open, interdependent world economy and isolate or "contain" nations opposing it (e.g., the Soviet bloc). Operationally, a vote *for* any of the following was considered a vote in favor of Cold War internationalism: military spending, foreign aid, arms sales, forward defense, overseas alliances, military intervention, international institutions, and presidential prerogative in the making of foreign policy.[31] The data set spans the Truman through Reagan years and includes all of the major foreign policy initiatives undertaken by a president that required approval by the House, and votes on every major foreign policy issue that reached the House floor. All of the votes included in the analysis were weighted equally.[32]

The historical data raise serious doubts about explanations of American foreign policy that give pride of place to party and ideology. While it is true that partisan rivalry rose sharply in the 1970s, and then intensified in the 1980s, it is not true that the 1940s and 1950s, the years of supposed bipartisanship, were free of the "scourge" of party politics. In fact, as figure 4.1 indicates, partisan conflict over foreign policy was often very pronounced in the early postwar period, especially when America was at war in Korea.[33] Moreover, as figure 4.2 shows, it is hard to attribute the surge in party conflict in the 1970s and 1980s to ideology. Ideological differences between the parties were as striking at the beginning of the "first" Cold War in the late 1940s and early 1950s as they were during the "second" Cold War that began in the late 1970s and early 1980s. The ideological stance of Republicans and Democrats certainly changed over time—indeed, they flip-flopped—but ideological polarization was a fact of life at the start of the Cold War, as well as at its end. Lastly, the partisan surge to which other analysts attach so much weight occurs *after* the "breakdown of consensus" over foreign policy. The issue that so deeply rent America in the late 1960s and early 1970s—Vietnam—did not divide its elected leaders along party lines. The level of partisan conflict during the Nixon years was unusually low, even when measured against the 1950s, which are remembered as the halcyon years of bipartisanship.

Those who stress party competition as a source of conflict over foreign policy are not wrong; party leaders do play politics with the national interest. The problem with party-based explanations of foreign policy is that they confuse symptoms with causes. In the 1980s, Republicans and Democrats did not disagree over foreign policy because of deeply felt ideological convictions about the national interest or, for that matter, about the proper constitutional division of authority over foreign affairs. Rather, party leaders espoused different ideologies—conservative versus liberal, hawk versus dove, Hamiltonian versus Jeffersonian—because they sought to appeal to constituencies that had distinct and different stakes in how the United States responded to international challenges. What made bipartisanship possible in the early 1950s was what enabled Roosevelt to prevail over western isolationists in the 1930s: the alliance between the urban Northeast and agrarian South. What made it so elusive in the 1980s was the collapse of this

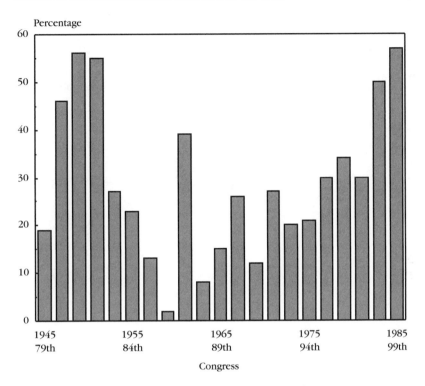

Percentage

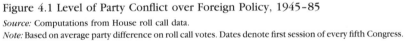

Figure 4.1 Level of Party Conflict over Foreign Policy, 1945–85

Source: Computations from House roll call data.

Note: Based on average party difference on roll call votes. Dates denote first session of every fifth Congress.

sectional alliance and the growing polarization of party competition between the rustbelt and the sunbelt.

A closer examination of the same House votes provides substantial support for this view. Tables 4.1 and 4.2 report results obtained by factor analysis—a standard technique used to reconstruct patterns of alignment from roll call data.[34] The analysis reveals a relatively clear two-factor pattern, with the first and second "dimensions" explaining over 70 percent of the total variance in the data.[35] The Truman, Eisenhower, Kennedy, and Johnson presidencies "load" high on the first dimension; the Nixon, Ford, Carter, and Reagan presidencies load on the second dimension. Put another way, there is a realignment over foreign policy. The domestic bases of Cold War internationalism changed in the late 1960s and early 1970s.[36] As the coalition that backed the exercise of American hegemony for the first half of the Cold War era unrav-

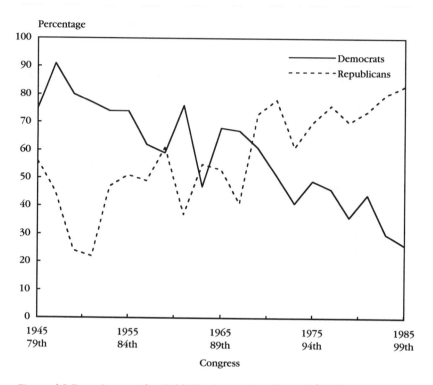

Figure 4.2 Party Support for Cold War Internationalism, 1945–85
Source: Computations from House roll call data.
Note: Dates denote first session of every fifth Congress.

eled, there was a shift in the geographic bases of support for an internationalist agenda combining military spending, liberalized trade, and forward defense. The geographic dimensions of this realignment are fleshed out in figures 4.3 through 4.5.[37] The Truman and Reagan years bracket the analysis historically; the Nixon map is used to highlight the regional bases of the realignment in House voting.

The figures reveal several things. First, it is clear that while the Cold War "consensus" included much of the country, it did not include all of it. Support was strongest in the South and the Northeast, especially in New England and the Middle Atlantic states. The pattern of alignment during the Truman years is thus quite similar to that of the Roosevelt years. Second, it is also apparent that the pattern of interstate alignment shifts dramatically over time, and that the new alignment parallels the popular distinction drawn between the manufacturing belt and the sunbelt. A comparison of the Truman and Nixon maps makes this clear. During the Nixon years, Cold War internationalism continued to enjoy solid support in the South, but it also won strong backing in the West, once the bedrock of isolationism. Support for the exercise of American power abroad was now weakest in the Northeast. Finally, voting patterns during the Nixon and Reagan years are similar. The rustbelt-sunbelt cleavage is starker during the Reagan presidency, but this fault line is already fully evident by the Nixon years. By the 1970s the North-South alliance was in serious disrepair. Support for continued American hegemony now rested in what commentators were soon calling the "Reagan coalition," an alliance of western and southern interests.

Table 4.1 Summary of Factor Analysis

Component	Eigenvalue	Percent Variance Explained	Cumulative Percent Variance Explained
1	4.187	52.3	52.3
2	1.729	21.6	73.9
3	0.745	9.3	83.2
4	0.516	6.4	89.6
5	0.354	4.4	94.0
6	0.227	2.8	96.8
7	0.152	1.9	98.7
8	0.089	1.3	100.0

Source: Computations from House roll call data.

Table 4.2 Varimax Rotated Coefficients and Variable Communalities

Presidency	Loadings on: Dimension 1	Dimension 2	Percent Variance Explained (100 × Communality)
Truman	.318	.711	60.7
Eisenhower	−.295	.879	86.0
Kennedy	−.320	.800	74.3
Johnson	−.596	.686	82.6
Nixon	.818	−.052	67.2
Ford	.898	−.064	81.1
Carter	.875	−.216	81.2
Reagan	.739	−.196	58.4

Source: Computations from House roll call data.

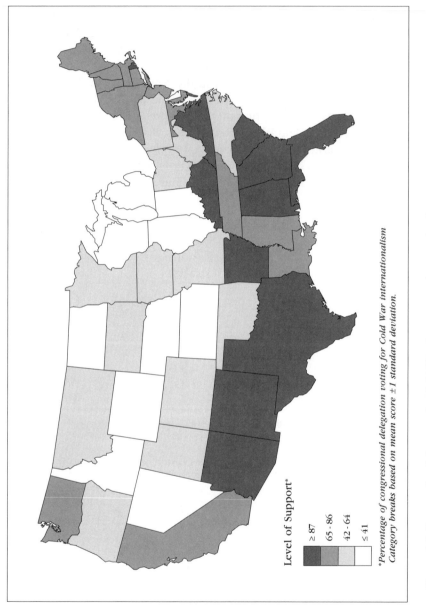

Level of Support*

≥ 87

65 - 86

42 - 64

≤ 41

*Percentage of congressional delegation voting for Cold War internationalism
Category breaks based on mean score ±1 standard deviation.

Figure 4.3 Congressional Support for Cold War Internationalism, 1947–48

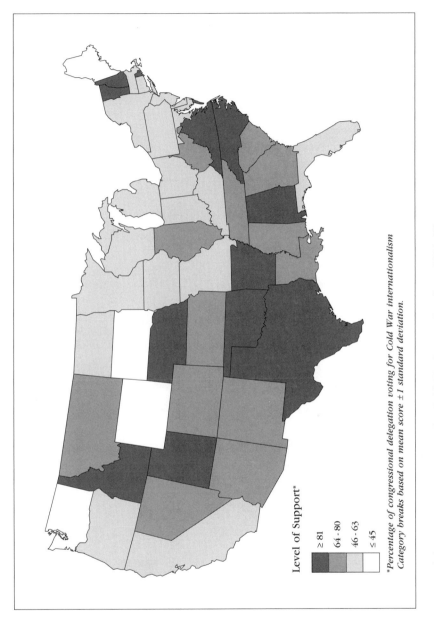

Level of Support*

≥ 81
64 - 80
46 - 63
≤ 45

*Percentage of congressional delegation voting for Cold War internationalism
Category breaks based on mean score ±1 standard deviation.

Figure 4.4 Congressional Support for Cold War Internationalism, 1971–72

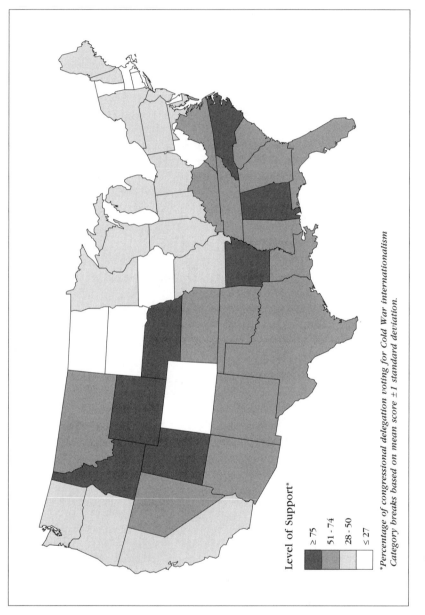

Level of Support*

≥ 75
51 - 74
28 - 50
≤ 27

*Percentage of congressional delegation voting for Cold War internationalism
Category breaks based on mean score ±1 standard deviation.

Figure 4.5 Congressional Support for Cold War Internationalism, 1983–84

The Sectional Bases of Party Conflict

The resurgence in party conflict over foreign policy in the post-Vietnam era was an artifact of America's changing political geography. The Democratic party, traditionally based in the South, had for all practical purposes become the party of the Northeast by 1980.[38] This shift is reflected in the declining number of Democratic seats in the House held by southerners. In 1947, the year the Marshall Plan for Europe was proposed, southern Democrats held over 60 percent of all Democratic seats.[39] In 1980, the southern share of Democratic seats had fallen to below 40 percent—the lowest level since Roosevelt broke the GOP's hold on the big cities to the North. The growing strength of the Republican party below the Mason-Dixon line meant that the South was sending fewer and fewer Democrats to Congress.[40] Meanwhile, changes in the regional bases of the Republican party meant more and more northern seats, especially those in the big northeastern cities, were going to the Democrats. As the Democratic party shifted North, the Republican party was moving West.[41] Long divided along East-West lines, the Republican party swung decisively toward the West in the 1970s. The results of the process that began in the 1960s with the Goldwater movement were manifest starkly: in Congress, a growing proportion of the Republicans' House seats were from western districts and increasingly, southern ones.[42]

The impact of these developments on America's foreign policy was striking. As the base of the Democratic party moved into the urban-industrial centers of the Northeast in the 1970s, areas that no longer backed Cold War internationalism, the party's support for an expansive definition of the national interest waned (fig. 4.6). By contrast, support for Cold War internationalism remained strong in the party's southern wing. The changing geography of the Democratic party explains why party leaders, in the words of Zbigniew Brzezinski, "became increasingly prone to the appeal of neo-isolationism."[43] The more politically dependent the Democratic party became on the aging Northeast, the more its party leaders found it politically necessary *and* politically useful to turn away from the *Pax Americana* their predecessors built, and to advocate a more "isolationist" foreign policy agenda. In short, it was politics, not ideology, that explains what partisan opponents characterized as the Democrats' move to the left. A similar argument can be made about the Republicans. The surge in Republican support for what Brzezinski aptly called "militant interventionism" reflected the growing strength of the West in the party (fig. 4.7). Just as Democratic politi-

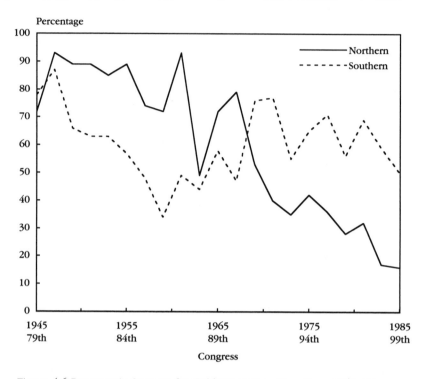

Figure 4.6 Democratic Support for Cold War Internationalism, 1945–85
Source: Computations from House roll call data.
Note: Dates denote first session of every fifth Congress.

cians saw political utility in distancing themselves from their party's internationalist past, Republican party leaders saw political advantage in embracing a more expansionist foreign policy agenda. Ronald Reagan may or may not have been a Cold War ideologue, but he certainly had his finger on the pulse of the West (and South) when he stressed the need for restoring American power.

Politicians may have deep convictions, but they also act strategically. This is as true for foreign policy as it is for domestic policy. In the post-Vietnam America, as in other periods, politicians treated ideas as political resources: as tools for mobilizing popular support and for dividing political opponents. Recognizing this, there is little mystery about why bipartisanship proved so elusive in the Reagan/Bush era. A Republican White House, seeking to mobilize support in the West and

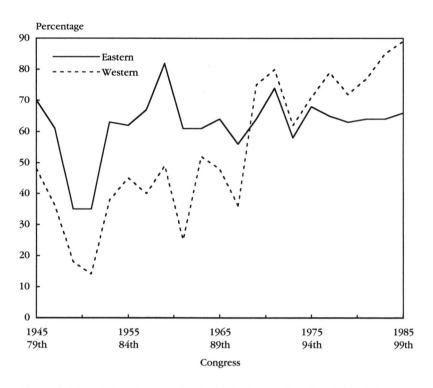

Figure 4.7 Republican Support for Cold War Internationalism, 1945-85
Source: Computations from House roll call data.
Note: Dates denote first session of every fifth Congress.

South, favored a foreign policy agenda that threatened the interests of a Democratic party that controlled the House and that sought to protect the interests of its core constituencies in the urban Northeast. This is why divided party government in the 1980s proved to be an impediment to consensus-building. In contrast to the late 1940 and 1950s, when presidents also had to cope with Congresses controlled by the other party, divided government intensified sectional differences in the post-Vietnam era.[44] Clashes between the party of the rustbelt and the party of the sunbelt masqueraded as fights over the prerogatives of the Executive and the Congress. The real question is not why the two parties, or even the two branches, did not see eye to eye but rather why the rustbelt and the sunbelt did not. A closer look at the politics of trade policy in the 1980s helps explain why.

Trade Policy and the "Paradox" of American Decline

In the 1980s political scientists scrutinized no paradox more intensely than the puzzle of America's continuing support for free trade in the face of declining competitiveness. If support for liberal trade had reflected America's economic preeminence in the first place, then it stood to reason that the country would turn toward protectionism as its economic standing weakened. By the 1970s, many scholars and observers were predicting just such an outcome.[45] Some were drawing ominous parallels to the 1920s, when the American market was abruptly closed off to foreigners after a period of trade liberalization under Woodrow Wilson. Those who made this prediction seemed to have the facts on their side. America was no longer as competitive as it once was. Its share of international trade had fallen from around 18 percent in 1950 to roughly 15 percent in 1970, and 12 percent by 1980.[46] Even more dramatic was the drop in world manufacturing exports: from nearly 30 percent when Dwight Eisenhower entered office to about 13 percent by the time Jimmy Carter was turned out of office.[47] America's share of international manufacturing output had also dropped, from 62 percent in 1953 to 44 percent by 1977. At the same time, America was no longer as dominant in the international monetary system. It is not surprising that many expected the United States to turn inward by the 1980s.

But America did not. Some nontariff barriers (e.g., subsidies, targeting, and government procurement) did increase. So did the number of petitioners seeking relief from foreign competition under Washington's unfair-trade practices statutes. Political pressure also mounted in Congress for trade reform and tougher policies toward countries that limited American access to their markets—most notably, Japan and the "Asian Tigers." Yet in the face of all this, the nation's trade policy remained decidedly open in the 1980s. And the institutional arrangements that had governed trade policy for decades remained intact. The White House still dominated the trade agenda. While the Reagan administration was often hostile toward international institutions and multilateralism, and while it did not shy away from selectively imposing quotas on foreign goods sold in the United States, it lost no opportunity to reaffirm the nation's commitment to the General Agreement on Tariffs and Trade (GATT) and the principle of liberal trade. Commitment to the principle of laissez-faire continued under President Bush. As veteran trade watcher I. M. Destler concluded in 1992, "[t]he system has held."[48] The question is why? What explains America's continuing adherence to principles of free trade in the face of declining competitiveness and mounting protectionist pressures from firms and workers hurt by global competition?

Various domestic-level explanations have been advanced: sectoral, institutional, and ideational. For sectoral analysts, the key is the internationalization of the American economy.[49] They argue that nation's steady integration into the international economy since World War II has dampened support for protectionism. Many of America's firms, even those facing serious import competition, have become so dependent on the world market that protectionist strategies are too costly and dangerous to pursue. Institutionalists take a different tack. They focus on the 1930s shift in tariff-making authority from Congress to the president and argue that the president's continuing dominance helps defuse pressures to erect tariff walls. These institutional arrangements insulate trade policy from Congress and the multitude of interests seeking protection from the vicissitudes of the market.[50] Still others stress the power of ideas, or more precisely, their "stickiness."[51] America, it is argued, learned painful lessons in the 1930s when the ultra-protectionist Smoot-Hawley tariff act unleashed a trade war and fueled the Great Depression. Those lessons were institutionalized in the nation's trade laws and internalized in norms governing the "do's and don'ts" of trade policy. The idea of open markets has thus taken on a life of its own. It helps keep the embers of protectionism from bursting into flames. Politicians fear a repeat of the 1930s and therefore have purposely made it hard to gamble with trade policy.

These accounts highlight important dimensions of American trade policy. America is more integrated in the world economy than it was in the past; the president is still the dominant player on trade matters; and free traders do regularly invoke the "lessons of the past." Still, these accounts are not satisfying. They are surprisingly apolitical. Trade politics may be less bareknuckled today than it was in the 1890s or the 1930s, but it remains a potent political issue. What is missing from existing attempts to resolve the paradox of American economic liberalism since the 1970s is an awareness of the larger "geopolitical" structures that undergird America's commitment to free trade. When one cuts to this level of analysis—the regional level—a rather different picture emerges. One sees that the effects of America's declining competitiveness in the world economy were not felt uniformly across the country, and that the nation's commitment to free trade reflects the same thing it has since the New Deal: the ability of the parts of the nation that gain the most from free, open, and stable trade to hold the line against protectionist forces. The difference between the current era and the 1930s is the "geopolitical" lineup. Now, it is the rapidly growing economies of the West, and to a lesser extent the South, that have the most to gain from free trade. Together, they form the backbone of the new Republican coalition, and make a powerful counterweight to the protectionist bloc arising in the once mighty northern core. The solution to the paradox of declining American hegemony lies here. It tells us a great deal about how America's political economy has changed since the 1930s.

America's New Geography

America dominated the world economy during the first two post-World War II decades. While much of the industrialized world was recovering from history's most destructive war, the United States was capturing resources and markets that would provide the basis for unprecedented economic growth and improvements in domestic standards of living. America, in economist John Kenneth Galbraith's words, was "the affluent society."[52] In the 1970s, however, the country witnessed a precipitous decline in its ability to create and sustain such affluence. The gross national product grew by only 2.9 percent per year in the 1970s, a far cry from the high rates of growth that characterized the "long boom" of the 1950s.[53] By the end of the decade, the typical American family with a $20,000 annual income had only 7 percent more real purchasing power—or a mere $25 more per week—than it had a full decade earlier. Other advanced industrialized nations also experienced declining growth rates during the 1970s, but America's was considerably lower than the average. By 1980, nine other industrialized countries had higher standards of living than the United States. In 1980, the domestic "misery index"—inflation plus unemployment—reached nearly 20 percent, almost three times its average during the 1960s. America was in trouble.

What was true of America as a whole was not equally true of all of its parts. Dramatic regional variations meant that some states were hit much harder than others, and those in the Northeast were hit hardest of all. The big manufacturing states of New York, Pennsylvania, Illinois, and Michigan suffered huge job losses. Plant shutdowns were commonplace; so were small business failures. While the number of

Table 4.3 Employment Growth Rate by Region, 1970-80[1]

Region	Mean	Std. Dev.	Minimum	Maximum
Northeast	18.9	10.4	−1.1	44.7
New England	24.7	11.9	14.2	44.7
Middle Atlantic	13.9	10.6	−1.1	28.1
Great Lakes	16.9	5.3	12.4	25.8
South	41.0	10.7	25.1	63.4
Southeast	41.6	12.4	25.1	63.4
Southwest	39.4	5.5	34.3	47.0
West	49.1	20.9	17.7	90.3
Great Plains	31.9	9.2	17.7	45.8
Mountain	65.8	18.9	36.0	90.3
Pacific Coast	44.7	4.3	40.1	47.4
United States	36.7	19.9	−1.1	90.3

Source: Based on data from the U.S. Department of Labor.
Note: See table 2.1 for regional groupings. Alaska and Hawaii are not included.
[1] Based on nonagricultural employment.

manufacturing jobs declined in all parts of the country, most of the losses were concentrated in the traditional northern core. In 1980 there were, for the first time, as many manufacturing jobs outside the "core" as inside it.[54] By contrast, many state economies in the South and West diversified and became more prosperous during the "stagnant" 1970s.[55] To be sure, there were some major exceptions: California, for example, posted higher than average unemployment rates during most of the decade. Overall, however economic growth rates were substantially higher in the South and West than in the Northeast (table 4.3). Total capital formation, investments in manufacturing, and high-technology employment grew more rapidly outside the old industrial heartland. The headquarters of many Fortune 500 corporations relocated to the sunbelt. And rates of migration from areas of low opportunity to faster-growing regions quickened. The big "winners" were the high growth states in the South and especially the West. The big losers were the slow-growing states in the Middle Atlantic and Great Lakes areas.[56]

For geographers, the 1970s were not just about American economic decline. They were also about regional "restructuring" and economic change. The process known as "deindustrialization" was hollowing out the northern core as labor and capital moved from the rustbelt to the sunbelt. These trends reflected various "push" and "pull" factors: reductions in transportation costs that allowed industrial production to move away from primary markets to areas with cost advantages; the diffusion of large-scale, high-technology production; the depletion of the local resource base in the Northeast; widespread use of air-conditioning in the South, which made the climate more appealing to northerners and made possible local productivity increases; and regional disparities in labor costs, energy prices, social welfare burdens, and local tax rates. Spatial disparities in federal spending and federal tax policies also played a role, as did the uneven regional consequences of rising American investment overseas. There is little question that the manufacturing belt suffered the most from the rapid migration of American firms to less developed countries in the 1960s and 1970s. The Third World, like the sunbelt, provided many advantages to northern-based firms: lower wage rates and tax advantages are the most obvious. Offshore production sites offered the additional advantages of providing access to protected foreign markets and imposing fewer workplace and environmental regulations on producers.

No less important was the uneven impact of America's declining commercial power. While some sectors and regions reaped the benefits of expanding trade, others were net losers.[57] Many semiskilled blue-collar workers who once enjoyed job security and good benefits were "displaced" by low-wage workers in the Third World or by equally skilled, well-paid workers in Europe or Japan. So were many in the ranks of middle management. Sectors such as autos, steel, textiles, semiconductors, and consumer electronics experienced net job and capacity losses, while others such as aircraft, computers, movies, and finance boomed. Altogether, American industries lost 23 percent of their share of world exports in the 1970s. The 1980s were no "kinder or gentler" for American workers. Areas hit hardest were those specializing in the production of nonmilitary capital goods and consumer durables—mostly the big cities in the manufacturing belt.[58] Chicago, Milwaukee, Cleveland, and Detroit suffered dramatic losses, as did smaller cities such as Flint, Peoria, and Gary. Because they were less dependent on the heavy industries that were taking a shellacking on international markets, sunbelt cities did much better.[59] So did the sunbelt overall. One business magazine identified the states most affected by the internationalization of trade in the 1970s as Massachusetts, Connecticut, Pennsylvania, Ohio, Michigan, Illinois, Indiana, and Wisconsin.[60] Table 4.4 reveals that process continued in the 1980s.[61] The Northeast

Table 4.4 Regional Vulnerability to International Competition, 1984[1]

Region	Mean[2]	Std. Dev.	Minimum	Maximum
Northeast	1.11	0.23	0.69	1.73
New England	1.20	0.35	0.69	1.73
Middle Atlantic	1.00	0.10	0.86	1.12
Great Lakes	1.11	0.13	0.99	1.28
South	0.78	0.26	0.45	1.26
Southeast	0.83	0.28	0.52	1.26
Southwest	0.66	0.17	0.45	0.86
West	0.95	0.29	0.42	1.71
Great Plains	0.93	0.42	0.42	1.71
Mountain	0.88	0.10	0.76	1.07
Pacific Coast	1.17	0.16	0.99	1.26
United States	0.96	0.29	0.42	1.73

Sources: Based on data from U.S. Department of Commerce and COMPUSTAT Annual Industrial Database.
Note: See table 2.1 for regional groupings. Alaska and Hawaii are not included.
[1] Measures vulnerability to foreign penetration in export markets. All calculations based on manufacturing employment.
[2] A value greater than 1 indicates high vulnerability to international competition, and a value less than 1 indicates low vulnerability.

was the region hardest hit by international market integration and declining relative competitiveness.

Meanwhile, there were important variations in the export-orientation of America's regional economies. Different regions inside the United States traded with different foreign markets. Table 4.5 shows how pronounced these differences in export-orientation were in the 1980s. It also underscores the importance of geography: in general, regional export-orientations reflected relative distance or proximity. The Northeast sent the vast majority of its exports to Canada and Europe. The Great Lakes region alone was shipping over 50 percent of its exports to Canada in the 1980s, while only 15 percent went to markets in Asia. By comparison, 44 percent of the Pacific Coast's exports were destined for Asian countries. Similarly, the Mountain states shipped a hefty 36 percent of their exports to the Asia trading group — well above the national average of 26.5 percent. Japan took nearly 20 percent of all of the West's exports. What was true of industry was also true of western agriculture. Over one-third of American agricultural exports went to Asia, with Japan alone absorbing 15 percent.[62]

Table 4.5 U.S. Industrial Exports by Region, 1987 (percentage shares)

Region of Production	Foreign Destination Area					
	North America	Latin America	Europe	Asia	Other	All
Northeast						
New England	23.7	5.2	39.6	25.6	5.9	100
Middle Atlantic	25.7	12.2	31.4	25.5	5.3	100
Great Lakes	52.6	8.1	20.1	15.3	3.9	100
South						
Southeast	19.2	21.1	31.3	23.0	5.6	100
Southwest	11.8	31.7	23.4	27.1	6.0	100
West						
Great Plains	38.8	6.4	25.9	24.2	4.7	100
Mountain West	22.1	5.3	32.3	36.2	4.2	100
Pacific Coast	11.3	8.9	30.3	44.1	5.4	100
United States	27.3	13.1	28.0	26.5	5.1	100

Source: Based on Rodney A. Erickson and David J. Hayward, "The International Flows of Industrial Exports from U.S. Regions," *Annals of the Association of American Geographers* 81 (1991): 371–90.
Note: For each region the rows add up to 100 percent except for rounding error. See table 2.1 for regional groupings. Due to differences in regional classification schemes, Arizona and New Mexico are included here as southwestern states. Arkansas and Louisiana are treated as southeastern states. Nevada is classified as a Pacific Coast state. Alaska and Hawaii are not included.

Asia was also an important market for the South. Here, however, Latin America and Europe remained the key export markets.

This explains a great deal about the politics of trade. By the 1980s, the Republicans, once the party of protection, had become the party of free trade. There is little mystery as to why: as the party was becoming increasingly "westernized," the West was becoming increasingly internationalized. While a free trade stance clearly posed some problems for Republican leaders trying to expand the party's base in the low-wage border states of the South, rapid growth in states like Florida, Georgia, Oklahoma, North Carolina, and Texas meant continuing support for liberal trade. The House voting alignment over trade policy in figure 4.8 makes this abundantly clear.[63] Not surprisingly, opposition to free trade was concentrated in the Northeast—the increasingly Democratic Northeast. For Republican strategists eager to exploit sectional tensions in the Democratic party, free trade was a powerful wedge issue. It also was a powerful weapon in the Reagan administration's war on organized labor. A strategy that allowed foreign goods to flood

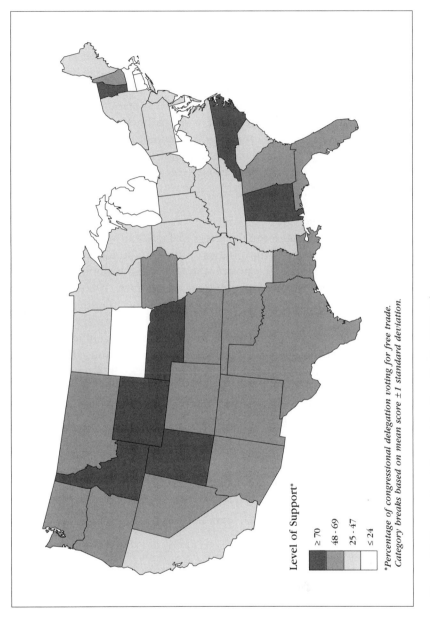

Level of Support*

≥ 70

48 - 69

25 - 47

≤ 24

*Percentage of congressional delegation voting for free trade.
Category breaks based on mean score ± 1 standard deviation.

Figure 4.8 Congressional Support for Free Trade, 1983–84

the American market meant increasing unemployment in the heavily unionized industries and cities of the core.[64] And as the unions lost jobs, and union membership rolls shrunk, organized labor lost power at the bargaining table with a key Republican constituency—big business. Democratic leaders were no less calculating. They understood only too well that job loss and plant shutdowns in the manufacturing belt spelled escalating social welfare costs, a shrinking tax base, and out-migration. Demands for "fairer trade," job retraining, and industrial policy became as obligatory in Democratic politics as demands for freer trade, "fast track procedures," and "FTAs" (free trade agreements) were in Republican circles.

The Great Auto Shakeout

A closer look at trade politics in Congress makes clear how this geopolitical reshuffling redefined the politics of trade. Nothing symbolized the erosion of the Northeast's position in the world economy and its political effects better than the auto crisis of the early 1980s and the sectional strife it unleashed in Congress. All of the ingredients that made trade policy a "hot button" issue in the 1980s were present in the debate over how best to respond to the crisis: the conflicting imperatives of the rustbelt's smokestack industries and the sunbelt's high-tech sectors; the erosion of the institutional checks in Congress on industry-specific and regionally targeted trade legislation; and the re-emergence of trade as a political weapon that each party used to fracture the other's sectional base and strengthen its own. The first skirmish in this new "trade war" was the battle to protect American auto workers from the flood of Japanese imports in the late 1970s and early 1980s. Others would follow: debates over extending the Generalized System of Preferences and tightening the restrictions on textile and apparel imports, fights over the Caribbean Basin Initiative and the 1988 Omnibus Trade Bill, and the battle over fast-track authority to negotiate a free-trade agreement with Mexico.

Automobiles had long symbolized American supremacy in the world economy. They were to twentieth-century America what railroads had been to the nineteenth century: powerful stimuli to growth and employment. In the 1980s this industry alone accounted for almost 4 percent of the Gross National Product and accounted directly or indirectly for one out of every six manufacturing jobs in the United States.[65] The auto industry was the downstream customer for many of the country's other critical industries. Auto manufacturing consumed 60 percent of the country's synthetic rubber production, 30 percent of its metal casings, 20 percent of its steel, and 11 percent of its primary aluminum.[66] The industry was the largest consumer of robotics and a very large consumer of electronics equipment, including audio electronics and engine controls. One did not have to be an economist to see that large-scale changes in the auto industry had a widespread and powerful impact on the economy.

For the first half of the twentieth century the United States was the unchallenged leader in world auto production. The vast majority of all motor vehicles produced in the world were made in America. It was not until the mid-1950s that the pattern of world auto production began to change. Between 1955 and 1965, European production grew threefold, spurred by the continent's rapid economic recovery from World War II and huge jumps in income. While America's share of world production fell from nearly 70 percent to 45 percent, Europe's rose from 24 to 39 percent.[67] In the 1960s the structure of world auto production changed again. Japan, once a relatively small producer, quickly emerged as a world leader. Japanese auto production tripled between 1965 and 1973. At the time of the 1973 Arab oil embargo, Japan was producing 18 percent of the world's autos. By the end of the decade, Japan's share of the world auto market had risen to 25 percent, Europe's was about 35 percent, and America's share had dropped to 32 percent and was continuing to slide downward.

The American auto industry stumbled badly during the 1970s. Domestic car sales dropped off sharply, falling from 9.3 cars in 1972 to 6.6 million in 1980.[68] Foreign imports quickly expanded to meet demand: imports doubled between 1969 and 1979 and by the end of the decade foreign car manufacturers held nearly 22 percent of the American market. In 1980 things went from bad to worse: by spring of that year, the auto industry had suffered its worst year since the Great Depression. Roughly 300,000 auto workers—some 40 percent of the industry's labor force—were laid-off, and approximately twice that number in auto-related industries like rubber, steel, and aluminum were idled.[69] Ford and General Motors suffered record losses, and Chrysler needed federal loans to avert bankruptcy. Facing weak markets, tough competition, excess capacity and high fixed costs, the Big Three began shuttering some of their older plants.

The industrial Northeast bore the brunt of the industry's shakeout. Fourteen plants were closed by 1984. Ten of these were located in the Great Lakes and Middle Atlantic states.[70] Detroit, the cradle of the

American auto industry, was hit especially hard by the wave of plant closings and slowdowns.[71] Between 1978 and 1982, the number working in the city's auto plants fell from 609,000 to 422,000—a 30-percent drop.[72] The result was massive unemployment. By 1982, unemployment in the Motor City had reached almost 16 percent. Among Detroit's black population, the rate of unemployment was a staggering 27 percent. Demand for social services swelled. By June 1981, 60 percent of Detroit's 1.2 million residents were on some form of public assistance.[73] Meanwhile, the local revenue base fell by $30 million, leaving the city $120 million in the red for fiscal 1981 and with projected losses of $150 million for fiscal 1982. By this point, the once-thriving center of the auto industry had joined New York, Cleveland, and others as a city in crisis. Mayor Coleman Young declared that Detroit was in "a state of emergency."[74]

The suddenness and magnitude of the downturn in the auto industry shocked Americans. Many were quick to blame the Japanese. They made an easy target. While auto imports doubled overall, domestic sales of Japanese cars had increased fivefold. By 1980 three out of every four imported automobiles were made in Japan.[75] Japan's stunning achievement was measured by the fact that it now held a larger share of the American auto market than either Ford or Chrysler.[76]

The truth of the matter was that Japanese competition alone did not explain the auto industry's declining fortunes. American government policies and the domestic auto industry itself were partly to blame. In the wake of the 1973 oil shock, the Big Three had failed to adapt to higher gasoline prices by building smaller, more fuel-efficient cars. Japanese firms, specializing in minicompact and subcompact cars, found a niche that they were able to exploit all the more quickly and efficiently because Washington continued to adhere to a relatively open market policy while offering special dispensations that allowed the Big Three to defer adjustment. Facing stiff import restrictions in Europe, the Japanese did the rational thing: they concentrated their export strategy on the American market. An overvalued dollar helped Japanese auto makers consolidate their position. Responding to the second oil shock of 1979, the Federal Reserve had adopted tight monetary policies, thereby raising the value of the dollar. Between 1978 and 1982 the dollar appreciated by 50 percent relative to the Japanese yen.[77] American consumers, who were seeking fuel-efficient vehicles, now found the Japanese imports both appealing and quite affordable.

The Big Three's troubles became intensely politicized. Talk of "a

Japanese threat" and American retaliation spread. The United Auto Workers (UAW), a union long committed to open trade, pressed for relief from foreign competition. In November 1979, when the number of laid-off auto workers surpassed 100,000, UAW President Douglas A. Fraser began publicly criticizing Japanese auto makers for ignoring the plight of the American worker. Frustrated by the situation, Fraser declared that UAW members would boycott Japanese cars unless Toyota and Nissan built assembly plants in the United States. In January 1980 the labor leader went a step further, telling Washington reporters that he was preparing a recommendation for legislation that would require automobile makers who sold more than 200,000 cars in the United States to build assembly plants in that country. One month later Fraser repeated these concerns and ideas in a well-publicized trip to Japan. Meeting with high-ranking industry, labor, and government officials, the union leader made it abundantly clear that the UAW's long-standing opposition to managed trade notwithstanding, the union would support congressional calls to impose import restrictions on Japanese cars unless Japanese manufacturers moved quickly to invest in the United States. Telling the Japanese that the root of the problem was high unemployment rates in the United States, Fraser offered to cooperate with Japanese manufacturers by making agreements on wages and related matters.

Fraser declared his trip to Japan a success, but it was clear that any movement by the Japanese would take time and that the situation in the auto industry was only getting worse. An astonishing 28 percent of UAW membership was now on layoff, and announcements of new plant closings or slowdowns came with almost daily regularity.[78] The UAW needed a quick fix. Shocked by the massive layoffs in the spring, the UAW and the Ford Motor Company filed an "escape clause" petition to the International Trade Commission (ITC) in the hopes that it would provide some relief in the form of import quotas, tariff increases, or the like. It was an election year, and labor's backers in Congress responded by holding hearings.

Meanwhile, Jimmy Carter and Ronald Reagan jockeyed for electoral advantage. Facing a challenge from Edward "Teddy" Kennedy, Massachusetts senator and long-time friend of labor, Carter responded by providing generous trade adjustment assistance for laid-off workers. Although Carter's nomination was never in serious jeopardy, Kennedy's short-lived candidacy did reveal how politically vulnerable the Georgian was in the industrial Northeast. This fact was not lost on the Republicans. Sensing an opportunity to divide the Democratic base in key electoral states like Michigan, Ohio, and Pennsylvania, Reagan promised in September "to try to convince the Japanese that . . . the deluge of their cars into the United States must be slowed."[79] Shortly after election day the ITC announced its decision: three-to-two against the UAW. In the end, the Commission concluded that the auto industry's woes had more to do with recession, higher oil prices, and consumer tastes than with Japanese imports.

Finding no relief, the UAW turned up the heat on Congress. Charles Vanik of Ohio, the sympathetic chairman of the Subcommittee on Trade of the House Ways and Means Committee, quickly won House passage of a bill authorizing the president to negotiate an orderly marketing agreement with Japan. The initiative then passed to the new Republican Senate and to the new chairman of the Finance Subcommittee on International Trade, John Danforth of Missouri. After a round of hearings in January 1981, Danforth introduced a bill that would impose statutory quotas on Japanese automobile imports for three years. The senator's reasons for pushing the bill were clear enough: Missouri was an important auto-producing state. The Japanese government signaled that it could live with the arrangement. The auto issue was not going to go away anytime soon, and the Danforth plan was a better deal than anything the UAW was offering. The main obstacle was the Reagan administration, which did not want to be closely associated with such a restrictive scheme. In the end, the White House yielded to Senate pressure. Reagan sent U.S. Trade Representative William E. Brock III to Tokyo in May to work out an arrangement by which Japan would "voluntarily" cut back on exports for at least two years.[80]

The agreement between Washington and Tokyo did not live up to advance billing. American auto sales continued to plunge while Japan's share of the American auto market edged further upward. In 1981 domestic auto sales fell 6 percent from their 1980 level. Japanese imports had risen to 2.3 million, giving them 21 percent of all car and truck sales in the United States.[81] Meanwhile, the number of auto workers dropped from the Big Three's payrolls continued to swell. Faced with even more layoffs, the UAW responded with H.R. 5133, a bill requiring foreign auto companies to either build more cars in the United States or reduce their auto sales here. Introduced by Richard L. Ottinger (D-NY) in 1982, the bill provided a rigid domestic-content formula: domestic content ratios would be based on the number of cars sold in the United States. The measure, had it become law, would have required auto makers to use a high percentage of American labor and parts in cars they sold in the United States.[82] Given current levels of sales, Toyota and Nissan cars would be required to have 70 to 75 percent domestic content by 1985, while smaller makers like Mazda and Honda would have to achieve ratios of between 20 and 40 percent. Major American makers would face a domestic content requirement of 90 percent, which would severely limit their ability to buy parts from abroad. Stiff quotas would be slapped on companies that failed to meet the bill's required ratios.

The ensuing fight set the stage for much of what would follow in the 1980s. The Reagan administration, committed to free-market solutions, worked hard to defeat the bill, calling it "the worst piece of economic legislation since the 1930s."[83] House Republicans prepared dozens of amendments designed to weaken or kill the bill.[84] Meanwhile, as the bill worked its way to the House floor, UAW lobbyists had succeeded in turning it into a test of lawmakers' support for American labor and "toughness" toward Japan. *Congressional Quarterly Weekly* dubbed the final vote in favor of the bill in December 1982 a "Christmas gift" for American labor and "ashes" for Japan.[85] Supporters claimed that the House vote sent a "clear signal" to Japan to change its trading practices. Yet the victory turned out to be largely a symbolic one. An amendment by lame-duck Rep. Millicent Fenwick (R-NJ) had seriously weakened the bill by making it possible for American courts to invalidate the measure on the grounds that it violated America's obligations under the GATT.[86] By the time the final roll was taken, the UAW-backed bill had lost much of its bite. "We just gutted the bill," gloated Phil Gramm, the voluble Texas Democrat, after the Fenwick amendment passed by a narrow 195–194 margin.[87] Gramm was half-right. The bill never reached the Senate floor and eventually faded from the trade scene. But not before it had polarized Congress and redefined the trade debate.

The final vote on H.R. 5133 was 215 to 182. By standard measures, it was a party line vote. A majority of Democrats voted for the legislation while a majority of Republicans voted against. Yet a closer look at the vote tally reveals how the "party vote" designation can hide a deeper line of cleavage. On this vote—as on so many other votes dealing with trade policy in the 1980s—party was a proxy for section. A declining, and increasingly Democratic, Northeast stood on one side. On the other side was a rising, and increasingly Republican, West (see fig. 4.9). Indeed, northeastern Democrats, who made up over 44 per-

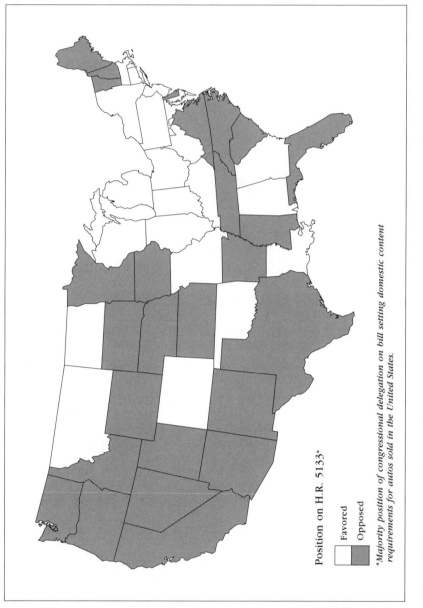

Position on H.R. 5133*

☐ Favored

▨ Opposed

*Majority position of congressional delegation on bill setting domestic content requirements for autos sold in the United States.

Figure 4.9 Congressional Support for Auto Domestic Content Legislation, December 15, 1982

cent of all Democrats in the 97th Congress, voted almost unanimously for imposing domestic content restrictions. By comparison, only 53 percent of the Democrats from the South backed the measure. On the Republican side of the aisle, it was western Republicans who voted overwhelmingly against the bill. Over 94 percent of them opposed the measure. Though few in number, northeastern Republicans accounted for nearly all Republican votes in favor of domestic content. Only in the South could it be said that Republicans and Democrats viewed the issue of domestic content differently. And even here the gap was not wide.

In the weeks leading up to the vote on H.R. 5133, dramatic public debate framed the issue in extreme terms. While there was no argument about the dismal financial condition of the American auto industry, proponents and opponents of the bill attributed the automakers' woes to different causes and disagreed sharply about how best to respond. Rustbelt Democrats placed the onus on the Japanese and the White House. "America," argued John Dingell, the Michigan Democrat and Chairman of the House Energy and Commerce Committee that marked up the bill, "plays by the Marquis of Queensbury's rules and the others have their knee in our groin."[88] Japan's "predatory practices" were part of the problem.[89] So too was the Reagan's administration's anachronistic commitment to laissez-faire. Richard Ottinger (D-NY) led the charge for labor and articulated northeasterners' frustration and anger: "[W]e have been acting like 'Uncle Sucker.' We have seen our entire industrial base eroded, and we have done nothing to counter it."[90] Something had to be done to slow and reverse the trend. True, many conceded, legislating domestic content was less than ideal as a solution. But as Don Bailey (D-PA) noted, there was no magic bullet. "This piece of legislation is not the best thing to do in an ideal sense. It is a necessary political vehicle to teach some lessons."[91]

How Japan would react to H.R. 5133 was an open question. For many northeastern lawmakers, it was also a secondary one. The bill had many other virtues, and one was symbolic: the crisis in the auto industry symbolized the plight of the Northeast.[92] What was happening to Detroit, the "birthplace of good times and bad," was happening to much of the region. Industry in all the big cities was being hammered by foreign competition. In the late 1970s and early 1980s, the Northeast suffered the brunt of the surge in imports, losing 346,138 manufacturing jobs or 56.3 percent of all jobs lost due to foreign competition.[93] The 1981–82 recession had devastated the Northeast. The region's machinery and equipment industries were "badly mauled."[94] Steel output dropped below 50 percent of capacity.[95] In December 1982, the low point of the recession, employment in motor vehicles was down 36 percent; steel, 45 percent; farm equipment, 40 percent; construction equipment, 36 percent; metalworking, 22 percent; and railroad equipment, 38 percent.[96] It is no wonder that rustbelt Democrats like Representative Tobey Moffet of Connecticut spoke passionately in defense of trade legislation like H.R. 5133. Addressing his colleagues on the House floor, Moffet laid out the dilemma facing congressmen from districts whose industries were once the envy of the international marketplace and whose workers were now reeling from the scourge of globalization and recession:

> [H]ow many of us, particularly from the Northeast, dwell on free trade? I cannot speak for Iowa, where maybe our friends are right. Maybe wheat trade is top thing on people's minds in Iowa or Nebraska, where maybe they really do believe in totally free trade and leaving the current situation the way it is. But I can tell the Members, being from the Northeast . . . that we have sat in too many coffee-shops and delicatessens across the table from auto workers who are out of work and without anything to tell them what we think should be done. . . . Members of Congress, Republican and Democrat, from those kinds of districts can no longer sit in those coffee-shops and talk to guys who have been thrown out on the street without offering some alternatives. There is just no more time for that. So this is an imperfect instrument to try to speak to their plight.[97]

From the perspective of northeastern lawmakers, another virtue of H.R. 5133 was more concrete. Many northeastern Democrats who were elected in November 1982 enjoyed the backing of labor. Union money, manpower, and votes helped them to win their seats, and the legislators could now return the favor by voting for the UAW-backed plan.[98] A final virtue of a vote in favor of H.R. 5133 was that it was, as one top House aide put it, a "free vote." Northeastern Democrats could support labor and send a signal to Japan without having to take any responsibility for the bill's effects: everyone knew that it would be defeated by the Republican Senate or vetoed by the Reagan White House.[99] H.R. 5133 was tailor-made to serve the political needs of rustbelt Democrats.

Sectional imperatives and party politics had thus fused over the trade issue. Just as free trade was a key element in the "New Right's" strategy to "Republicanize" the sunbelt South, Democratic party leaders used protectionism during the peak years of recession in the early 1980s to fortify their base in the Northeast and solidify the party's control of Congress. Similar logic shaped the behavior of congressmen from the West.

Western congressmen mounted an impassioned attack on domestic content legislation. They conjured up visions of a trade war, drawing ominous comparisons to the 1930s. "Let us not forget Smoot-Hawley," argued James Jones (D-OK). "Let us not forget the last worldwide depression which it sparked. Let us not repeat that mistake again today by passing this legislation."[100] Raising the specter of Japanese retaliation, western lawmakers catalogued what the bill might mean for western agriculture and industry. A trade war would be devastating for western farmers. Calling the bill "the Soviet grain embargo No. II," Douglas Bereuter, Republican of Nebraska, claimed that its "impact would be at least as deleterious for American agriculture and the country as the original Carter grain embargo."[101] Wheat, corn, and soybeans were all now highly dependent on foreign markets. So were many of the region's high-tech electronic and aerospace industries, along with its service-oriented industries such as banking and insurance. Democrat Dan Glickman of Kansas, whose district was a large producer of airplanes and wheat, spoke for both: "My district lives on exports. We survive on exports, and we will die as a result of a lack of exports."[102]

Glickman's views were a sharp reminder of how much the West's position in the world economy had changed since the 1930s. Western interests were now heavily dependent on foreign markets, and the Pacific Basin was the region's key export market. In fact, as one careful study of regional trade flows concluded, no other region of the country was more integrated into the Asian market or more vulnerable to a trade war with Japan than the West.[103] Western agriculture was especially vulnerable to any disruption of trade with Asia. Exports of American agricultural products had increased from $7 billion in 1970 to $41 billion in 1980.[104] Over 36 percent of these sales were made to Asian countries. Japan alone took 15 percent of all American farm exports. It made large oilseed and wheat purchases and was the largest single market for feed grains. What was true of sales to Japan was true American agricultural exports more generally. Grain led all other commodities.[105] At decade's end, western grains accounted for 44 percent of all American agricultural exports. Oilseeds came next at 23 percent. The fact that cotton now accounted for only 7 percent of all agricultural exports was one measure of how much American farm production and farm interests had changed since the 1930s.

Once the self-appointed guardians of the home market, western lawmakers were now fervent advocates of free trade. Given the region's dependence on export markets, and especially the growing Asian market, it is not surprising that so many of them opposed H.R. 5133. Any legislation that might invite Japanese retaliation, or create an opening for more restrictive trade legislation, was to be avoided.

The farm crisis that hit western farmers in the early 1980s only reinforced western lawmakers' commitment to free trade. The very conditions that been so beneficial to farmers in the 1970s—rising global demand and a weak dollar—had reversed themselves.[106] Global farm output jumped and the dollar rose sharply. Major wheat competitors such as Canada, Australia, and Argentina captured larger shares of the export trade by adopting aggressive marketing strategies that included lower prices and attractive credit arrangements. International demand for grains produced by farmers in the American West plummeted. Having expanded operations in the boom years, western farmers now found themselves burdened by unserviceable debt.[107] Export-oriented counties were especially hard hit. Land values dropped as farm incomes and farm-sector growth prospects diminished. In this predicament the last thing western farmers needed was a trade war with Japan. And the last thing their representatives in Washington needed was to appear indifferent to the farmers' plight. Democrat Glickman understood this only too well, and that is why he and other Democrats from the Great Plains and Mountain West crossed party lines to vote against H.R. 5133 and against their own party leaders.

The fight over domestic content was not just about Japan, auto parts, and jobs. More fundamentally, it was about America and its changing economic geography. As Norman Shumway (R-CA) put it, "We must recognize that the fundamental nature of our economy is changing; that the so-called smoke-stack industries will play a relatively less prominent role in the future."[108] On this there was little disagreement. The real question was what the future would look like, and what role the government would play in getting us there. For northeastern lawmakers the answer was obvious: federal intervention to ease economic restructuring. Domestic content legislation was just one of many devices they employed to shift the burden of regional restructuring to others: the South, the West, the Japanese. And it was precisely this "solution" that infuriated the bill's opponents. Over and over again, they stressed the redistributive character of H.R. 5133. For Charles Pashayan, Republican of California, the bill was nothing less than a transfer payment: "[I]t's principal effect is really to transfer jobs within this country from one group to another."[109] Income would be transferred from more dynamic export-oriented sectors to older, increasingly noncompetitive ones. Phil Gramm, the Texas Democrat, agreed. "[T]his is not a job-creation bill," he asserted. "This is a job-transfer bill. . . . It transfers jobs from those industries, that have been competitive, that have been responsible, to those that are not. And in the long run, it is self-defeating."[110]

When western lawmakers extolled the virtues of open markets and unfettered trade, they were talking the language of regional economic conflict. The same was true of northeastern politicians when they spoke out about the need to save American jobs from foreign predators and to "level the playing field." Both were concerned about who would shoulder the costs of America's economic restructuring in the 1980s. Westerners sought to "localize" those costs in the Northeast, while northeasterners sought to nationalize the costs by spreading them more broadly. In the 1980s, as in earlier periods, politicians made their case for or against trade legislation on the basis of what was in "the national interest." Yet oftentimes, it was as if they were saying, "What is good for my region is good for the country."

The fight over domestic auto content legislation was representative of fights over all major trade issues of the 1980s. Table 4.6 summarizes the regional vote on five key trade issues taken up by Congress during the Reagan and Bush years: the Auto Domestic Content Rule, the Caribbean Trade Plan, the Textile Import Quotas Bill, the Omnibus Trade and Competitiveness Act of 1988, and the vote on the North American Free Trade Agreement (NAFTA). In the analysis, each vote was coded so that it could be understood as a vote for greater responsiveness to the needs of import-sensitive or import-injured industries and as a vote for a larger role for Congress in shaping trade policy. Support for more restrictive or protectionist trade policies was strongest in the Northeast, while support for free trade was greatest in the West. The South, once the nucleus of the free trade bloc, now lay in between. On some issues, most notably import quotas on textiles, southern lawmakers sided with their colleagues from the Northeast; on others, such as the Auto Content Rule and Bush's proposed American-Mexican free trade zone, southerners aligned with westerners.

Table 4.6 Regional Support for Protectionism, 1981–91 (percentage)

Region	Domestic Auto Content[1]	Caribbean-Basin Initiative[2]	Textile Import Quotas[3]	Omnibus Trade Bill[4]	NAFTA[5]
Northeast					
New England	76.2	65.2	91.3	69.6	68.9
Middle Atlantic	74.1	70.9	79.5	63.7	34.6
Great Lakes	69.5	46.2	56.6	57.0	54.4
South					
Southeast	33.3	32.9	82.7	51.9	55.3
Southwest	40.5	27.5	61.4	48.9	11.2
West					
Great Plains	37.5	58.1	34.4	39.4	56.7
Mountain West	23.5	41.7	22.7	29.2	33.3
Pacific Coast	40.4	54.7	33.3	28.1	35.7

Source: Computations from House roll call data.

Note: See table 2.1 for regional groupings. Alaska and Hawaii are not included.

[1] Final vote on bill to require automakers to use set percentages of American labor and parts in automobiles sold in the United States. A vote for the bill is a vote for more restrictive trade. December 15, 1982.

[2] Vote on rule prohibiting labor-backed amendments to (restrictions on) President Reagan's Caribbean Basin Initiative. A vote against the rule is a vote for more restrictive trade. July 13, 1983.

[3] Final vote on bill imposing new quota restrictions on textile imports. A vote for the bill is a vote for more restrictive trade. October 10, 1985.

[4] Vote on Gephardt (D-MO) Amendment establishing a mechanism to impose import barriers against countries that failed to reduce their large bilateral trade surpluses with the United States. A vote for the amendment is a vote for more restrictive trade. April 29, 1987.

[5] Vote on a resolution to disapprove President Bush's request for fast-track authority to begin negotiations with Mexico to create a North American free-trade zone and revive negotiations on the General Agreement on Tariffs and Trade (GATT). A vote for the resolution is a vote for more restrictive trade. May 23, 1991.

During the Cold War years the South had shed its centuries-long dependence on agriculture. Leading all American regions in economic growth, the South registered impressive gains in its share of the nation's value added and manufacturing employment.[111] Total nonagricultural employment expanded rapidly, at a rate second only to that of the fast-growing western states of California, Oregon, and Washington. Employment in manufacturing firms expanded faster in the South than in any other part of nation. Yet for all its spectacular growth, in 1980 the South remained the nation's premier low-wage region. The region's strides in high-wage industries such as electronics, automobiles, chemicals, rubber and plastics, and nonelectrical machinery were clustered in Texas, Florida, Tennessee, and North Carolina. Low-wage industries like textiles, apparel, leather, and lumber continued to account for over 40 percent of all manufacturing jobs in states such as Virginia, South Carolina, Mississippi, and Alabama. Although low-wage industries' share of the South's economy had declined considerably since World War II, during this period the region had nonetheless increased its share of all low-wage industries in the United States.

Many of the South's manufacturers competed with foreign low-wage industry. This helps explain why southern industry was less export-oriented than the rest of the United States. It also helps explain why many of the South's representatives in Washington no longer automatically rejected schemes designed to restrict access to the American market. When import penetration (imports as a percentage of domestic production) hurt domestic low-wage industry, the South bore a disproportionate share of the cost.[112] In 1984, the average import penetration ratio for manufacturing nationwide was 10 percent. There was however variation across sectors. In the apparel industry the ratio was twice the national manufacturing average, and nearly 50 percent of apparel industry employment was located in the South. Leather goods had an import-penetration ratio of 44 percent. In this industry, 20 percent of the nation's jobs were in the South. The structure of the southern economy in the 1980s explains why southern lawmakers found themselves aligning with the free-trade West on some trade issues, and the protectionist Northeast on others.

The Trade Policy-Making System

In the early postwar decades Congress was "remarkably restrained" in the exercise of its constitutional authority to "regulate commerce with foreign nations."[113] This pattern dates to 1934, when Congress approved the Reciprocal Trade Agreements Act and thereby relinquished its tariff-making authority to the president. Chief executives were authorized to negotiate lower tariffs with foreign governments for particular items and to implement these agreements through executive order. Presidential dominance in trade policy persisted through the end of the 1960s. Each White House request to renew or extend executive authority to negotiate tariff revisions was approved by Congress by hefty vote margins. House and Senate members did frequently take advantage of the White House's requests for new trade authority "to set guidelines regulating how much tariff levels could be changed, by what procedures, and with what exceptions," but none of this seriously threatened the president's primacy in making trade policy.[114] Although

lawmakers debated trade questions, few introduced legislation to protect specific industries. When they did, such initiatives usually died qui-
etly in committee. In most instances, industries and groups seeking
some kind of subsidy or relief from Congress were referred elsewhere,
usually to the International Trade Commission (ITC), the chief agency
for administering trade relief. With few exceptions—most notably in
the cases of textiles, shoes, and steel—Congress refrained from the
kind of product-specific lawmaking that had given the country Smoot-
Hawley.

Executive dominance in international trade matters in the 1950s
and 1960s was made possible by two things: the economic strength of
U.S. industries, and the enduring political strength of the 1930s alliance
between the industrial Northeast and agrarian South. Predominance of
this free-trade alliance in Congress rendered international trade a non-
partisan issue—the leaders of both parties advocated freer trade.[115] This
consensus gave presidents considerable room to maneuver in the trade
policy arena.[116] Meanwhile, Congress's strong committee system put
enormous agenda-setting and procedural power in the hands of the
committee chairmen from the Northeast and South who dominated
the pivotal Ways and Means and Finance committees.[117] Because few
domestic industries faced an immediate threat from foreign competition, there was little pressure on Congress to break from this system.
Congress's "voluntary restraint" on foreign trade during this period was
thus no accident.[118] Delegating authority to chief executives who favored trade liberalization served the interests of northeastern and
southern lawmakers. Seeing little sectional advantage in playing the
"trade card," party leaders were forced to look elsewhere for electoral
issues. Republican and Democratic platform positions on trade con-
verged, rivalry on the House and Senate floor waned, and bipartisanship was the norm in committee deliberations over trade.[119]

This system broke down in the 1970s. Industry pressure for protection was increasing while the institutional arrangements that had long
insulated trade decisions from such pressure were fraying. A reform-
minded Congress began dispersing power, weakening Ways and Means
and creating opportunities for other committees to extend their reach
into trade policy.[120] Congressional proceedings grew more fractious
and floor votes became more partisan.[121] Demands for fairer trade,
sectoral reciprocity, and domestic content ratios escalated.[122] In the
1980s the trend accelerated. Following Congress's revision of the trade
grievance procedure in 1979, the number of "unfair trade" cases

exploded under Reagan and Bush. Meanwhile, lawmakers demanded even tougher executive action to open markets overseas and to use access to the American market as a bargaining chip in trade negotiations. The number of protectionist trade bills introduced in Congress rose dramatically in the Nixon, Ford, and Carter years, and soared during the 1980s. During the Bush and Reagan administrations, hundreds of bills were introduced each Congress and floor votes on product-specific restrictions became more commonplace.

The president's ability to keep trade policy on a liberal course was severely tested in the 1980s. Yet the executive-centered trade system created in the 1930s did hold. Congress did continue to delegate broad powers to the president, but as I. M. Destler observed, "it did so more grudgingly, with more detailed demands and timetables, which constrained administration flexibility."[123] In Congress there was considerably more partisan rancor over trade policy-making authority.[124] Democrats, once champions of executive prerogative, had become strong advocates of congressional activism in this area. The Republicans were now the biggest defenders of presidential authority.

The Sectional Bases of Trade Conflicts
Partisan conflict over both substance and procedure in the area of trade policy reflected fundamental changes in the geography of free trade. Democratic support for protectionism was strongest in the Northeast; Republican support for free trade was greatest in the West and South.[125] During the 1970s, the North-South alliance underlying America's commitment to liberal trade came unglued. By the 1980s a new line of cleavage had emerged: one dividing the country along East-West lines.[126] This realignment over trade altered the relationship between party, ideology, and section that had dominated America's trade politics for nearly half a century. Now the prototypical proponent of freer trade was a laissez-faire Republican lawmaker from a high-growth sunbelt state specializing in trade with the Pacific Rim. The protectionist archetype was a pro-labor, liberal Democrat from a slow-growing, heavily urbanized state suffering from "deindustrialization." The regional bases of the parties were rapidly changing, and with it came a realignment in party ideology on trade matters.

The change is revealed in congressional votes on trade questions. The result of a cross-sectional analysis of voting in the House for 1983–84 is summarized in table 4.7. The dependent variable is state support for free trade—the same measure that was used to generate figure 4.8.

Table 4.7 Analysis of House Support for Free
Trade, 1983–84

Intercept	0.850
(Prob > |T|)	(0.001)
Trade vulnerability	−0.100
	(0.010)
State growth	0.280
	(0.003)
Liberal	−0.002
	(0.021)
Democratic	−0.490
	(0.001)

Adjusted R^2: 0.800
Method: ordinary least squares
N: 48

Two independent economic variables are included: they measure rate
of economic growth (*State Growth*) and vulnerability to international
competition (*Trade Vulnerability*).[127] The model includes two political
variables as well: *Liberal* and *Democratic*. *Liberal* is simply the average
vote score compiled by Americans for Democratic Action (ADA)—a
"liberal" watchdog organization whose membership base is overwhelmingly northeastern—for each state delegation in the Senate.[128] It
is a commonly used measure of support for liberal causes (e.g., labor,
civil rights, welfare aid) in voting studies. *Democratic* is simply the
percentage of Democrats in a state's House delegation, the assumption
being that Democratic and Republican states would, generally speaking, line up on opposite sides: heavily Democratic ones favoring protection; Republican ones backing free trade.

The results are striking. Parameter estimates uniformly conform to
expectations—i.e., the prototypical free trader and protectionist—and
fall well within standard boundaries of statistical significance. There
are three primary observations to made based on figure 4.8 and table
4.7. First, there are clear regional differences in the political consequences of the internationalization of the American economy. High
growth, internationally competitive states backed free-trade policies,
while low-growth, relatively uncompetitive states supported policies
and programs aimed at protecting workers and firms from foreign competition (i.e., domestic content laws, trade adjustment assistance, trade-
remedy laws, etc.). Second, the historic positions of the political parties

have been reversed: elected officials from strongly Democratic states voted against liberal orthodoxy on trade matters, while Republican lawmakers were the ones who saw the advantages of "comparative advantage." Finally, in contrast to the 1930s, when much of the industrial Northeast had a stake in freer trade, by the 1980s the northern core was strongly protectionist, much as it had been in the late nineteenth and early twentieth centuries. By contrast, the West, the bedrock of trade protectionism in the 1930s, had become the most free-trade-oriented region, surpassing the South, which on balance stood somewhere between the protectionist Northeast and free-trade West.

The political logics of coalition-building and promoting constituents' interests thus go far in resolving the paradox of American support for an open international economy in the 1970s and 1980s. The Republicans exercised their growing power in Washington to champion freer trade and thus to cater to their expanding base in the West. To a large extent, their vision of "the national interest" prevailed. In building winning foreign policy coalitions, the challenge Republican leaders faced was figuring out how to keep the South in tow. Here, the key was not laissez-faire; it was military Keynesianism. This explains why Ronald Reagan and the Republicans engaged in what one of their own called "voodoo economics": increased defense spending may have violated the tenets of free trade, but "bad economics" made for good Republican politics. This explanation is simpler and more concrete than sectoral, institutional, and ideational explanations of United States support for freer trade in the era of rustbelt decline and waning American hegemony in the international system.

The Politics of Guns and Butter: The Reagan Buildup

There were few more divisive issues in the 1980s than national security. Although the public gave Reagan high marks as a "strong leader," his defense policies were the object of anxiety, derision, and conflict. In Congress, battles over issues such as the B-1 bomber, the MX missile, and "Star Wars" split lawmakers along sectional lines. Politicians from the Northeast, mostly Democrats, argued that the buildup was unnecessary, destabilizing, and wasteful. They agreed that America faced new international challenges and threats but argued that those challenges were more economic than military in nature: they had more to do with the nation's declining economic competitiveness than Soviet advantages in missile throw-weight, or even "communist gains" in the Third World. However potent those arguments were in the Northeast, they carried little weight in the sunbelt. Lawmakers from the South and West, Democrats as well as Republicans, dismissed the idea that the United States was suffering from economic decline. America's problem, they argued, was weak leadership. A "decade of neglect" had left the nation vulnerable to Soviet political intimidation and had seriously compromised its ability to check unrest in regions that were, they argued, of vital national interest: Central America, Southern Africa, and the Persian Gulf.

What explains these conflicts? Why did the Reagan buildup spark such heated debate over America's priorities? This book argues that debates over defense spending, like debates over foreign policy more generally, are grounded in conflicts of interest; they are grounded in uneven growth and development. Politicians face difficult trade-offs when thinking about defense policy. They weigh the economic benefits of federal military spending against *opportunity costs*. Politicians' assessments of the benefits and costs of military spending vary "across space and over time;" what remains constant is their preoccupation with anticipating how defense policies might affect the interests they represent in the medium- to long-run. In this section, I show that this was as true for the 1980s as it was one-hundred years earlier.[129] As in the great debate over naval expansion in the 1890s, politicians' views about America's security needs in the 1980s were grounded in conflicting sectional imperatives. Issues of national defense were seen in redistributive terms: a gain for one region was seen as a loss for another (at least by those representing the regional "loser"). What changed over the course of a century were the regional winners and losers. The Northeast, once the champion of large defense outlays, was now an ardent foe. The South, which waxed Jeffersonian on matters of defense one hundred years before, now spoke Hamilton's language. Defense expenditures that had once levied a harsh tax on southern income were now critical to southern growth. The West, at best a lukewarm enthusiast of military outlays in the 1930s, now championed defense spending.

Seen in this light, one of the "puzzles" of the Reagan/Bush years becomes less puzzling. In the 1980s, as in the 1970s, scholars looked hard for evidence to support the "military-industrial complex" thesis. Working within the framework of the "pork barrel" or distributive-politics model, they looked for links between politicians' views about national defense—hawk versus dove, conservative versus liberal—and the geographic distribution of military contracts, bases, and payrolls.[130] Searching for clues in congressional voting records, analysts found no direct or enduring connection. Many concluded that politicians' views on matters of national defense had very little to do with whether (or how much) their districts or states benefited from military spending. Most concluded that ideology drove politicians' views about defense.

This judgment is premature. It is based on a conception of interests that is far too narrow and a view of politicians that is far too simple. In particular, it ignores the important role that "cost" plays in politicians' judgments about what is good public policy. As James Q. Wilson pointed out in *Political Organization,* members of Congress are attentive to costs as well as benefits.[131] They are risk-averse: they seek to secure benefits (i.e., jobs, services, markets) at the lowest possible cost. When one factors in not only the economic benefits but also the opportunity costs of defense spending, the politics of defense spending during the Reagan years looks very different.

Regional Inequity and Federal Dollars

On September 1, 1976, two dozen members of Congress from states in the Northeast attended a meeting called by Michael Harrington, a Democratic firebrand from Boston. The congressmen were convinced that their districts and states were being shortchanged by Washington. Federal policies, they claimed, were regionally biased: they were catering to the interests of the South and West. By the time the meeting adjourned that day, the group had formed the Northeast-Midwest Congressional Coalition—a bipartisan congressional caucus devoted to work on pressing issues that affected the economic fortunes of the aging industrial heartland. Though they were chiefly concerned about the regional distribution of federal funds, their critique of Washington's funding practices was informed by an acute understanding of the fact that the northern core's position in the international economy was declining, and it was losing "economic share" in the national economy to the states south of the Mason-Dixon line and west of the Mississippi. Kirkpatrick Sale stated the case when he declared in 1975 that there had been a "power shift" from the Northeast toward the South and West. He, like Harrington and his followers, was onto something.[132]

What was perhaps most remarkable about the Northeast's relative decline was its pace. By most measures the region's dominance in the national economy, and for that matter the world economy, was secure as recently as the Korean War. In 1950, the Northeast still encompassed 49 percent of the nation's population and no less than 68 percent of its manufacturing employment.[133] The country's technological know-how was still heavily concentrated in the region, as were the vast majority of the nation's Fortune 500 industrial corporations. With the Northeast reaping the largest share of American economic growth, the rest of the country was seen, as geographer Edward Ullman put it, as fighting "for the remainder in a manner not unlike a pack of hungry dogs fighting over a dry bone."[134] The South, despite the huge economic gains it made during World War II, remained an industrial backwater in 1950. With 30 percent of the nation's population, it still held less than 20 percent of the nation's manufacturing jobs, and most of these were low-wage jobs.[135] The economic situation in the West was brighter, but with a few exceptions (most notably California) the region remained what Ullman called a "fringe area." Like the South, the West in the 1950s was a region "remote from the center of the system and the self-generating momentum of the center."[136]

Thirty years later the center of economic activity had shifted from the core area to the fringe areas.[137] Population change figures indicated that the most rapidly growing areas during the intervening decades were all in the South and West.[138] Over this same period the regional distribution of national income also changed significantly. The Northeast's share of national income dropped from 52.3 percent to 42.0 percent.[139] Employment data tell the same story as population and income statistics.[140] The weak performance of the Northeast reflected not only its high share of low-growth industries like manufacturing but also its low share of high-growth industries, particularly mining, finance and insurance and real estate, and services.[141] These high-growth industries helped drive the rapid economic ascendance of the sunbelt.

For years the Northeast had been losing its long-standing lead in population, income, and jobs to the South and West. The obvious question is why did the region's leaders wait until the 1970s to go on the offensive? The short answer is oil. Between 1970 and 1981 crude oil prices jumped from less than $5 per barrel to just under $40 per barrel.[142] Like the great fall in world grain prices one hundred years earlier, the huge 1973 rise in oil prices had an uneven geographic impact inside the United States. The Northeast, which depended on oil for nearly 80 percent of its energy needs, suffered the most. Northern industries, already suffering from high labor and energy costs, were suddenly faced with staggering increases in operating expenses and uncertainty about the future supply of oil. In the Great Recession of 1975, thousands of workers in the Northeast were laid off and small-business bankruptcy rates soared.[143] Although the 1973 Arab oil embargo meant higher fuel prices for all regions, the energy-rich South and West reaped windfall gains from the rise in energy prices. Income flowed out of energy-deficit states like Massachusetts, Michigan, and New York into energy-surplus states such as Colorado, Louisiana, and Texas. So did labor, as the pace of out-migration from the Northeast quickened. The geographic "terms of trade" shifted. Commodity exchange ratios, which once heavily favored the "core," now strongly tilted toward the "periphery." William Miernyk wrote that "in 1970, for example, 4.9 million cubic feet of Texas natural gas would buy 1,000 pounds of New York butter. By 1978, 1.1 million cubic feet of Texas gas would buy 1,000 pounds of New York butter."[144]

A little over a decade before, a major regional study had declared that "[t]he most striking feature in the history of American manufacturing is the enduring strength of the Northeast."[145] By the American bicentennial in 1976 this was no longer true. Relative decline in many areas of the Northeast gave way to absolute decline. Between 1970 and 1980, the region lost over 567,000 manufacturing jobs, 311,486 of them in metals industries, electrical machinery, and transportation equipment.[146] Many of these jobs were lost after 1975. "The states worst affected—Michigan, New Jersey, New York, Ohio, and Pennsylvania—lost employment in every major manufacturing sector."[147] In some areas unemployment rates threatened to approach the record levels of the Great Depression. The White House under Gerald Ford offered reassurances about the economy, but the recession dragged on. Northeastern politicians came under increasing pressure from business and labor to do something to solve the economic crisis.

Elected officials in the Northeast went into action. In June 1976, governors of seven northeastern states launched the first salvo in a sectional battle that *Business Week* dubbed "the Second War Between the States."[148] Raising the specter of the "cancer of depressed Appalachia" spreading throughout the Northeast, the coalition demanded massive infusions of federal moneys to stimulate recovery and reverse the desperate conditions in their cities.[149] "As the nation in the past recognized the development needs of the Western frontiers and the rural South," the governors argued, "so now the nation must acknowledge a similar commitment to the older yet still vibrant Northeast."[150] The formation of Harrington's Northeast-Midwest Coalition followed a few months later, as did other political organizations during Jimmy Carter's years in the White House. By the beginning of 1979, no less than twelve coalitions had formed to pressure Washington to help the Northeast regroup and chart a new economic course.[151] On Capitol Hill the Northeast-Midwest Coalition mobilized to reverse the regional "terms of trade." Membership in the organization swelled. By 1978 the organization had over 213 members, nearly half the membership of the House.

Inevitably, the South and West responded.[152] Southern lawmakers like John Buchanan (D-AL) urged their colleagues to develop "a countervailing force."[153] Senator Russell Long (D-LA) reinforced the point: "If our people don't get along and start working together, then we're going to suffer for it."[154] A beefed-up Southern Growth Policies Board was the South's answer. Originally established in 1971 to plan for growth and change in the region, the Board's focus quickly expanded in the mid-1970s as southern leaders searched for ways to counter charges about federal bias and interregional inequity. After decades of being the underdog in fights over Washington's fiscal priorities, southern lawmakers suddenly found themselves on the political defensive, searching for ways to explain away an apparent pro-southern tilt in federal spending. Was the federal government siphoning-off much needed capital from the struggling Northeast and pumping it into the booming South? By the late 1970s, this question more than any other was at the center of the growing conflict between the rustbelt and sunbelt—a struggle over federal resources that was increasingly viewed in zero-sum terms.[155]

The debate was fueled by the popular press, which began to evaluate national economic trends in the context of regional disparities in growth. In February 1976, the *New York Times* ran a front-page series arguing that the South was the largest and fastest growing region in the country, and that much of the region's growth was a result of a favorable balance of payments with the federal government.[156] The controversy sparked by this series was fueled by *Business Week*'s much-ballyhooed story about the population drain from the Northeast to the South and West.[157] This migration was attributed to lower wages, lower utility costs, and lower state and local taxes in the growing regions, as well as regional biases in federal flow-of-funds accounts. Next came a highly publicized article in the *National Journal* that argued that states from the sunbelt were receiving far more from Washington in grants and spending than they paid in federal taxes.[158] The implication was that such inequities were at least partly responsible for regional disparities in growth.

The issue of federal bias quickly emerged as the central one in Congress. Like southern members a century earlier, northern lawmakers now charged that federal policy was the chief culprit in creating their region's problems. Federal spending trends associated with defense spending provoked the most controversy. In the 1970s, the defense portion of the federal budget alone accounted for an estimated net loss of over $25 billion in revenues for the Northeast.[159] Without the "inequitable burden" of defense spending, the Northeast would have held its own in the federal budget. Some charged that the shift in the regional allocation of defense spending was politically motivated and traced this strategy to the Nixon administration's desire to create political patronage in the South and West—the electoral base of the Republican party.[160] Yet the tilt toward the sunbelt continued during the Carter years. Counter-pressures to redirect federal spending toward the manufacturing belt intensified. Elected officials from the Northeast, most of them Democrats, pursued a two-pronged strategy. They combined attempts to cut the Pentagon budget with various proposals to reformulate and liberalize criteria for allocating or targeting federal funds for revenue sharing, highway construction, unemployment compensation, and so forth.[161]

The Reagan Buildup

Fights over the Reagan buildup are best understood in this context. Between 1980 and 1985, military spending authority jumped from $143.9 billion to $294.7 billion. In inflation-adjusted dollars this represented a increase of almost 55 percent. In 1986, the apex of the Reagan buildup in terms of outlays, the military consumed $273 billion, a 48-percent increase over 1980 in constant dollars. Significantly, research and development of new high-tech weapons systems (e.g., the "stealth" bomber, ballistic missile defense, precision-guided munitions, etc.) absorbed a large portion of the increase.[162] In 1980, the Pentagon spent roughly 64 percent of its budget on operations. The remaining 36 percent went for new investment. These funds were lavished on high-tech growth industries.[163] By 1986, investments accounted for over 50 percent of the military budget, nearly 160 percent more in dollar terms than when Reagan took office.[164]

The main beneficiaries of the administration's high-tech defense

Table 4.8 Jobs Created and Lost through Military Buildup, 1981–85[1]

Region	Mean[2]	Std. Dev.	Minimum	Maximum
Northeast	1.08	1.71	0.07	6.77
New England	1.71	2.51	0.22	6.77
Middle Atlantic	0.98	1.38	0.07	3.42
Great Lakes	0.42	0.34	0.15	0.90
South	2.06	3.32	−0.26	12.47
Southeast	2.44	0.86	−0.17	12.47
Southwest	1.11	1.20	−0.26	2.36
West	1.65	1.59	0.13	5.12
Great Plains	1.37	1.89	0.18	5.12
Mountain	1.90	1.58	0.13	4.38
Pacific Coast	1.70	1.25	0.26	2.47
United States	1.58	2.26	−0.26	12.47

Source: Based on data from Marion Anderson, Michael Frisch, and Michael Oden, *The Empty Pork Barrel: The Employment Cost of the Military Build-up, 1981–1985* (Lansing, Mich.: Employment Research Associates, 1986).
Note: See table 2.1 for regional groupings. Alaska and Hawaii are not included.
[1] Based on manufacturing employment.
[2] A value greater than 1 indicates job growth; a value less than 1 indicates job loss.

strategy, measured in terms of gains in industrial employment from the Reagan buildup, were concentrated in the sunbelt, particularly in the South and West (table 4.8).[165] This means that the geography of defense production had changed dramatically since the 1930s. The industrial heartland had long been the locus of production of military hardware. During World War II, military production was concentrated in the Northeast, especially in the Great Lakes states, as well as in the emerging centers of West Coast production, California and Washington.[166] During the early years of the Cold War, the Northeast continued to receive over 60 percent of all prime military contracts.[167] Military spending continued to be concentrated in the Great Lakes region, with secondary concentrations in New England and the Mid-Atlantic states and the Pacific Coast. Gradually, however, the pattern of military spending shifted away from the Northeast and toward the South and West. By the Nixon years the manufacturing belt's share of defense contracts had fallen to about 37 percent. Meanwhile, the sunbelt received 54 percent.[168] In the 1980s the shift in defense spending toward the sunbelt accelerated. The Northeast's share fell to 34 percent, the sunbelt's rose to 58 percent. Big industrial states like Michigan, Ohio, and New Jersey that had once dominated the defense procurement sweepstakes had dropped out of the "top ten" defense producing states, while sunbelt competitors such as Texas, Missouri, Florida, Maryland, and Virginia had joined this elite club.[169] In the Northeast, only New York, Connecticut, and Massachusetts bucked the trend of a regional shift in defense spending toward the South and West.

The sunbelt proved to be the primary beneficiary of federal Cold War-related spending for several reasons.[170] The American military's growing reliance on highly capital- and technology-intensive weapons systems generated a "new locational logic."[171] Changes in Pentagon strategy and doctrine meant less demand for the traditional weapons industries—tanks, ordnance, shipbuilding—that had long been the "bread and butter" of the industrial heartland.[172] Sunbelt elites were quick to capitalize on this shift in military strategy. Local boosters—city officials, land developers, venture capitalists—acted as catalysts, drafting strategic plans, assembling land and offering inducements, and lobbying Congress. Military contractors seeking to reduce production costs found cost advantages in building their plants outside the Northeast, especially in the South. Labor costs and wages were low in the South, and the southern labor force was much less unionized than the North's. "Moreover, many of the products manufactured by military contractors were consumed at military bases, which themselves tended to be located south of the Mason-Dixon line."[173] The sunbelt's political clout reinforced this pattern. Powerful Southern congressional committee chairs used their clout and prerogative to funnel federal dollars into their home districts, bringing home the bacon in the form of weapons and supply contracts and military bases.

Most of the politicians from the South and West—many of whom were Democrats—backed the Republican buildup, and for good reason: they enjoyed most of the benefits and paid few of the costs. The big losers were located in the Northeast, especially in the older, smokestack economies of the Middle Atlantic and Great Lakes areas.[174] Here is where the "substitution effects" of the Reagan buildup—the civilian jobs lost—were most keenly felt.[175] Elected officials from the Northeast questioned the strategic merits of Reagan's military doctrines and programs. They also opposed the redistributive consequences of such large defense outlays and investments in high-tech weapons systems. Many viewed the Reagan military buildup as a de facto regional development policy for the sunbelt.

Struggles over jobs and defense dollars were also waged as sectional battles over broad strategic visions and definitions of the national interest. In the 1980s, as before, politicians' views of America's place in the world were shaped by the position of their home region in the world economy. The West and the South, the parts of the country that were now the most internationally competitive, were the strongest supporters of military and defense policies designed to guarantee continued American hegemony in the international system—forward defense, military aid, and heavy defense spending. Since these regions stood to reap most of the benefits of an activist foreign policy to assert American leadership, both in terms of its hoped-for effects on international commerce and its domestic spin-offs in the form of military procurement, southern and western lawmakers had a double-incentive to back the Reagan administration's efforts to make America's overseas military presence more visible. The situation facing lawmakers from the Northeast was quite different. Once at the cutting edge of international competition, the region was now losing "market share" to foreign competitors and clamoring for federal relief. Lawmakers from the Northeast were no longer willing to pay "overhead charges" of international leadership, which came in the form of heavy American defense and military aid expenditures.

Individual politicians also had the narrowest of electoral incentives for fighting over the defense budget. When lawmakers from the Northeast argued that the rearmament program was excessive and wasteful and proposed defense cutbacks, they were appealing to constituents in an era of sluggish growth in the region's big urban states. Voters in these states were sensitive to the social costs of the Reagan buildup, which many perceived to be high. Whereas sunbelt politicians feared appearing weak on national security, lawmakers from the rustbelt feared appearing weak or indifferent when it came to fighting for the material needs of their constituents (e.g., jobs, services, housing, taxes, and so on), especially since Reagan's tax cuts benefited higher income states the most, particularly those in the sunbelt.[176]

This is why "guns-versus-butter" trade-offs were prominent themes in the debates over Reagan's defense policies. Many of those who opposed the build-up believed that it disproportionately benefited the South and West, and they were right. What lawmakers from the sunbelt claimed was an unintended consequence of Reagan's efforts to make America's overseas military presence more visible, northern Democrats saw as a sunbelt-oriented industrial policy veiled in the garb of national security.[177] They saw it as a Republican "wedge": a policy designed to split Democrats along sectional lines and solidify the Republicans' political base in the South and West. At times the politics of defense in the Reagan years took shape as a partisan stand-off and appeared as a war of ideas between the parties. The basic alignments, however, were actually much simpler. Lawmakers from sluggish economies stressed domestic priorities; politicians representing robust ones championed a "strong defense."

An analysis of voting in the House of Representatives supports this view. Figure 4.10 summarizes the voting alignment over the Reagan buildup.[178] It shows that the debate over the administration's military policies broke down along sectional lines. Support for the White House's military policies was strongest in the South and West. Opposition was concentrated in the Northeast, and was especially strong in New England. The only regional exceptions are in the Great Lakes region, where Illinois (mean = 54 percent) and Indiana (mean = 57 percent) have support scores ranging as high as some states from the South. When the rest of the lower forty-eight states are included, it is also evident that the voting pattern in the Pacific Coast is similar to the pattern in the industrial Midwest. The Mountain West and the Great Plains are less homogeneous, with pockets of great support (e.g., Idaho, Nebraska, Utah, and Wyoming) and areas much less supportive (e.g., Iowa, North Dakota, and South Dakota). The average score in the manufacturing belt is 36 percent; the mean score in the sunbelt region is 67 percent. The national average is 52 percent.

These results are suggestive. More systematic analysis reveals that the conflict over the Reagan buildup was in fact interest-driven. Table 4.9 summarizes the results obtained through a cross-sectional analysis of voting in the 98th Congress. The dependent variable in the model is state support for Reagan's military policies—the same measure used to generate figure 4.10. Three independent economic variables are included: they measure the employment gains from the Reagan buildup (*Defense Gain*), rate of economic growth (*State Growth*), and vulnerability to international competition (*Trade Vulnerability*).[179] *Defense Gain* is the same measure used to generate table 4.8. *State Growth* measures the relative capacity of state economies to bear the social burden or costs of the Reagan military buildup. From the standpoint of national security, *Trade Vulnerability* measures the relative sensitivity of state delegations to the potential opportunity costs to state econ-

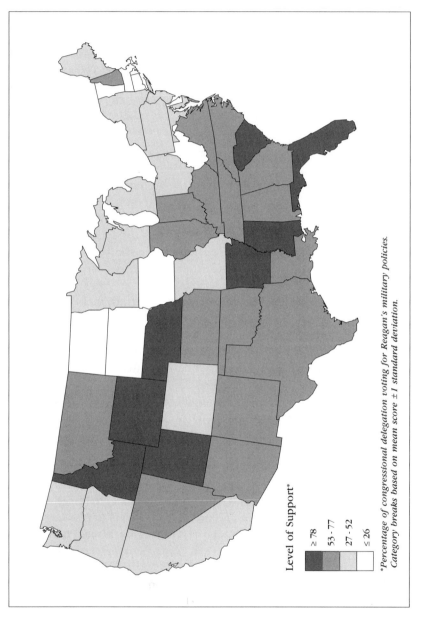

Level of Support*

≥ 78
53 - 77
27 - 52
≤ 26

*Percentage of congressional delegation voting for Reagan's military policies.
Category breaks based on mean score ±1 standard deviation.

Figure 4.10 Congressional Support for Military Buildup, 1983–84

Table 4.9 Analysis of House Support for
Military Buildup, 1983–84

Intercept	0.880
(Prob > |T|)	(0.001)
Defense gain	0.039
	(0.001)
Trade vulnerability	−0.220
	(0.001)
State growth	0.243
	(0.089)
Liberal	−0.002
	(0.028)
Democratic	−0.320
	(0.001)

Adjusted R^2: 0.652
Method: ordinary least squares
N: 48

omies of strategic policies to maintain American "hegemony" and promote international economic stability and trade. The model also includes the two political variables used in the preceding section: *Liberal* and *Democratic*. Again, *Liberal* is simply an index measuring support for liberal causes like labor, civil rights, and social welfare. *Democratic* is simply the percentage of Democrats in a state's House delegation, the assumption being that Democrats were, generally speaking, less inclined to support the Reagan buildup.

The analysis indicates that political support for the military buildup in the 1980s varied geographically and that local economic considerations were a decisive factor. The model supports the central argument that during the 1980s, as in other periods, politicians judged defense policies in terms of their opportunity costs as well as their benefits. The typical opponent of Reagan's national security agenda was a liberal Democrat from a slow growing, heavily urbanized state suffering from "deindustrialization." The profile of a pro-defense lawmaker was a representative from a fast growing, sunbelt state specializing in the production of military goods and holding its own in international markets.

Analysts who stress the importance of party and ideology in understanding the battles over defense spending in the post-Vietnam era are not completely off the mark. In the 1980s, party politics and ideological conflict reinforced a pattern of regional alignment whose roots can be traced to the 1960s, when economic power began to shift from the once-dominant northern core to the southern and western periphery. National security was an ideologically charged, partisan "hot button" issue in the 1980s for the same reason that it had been so divisive in the 1890s and 1930s: defense spending was viewed in *redistributive* terms.

Conclusion

Once the champion of Cold War internationalism, the urban-Northeast had become the defender of neo-isolationism by the 1980s, unwilling to pay the "overhead charges" of international stability and economic openness: large defense budgets, low tariff barriers, and extensive overseas commitments. Caught in the throes of "deindustrialization," political leaders in the largely Democratic Northeast backed a policy of continued "strategic retrenchment." They combined appeals for defense cutbacks with demands for increased protection from foreign imports and greater congressional control over the nation's warmaking capacity. In the 1980s, it was the once-solid Democratic South and the Republican West—America's newest industrialized regions—that had the most to gain from foreign policies that deployed American military power to check threats to international stability and that promoted the free movement of capital, goods, and currencies. Whatever effect defense spending had on economic competitiveness in the Northeast, it was an engine of rapid growth in America's sunbelt.

A strategy calling for increased defense spending and freer trade was a boon to Republican politics in the sunbelt. Both tenets appealed to their core sunbelt constituencies—aerospace, agribusiness, electronics, oil, construction, and real estate. Meanwhile, by pushing a foreign policy agenda antithetical to the interests of the Northeast, Republicans leaders heightened North-South tensions within the Democratic party and moved one step closer to cementing the sectional coalition that had eluded agrarians nearly one hundred years earlier: the Southern-Western alliance. In the foreign policy arena, the result of Republican success was the reversal of the 1970s decade of foreign policy retrenchment and the reassertion of American "leadership" in the international arena.

This analysis of foreign policy change in the 1980s goes far beyond conventional treatments that explain the reassertion of American power from the "outside-in," that is, as determined by events at the international level. Realist accounts identify international trends (growing Soviet power) and events (the Sandinista revolution in Nicaragua, the fall of the Shah of Iran, the Russian invasion of Afghanistan) as the sources of foreign policy change. The trouble with this "level of explanation" is not that it focuses on the international setting. The international situation facing America mattered in the 1980s, just as in the 1890s and 1930s. The problem is that the meaning of international trends and events—indeed, even what trends and events were meaningful—varied regionally in the United States. Anticipating the arguments developed and popularized by historian Paul Kennedy and others later in the decade, rustbelters defined the threat to the United States in the early 1980s in economic, as opposed to military, terms and stressed the need for the federal government to assume a larger, more active role in restoring American productivity and competitiveness in the world economy. For politicians who hailed from the sunbelt, those solutions were unattractive. The region's firms, workers, and voters had much less to fear from foreign competition and much to gain from a foreign policy that defined the principal threat in strategic-military terms and placed a premium on countering it.

Reversing the Rankean dictum on the primacy of foreign policy, this chapter argues that politicians in the 1980s thought about foreign policies the same way they thought about domestic politics: in terms of how they affect the interests of constituencies they represent and seek to mobilize. Put another way, political leaders treated matters of foreign policy—from national defense to international trade to foreign aid—as political resources. In the 1980s as in earlier periods, foreign policies were instruments of coalition building, party building, and electioneering, and for solving domestic political problems in ways that would protect or enhance the political standing of elected representatives, political parties, or presidents.[180]

Institutional explanations of American foreign policy are attentive to domestic-level constraints, but like realist accounts they misspecify the sources of foreign policy change and conflict. They forget that during the Reagan years, like other periods of American history, politics was not divorced from place. Fights over foreign policy during the 1980s were highly partisan, and analysts who point to this fact to explain the difficulties Republican leaders experienced in implementing their policies do have a point. What is missing from their accounts is an explanation for *why* the Republicans and Democrats disagreed so much over foreign policy. Analysts who fall back on ideology, noting for instance that Republicans were "tougher" on national defense and less protectionist in outlook than Democrats, only beg the question. They forget that it was the Democrats in the late 1940s who put together the policy package of military Keynesianism and laissez-faire trade that Republicans resurrected and pushed in the late 1970s and early 1980s. In order to explain the rise in party conflict over foreign policy and the changing ideological orientation of Republican and Democratic politicians, one must enter the realm of interests. It is here, in the shifting sectional bases of the parties, that the logic of party competition and conflict over foreign policy in the 1980s is found.

CHAPTER FIVE

Geopolitics and Foreign Policy

Statesmen in the future, as in the past, will achieve their leadership
by voicing the interests and ideas of the sections which have shaped
these leaders, and they will exert their influence nationally by making
combinations between sections and by accommodating their policy to
the needs of such alliances.

FREDERICK JACKSON TURNER, 1908

Introduction

Every era has writers who make America think hard about its place in
the world. In July 1893, a young historian from the University of Wisconsin, speaking at the Columbia Exposition at the Chicago World's
Fair, read a paper to a group of American historians.[1] No historian ever
penned a paper that so profoundly shook the nation's intelligentsia or
aroused the popular mind.[2] Writing in the midst of economic crisis and
populist insurgency, Frederick Jackson Turner sketched-out his famous
"frontier thesis," a historical interpretation of American political development suggesting that the nation's unique and true democracy was
the product of an expanding frontier. Westward expansion had been
the formative influence on American life: like a safety valve it re-
lieved the social and political tensions that came with rapid and uneven
growth. The problem, Turner declared, was that the frontier was disappearing. Americans were entering a new period in their history. No
longer would they be able to turn to the West to avoid the intractable
problems of a closed society. America's exceptional years were over.
It now faced the same choice that confronted other great nations in
the throes of economic depression and political upheaval: it could learn
to live as a self-contained society, with all that implied about redistributing wealth and power, or find new areas for expansion overseas.[3] Opting for the latter, the country broke its long-standing tradition of self-

isolation and embraced a vigorous, nationalistic, and imperial foreign policy.

A half-century later another writer, the prominent publisher Henry Luce, called America's attention to a new challenge and a new frontier. In a series of widely read editorials, Luce proclaimed an "American Century."[4] Claiming that the United States had passed up "a golden opportunity" after World War I "to assume the leadership of the world," he called on the American people to help Franklin Roosevelt succeed where Woodrow Wilson had failed. It was time for Americans "to accept wholeheartedly our duty and our opportunity as the most powerful and vital nation in the world." Isolationism and economic nationalism, he asserted, were disastrous, self-defeating policies. They had opened the door to aggression overseas and fueled the economic crisis that threatened democracy at home. If the United States was to preserve its way of life, it had to use its tremendous power to create an international capitalist marketplace that would be open to all, and that would embody the country's ideals of freedom, justice, and opportunity. Only a nation as powerful, and that enjoyed as much moral authority, as the United States could provide the leadership necessary to turn back the Axis powers, restore the peace, and build this new liberal world order. Henry Luce's vision was a commanding one: it became America's vision. His call to national greatness became the credo of American foreign policy and lay at the heart of the postwar order— the *Pax Americana.*

In the 1980s, no book spoke more to Americans' concerns about their place in the world than Paul Kennedy's. An unexpected bestseller, *The Rise and Fall of Great Powers* told a story of an America in decline, of a country that was living beyond its means.[5] As Kennedy saw it, the United States was suffering from the same ailment that had plagued Spain in the seventeenth century, France in the eighteenth, and Great Britain more recently: "imperial overstretch." The American century was over. The ambitious internationalist agenda that America's leaders set in the early Cold War years had led the country to invest scarce resources in ways that proved damaging over the long haul. The result was the gradual erosion of American power, measured in the standard ways (share of international growth, percent of world trade, share of international resources). Though it was still the world's leading power, America's overseas commitments now outdistanced its domestic capacity to sustain them. Kennedy's book was not a clarion call like

Luce's but a warning more in the tradition of Turner's famous paper. Kennedy suggested that America could avoid the fate of other great powers if it acted wisely and brought its commitments in alignment with its strengths. Its overseas strategic burdens had to be reduced and its domestic industrial plant had to be revitalized. Once again, America had to redefine its priorities.

Taken together, these three books trace a trajectory arcing across the twentieth century: the rise and decline of the *Northeast* in the world economy. Like Turner's expansionism and then Luce's liberal-internationalism, Kennedy's "declinism" described the interests and needs of America's industrial heartland.[6] Seen from afar, it is easy to confuse the Northeast's story with America's and to see the evolution of American foreign policy over the last century as a series of logical, almost inevitable, phases—a kind of chronicle of the nation's changing position in the international system. Many scholars do just this. In reality, of course, the tale of the Northeast is only part of the story, and the story itself was anything but predestined. It took politics to make America great. The nation's foreign policy is borne of conflict, and deep conflicts spring from uneven growth and development. It turns out that America is no exception to the "law of uneven development."[7] Its politics are not only about national identity or constitutional order; they are also about the distribution of wealth and power between rising and declining regions of the country. Scholars who ignore this reality miss the big structures and processes that have moved American foreign policy in the twentieth century, and that are carrying it into the next. In the end, the view that Turner reached toward the end of his life was right: sectionalism, not the frontier, is America's enduring political reality.

This book offers a new way of thinking about American foreign policy and the larger "geopolitical" forces that drive, shape, and animate it. It is a not a study of palace politics, bureaucratic gamesmanship, or "iron triangles." Rather it is an analysis of the larger macropolitical context within which politics "inside the Beltway" takes place. Looking through Turner's lenses on American politics, it reconstructs the great battles that have been waged over United States foreign policy in the twentieth century. The goal is to bring a sense of politics back into a field of study that far too often leaves out the stuff that comprises the warp and woof of American politics: party competition, coalition-building, logrolling, and struggles over the federal purse. The tendency of students of American politics to treat foreign policy analysis as though it were a distant relative, or even worse, an orphan, has not made the task any easier. It too is based on a mistaken premise: that what happens "out there" does not matter much "back here." It is as if these two domains—the international and the domestic—ran on separate tracks, like two trains rushing past each other toward their own destinations. This book shows that the two domains are interdependent. American foreign policies are determined by struggles that are typically assigned to the realm of domestic politics. Domestic political struggles, in turn, are often rooted in America's uneven integration into the international economy. And in the end, policy is made by politicians, who attend to the *local* consequences of policies and issues, be they foreign or domestic.

Ideas, Institutions, and Interests

Alexis de Tocqueville posed a big question that has claimed the attention of scholars ever since: Why is American foreign policy so conflict-prone? Why does a country as big and powerful as the United States so often behave as if it were weak and confused? This book challenges the ways American scholars have come to answer these questions. Where others stress the importance of ideas and institutions in explaining foreign policy conflicts, I give pride of place to interests. A comparative historical analysis shows that neither ideas nor institutions pack the explanatory punch needed to do the job. Once interests are taken into account, theories that place the burden of explanation on culture or the constitution collapse in on themselves. In the debates of the 1890s, 1930s, and 1980s, ideas were grounded in interests. As interests changed over time, so too did the values that regional elites espoused: the Hamiltonians of one era were Jeffersonians of another, and vice versa. Cultural explanations are static and therefore cannot explain these changes. Institutional explanations also fall short. In each of these periods, the most persistent and divisive conflicts were drawn along geographic "fault lines," not institutional boundaries. The Congress itself was deeply divided over foreign policy, and these conflicts were structured along sectional lines. The same was true of the parties. One or both were themselves divided over foreign policy—and those divisions were sectional in nature. In the final analysis, America's divided constitutional order and two-party system do not so much "invite" or cause struggle as permit it to flourish once it has arisen. And divisive conflicts over the basic direction of the nation's foreign policy spring from the helix of uneven growth. As one astute constitutional scholar observes: "If we could always agree where our true interests lie, the untidiness inherent in the Constitution would matter little."[8]

Explanations of American foreign policy that rest on ideas and institutions confuse symptoms with causes. Each approach is handicapped by its view of politicians. Cultural explanations view America's elected officials as though they were little more than surrogates of the Founding Fathers: poor substitutes to be sure, but substitutes nonetheless. Politicians are reduced to ideas, and politics is reduced to the clash of ideas. This is a very apolitical view of politics. Politicians may have strongly held beliefs but, they also have interests. For them, ideas are also political resources: instruments for mobilizing voters, building coalitions, and translating interests into foreign policy. When Republican leaders like James G. Blaine and Theodore Roosevelt waxed Hamiltonian, linking overseas expansion to national greatness, they were also playing politics, searching for ways to divide Populists along sectional lines and strengthen the party's control over the machinery of national government. Scholars who do not see "the national interest" as inherently political not only misread the present, they also view the past through rose-colored glasses.

Many institutionalists recognize that there is a strategic dimension to politics. They see political leaders, executives as well as legislators as strategic actors who are self-interested. Politicians seek power, influence, and approbation (votes) first; matters of principle come second. The problem with this view is not that it focuses on institutions per se, or that it insists that presidents and congressmen seek to protect and expand their institutional prerogatives and resources. Analysis of institutions is necessary; assumptions about political self-interest are sensible. The trouble with this view of American politics is that it strips away the larger socioeconomic context within which fights over institutional prerogative are played out. Institutionalists flesh out the "agents" that culturalists caricature, but like culturalists, their conception of "structure" is narrow and insufficiently contextualized. In each of the historical periods studied here, politicians were constrained by the harsh realities of economics. Their policy preferences reflected this essential but often disregarded fact. So did their attitudes toward the "proper" division of constitutional authority. As the case of the 1930s so amply demonstrates, politicians who represented parts of the country that stood to benefit most from the restoration of international order and liberal trade were only too happy to concede constitutional authority over foreign policy to a president committed to the cause of internationalism. The prospective "losers" did what those who see the proverbial writing on the wall always do: they fought hard to protect their constitutional prerogatives and the interests of those who depended on their power and influence in the Congress. Fifty years later, when the "losers" inherited control over the White House, they were transformed into enthusiastic advocates of a strong presidency.

Beyond Realism and *Innenpolitik*

A sectional approach explains why American foreign policy-making is so conflict-prone. It also offers new insight into the sources of foreign policy change. The field of international relations is divided between those who explain foreign policy change in terms of international opportunities and constraints, and those who argue that the fundamental parameters and impulses that shape foreign policy are rooted in the domestic political economy. In these research traditions, America has become a "critical case"—a testing ground for theory-building and a case in point for political argument. For Realists who wish to show that the international system, and a nation's position within it, is decisive in explaining the external behavior of nation-states, the United States, with its fragmented and decentralized political system, is considered the "hard test." If the theory holds for America, the canonical "weak state," then it must hold for other countries as well—nations with stronger, more centralized decision-making structures. For those who think about foreign policy from the "inside out" and wish to show that socioeconomic structure is crucial in shaping a nation's foreign policy, studying the United States has its methodological advantages as well. What better place to show that economic structure matters than in the United States, the "classless society."

Each approach has strengths and weaknesses. Realists draw our attention to the importance of international constraints, pressures, and opportunities in explaining a state's foreign policy. Big changes on the "outside" can lead to big changes on the "inside." One cannot begin to explain the shift in American foreign policy during the 1890s, 1930s, or 1980s without taking the international setting, with all its attendant pressures and possibilities, into account. The external environment matters. Where Realists go astray is in assuming that the internal consequences of international forces are spatially uniform. They are not, especially in countries as regionally diverse as the United States. Uneven growth means that the implications of international developments vary internally within the United States. For northern industrialists and southern cotton growers in the late nineteenth century, for example, the decline of British hegemony meant very different things: for the former it opened possibilities for commercial expansion; for the latter it threatened an already-weakened liberal trading order on which the South was vitally dependent. The point is this: the implications of changes in the external environment are indeterminate when it comes to explaining grand strategy.[9] International effects vary regionally, and must be translated into policy via a complex and competitive political process. During periods of transition in American foreign policy, this indeterminacy is conspicuous. It is manifest in bitter domestic struggles over policy and, at a deeper level, in conflicts over the very meaning of "the national interest."

Because Realists cast their analysis at the national level, and miss crucial geographic variations in the effects of external forces, they cannot explain how changes on "the outside" produce big changes on "the inside." They assume what needs to be shown: why one view of how America should respond to changing international conditions and circumstances triumphs over another. This is not simply an empirical inconvenience, a price that must be paid for building parsimonious theory. It cuts to the heart of the Realist project. Without a model that shows how conflicts over the meaning of international trends and events are mediated politically, they cannot account for what they purport to explain: programmatic changes in policy. In the final analysis, it is the realities of power inside a country, not the distribution of power in the international system, that determine the course of the nation's foreign policy. This is why America of the 1920s "failed" to assume a leading role in world affairs, and why America of the 1930s ultimately rose to the challenge. In the first instance, Republican leaders were unable to overcome sectional divisions within their party— divisions between regions that faced different international imperatives. The political earthquake of 1932 that put Roosevelt in the White House cleared the way for a new political alignment—a North-South alliance—that would preside over the creation of Henry Luce's American Century.

Foreign policy is not just about the world out there; it is also about politics here at home. In each period, foreign policy was used to solve political crises caused by economic upheaval. This is the reality that concerns those schooled in the tradition of *Innenpolitik* and its "Beardsian" variant on this side of the Atlantic. It views the strategic rationales of statesmen with a healthy dose of skepticism, and rightly roots foreign policy in the domestic social and economic structure of states. Those who attack scholars working in this genre for "reducing everything to material interests" miss the mark. This charge is simply not true: it remains an unfair criticism no matter how often it is repeated by scholars wedded to traditional and even so-called post-revisionist histories of American foreign policy. America's *Innenpolitikers* focus on linkages between ideology and economics. That is their great contribution to a field that far too often would have us believe that there was no connection whatsoever between the two. The trouble with the revisionist *Innenpolitik* accounts of foreign policy lies elsewhere. In exposing the limitations of traditional histories, they overdraw their case. They too assume what needs to be shown: how consensus is derived.[10] Revisionists study periods that were rent with political conflict over the direction of U.S. foreign policy. Typically, they try to finesse the issue by treating those fights as merely disputes over tactics between men who shared a common view of the national interest. This does an injustice to those who fought these battles, and a disservice to those who might learn from them. In America, as elsewhere, struggles over ends are fought out as battles over means.

Sectoral analysts have refined structuralist models of how domestic economic interests shape American foreign policy. They recognize that capitalists are not a monolithic bloc, and are attuned to the fact of uneven growth. Even so, this version of *Innenpolitik* has its limitations as a general model of foreign policy-making. It does not explain how business preferences are translated into policy outcomes. It is impossible to show that U.S. "grand strategy" is derived directly from the needs of America's capitalists. The fact that big business is often internally divided over questions of foreign policy forces politicians to maneuver and gives them room to do so. Meanwhile, in an economy as large and complex as America's, distinctions between "segments" of business *are* extremely important in thinking about how foreign policy is made, but just as important is a factor sectoralists neglect: the uneven *regional* distribution of industry, agriculture, and services. Sectoralists ironically buy into the myth of nationalization propagated by modernization theorists: that is, the idea that in the United States, as in other advanced industrial nations, the politics of place is a relic of the past. As geographer John Agnew points out, this "confuses a process with an outcome."[11] Indeed, despite decades of convergence in per capita incomes, the percentage of manufacturing employment, and heightened capital mobility, the American economy is marked by high degrees of regional specialization and differentiation. Popular images such as the "manufacturing belt," the "farm belt," the "sunbelt" capture this regional dimension of the national economy. These distinctions impose structure on the nation's politics, including the politics of foreign policy.

Like Realists, and like other *Innenpolitikers,* sectoral analysts theorize at the national level. In practice, however, their analyses are limited to the manufacturing belt. As this account of the 1930s shows, the triumph of internationalism cannot be explained by focusing only on the divisions within industry, or by ignoring the problems posed by America's weak state. In the 1930s, as in other periods, industrial interests—big and small, capital-intensive and labor-intensive, export-oriented versus import-oriented—had to contend with representatives of agrarian interests who occupied powerful positions at the national level. Roosevelt's genius, like Blaine's before him, lay in splitting agrarians' ranks along sectional lines. This time, the rural West was sacrificed to hold the agrarian South in tow. Without southern support, Roosevelt understood that he could not proceed down the internationalist path that the Eastern Establishment now so desperately wanted to walk. The point is that in a political system where power is as spatially decentralized as it is in the United States, political leaders pay close attention to the geographic implications of policies. During the 1930s, and more recently in the 1980s, political leaders put together foreign policy packages that were tailored to the needs of regionally specific interests. Sectoralists are interested in explaining programmatic transformations in foreign policy, and America's weak state *does* make it hard to initiate this kind of change. Institutionalists are not wrong to stress this, and this point can enrich sectoral analysis. What the analysis presented here shows is that it is at the regional level that the "building blocs" of winning political coalitions in America are found, and where the mediations between the international and the domestic, the "outside" and the "inside," lie. In this respect the present is no different than the past.

Déjà Vu All Over Again

Once again, America faces uncertain times. The country's leaders rejoice over the end of the Cold War, but they are divided over its meaning. For every one who claims that the collapse of communism and the opening of Central Europe offer new opportunities for America to solve its domestic economic and social problems, there is another who warns against excessive optimism about the future of international politics. Nowhere were these views more thoroughly aired, and the battle lines more sharply delineated, than in congressional debates over the defense budget and the so-called peace dividend in the early 1990s. The huge budget and trade deficits, coupled with the absence of a formidable foe on the international scene, made it hard to avoid the issue. Faced by the global realignment that began in *Mittleuropa* in 1989, even the most vigilant guardians of the military purse on Capitol Hill recognized that defense cutbacks in the budget were inevitable. The issue was how much should be cut and what should be done with the savings. The divisive question on the House and Senate floors was this: Should the savings be channeled into public investment (education, job training, and infrastructure) or be used to spur private consumption through deficit reduction or tax relief? Viewed from an economic perspective, these were matters of efficiency; seen from a political vantage point, these arguments were about power and the redistribution of wealth.

The debate over America's defense needs had a familiar ring, for its politics were well rehearsed. The debate pitted America's oldest region—the industrial Northeast—against its newest industrial regions—the South and West.[12] Politicians from the urban Northeast, mostly Democrats, led the chorus urging large-scale reductions in the Pentagon's budget and increased spending on neglected domestic programs and problems. Drawing on arguments popularized by "declinists" like Paul Kennedy, the neo-Keynesians of the North defined the threat to the United States in economic, not military, terms. They were the ones who looked to government to lead the way in restoring American competitiveness in the world economy. On the other side were the "sunbelters," the Gingrichs and Armeys, the lions of laissez-faire, who "liberated" Congress in 1994 from the clutches of the rustbelt politicians. They were the ones who cautioned America to pursue a more gradual and limited "downsizing" of the military, one that would not eviscerate the nation's military-industrial base or jeopardize its long-term ability to quickly project military power abroad. Whatever savings the country might derive from cutting the defense budget, they argued, should be used to reduce the huge federal deficit or cut personal income taxes, rather than to fund inefficient and costly Great Society-style domestic social and economic programs.

Like the debate over America's military buildup at the end of the last century, the debate over the "build-down" at the end of this one was framed in ideological terms. This time, however, it was the threat of fiscal insolvency, rather than the meaning of Treasury surpluses, that was the touchstone of public discourse. Most Democrats claimed that increased public investment would lead to deficit reduction; most Republicans insisted that tax cuts were the answer. Yet as before, lawmakers' positions today are shaped less by the abstract merits of various proposals for turning the peace dividend into fiscal solvents than by political competition for regional and partisan advantage. This is because different parts of the country had different stakes in how the savings were allocated. When Democrats made the case for increased public investment, they were speaking to the interests of their electoral base: the sluggish, densely overpopulated economies of the Northeast. By the same token, Republicans who insisted that private incentives offered the most efficient route to economic growth and deficit reduction knew only too well that those arguments played well in the South and West—regions that do not bear the heavy burden of the urban decay, industrial decline, and welfare dependency that confront Democrats from the "core." The commotion over the peace dividend is a reminder of how much the politics of American foreign policy have changed in the last century, and of how much they have remained the same.

Notes

Chapter One

1. See, for example, Paul Kennedy, *The Rise and Fall of the Great Powers: Economic Change and Military Conflict from 1500 to 2000* (New York: Random House, 1987), 529; Joseph S. Nye, Jr., *Bound to Lead: The Changing Nature of American Politics* (New York: Basic Books, 1990), 219–30.

2. Alexis de Tocqueville, *Democracy in America,* 2 vols. (New York: Alfred A. Knopf, 1945); Walter Lippmann, *The Public Philosophy* (Boston: Little, Brown, 1955); George F. Kennan, *The Cloud of Danger: Current Realities of American Foreign Policy* (Boston: Little, Brown, 1977). For a general overview of this and related literature see Miroslav Nincic, *Democracy and Foreign Policy: The Fallacy of Political Realism* (New York: Columbia University Press, 1992), 1–24. On the national interest see W. David Clinton, *The Two Faces of National Interest* (Baton Rouge: Louisiana State University Press, 1994).

3. The standard references on the consequences for American diplomacy are Hans J. Morgenthau, *In Defense of the National Interest* (New York: Alfred Knopf, 1951); Henry Kissinger, *The Necessity for Choice: Prospects of American Foreign Policy* (New York: Harper and Row, 1960); George F. Kennan, *American Diplomacy: 1900–1950* (Chicago: University of Chicago Press, 1950); Stanley Hoffmann, *Gulliver's Troubles; or, the Setting of American Foreign Policy* (New York: McGraw-Hill, 1968). For a contrary view see Kenneth N. Waltz, *Foreign Policy and Democratic Politics: The American and British Experience* (Boston: Little, Brown, 1967).

4. This formulation is best expressed in Felix Gilbert's classic *To the Farewell Address: Ideas of Early American Foreign Policy* (Princeton: Princeton University Press, 1961). See also Michael H. Hunt, *Ideology and U.S. Foreign Policy* (New Haven: Yale University Press, 1987); Samuel P. Huntington, *American Politics: The Promise of Disharmony* (Cambridge: Harvard University Press, 1981); Walter A. McDougall, *Promised Land, Crusader State: The American Encounter with the World since 1776* (Boston: Houghton Mifflin, 1997); Robert Osgood, *Ideals and Self-Interest in America's Foreign Relations* (Chicago: University of Chicago Press, 1953); Paul Seabury, *Power, Freedom, and Diplomacy: The Foreign Policy of the United States* (New York: Random House, 1963); Robert Strausz-Hupé, *Democracy and American Foreign Policy: Reflections on the Legacy of Alexis de Tocqueville* (New Brunswick, N.J.: Transaction, 1995).

5. Edwin Corwin's *The President's Control of Foreign Relations* (Princeton:

Princeton University Press, 1917) is the touchstone here. See also Louis Henkin, *Foreign Affairs and the Constitution* (New York: Norton, 1972); George C. Edwards, III, and Wallace Earl Walker, eds., *National Security and the U.S. Constitution: The Impact of the Political System* (Baltimore: Johns Hopkins University Press, 1988); Harold Hongju Koh, *The National Security Constitution: Sharing Power after the Iran-Contra Affair* (New Haven: Yale University Press, 1990); Theodore J. Lowi, *The End of Liberalism: The Second Republic of the United States* (New York: W. W. Norton, 1969); Michael Mastanduno, "The United States Political System and International Leadership: A 'Decidedly Inferior' Form of Government," in *American Foreign Policy: Theoretical Essays,* 2d ed., edited by G. John Ikenberry (New York: HarperCollins, 1996), 328-48. For a good discussion of the relationship between American institutions and American strategy see Aaron Friedberg, "Is the United States Capable of Acting Strategically?" *Washington Quarterly* 14 (winter 1991): 5-23.

6. On this distinction and its impact on foreign policy-making see Stephen D. Krasner, *Defending the National Interest: Raw Materials Investments and U.S. Foreign Policy* (Princeton: Princeton University Press, 1978), 63-64; David A. Lake, *Power, Protection, and Free Trade: International Sources of U.S. Commercial Strategy, 1887-1939* (Ithaca: Cornell University Press, 1988), 69-72; Jack Snyder, *Myths of Empire: Domestic Politics and International Ambition* (Ithaca: Cornell University Press, 1991), 51. For a more general discussion of relationship between political institutions and governance in the United States see John E. Chubb and Paul E. Peterson, "American Political Institutions and the Problem of Governance," in *Can the Government Govern?* ed. John E. Chubb and Paul E. Peterson (Washington, D.C.: Brookings Institution, 1989), 1-43.

7. The terms "sectional" and "regional" are used interchangeably.

8. In making this assumption, I follow a vast literature on the study of American politics. A seminal work is David R. Mayhew, *Congress: The Electoral Connection* (New Haven: Yale University Press, 1974).

9. Among the works that best represent this tradition are E. H. Carr, *The Twenty Years' Crisis, 1919-1939: An Introduction to the Study of International Relations* (1939; reprint, London: Macmillan, 1962); Hans J. Morgenthau, *Politics among Nations: The Struggle for Power and Peace,* 5th ed. (New York: Knopf, 1973); Arnold Wolfers, *Discord and Collaboration: Essays on International Politics* (Baltimore: Johns Hopkins University Press, 1962); Kenneth N. Waltz, *Theory of International Politics* (New York: Random House, 1979); Robert Gilpin, *U.S. Power and the Multinational Corporation* (New York: Basic Books, 1975); Krasner, *Defending the National Interest.*

10. Kenneth N. Waltz, "A Response to My Critics," in *Neorealism and Its Critics,* ed. Robert O. Keohane (New York: Columbia University Press, 1986), 329.

11. The classic accounts are John A. Hobson, *Imperialism; A Study* (1902; reprint, London: Allen and Unwin, 1938); Joseph Schumpeter, "The Sociology of Imperialism," in *Imperialism and Social Classes,* trans. Heinz Norden (New York: Augustus M. Kelley, 1951), 3-83; Eckart Kehr, *Battleship Building and Party Politics in Germany, 1894-1901: A Cross Section of the Political, Social, and*

Ideological Preconditions of Germany Imperialism, trans. Pauline R. Anderson and Eugene N. Anderson (1930; reprint, Chicago: University of Chicago Press, 1973). See also Arno J. Mayer, "Internal Causes and Purposes of War in Europe, 1870-1956: A Research Assignment," *Journal of Modern History* 41 (September 1969): 291-303.

12. Some of the earliest and best work in this tradition includes Lloyd C. Gardner, *Economic Aspects of New Deal Diplomacy* (Madison: University of Wisconsin Press, 1964); Walter LaFeber, *The New Empire: An Interpretation of American Expansion, 1860-1898* (Ithaca: Cornell University Press, 1963); Thomas J. McCormick, *China Market: America's Quest for Informal Empire, 1893-1901* (Chicago: Quadrangle Books, 1967); William Appleman Williams, *The Roots of the Modern American Empire: A Study of the Growth and Shaping of Social Consciousness in a Marketplace Society* (New York: Random House, 1969).

13. See, for example, Joyce Kolko and Gabriel Kolko, *The Limits of Power: The World and United States Foreign Policy, 1945-1954* (New York: Harper and Row, 1972).

14. See, for example, Bruce Cumings, *The Origins of the Korean War,* vol. 2, *The Roaring of the Cataract, 1947-1950* (Princeton: Princeton University Press, 1990); Lynn Eden, "Capitalist Conflict and the State: The Making of United States Military Policy in 1948," in *Statemaking and Social Movements: Essays in History and Theory,* ed. Charles Bright and Susan Harding (Ann Arbor: University of Michigan Press, 1984), 233-61; Thomas Ferguson, "From Normalcy to New Deal: Industrial Structure, Party Competition, and American Public Policy in the Great Depression," *International Organization* 38 (winter 1984): 41-94; Jeffry A. Frieden, "Sectoral Conflict and U.S. Foreign Economic Policy, 1914-1940," *International Organization* 42 (winter 1988): 59-90; Peter Gourevitch, "International Trade, Domestic Coalitions, and Liberty: Comparative Responses to the Crisis of 1873-1896," *Journal of Interdisciplinary History* 8 (fall 1977): 281-313; Franz Schurmann, *The Logic of World Power: An Inquiry into the Origins, Currents, and Contradictions of World Politics* (New York: Pantheon Books, 1974). For a related approach see Ronald Rogowski, *Commerce and Coalitions: How Trade Affects Domestic Political Alignments* (Princeton: Princeton University Press, 1989).

15. This is obvious in the case of realist accounts of foreign policy change, but it is also true in the case of sectoral approaches. While these make allowances for transnational processes, they nevertheless make few allowances for geography. This is surprising given the extent to which industrial sectors are regionally concentrated in the United States. For an exception see James Kurth's "Between Europe and America: The New York Foreign Policy Elite," in *Capital of the American Century: The National and International Influence of New York City,* ed. Martin Shefter (New York: Russell Sage, 1993), 71-94.

16. John Agnew, *The United States in the World-Economy: A Regional Geography* (Cambridge: Cambridge University Press, 1987); D. W. Meinig, *The Shaping of America: A Geographical Perspective on 500 Years of History,* vols. 1 and 2 (New Haven: Yale University Press, 1986-93); Carville Earle, *Geographical Inquiry and American Historical Problems* (Stanford: Stanford University Press,

1992). These and other works deemphasize national boundaries and prioritize the analysis of regional economies. In this way they parallel—and in fact draw on—other transnational histories, most notably Wallerstein's treatment of the modern world economy and the *Annales* School's account of the rise of nation-states. See Immanuel Wallerstein, *The Capitalist World-Economy* (Cambridge: Cambridge University Press, 1979); Fernand Braudel, *The Mediterranean and the Mediterranean World in the Age of Philip II*, 2 vols., trans. Sian Reynolds (New York: Harper and Row, 1972–73); and the contributions in Eugene D. Genovese and Leonard Hochberg, eds., *Geographic Perspectives in History* (New York: Basil Blackwell, 1989). For a good discussion of the relevance of these and other transnational approaches to America's historical development see Ian Tyrrell, "American Exceptionalism in an Age of International History," *American Historical Review* 96 (October 1991): 1031–55.

17. The main exception here is Schurmann. See his *The Logic of World Power*. See also Kurth, "Between Europe and America."

18. V. O. Key, *Politics, Parties, and Pressure Groups* (New York: Thomas Y. Crowell, 1964), 229.

19. E. E. Schattschneider, *The Semisovereign People: A Realist's View of Democracy in America* (New York: Holt, Rinehart and Winston, 1960); Walter Dean Burnham, *Critical Elections and the Mainsprings of American Politics* (New York: W. W. Norton, 1970).

20. Most of the work on sectionalism and foreign policy is historiographic and section specific. There is much excellent work in this tradition. See, for example, Ray A. Billington, "The Origins of Middle Western Isolationism," *Political Science Quarterly* 60 (March 1945): 44–64; Edward W. Chester, *Sectionalism, Politics, and American Diplomacy* (Metuchen, N.J.: Scarecrow Press, 1975); Wayne S. Cole, *Roosevelt and the Isolationists, 1932–45* (Lincoln: University of Nebraska Press, 1983); Justus D. Doenecke, *Not to the Swift: The Old Isolationists in the Cold War Era* (Lewisburg, Pa.: Bucknell University Press, 1979); George L. Grassmuck, *Sectional Biases in Congress on Foreign Policy* (Baltimore: Johns Hopkins University Press, 1951); Alfred O. Hero, Jr., *The Southerner and World Affairs* (Baton Rouge: Louisiana State University Press, 1965); Charles O. Lerche, Jr., *The Uncertain South: Its Changing Patterns of Politics in Foreign Policy* (Chicago: Quadrangle Books, 1964); Leroy N. Rieselbach, *The Roots of Isolationism* (Indianapolis: Bobbs-Merrill, 1966).

21. Frederick Jackson Turner, *The Significance of Sections in American History* (New York: Holt, Rinehart and Winston, 1932). The quote is from Turner's typescript, "The Significance of the Section in the U.S.," May 1922, cited in Michael C. Steiner, "The Significance of Turner's Sectional Thesis," *Western Historical Quarterly* 10 (October 1979): 440.

22. Quoted in Steiner, "Significance of Turner's Sectional Thesis," 458.

23. For Turner and his disciples, sectionalism was simultaneously a source of strife and "an alternative to 'toxic' European nationalism." It was America's cross and America's salvation. Steiner, "Significance of Turner's Sectional Thesis," 458.

24. See Agnew, *The United States in the World-Economy;* J. Clark Archer and Peter J. Taylor, *Section and Party: A Political Geography of American Presidential Elections* (New York: John Wiley, 1981); Richard Franklin Bensel, *Sectionalism and American Political Development, 1880-1980* (Madison: University of Wisconsin Press, 1984); Ann R. Markusen, *Regions: The Economics and Politics of Territory* (Totowa, N.J.: Rowman & Littlefield, 1987).

25. Bensel, *Sectionalism and American Political Development,* 4.

26. See Sidney Tarrow, *Between Center and Periphery: Grassroots Politicians in Italy and France* (New Haven: Yale University Press, 1977); William Brustein, *The Social Origins of Political Regionalism: France, 1849-1981* (Berkeley and Los Angeles: University of California Press, 1988); Michael Hechter, *The Microfoundations of Macrosociology* (Philadelphia: Temple University Press, 1983).

27. On the macro-micro distinction see J. Clark Archer, "Macrogeographical versus Microgeographical Cleavages in American Presidential Elections: 1940-1984," *Political Geography Quarterly* 7 (1988): 111-25. For a contrary view on the importance of regional culture see Daniel J. Elazar, *American Federalism: A View from the States* (New York: Thomas Y. Crowell, 1972). For a critique of Elazar's approach that takes it on its own terms see Richard J. Ellis, *American Political Cultures* (New York: Oxford University Press, 1993), 65-69.

28. The best single account of this process is David R. Meyer, "The National Integration of Regional Economies, 1860-1920," in *North America: The Historical Geography of a Changing Continent,* ed. Robert D. Mitchell and Paul A. Groves (London: Hutchinson, 1987), 321-46. See also Paul Krugman's *Geography and Trade* (Cambridge: MIT Press, 1991), especially 1-34.

29. As Agnew points out, those who assume that sectionalism has been displaced by the "nationalization" of the American political economy "confuse a process with an outcome." Agnew, *United States in the World-Economy,* 94. See also Ann R. Markusen, *Profit Cycles, Oligopoly, and Regional Development* (Cambridge: MIT Press, 1985); Richard Peet, "The Geography of Class Struggle and the Relocation of United States Manufacturing Industry," in *International Capitalism and Industrial Restructuring,* ed. Richard Peet (Boston: Allen and Unwin, 1987), 40-71.

30. On the general topic of uneven regional growth see Neil Smith, *Uneven Development: Nature, Capital and the Production of Space* (Oxford: Basil Blackwell, 1984).

31. For a discussion see Michael J. Healey and Brian W. Ilbery, *Location and Change: Perspectives on Economic Geography* (Oxford: Oxford University Press, 1990), 45-68. The classic application of this approach to the United States is Douglas C. North, *The Economic Growth of the United States, 1790-1860* (Englewood Cliffs, N.J.: Prentice-Hall, 1961).

32. On the regional consequences of technological innovation see Michael Storper and Richard Walker, *The Capitalist Imperative: Territory, Technology, and Industrial Growth* (Oxford: Basil Blackwell, 1989); John Rees and Howard Stafford, "Theories of Regional Growth and Industrial Location: Their Relevance

for Understanding High-Technology Complexes," in *Technology, Regions and Policy,* ed. John Rees and Howard Stafford (Totowa, N.J.: Rowan and Littlefield), 23–50. On the role of labor markets see Doreen Massey, *Spatial Divisions of Labor: Social Production and the Geography of Production* (New York: Methuen, 1984).

33. A review of the issues and literature can be found in Iain Wallace, *The Global Economic System* (London: Unwin Hyman, 1990). For specific reference to the United States see Agnew, *The United States in the World-Economy.*

34. On the importance of the state in analyzing regional development see, for example, Robert J. Johnston, "The State, Political Geography, and Geography," in *New Models in Geography,* ed. Richard Peet and N. J. Thrift (London: Unwin Hyman, 1989), 1:292–309; Robert Sack, "Territorial Bases of Power," in *Political Studies from Spatial Perspectives,* ed. Alan Burnett and Peter Taylor (New York: John Wiley, 1981). For a discussion of the role of the state in the American context see Markusen, *Regions,* 32–39; Norman J. Glickman, *The Urban Impacts of Federal Policies* (Baltimore: Johns Hopkins University Press, 1980).

35. Export dependence refers to the net balance of regional exports to regional imports, as well as to the relative importance of these exports vis-à-vis total regional production. Thus, a region's export dependence measures its sensitivity to reductions in regional sales abroad.

36. The logic here is similar to that developed in sectorally based models of foreign economic policy. See, for example, Peter Gourevitch, *Politics in Hard Times: Comparative Responses to International Economic Crises* (Ithaca: Cornell University Press, 1986), especially 55–60; Frieden, "Sectoral Conflict and U.S. Foreign Economic Policy"; and Ferguson, "From Normalcy to New Deal."

37. In the nineteenth century, England functioned as the world's hegemon; since 1945, America has. The seminal account is Charles P. Kindleberger, "Dominance and Leadership in the International Economy: Exploitation, Public Goods, and Free Rides," *International Studies Quarterly* 25 (1981): 242–54. See also the discussions in Robert Gilpin, *The Political Economy of International Relations* (Princeton: Princeton University Press, 1987); Robert O. Keohane, *After Hegemony: Cooperation and Discord in the World Political Economy* (Princeton: Princeton University Press, 1984). My thinking on this issue was sharpened by Thomas J. McCormick's provocative rendition of the theory from a world systems perspective. See his "World Systems," *Journal of American History* 77 (June 1990): 125–32.

38. There is a large literature on the regional consequences of defense expenditures. See, for example, Ann R. Markusen et al., *The Rise of the Gunbelt: The Military Remapping of Industrial America* (New York: Oxford University Press, 1991); Breandán Ó hUallacháin, "Regional and Technological Implications of the Recent Buildup in American Defense Spending," *Annals of the Association of American Geographers* 77 (spring 1987): 208–23; Marion Anderson, Michael Frisch, and Michael Oden, *The Empty Pork Barrel: The Employment Cost of the Military Build-up, 1981–1985* (Lansing, Mich.: Employment Research Associates, 1986); John Rees, "The Impact of Defense Spending on Regional Industrial Change

in the United States," in *Federalism and Regional Development*, ed. George Hoffman (Austin: University of Texas Press, 1981), 193–222.

39. See Markusen et al., *Rise of the Gunbelt*.

40. Peter Trubowitz and Brian E. Roberts, "Regional Interests and the Reagan Military Buildup," *Regional Studies* 26 (October 1992): 555–67. See also Ben Baack and Edward John Ray, "The Political Economy of the Origins of the Military-Industrial Complex in the United States," *Journal of Economic History* 45 (June 1985): 369–75.

41. The literature here is large. See, for example, Robert A. Bernstein and William A. Anthony, "The ABM Issue in the Senate, 1968–1970: The Importance of Ideology," *American Political Science Review* 68 (1974): 1198–1206; James Clotfelter, "Senate Voting and Constituency Stake in Defense Spending," *Journal of Politics* 32 (1970): 979–83; James M. Lindsay, "Parochialism, Policy, and Constituency Constraints: Congressional Voting on Strategic Weapons Systems," *American Journal of Political Science* 34 (1990): 936–60; Kenneth R. Mayer, *The Political Economy of Defense Contracting* (New Haven: Yale University Press, 1991); Wayne Moyer, "House Voting on Defense: An Ideological Explanation," in *Military Force and American Society*, ed. Bruce Russett and Alfred Stepan (New York: Harper and Row, 1973) 106–41; Barry S. Rundquist, "On Testing a Military Industrial Complex Theory," *American Politics Quarterly* 6 (1978): 29–53; Bruce Russett, *What Price Vigilance?* (New Haven: Yale University Press, 1970).

42. This argument is in no way limited to narrow procurement issues. As I show, it holds for broader strategic issues as well—issues having to do with military commitments, foreign intervention, and overseas military deployments. This is because there is a close relationship between choices about broad strategic matters and pork barrel issues: the strategic agenda affects the overall size and composition of the defense budget. On the relationship between strategy and defense budgets see Arnold Kanter, *Defense Politics: A Budgetary Perspective* (Chicago: University of Chicago Press, 1975). See also the discussion in Trubowitz and Roberts, "Regional Interests and the Reagan Military Buildup."

43. See, for example, Samuel P. Hays, *The Response to Industrialism, 1885–1914*, 13th ed. (Chicago: University of Chicago Press, 1971), 132–36.

44. This phrase is from Peter Gourevitch, *Politics in Hard Times*, p. 239.

45. See John W. House, ed., *United States Public Policy: A Geographical View* (Oxford: Clarendon Press, 1983); Stanley D. Brunn, *Geography and Politics in America* (New York: Harper and Row, 1974).

46. See Markusen, *Regions*. See also David W. Brady, *Critical Elections and Congressional Policy Making* (Stanford: Stanford University Press, 1988), 1–19. A similar view of the state as fragmented and weak (developed from a national rather than regional perspective) informs much contemporary research in international relations that uses the United States as a "case study." See Peter Katzenstein, "International Relations and Domestic Structures: Foreign Economic Policies of Advanced Industrial States," *International Organization* 30 (winter 1976): 1–45; Krasner, *Defending the National Interest*, 55–90.

47. Burnham, *Critical Elections*, 176.

48. Burdett A. Loomis, "Congressional Caucuses and the Politics of Representation," in *Congress Reconsidered,* 2d ed., edited by Lawrence C. Dodd and Bruce I. Oppenheimer (Washington, D.C.: Congressional Quarterly Press, 1981), 204–20.

49. James T. Patterson, *Congressional Conservatism and the New Deal: The Growth of the Conservative Coalition in Congress, 1933–1939* (Lexington: University of Kentucky Press, 1967).

50. Samuel Beer, "The Modernization of American Federalism," *Publius* 3 (1973): 49–95; John W. House, "The Policy Arena," in House, *United States Public Policy,* 1–33; Ronan Paddison, *The Fragmented State: The Political Geography of Power* (New York: St. Martin's Press, 1983).

51. Archer and Taylor, *Section and Party,* 112.

52. See, for example, Schattschneider, *Semi-Sovereign People,* especially 60–94; Archer and Taylor, *Section and Party,* 110–13. For the perspective of a former practitioner of the "art" see Kevin P. Phillips, *The Emerging Republican Majority* (Garden City, N.Y.: Anchor Books, 1970).

53. Years ago Arthur Holcombe put this point as well as anyone could: "[N]ational parties, which are built up in the manner described by Tocqueville—that is, through the combination of such interests as can be collected around and amalgamated with those of its leaders—must rest upon the support of interests which are, or might be, able to dominate the politics of particular localities or sections of the country. National politics is inseparable from sectional politics." He went on to add that "[n]ational parties cannot be maintained by transitory impulses or temporary needs. They must be founded upon permanent sectional interests, above all upon those of an economic character." See Arthur N. Holcombe, *The Political Parties of To-Day: A Study in Republican and Democratic Politics* (New York: Harper & Brothers, 1924), 40.

54. For examples, see Elizabeth Sanders, "Industrial Concentration, Sectional Competition, and Antitrust Politics in America, 1880–1980," in *Studies in American Political Development,* ed. Karren Orren and Stephen Skowronek (New Haven: Yale University Press, 1986), 1:142–214.

55. Archer and Taylor, *Section and Party;* Bensel, *Sectionalism and American Political Development;* Carville, *Geographical Inquiry and American Historical Problems.*

56. Burnham, *Critical Elections.*

57. On the distinction between "society-centered" and "state-centered" approaches to foreign policy-making see G. John Ikenberry, David A. Lake, and Michael Mastanduno, "Introduction: Approaches to Explaining American Foreign Economic Policy," *International Organization* 42 (winter 1988): 1–14.

58. Both attach great weight to societal interests in explaining state behavior, and each starts from the assumption that in the main, politics is about wealth, power, and the means for producing, distributing, and redistributing it. For those working within the tradition of class analysis, the unit of analysis is typically groups, strata, or sectors. Class-based explanations are most closely associated

with Charles A. Beard and his famous *An Economic Interpretation of the Constitution of the United States* (New York: Macmillan, 1941). Beard's views were influenced by Kehr. See note 11 above.

59. Turner, *Significance of Sections,* 32.

60. Harvey S. Perloff et al., *Regions, Resources, and Economic Growth* (Baltimore: Johns Hopkins Press, 1960), 4.

61. "The Northeast" refers to states in New England, the Middle Atlantic, and the Great Lakes areas: Connecticut, Delaware, Illinois, Indiana, Maine, Maryland, Massachusetts, Michigan, New Hampshire, New Jersey, New York, Ohio, Pennsylvania, Rhode Island, Vermont, and Wisconsin. "The South" includes states from the Southeast and Southwest: Alabama, Arkansas, Florida, Georgia, Kentucky, Louisiana, Mississippi, North Carolina, Oklahoma, South Carolina, Tennessee, Texas, Virginia, West Virginia. "The West" refers to states from the Great Plains, Mountain West, and Pacific Coast: Arizona, California, Colorado, Idaho, Iowa, Kansas, Minnesota, Missouri, Montana, Oregon, Nebraska, Nevada, New Mexico, North Dakota, South Dakota, Utah, Washington, and Wyoming. Alaska and Hawaii are not included.

62. Moreover, much of the aggregate economic data that is so crucial to telling this story uses comparable regional categories or related subregional groupings.

63. The phrase is loosely adapted from J. David Greenstone, "Political Culture and American Political Development: Liberty, Union, and the Liberal Bipolarity," in Orren and Skowronek, *Studies in American Political Development,* 1: 1-49.

64. The phrase is Samuel P. Huntington's, *Political Order in Changing Societies* (New Haven: Yale University Press, 1968), 110.

65. This "version" of the argument is underdeveloped in the foreign policy literature.

66. The decision to focus on the House, as opposed to the Senate, is largely one of analytic convenience. Since the unit of aggregation is "states," state delegations in the lower chamber are most suitable from a methodological standpoint. In principle, this choice entails some cost in generalizability, due to differences in the institutional structures and, most important from the standpoint of foreign policy, the constitutional prerogatives of the House and Senate. As a practical issue, this proves to be less of a problem. All of the issues covered in the study were debated and voted in both chambers. Moreover, in several instances the "key" votes were in the House, not the Senate.

67. Turner made the same methodological move. He and his followers relied heavily on roll calls to illustrate sectional competition. For Turner, this was a second-best solution: he believed that sectionalism was even more pervasive at other, less public and more informal stages of the legislative process, most notably in committee chambers.

68. Bensel, *Sectionalism and American Political Development,* 7.

69. I use "foreign intervention" when referring to issues concerning territorial expansion, overseas commitments, and military intervention.

Chapter Two

1. Robert Wiebe, *The Search for Order, 1877–1920* (New York: Hill and Wang, 1967), 225. On the changing role of the national government in foreign affairs during the 1890s see also Emily S. Rosenberg, *Spreading the American Dream: American Economic and Cultural Expansion: 1890–1945* (New York: Hill and Wang, 1982); Robert L. Beisner, *From the Old Diplomacy to the New, 1865–1900* (Arlington Heights, Ill.: Harlan Davidson, 1986).

2. Constant (1958) dollars. The first figure is an average for 1869–78. The second is for 1898. Bureau of the Census, *Historical Statistics of the United States, Colonial Times to 1970,* 2 vols. (Washington, D.C., 1975), Series F 1-5.

3. The figures are taken from David M. Pletcher, "1861–1898: Economic Growth and Diplomatic Adjustment," in *Economics and World Power: An Assessment of American Diplomacy since 1789,* ed. William H. Becker and Samuel F. Wells, Jr. (New York: Columbia University Press, 1984), 120. For more general surveys of this growth see Gerald Gunderson, *A New Economic History of America* (New York: McGraw-Hill, 1976); Harold G. Vatter, *The Drive to Industrial Maturity: The U.S. Economy, 1860–1914* (Westport, Conn.: Greenwood, 1975).

4. Bureau of the Census, *Historical Statistics,* Series U 213-24.

5. These are summarized in Rosenberg, *Spreading the American Dream,* 23–28.

6. There is a large literature on the "overproduction thesis" and its impact on American politics at the end of the nineteenth century. See Thomas J. McCormick, *China Market: America's Quest for Informal Empire, 1893–1901* (Chicago: Quadrangle Books, 1967); Walter LaFeber, *The New Empire: An Interpretation of American Expansion, 1860–1898* (Ithaca: Cornell University Press, 1963); William Appleman Williams, *The Roots of the Modern American Empire: A Study of the Growth and Shaping of Social Consciousness in a Marketplace Society* (New York: Random House, 1969); James Livingston, *Origins of the Federal Reserve System: Money, Class, and Corporate Capitalism, 1890–1913* (Ithaca: Cornell University Press, 1986).

7. The terms "northern core" and "southern periphery" are from Richard Franklin Bensel, *Sectionalism and American Political Development, 1880–1980* (Madison: University of Wisconsin Press, 1984).

8. LaFeber, *New Empire,* 58.

9. Naval historians generally regard 1890 as the "pivotal" or "benchmark" year in the development of the modern American navy. On the distinction between the navy of the 1880s and 1890s, see, for example, George W. Baer, *One Hundred Years of Sea Power: The U.S. Navy, 1890–1990* (Stanford: Stanford University Press, 1994), 1–2, 9–26; Robert L. O'Connell, *The Cult of the Battleship and the Rise of the U.S. Navy* (Boulder: Westview Press, 1991), 60–71; Harold Sprout and Margaret Sprout, *The Rise of American Naval Power, 1776–1918* (Princeton: Princeton University Press, 1939), 213.

10. Lightly armored cruisers were "useful in deterring commercial states

from aggression," but they did not, the secretary argued, "constitute a fighting force." To wage "even a defensive war with any hope of success," he continued, "we must have armored battleships." What was needed was a fleet "able to divert an enemy's force from our coast by threatening his own, for a war, though defensive in principle, may be conducted most effectively by being offensive in its operations." See *Annual Report of the Secretary of the Navy, 1889,* 51st Cong., 1st sess., H. Ex. Doc. No. 1, pt. 3. The secretary's report was premised on the notion that the very character of naval warfare was undergoing a "sea change," and that in the near future only seagoing, capital ships would provide a credible deterrent to foreign pressure and aggression. Along these lines, the report also marked a significant change in how naval requirements were to be determined in the future. They would be based on comparisons of relative strength with selected foreign navies. On the significance of Secretary Tracy's report see Benjamin Franklin Cooling, *Benjamin Franklin Tracy: Father of the Modern American Fighting Navy* (Hamden, Conn.: Archon Books, 1973), 75–78; Walter R. Herrick, Jr., *The American Naval Revolution* (Baton Rouge: Louisiana State University Press, 1966), 54–68.

11. The secretary called for the construction of twenty battleships—twelve for the Atlantic, eight for the Pacific. In addition, Tracy included a proposal to build twenty coast-defense ships, along with twenty-nine cruisers and a number of torpedo boats. The cruisers and torpedo boats were justified as necessary "adjuncts" to a battleship-based fleet.

12. As a share of the total naval budget, the procurement of steel ships rose from a little over 13 percent in 1885 to 35 percent in 1895. By 1905, roughly 39 percent of the Navy's annual budget was spent on the construction of new steel ships. By comparison, military pay's share of the naval budget dropped from 43 percent in 1885 to just over 26 percent in 1895. By 1905, military pay accounted for a little less than 17 percent of the Navy's budget. See Ben Baack and Edward John Ray, "Special Interests and the Nineteenth-Century Roots of the U.S. Military-Industrial Complex," in *Research in Economic History,* ed. Paul Uselding (Greenwich, Conn.: JAI Press, 1988), 11:153–69, 156.

13. Secretary Tracy quoted in LaFeber, *New Empire,* 127.

14. For Boutelle's comments see *Cong. Rec.,* 51st Cong., 1st sess., 1890, 21, pt. 4:3161–65.

15. The 1890 Navy bill also provided for the construction of two cruisers and one light torpedo boat.

16. *Cong. Rec.,* 51st Cong., 1st sess., 1890, 21, pt. 4:3160–71.

17. On the initial debate over the relative advantages of an offensive battleship and coastal defense navy see *Cong. Rec.,* 51st Cong., 1st sess., 1890, 21, pt. 4:3161–72, 3216–23, and 3256–74.

18. William Oates (D-AL), *Cong. Rec.,* 51st Cong., 1st sess., 1890, 21, pt. 4: 3258.

19. During the depression years of the 1890s, the issue of naval reform also became embroiled in the debates over the power of the "trusts." In 1894 the Cleveland administration uncovered similarities in the contract prices and size of

orders placed with the Carnegie and Bethlehem steel mills. The administration concluded that the two firms had conspired against competitors and called for a reduction in their prices. They refused. This led to congressional hearings and protests by populists. The issue was revived in 1898 when it became clear that the American government was paying considerably more than foreign governments for armor plating. For a review of these episodes see Benjamin Franklin Cooling, *Gray Steel and Blue Water Navy: The Formative Years of America's Military-Industrial Complex, 1881–1917* (Hamden, Conn.: Archon Books, 1979), 113–60.

20. For a discussion of Mahan's ideas and their impact see Baer, *One Hundred Years of Sea Power*, 1–2, 9–33; LaFeber, *New Empire*, 85–95; Sprout and Sprout, *Rise of American Naval Power*, 202–22.

21. Representative Thomas A. E. Weadock of Michigan, *Cong. Rec.,* 53d Cong., 3d sess., 1895, 27, pt. 3:2259. See also the speeches by Representatives Jonathan Dolliver of Iowa and Robert Adams, Jr., of Pennsylvania, *Cong. Rec.,* 53d Cong., 3d sess., 1895, 27, pt. 3:2250, 2306. In the Senate, Orville Platt of Connecticut summarized the position of many of his colleagues when he observed:

> Not only respect for us depends upon the Navy, but commercial supremacy depends upon a proper and adequate naval force, a force proportioned to the magnitude of the country, to its resources, to its aims, to its purposes. No nation that does not maintain a navy can obtain commercial supremacy. Foreign trade flourishes where there is an adequate and proper navy to defend and protect it, or languishes where the navy is insufficient to protect and defend it. We of this country desire commercial supremacy. (*Cong. Rec.,* 53d Cong., 3d sess., 1895, 27, pt. 3:3045)

22. In addition, Congress authorized the construction of twelve torpedo boats, four monitors, and one gunboat.

23. Three battleships were authorized in 1899: the *Virginia, Nebraska,* and *Georgia.* Congress also authorized the construction of three armored cruisers and six protected cruisers. The other two battleships, the *New Jersey* and *Rhode Island,* were authorized in 1900, along with six cruisers and six submarines.

24. *Cong. Rec.,* 53d Cong., 3d sess., 1895, 27, pt. 3:2242.

25. Representative William S. Holman (R-IN), *Cong. Rec.,* 51st Cong., 1st sess., 1891, 21, pt. 11, app.:178.

26. *Cong. Rec.,* 51st Cong., 1st sess., 1891, 21, pt. 11, app.:3171.

27. Ibid., 3045.

28. See, for example, Lance Buhl, "Maintaining 'An American Navy,' 1865–1889," in *In Peace and War: Interpretations of American Naval History, 1775–1984,* ed. Kenneth J. Hagan (Westport, Conn.: Greenwood, 1984), 145–73; Mark Shulman, *Navalism and the Emergence of American Sea Power, 1882–1893* (Annapolis: Naval Institute Press, 1995); Allen R. Millett and Peter Maslowski, *For the Common Defense: A Military History of the United States* (New York: Free Press, 1984), 233–66; Edward Rhodes, "U.S. Strategic Adjustment in the 1890s" (paper presented at the Social Science Research Council Research Workshop, *The Politics*

of Strategic Adjustment: Ideas, Institutions, and Interests, Austin, Tex., 23–24 April 1994).

29. Figure 2.2 is based on an index of state support for naval buildup. Principal components analysis was used to construct the index or scale. Only votes that loaded on the first component (i.e., where the loading was greater than 0.60) were used. (A total of 18 votes made the cutoff.) One vote was then selected to define support for the naval buildup. The direction of every other roll call vote was determined by its sign of correlation with this roll call. The position of each representative on the votes in the analysis was then identified and a mean support score was calculated for the representatives for each state. Following convention, paired votes and announced positions were treated as formal votes. Territories that were not already incorporated as states by 1890 are not included in the analysis.

30. The mean for northeastern and southern states is 78.8 percent and 33.1 percent, respectively.

31. The changing composition of American exports and its implications for the nation's foreign policy are discussed more fully below. For quantitative support see Ben Baack and Edward John Ray's insightful analysis of congressional voting on naval appropriations, "The Political Economy of the Origins of the Military-Industrial Complex in the United States," *Journal of Economic History* 45 (June 1985): 369–75.

32. See Cleona Lewis, *America's Stake in International Investments* (Washington, D.C.: Brookings Institution, 1938), 606.

33. This is one of the main conclusions reached by Baack and Ray in their analysis of the political geography of naval spending. "Special Interests and the Nineteenth-Century Roots of the U.S. Military Industrial Complex," 167. On the connection between military power and foreign investment see Jeffry A. Frieden, "The Economics of Intervention: American Overseas Investments and Relations with Underdeveloped Areas, 1890–1950," *Comparative Studies in Society and History* 31 (January 1989): 55–80.

34. This is a prominent theme in Benjamin Franklin Cooling's account of the steel industry and its role in the naval buildup in *Gray Steel.*

35. Naval shipbuilding also had a salutary effect on the commercial shipbuilding industry during the period. As one analyst at the time observed:

> The policy of the Government in building up a Navy has created a condition favorable to the increase of commercial tonnage, rather than acted as the cause of this increase. Building of war ships created plants prepared to turn out merchant ships. Between that and the actual building of a merchant marine lies a not very deep gulf, which progress in the iron and steel industries of the United States has gradually been filling up. The very fact that iron merchant shipbuilding remained practically dead in the United States so far as ocean trade was concerned until a few years ago, shows very well that the development of naval shipbuilding has at least laid the basis for a possible development of American

merchant shipbuilding. (J. F. Crowell, "Shipping Industry of the United States; Its Relation to the Foreign Trade," in *Monthly Summary of Commerce and Finance of the United States* [Washington, D.C.: GPO, 1901], 1373–1411, 1391)

36. Sprout and Sprout, *Rise of American Naval Power*, 194.

37. The value of heavily armored battleships was certainly not lost on Andrew Carnegie, the voracious Captain of Industry, who candidly observed, "There may be millions for us in armor" (Cooling, *Benjamin Franklin Tracy*, 92). The irony here is that Carnegie was a vocal opponent of imperialist expansion. Apparently, he mastered the distinction between the "need" to develop tools of war and decisions to actually use them. See also Walter LaFeber, *The American Search for Opportunity, 1865–1913* (Cambridge: Cambridge University Press, 1993), 31–36.

38. See Cooling, *Gray Steel*, tables 5, 6, and 9. Estimates for regional steel output (measured in pig iron) are from Harvey S. Perloff et al., *Regions, Resources, and Economic Growth* (Baltimore: Johns Hopkins Press, 1960), 210.

39. For a discussion of this issue see Cooling, *Benjamin Franklin Tracy*, 102–24.

40. Cooling, *Gray Steel*, 88.

41. For a discussion of the impact of the depression on the naval debate see LaFeber, *New Empire*, 231–35. See also Cooling, *Gray Steel*, 120–21.

42. See John Legler, *Regional Distribution of Federal Receipts and Expenditures in the Nineteenth Century: A Quantitative Study* (New York: Arno, 1977), 77.

43. Crowell, "Shipping Industry of the United States," 1411.

44. On western attitudes toward overseas commerce see Salvatore Prisco III, *John Barrett, Progressive Era Diplomat: A Study of a Commercial Expansionist, 1987–1920* (Tuscaloosa: University of Alabama Press, 1973), 13–30.

45. While these states were still major raw materials producers, by 1870 they had also achieved the greatest concentration of manufacturing-service activities outside the Northeast. For supporting data see Perloff et al., *Regions, Resources, and Economic Growth*, 170–90, especially 182–84.

46. Senator Orville Platt (R-CT), *Cong. Rec.*, 53d Cong., 3d sess., 1895, 27, pt. 4:3045.

47. On western attitudes toward the British market see Morton Rothstein, "America in the International Rivalry for the British Wheat Market, 1860–1914," *Mississippi Valley Historical Review* 47 (December 1960): 401–18.

48. An obvious exception here was Congressman Hilary Herbert of Alabama, who was chairman of the Naval Affairs Committee in the early 1890s. A convert to Secretary Tracy's naval reform program, Herbert went on to assume the position of secretary of the navy during the Cleveland administration. As secretary, Herbert used his considerable influence to move a somewhat reluctant Cleveland to pursue the program begun by the Harrison administration. For an account of Secretary Herbert's tenure in office see Herrick, *The American Naval Revolution*, 153–92.

49. Computed by author from *Congressional Directory,* selected years.

50. See Matthew Simon and David Novack, "Some Dimensions of the American Commercial Invasion of Europe, 1871-1914: An Introductory Essay," *Journal of Economic History* 24 (December 1964): 591-605; William K. Hutchinson, "Regional Exports of the United States to Foreign Countries: A Structural Analysis, 1870-1910," in *Research in Economic History,* ed. Paul Uselding (Greenwich, Conn.: JAI Press, 1986), 10:131-54.

51. See Thomas Coode, "Southern Congressmen and the American Naval Revolution, 1880-1889," *Alabama Historical Quarterly* 30 (fall-winter 1968): 108-9.

52. The surplus, and more generally the tariff, was a persistent theme in the debates over the navy. Even in the mid-1890s, when many contended that government revenues were no longer sufficient to cover increased naval expenditures, the issue continued to provoke heated debate. See, for example, the House and Senate floor debates in 1896 over the House Committee on Naval Affairs' proposal to authorize the construction of four more battleships and fifteen torpedo boats. *Cong. Rec.,* 54th Cong., 1st sess., 1896, 28, pt. 4:3193-203; pt. 5:4502—23; pt. 5:4847-56.

53. Oates, a leading opponent of the battleship navy, continued: "The right thing to do is to revise the tariff and reduce taxation and modify the internal-revenue laws so that there will be no surplus in the Treasury; leave the surplus in the pockets of the people, where it rightly belongs." *Cong. Rec.,* 51st Cong., 1st sess., 1890, 21, pt. 4:3259.

54. For a similar interpretation see Baack and Ray, "Special Interests and the Nineteenth-Century Roots of the U.S. Military-Industrial Complex," 167. On the relationship between the protective tariff and veteran's pensions see Bensel, *Sectionalism and American Political Development,* 62-73.

55. *Cong. Rec.,* 51st Cong., 1st sess., 1890, 21, pt. 4:3169.

56. While implicitly acknowledging that naval appropriations were not regionally neutral, Lodge assured his colleagues from agrarian states that

> I stand ready and have always stood ready in this House when the representatives of other sections have come to us and urged us, year after year, to put millions of dollars into the improvement of the Mississippi River for the protection of that great region, I have always been glad to see such appropriations voted. I have always been glad to take part in such action. Now, when the people of the coast come and ask for defense I do not believe it is the time for members from other states to talk about "inherent defenses" which are never defined and which, so far as I can see, consist chiefly in residence in the interior of the country. (*Cong. Rec.,* 51st Cong., 1st sess., 1890, 21, pt. 4:3268)

57. *Cong. Rec.,* 51st Cong., 1st sess., 1890, 21, app.:178.

58. Numerous accounts of the debates over imperialism interpret the conflict in cultural or ideological terms. See, for example, Robert Osgood, *Ideals and Self-Interest in America's Foreign Relations: The Great Transformation of the Twen-*

tieth Century (Chicago: University of Chicago Press, 1953), 29–70; Michael H. Hunt, *Ideology and U.S. Foreign Policy* (New Haven: Yale University Press, 1987), 36–45; Akira Iriye, *From Nationalism to Internationalism: US Foreign Policy to 1914* (London: Routledge and Kegan Paul, 1977), 53–191.

59. See Harold Hongju Koh, *The National Security Constitution: Sharing Power after the Iran-Contra Affair* (New Haven: Yale University Press, 1990), 84–93, and Henry Bartholomew Cox, *War, Foreign Affairs, and Constitutional Power: 1829–1901* (Cambridge, Mass.: Ballinger, 1984), 247–331.

60. The immediate issue in this case was whether the president had inherent constitutional power to protect federal judges. The justices, however, went much further by declaring in a 6–2 vote that the president's inherent constitutional power to carry out acts of Congress or enforce treaties included "the rights, duties, and obligations growing out of the Constitution itself, *our international relations,* and all the protection implied by the nature of the government under the Constitution." In re Neagle, 135 U.S. 1, 64 (1890) (emphasis added), as cited by Walter LaFeber, "The Constitution and U.S. Foreign Policy: An Interpretation," in *Alternative Perspectives on the U.S. Constitution,* ed. Jules Lobel (New York: Monthly Review Press, 1988), 242. For a discussion of the case and its significance for American foreign policy see ibid., 221–48.

61. For a good treatment of northern-based anti-imperialist sentiment see Robert L. Beisner, *Twelve against Empire: The Anti-Imperialists, 1898–1900* (Chicago: University of Chicago Press, 1968). See also E. Berkely Tompkins, *Anti-Imperialism in the United States: The Great Debate, 1890–1920* (Philadelphia: University of Pennsylvania Press, 1970).

62. On the position of the southern press see Edward L. Ayers, *The Promise of the New South: Life after Reconstruction* (New York: Oxford University Press, 1992), 332–33.

63. See David Healy, *U.S. Expansionism: The Imperialist Urge of the 1890s* (Madison: University of Wisconsin Press, 1970), 232–47. See also McCormick, *China Market,* 52; LaFeber, *New Empire,* 416.

64. Nor was territorial expansion itself a problem. As David Healy notes, "while there were many anti-imperialists in America, there were few anti-expansionists." Few late-nineteenth-century lawmakers actually questioned the desirability of additional territory. What they disagreed over was what the political status of the new possessions should be or, more precisely, whether the acquisition of islands in the Caribbean and Pacific should be treated differently from the areas destined for statehood on the continent. At the very time southern representatives were opposing the acquisition of Cuba, Hawaii, Puerto Rico, and the Philippines, they were urging Congress to grant statehood to the territories of Arizona, Oklahoma, and New Mexico, an idea that enjoyed considerably less enthusiasm among congressional delegations from the Northeast. Healy, *U.S. Expansionism,* 49. See also Bensel, *Sectionalism and American Political Development,* 90–93.

65. On the early history of American-Hawaiian relations see Merze Tate, *The United States and the Hawaiian Kingdom: A Political History* (New Haven: Yale University Press, 1967), 1–26.

66. Quoted in Walter LaFeber, *The American Age: United States Foreign Policy at Home and Abroad since 1750* (New York: W. W. Norton, 1989), 108.

67. On the effects of reciprocity see Merze Tate, *Hawaii: Reciprocity or Annexation* (East Lansing: Michigan State University Press, 1968), 108–34, 215–67.

68. The account that follows draws heavily on Thomas J. Osborne, *"Empire Can Wait": American Opposition to Hawaiian Annexation, 1893–1898* (Kent, Ohio: Kent State University, 1981) and Julius W. Pratt, *Expansionists of 1898: The Acquisition of Hawaii and the Spanish Islands,* 2d ed. (Chicago: Quadrangle Books, 1964).

69. The McKinley Tariff also placed a bounty of two cents for sugar produced by domestic growers, thereby undercutting any natural foreign price advantage.

70. Grover Cleveland was first elected President in 1884. After losing his reelection bid in 1888 to Benjamin Harrison, he won the presidency for a second time four years later.

71. Cleveland sent word to key Democrats in the Senate that he wished the treaty to be blocked temporarily. Even Democrats in favor of annexation could support such a move: by delaying Senate consideration for a few months, the Democrats could claim credit for a treaty negotiated by the Republicans.

72. The House bill contained two important clauses. One had to do with the question of annexation; the other concerned former Minister Stevens's role in the overthrow of the Hawaiian monarchy. Stevens was condemned in the resolution for "illegally aiding" in the *coup d'état.*

73. One was Cleveland's much criticized decision to recall the *U.S.S. Philadelphia* from Honolulu, leaving the island without an American warship for the first time in many years. Another was the failed royalist uprising of January 1895 in Honolulu by the Queen's friends and supporters.

74. In late 1894, the British government asked the Hawaiian government for the lease of Necker Island as a mid-sea station for a trans-Pacific telegraphic cable linking Canada and Australia. The Hawaii government was inclined to grant the request, but under existing treaty arrangements with the United States it could not lease its own territory to a foreign power without American consent. On the debate over the cable subsidy see Osborne, *"Empire Can Wait,"* 82–84; Pratt, *Expansionists of 1898,* 203–6.

75. Like Hawaii, Samoa was the object of great power rivalry. Germany, Britain, and the United States all had an interest in securing the harbor of Pago Pago. The rivalry reached a flash point in 1887 when Germany and Britain attempted to cut a deal that threatened American claims. It was temporarily resolved under the Berlin General Act of 1889. The treaty effectively divided the islands into a tripartite protectorate while nominally recognizing Samoan independence.

76. In the Senate, the measure passed by a vote of 36 yeas to 25 nays, with 26 abstentions. In the House the measure was rejected by a vote of 152 to 114. More than half of the voting representatives from the Northeast backed the cable-laying measure. For Lodge's comment see *Cong. Rec.,* 53d Cong., 3d sess., 1895, 27, pt. 4:3082–84.

77. On the nineteenth-century world economy see Walt Rostow, *The World*

Economy: History and Prospect (Austin: University of Texas, 1978), 123–62; Charles Kindleberger, "The Rise of Free Trade in Western Europe, 1820–75," *Journal of Economic History* 35 (1975): 20–55. On the political and strategic dimensions of the *Pax Britannica* see Paul Kennedy, *The Rise and Fall of the Great Powers: Economic Change and Military Conflict from 1500 to 2000* (New York: Random House, 1987), 143–93.

78. For a general discussion see E. J. Hobsbawm, *The Age of Empire, 1875–1914* (New York: Pantheon Books, 1987), 34–55. See also Hans Rosenberg, "The Depression of 1873–1896 in Central Europe," *Journal of Economic History* 13 (1943): 58–73.

79. The Cobden-Chevalier Treaty effectively formed a European free trade or low-tariff "regime" that included most of the nations on the continent.

80. Hobsbawm, *Age of Empire*, 56–83; Kennedy, *Rise and Fall*, 194–274.

81. In a widely read article entitled "Hawaii and Our Future Sea Power," Mahan argued that the choice facing America over Hawaii was a historic one: "The United States finds herself compelled to answer a question—to make a decision—not unlike and not less momentous than that required of the Roman Senate, when the Mamertine garrison invited it to occupy Messina, and so abandon the hitherto traditional policy which had confined the expansion of Rome to the Italian peninsula." *Forum* 15 (March 1893): 1. For a good discussion of the views that Mahan and other military strategists shared on the importance of Hawaii see Allen Lee Hamilton, "Military Strategists and the Annexation of Hawaii," *Journal of the West* 15 (April 1976): 81–91.

82. Starting from the Mahan-like assumption that commercial power was a key to national power, Draper went on to expound the doctrine of sea power:

> If the United States aim at commercial supremacy in the Pacific, its trade must have such assurances, and a first necessity is the acquisition of bases for the protectors. Not only Hawaii is needed, but Samoa (distant 2,260 miles); a station at the mouth of the canal (say, 4,200 miles from Honolulu and 3,000 from San Francisco); and another at the Straits of Magellan (distant 4,000 miles from the isthmus, and 5,000 from Samoa). With these bases, a properly organized fleet, of sufficient size to keep the communications open between them, will hold the Pacific as an American ocean, dominated by American commercial enterprise for all time. (*Cong. Rec.,* 53d Cong., 2d sess., 1894, 26, pt.2:1847–48)

83. Annexation was not the only way to establish "control" over Hawaii, but most imperialists believed it was the most viable one. Reciprocity treaties, they cautioned, were terminable: the Hawaiian government could abrogate existing or supplemental treaties. They were thus viewed as an unreliable method for guaranteeing the permanent availability of Pearl Harbor as a coaling station. Moreover, there was some question as to whether the harbor could be defended adequately without controlling the entire archipelago. The alternative of establishing an American protectorate over the islands was rejected because even if the Hawaiian government agreed to such an arrangement it would raise international complications.

As an American protectorate, Hawaii could still conduct its own affairs; as Hawaii's protector, the U.S. government could easily become involved with any nation that made demands on Hawaii. By annexing Hawaii, these problems could be avoided.

84. Hamilton, "Military Strategists and the Annexation of Hawaii," 82.

85. At the time, the average battleship had a range of about five thousand miles at a speed of ten knots. Unless one of the other nations—Britain, Japan, China, Russia, or Spain—fielding navies in the Pacific gained control over the islands, this meant that their ships could not attack (or credibly threaten to attack) the United States without refueling at sea—a hazardous and impractical option. This argument was skillfully made by Lodge in a dramatic eleventh-hour attempt to win funding for the cable. See *Cong. Rec.,* 53d Cong., 3d sess., 1895, 27, pt. 4:3082–84.

86. As Julius Pratt pointed out long ago, the business community's interest in overseas markets did not automatically translate into support for the use of military force or colonial rule. Short of this, however, the historical evidence indicates that much of American business supported efforts to expand trade and investment in South America and Asia. See Pratt, *Expansionists of 1898,* 230–78. On the general attitude of American business toward overseas expansion in the nonindustrialized world see, for example, LaFeber, *New Empire,* 176–96, and Healy, *U.S. Expansionism,* 159–77.

87. So was the geography of American imports. Manufactured goods, historically the leading group of imports into the United States, declined in the late nineteenth century. This trend was partly the result of the very high tariff barriers that Congress reimposed on European manufactures after the Civil War. It also reflected the rapid growth and diversification of the American economy as factories and mills became increasingly dependent on imported crude materials such as rubber, hides, silk, wool, diamonds, and tin. As a result, American import trade gradually shifted out of the European orbit. Imports from Europe declined while imports from underdeveloped parts of the world increased. Emory R. Johnson et al., *History of Domestic and Foreign Commerce of the United States* (New York: Burt Franklin, 1915), 2:78–81.

88. The following nations were among the leading non-European importers of American products: Canada, Mexico, Argentina, South Africa, Japan, China, and Australia. See Johnson et al., *History of Domestic and Foreign Commerce,* 2:74–76.

89. Manufactures as a share of total exports to Europe also increased in the period, but not nearly as sharply.

90. See Johnson et al., *History of Domestic and Foreign Commerce,* 2:90. Furthermore, as Johnson and his colleagues noted European imports of American manufactures consisted chiefly of manufactured foodstuffs and semi-manufactures. When it came to finished manufactured goods, the European market was limited; it was the underdeveloped markets outside the Old World that accounted for most of the increase in the sale of high-end finished goods.

91. *Cong. Rec.,* 55th Cong., 2d sess., 1898, 31, pt. 6:5905.

92. Ibid., 6007.

93. Henry Cabot Lodge put it succinctly: "The sea power has been one of

the controlling forces in history. Without the sea power no nation has been really great. Sea power consists, in the first place, of a proper navy and a proper fleet; but in order to sustain a navy we must have suitable posts for naval stations, strong places where a navy can be protected and refurnished." *Cong. Rec.*, 53d Cong., 3d sess., 1895, 27, pt. 4:3082.

94. See Walter Karp, *The Politics of War: The Story of Two Wars Which Altered Forever the Political Life of the American Republic (1890–1920)* (New York: Harper and Row, 1979), 3–27.

95. Champ Clark (D-MO), *Great Debates in American History*, ed. Marion Mills Miller (New York: Current Literature, 1913), 3:207–8.

96. *Cong. Rec.*, 55th Cong., 2d sess., 1898, 31, pt. 6:5890.

97. To those northerners who proclaimed that Jefferson himself had stretched, if not violated, the Constitution to make the Louisiana Purchase, southerners replied that the territory was neither sovereign, nor did it lie thousands of miles from the closest border. Hawaii was a sovereign nation; Louisiana was a French territory.

98. On southern attitudes toward Hawaiian annexation see Gregory Lawrence Garland, "Southern Congressional Opposition to Hawaiian Reciprocity and Annexation, 1876–1898" (master's thesis, University of North Carolina, 1983); Osmos Lanier, Jr., "Anti-Annexationists of the 1890s" (Ph.D. diss., University of Georgia, 1965); Tennant S. McWilliams, *The New South Faces the World: Foreign Affairs and the Southern Sense of Self, 1877–1950* (Baton Rouge: Louisiana State University Press, 1988), 16–46. On the larger question of southern opposition to imperialism see Edwina C. Smith, "Southerners on Empire: Southern Senators and Imperialism, 1898–99," *Mississippi Quarterly* 31 (winter 1977–78): 89–107; Karp, *Politics of War*, 14–27, 104–16.

99. One important reason for the regional disparity was the high level of specialization and trade between the Northeast and the West. Compared to the Northeast, the South was virtually self-sufficient in foodstuffs, which sharply limited its potential interregional links with the West. On this matter see Albert Fishlow, "Antebellum Interregional Trade Reconsidered," in *New Views of American Economic Development*, ed. Ralph Andreano (Cambridge: Harvard University Press, 1965), 187–200; William K. Hutchinson and Samuel Williamson, "The Self-Sufficiency of the Antebellum South: Estimates of the Food Supply," *Journal of Economic History* 31 (September 1971): 591–612; Diane Lindstrom, "Southern Dependence upon Grain Supplies: A View of the Trade Flows, 1840–1860," in *The Structure of the Cotton Economy of the Antebellum South*, ed. William Parker (Washington, D.C.: Agricultural History Society, 1970), 101–13.

100. William K. Hutchinson, "Regional Exports to Foreign Countries: United States, 1870–1914," in *Research in Economic History*, ed. Paul Uselding (Greenwich, Conn.: JAI Press, 1982), 7:133–237, 155. See also Simon and Novack, "Some Dimensions of the American Commercial Invasion of Europe"; Hutchinson, "Regional Exports of the United States to Foreign Countries"; David F. Good, "Uneven Development in the Nineteenth Century: A Comparison of the Habsburg Empire and the United States," *Journal of Economic History* 96 (March 1986): 137–51.

101. Bensel, *Sectionalism and American Political Development,* 92. See also Smith, "Southerners on Empire."

102. *Cong. Rec.,* 55th Cong., 2d sess., 1898, 31, pt. 6:5903.

103. There were some obvious exceptions, such as Senators John Tyler Morgan (D-AL) and Joseph Brown (D-GA) and Congressmen Hilary Herbert (D-AL), Joseph H. Wheeler (D-AL), and J. Fred Talbot (D-MD), who were also proponents of New South industrialization and advocates of territorial expansion and naval expenditures. But as Joseph Fry repeatedly points out in his excellent biography of John Tyler Morgan, chairman of the Senate Foreign Affairs Committee and a champion of imperialism, such views were exceptional in the South and lay outside the mainstream of southern opinion. See Joseph Fry, *John Tyler Morgan and the Search for Southern Autonomy* (Knoxville: University of Tennessee Press, 1992). For other accounts of the foreign policy orientation of the New South movement see Tennant S. McWilliams, "The Lure of Empire: Southern Interest in the Caribbean, 1877–1900," *Mississippi Quarterly* 29 (winter 1975–76): 43–63; O. Lawrence Burnette, Jr., "John Tyler Morgan and Expansionist Sentiment in the New South," *Alabama Review* 43 (1965): 163–82; Patrick J. Hearden, *Independence and Empire: The New South's Cotton Mill Campaign, 1865–1901* (DeKalb: Northern Illinois University Press, 1982).

104. Treatments of southern politics after Reconstruction revolve around C. Vann Woodward's *Origins of the New South, 1877–1913* (Baton Rouge: Louisiana State University Press, 1951). Woodward's account, which emphasized the demise of the old planter elite and the rise of a new urban, industrial, professional elite in explaining post–Civil War politics in the South, has been repeatedly challenged. It now seems clear that Woodward's view of the disjuncture in southern political life was overstated, that the planter class was still a powerful political force in southern society, and that in most cases southern Democrats in Congress aligned themselves with agrarian-minded interests rather than industrially oriented ones. Leading the field here are James Tice Moore's "Redeemers Reconsidered: Change and Continuity in the Democratic South, 1870–1900," *Journal of Southern History* 44 (August 1978): 357–78, and William Cooper's *The Conservative Regime: South Carolina, 1877–1890* (Baltimore: Johns Hopkins University Press, 1968). For a balanced survey of this issue and the relevant literature see Howard N. Rabinowitz, *The First New South, 1865–1920* (Arlington Heights, Ill.: Harlan Davidson, 1992), 72–131. On the political orientation of southern Democrats during this period see Carl V. Harris, "Right Force or Left Fork? The Section-Party Alignments of Southern Democrats in Congress, 1873–1897," *Journal of Southern History* 42 (November 1976): 471–506.

105. C. Vann Woodward, *The Burden of Southern History* (Baton Rouge: Louisiana State University Press, 1960), 150.

106. This point was first made by Christopher Lasch in his seminal "The Anti-Imperialists, the Philippines, and the Inequality of Man," *Journal of Southern History* 24 (August 1958): 319–31. It should be noted that northern and southern politicians typically drew different conclusions from the presumption of racial superiority. Northerners invariably argued that it was Americans' duty to uplift

and care for the "backward and benighted savages" of Hawaii, Cuba, Puerto Rico, and the Philippines. By contrast, southerners voiced fears about the social and political consequences of allowing "tropical peoples" into the United States. Southern lawmakers were also quick to attack northerners' racially laden arguments for colonialism as hypocritical. They repeatedly pointed out that many of the same individuals who had preached the doctrine of racial equality in the United States and opposed southern racist practices now claimed that some "colored peoples" were not fit for self-government. On the role of racism in the debate over imperialism see also Hunt, *Ideology and U.S. Foreign Policy,* 77–90; J. Rogers Hollingsworth, *The Whirligig of Politics: The Democracy of Cleveland and Bryan* (Chicago: University of Chicago Press, 1963), 149–50; Healy, *U.S. Expansionism,* 39–41, 240–41.

107. The Force Bill was one of the methods Republicans used to try to weaken the Democrats' hold on the South. For years, southern states counted virtually all voting-age citizens when determining their representation in Congress, but then used stringent registration laws or poll taxes to disenfranchise many of those same citizens. As a result, southern states were overrepresented in Congress: one vote in a congressional election in Georgia or South Carolina carried the same weight as five votes in Minnesota, four votes in New Hampshire, or three votes in Wisconsin. There were two basic ways to solve the imbalance: adjust southern congressional representation or open up elections to all qualified voters. The Force Bill emphasized the latter. Under its terms, federal circuit courts would be authorized to supervise elections if one hundred voters in a congressional district or a city of twenty thousand believed there was election fraud and petitioned the court. Although the bill applied to all districts and regions of the country, and employed legal sanctions rather than physical force, it set off the most intense sectional conflicts in Congress since the end of Reconstruction. After passing the House on a highly sectional vote, Lodge's bill died in the Senate. Southern senators were able to win postponement of floor consideration of the bill, effectively killing the bill, by trading votes with pro-silver members from the West and northerners interested in winning some measure of southern support for revising the tariff. For a discussion of the bill's history and the southern reaction see R. Hal Williams, *Years of Decision: American Politics in the 1890s* (New York: Alfred A. Knopf, 1978), 29–32; Bensel, *Sectionalism and American Political Development,* 73–88; Stanley P. Hirshson, *Farewell to the Bloody Shirt: Northern Republicans and the Southern Negro, 1877–1893* (Bloomington: Indiana University Press, 1962), 200–46.

108. See also Bensel, *Sectionalism and American Political Development,* 71, table 3.2.

109. The connection between overproduction and tariff revision is explored most systematically by Tom E. Terrill, *The Tariff, Politics, and American Foreign Policy, 1874–1901* (Westport, Conn.: Greenwood).

110. The use of reciprocity by the United States was not in itself novel. American officials had signed reciprocity treaties with Canada and Hawaii in the past

and the principle had been applied to negotiations over commercial shipping for a long time. It was not, however, until the Tariff Act of 1890 that reciprocity became a full-blown strategy for promoting commercial expansion. For a review of the history of reciprocity see Robert Freeman Smith, "Reciprocity," in *Encyclopedia of American Foreign Policy*, ed. Alexander DeConde (New York: Charles Scribner, 1978), 3:867–81.

111. John Sherman, *Recollections of Forty Years in the House, Senate and Cabinet* (Chicago: Werner, 1895), 2:1085.

112. See Smith, "Reciprocity," 874–77.

113. Thomas J. McCormick, *China Market,* 43.

114. *Cong. Rec.,* 55th Cong., 1st sess., 1897, 30, pt. 2:482.

115. A bargaining tariff is one with flexible rate schedules that gives the president the authority to change the rates on some or all imports from any country in order to persuade that country to give more favorable treatment to its imports of American goods. There are two different approaches: the "penalty" method and the "concession" method. Under the penalty approach, Congress gave the president the power to raise duties on a nation whose goods entered the United States at favorable rates, unless that nation offered American products better treatment. Under the concession method Congress authorized the president to lower the rates of duties against imports from another country to persuade the country to treat American goods better. At the beginning of the 1890s the United States relied exclusively on the penalty method. Secretary Blaine preferred the concession approach, but Congress granted the president only the authority to remove goods from the free list. Later in the decade, the president was granted separate authority for using each method.

116. On the importance of South America as a target of reciprocity see David M. Pletcher, "Reciprocity and Latin America in the Early 1890s: A Foretaste of Dollar Diplomacy," *Pacific Historical Review* 47 (February 1978): 53–89. Pletcher's views about the primacy of South American markets are shared by others. See McCormick, *China Market;* Terrill, *Tariff;* LaFeber, *New Empire;* Williams, *Roots of the Modern American Empire.*

117. See Johnson et al., *History of Domestic and Foreign Commerce,* 2:95–97.

118. As historian Samuel P. Hays notes, debates over principle "merely obscured the more basic dissensions among the producers of various sections." From *The Response to Industrialism, 1885–1914,* 13th ed. (Chicago: University of Chicago Press, 1971), 133.

119. The two standard histories of American tariff policy are Frank W. Taussig, *The Tariff History of the United States,* 8th ed. (New York: Putnam, 1931) and Edward Stanwood, *American Tariff Controversies in the Nineteenth Century* (Boston: Houghton Mifflin, 1903). For accounts that place the tariff in a larger foreign policy context see Terrill, *Tariff,* 159–209; LaFeber, *New Empire,* 112–21, 159–72, 374–79; McCormick, *China Market,* 39–51; David A. Lake, *Power, Protectionism, and Free Trade: International Sources of U.S. Commercial Strategy, 1887–1939* (Ithaca: Cornell University Press, 1988), 91–118.

120. Agreement was reached with an eleventh nation, France, through an informal commercial arrangement concluded by an exchange of notes. Efforts to reach agreements with Mexico, Argentina, and Peru proved unsuccessful. Lake, *Power, Protectionism, and Free Trade*, 101.

121. Ibid., 116. Most of the goods placed on the free list by the House simply vanished in the Senate version, while rates were raised on goods on the protected list. Moreover, by taking sugar off the free list to appease domestic sugar interests, the Senate version cut the legs out from under the reciprocity agreements signed by the Harrison administration.

122. *Speeches and Addresses of William McKinley from March 1, 1897 to May 30, 1900* (New York: Doubleday & McClure, 1900).

123. For a discussion of the connection between reciprocity and the silver question see Lewis L. Gould, "Diplomats in the Lobby: Franco-American Relations and the Dingley Tariff of 1897," *Historian* 39 (August 1977): 659–80. Gould argues that the reciprocity provisions aimed at Europe were inserted to win French backing for international bimetallism—a Republican party pledge designed to weaken domestic support for free silver in the West.

124. Under this provision the President could also negotiate the transfer to the free list of goods not produced in the United States.

125. These were called the "Kasson Treaties," named after John A. Kasson, a seasoned congressman and diplomat who headed a special reciprocity team in the State Department. Kasson also signed reciprocity treaties with Great Britain for Barbados, British Guiana, Turks and Caicos Islands, Trinidad, and Bermuda; Denmark for St. Croix; and with the Dominican Republic and Nicaragua. Lake, *Power, Protectionism, and Free Trade*, 129–31.

126. James D. Richardson, comp., *A Compilation of the Messages and Papers of the Presidents*, 10 vols. (New York: Bureau of National Literature, 1902), 10:396.

127. Andrew Carnegie, "What Would I Do with the Tariff If I Were Czar," *Forum* 19 (March 1895): 24. Industrialists like Carnegie were at the forefront of efforts in the business community to mobilize political support for reciprocity. Similar sentiments were apparently expressed by merchant capitalists and international bankers centered in the large port cities of Boston, Philadelphia, and especially New York. However, it is probably fair to say that most merchants and bankers saw reciprocity as a first step toward a more desirable policy of liberal trade. On this see Paul Wolman, *Most Favored Nation: The Republican Revisionists and U.S. Tariff Policy, 1897–1912* (Chapel Hill: University of North Carolina Press, 1992), 5; Samuel T. McSeveney, *The Politics of Depression: Political Behavior in the Northeast, 1893–1896* (New York: Oxford University Press, 1972), 39.

128. As cited in Martin J. Sklar, "The N.A.M. and Foreign Markets on the Eve of the Spanish-American War," *Science and Society* 23 (1959): 158.

129. Wolman, *Most Favored Nation*, 209.

130. *Cong. Rec.*, 55th Cong., 1st sess., 1897, 30, pt. 2:135.

131. "Protection and the Formation of Capital," *Political Science Quarterly* 23 (June 1908): 228.

132. Throughout the nineteenth century customs duties were by far the most important source of federal revenue. The other main sources of revenue were sales of federal lands and internal excise taxes. Even if conservatively estimated on a per capita basis, federal expenditures were generally higher in the Northeast (and the West) than in the South. See Lance E. Davis and John Legler, "The Government in the American Economy, 1815-1902," *Journal of Economic History* 26 (December 1966): 514-52, table 1.

133. Walter Prescott Webb once described the tariff and military pensions "as inseparable as Gold Dust twins." See his tract, *Divided We Stand: The Crisis of a Frontierless Democracy,* rev. ed. (Austin: Acorn Press, 1944), 13. For a brilliant treatment of the relationship between the tariff and pensions, and the underlying sectional logic, see Bensel, *Sectionalism and American Political Development,* 62-73.

134. Or as Albert Hopkins of Ways and Means put it a few years later: "the principle of reciprocity is in perfect harmony with the doctrine of protection." *Cong. Rec.,* 55th Cong., 1st sess., 1897, 30, pt. 2:135. Blaine, as cited by Edward P. Crapol, *America for Americans: Economic Nationalism and Anglophobia in the Late Nineteenth Century* (Westport, Conn.: Greenwood Press, 1973), 174.

135. The following discussion owes much to William Appleman Williams's cogent analysis. See *Roots of the Modern American Empire,* 319-37.

136. As a purely electoral strategy, reciprocity is more difficult to assess. Many historians attribute the Republicans' heavy losses in the midterm election of 1890 to the McKinley tariff. It is generally conceded, however, that reciprocity was one of the few popular elements in the law. Indeed, the Republican party made reciprocity a key feature of their 1896 platform.

137. As cited in Williams, *Years of Decision,* 39.

138. On the farmer and fears of overproduction see Rothstein, "America in the International Rivalry for the British Wheat Market," especially 402-7. More generally see Williams, *Roots of the Modern American Empire.*

139. My thinking here has been strongly influenced by Howard R. Smith's stimulating "The Farmer and the Tariff: A Reappraisal," *Southern Economic Journal* 21 (October 1954): 152-65.

140. See Gould, "Diplomats in the Lobby," 659-80, for a discussion of the ways McKinley used reciprocity to win the support of western silver interests.

141. "Reciprocity—Why Southward Only?" *Forum* 11 (May 1891): 268-75. Mills was attacking the Harrison administration and the reciprocity provisions entailed in the McKinley Tariff. Similar criticisms were levied against the McKinley administration and the Dingley Tariff. As Charles F. Cochran (D-MO) observed, the Dingley bill's reciprocity provisions were not aimed at "the great states of Europe, that consume the surplus agricultural products of this country, but with some of the Spanish-American countries and with some of the small islands adjacent to our coast." *Cong. Rec.,* 55th Cong., 1st sess., 1897, 30, pt. 2:199. See also

Cong. Rec., 55th Cong., 1st sess., 1897, 30, pt. 2:9536, 10633. There were exceptions, of course. Those who represented textile- and steel-producing areas of the South called for greater export trade with South America and East Asia. A few advocated policies, like tariff reciprocity and naval reform, that most southern representatives and senators opposed. See Hearden, *Independence and Empire,* 53–67.

142. On this important point see Morton Rothstein, "The New South and the International Economy," *Agricultural History* 57 (October 1983): 385–402. See also Calvin B. Hoover and B. U. Ratchford, *Economic Resources and Policies of the South* (New York: Macmillan, 1951), 422.

143. On southern attitudes toward the tariff in the nineteenth century see M. Ogden Phillips, "The Tariff and the South," *The South Atlantic Quarterly* 32 (October 1933): 375–86. On the South's dependence on international markets see Fred A. Shannon, *The Farmer's Last Frontier: Agriculture, 1860–1897* (New York: Farrar and Rinehart, 1945), 110–11. See also Good, "Uneven Development in the Nineteenth Century," especially table 6.

144. How serious the "threat" posed by Indian and Egyptian cotton producers actually was is open to question. What is not is that southern politicians acted as if the danger were real and present. See, for example, *Cong. Rec.,* 51st Cong., 1st sess., 1890, 21, pt. 5:4395; pt. 10:9536. According to Rothstein, "the only market condition that changed" for southern farmers in the late nineteenth century "was that competition in European and Asian markets from other cotton-growing countries, particularly India and Egypt, had become more pronounced; a condition offset only in part by the growth of domestic demand." See Rothstein, "The New South and the International Economy," 398–99.

145. Bensel, *Sectionalism and American Political Development,* 62. Even advocates of the New South, like Representative John L. McLaurin (D-SC), echoed this sentiment: "Since 1861 we have been living under the operation of a protective tariff, and during that entire period the people of the South have been laboring against unfair discrimination. It is this unfair discrimination of which I complain in this bill and would see removed, and in its place established a just and fair reciprocity between the sections." *Cong. Rec.,* 55th Cong., 1st sess., 1897, 30, pt. 1:182–91, 199, 205; pt. 3, app.:104, 349. For related criticisms of the tariff system see *Cong. Rec.,* 51st Cong., 1st sess., 1890, 21, pt. 5:4265, 4395; pt. 10:10055; pt. 11:10633, 10635–36; *Cong. Rec.,* 55th Cong., 1st sess., 1897, 30, pt. 1:182–91, 199, 205, app.:104, 349.

146. This position is often associated with President Cleveland. It is true that Cleveland embraced this position at the end of his first administration but he was a latecomer. The "low tariff" movement was centered in the House and led by a number of prominent southerners like John C. Carlisle (D-KY), William C. P. Breckinridge (D-KY), Clifton Breckinridge (D-AR), Roger Q. Mills (D-TX), and William Wilson (D-WV). In contrast to Cleveland, who viewed duty-free raw materials as a way to appeal to segments of northern industry, these congressmen saw tariff reductions as a way solve the problem of agricultural overproduction and expand

the Democrat's political base in the West. On this point see Williams, *Roots of the Modern American Empire,* 314-16.

147. *Cong. Rec.,* 51st Cong., 1st sess., 1890, 21, pt. 5:4397.

148. See Wolman, *Most Favored Nation,* 4-5; Terrill, *Tariff,* 187-88; McSeveney, *Politics of Depression,* 89-90.

149. The 1894 Wilson-Gorman Act included a 2 percent tax of income in excess of $4,000. Although it was ruled unconstitutional by the Supreme Court in 1895, many in the South and West found a graduated income tax appealing as a way to redistribute wealth. It was common knowledge that the Northeast would have shouldered a disproportionate share of the tax. See Ben Baack and Edward John Ray, "Special Interests and the Adoption of the Income Tax in the United States," *Journal of Economic History* 45 (September 1985): 607-25.

150. For a discussion of this point see Williams, *Roots of the Modern American Empire,* 314-16.

151. See John A. S. Grenville and George B. Young, *Politics, Strategy and American Diplomacy* (New Haven: Yale University Press, 1966); Ernest May, *Imperial Democracy: The Emergence of America as a Great Power* (New York: Harcourt Brace Jovanovich, 1961); Pratt, *Expansionists of 1898.*

152. *The American Commonwealth,* 3d ed. (New York: Macmillan, 1894), 1:310.

153. "Diplomacy and War Plans in the United States, 1890-1917," in *Essays on the History of American Foreign Relations,* ed. Laurence B. Gelfand (New York: Holt, Rinehart and Winston, 1972), 240.

154. On their larger strategy see E. E. Schattschneider, *The Semi-Sovereign People* (New York: Holt, Rinehart and Winston, 1960), 73. See also Walter Dean Burnham, "The System of 1896: An Analysis," in *The Evolution of American Electoral Systems,* ed. Paul Kleppner (Westport, Conn.: Greenwood Press, 1981), 147-202; Paul Kleppner, *Continuity and Change in Electoral Politics, 1893-1928* (New York: Greenwood Press, 1987).

Chapter Three

1. Francis L. Loewenheim, Harold D. Langley, and Manfred Jonas, eds., *Roosevelt and Churchill: Their Secret Wartime Correspondence* (New York: Saturday Review Press, 1975), 122-26.

2. *The Public Papers and Addresses of Franklin D. Roosevelt* (New York: Russell and Russell, 1969), 9:633-44.

3. Warren F. Kimball, *The Most Unsordid Act: Lend-Lease, 1939-1941* (Baltimore: Johns Hopkins University Press, 1969), 129.

4. For Roosevelt's views on Lend-Lease see Robert Dallek, *Franklin D. Roosevelt and American Foreign Policy, 1932-1945* (New York: Oxford University Press, 1979), 252-60.

5. Kimball, *Most Unsordid Act,* 164.

6. Ibid., 167.

7. House Committee on Foreign Affairs, *Hearings on H.R. 1776: A Bill Further to Promote the Defense of the United States, and for Other Purposes* (Washington, D.C.: GPO, 1941), 77:1, 3–10.

8. Cited in Wayne S. Cole, *Senator Gerald P. Nye and American Foreign Relations* (Minneapolis: University of Minnesota Press, 1962), 181.

9. Historian Thomas J. McCormick describes this era in these terms. For a concise and illuminating account of the world economy in the 1930s, see his *America's Half-Century: United States Foreign Policy in the Cold War,* 2d ed. (Baltimore: Johns Hopkins University Press, 1995), 28–33.

10. On Republican foreign policy during the 1920s see Joan Hoff Wilson, *American Business and Foreign Policy, 1920–1933* (Lexington: University Press of Kentucky, 1971); Melvyn P. Leffler, *The Elusive Quest: America's Pursuit of European Stability and French Security, 1919–1933* (Chapel Hill: University of North Carolina Press, 1979); Ellis W. Hawley, *The Great War and the Search for a Modern Order: A History of the American People and Their Institutions, 1917–1933* (New York: St. Martin's Press, 1979).

11. *The Diplomacy of the Dollar: First Era, 1919–1932* (Baltimore: Johns Hopkins University Press, 1950).

12. See her *Spreading the American Dream: American Economic and Cultural Expansion, 1890–1945* (New York: Hill and Wang, 1982), 169–201.

13. On the expansion of executive powers in the 1930s see Wilfred E. Binkley, *President and Congress,* 3d ed. (New York: Vintage Books, 1962), 289–336; Louis William Koenig, *The Presidency and The Crisis: Powers of the Office from the Invasion of Poland to Pearl Harbor* (New York: King's Crown Press, 1945); Harold Hongju Koh, *The National Security Constitution: Sharing Power after the Iran-Contra Affair* (New Haven: Yale University Press, 1990), 93–100.

14. Godfrey Hodgson, *The Colonel: The Life and Wars of Henry Stimson, 1867–1950* (New York: Alfred A. Knopf, 1990).

15. Ibid., 140, 388.

16. This was also true for elected officials from San Francisco and Los Angeles. In many respects, these two western "Goliaths" had more in common with the big northeastern metropolises than they did with the rest of the West. See Richard Franklin Bensel, *Sectionalism and American Political Development, 1880–1980* (Madison: University of Wisconsin Press, 1984), 37, 411.

17. Bureau of the Census, *Historical Statistics of the United States, Colonial Times to 1970,* 2 vols. (Washington, D.C., 1971), Series U 213-24.

18. Between 1897 and 1914, U.S. direct investments abroad more than quadrupled, rising from an estimated $634 million to $2.6 billion. Cleona Lewis, *America's Stake in International Investments* (Washington, D.C.: Brookings Institution, 1938), 605.

19. Matthew Simon and David E. Novack, "Some Dimensions of the American Commercial Invasion of Europe, 1871–1914: An Introductory Essay," *Journal of Economic History* 24 (December 1964): 602.

20. Bureau of the Census, *Historical Statistics,* Series U 213-24.

21. On the European reaction see David E. Novack and Matthew Simon, "Commercial Responses to the American Export Invasion, 1871–1914: An Essay in Attitudinal History," *Explorations in Entrepreneurial History* 3 (winter 1966): 121–47.

22. Simon and Novack, "Some Dimensions of the American Commercial Invasion of Europe," 604.

23. Bensel, *Sectionalism and American Political Development,* 107.

24. Lewis, *America's Stake in International Investments,* 447.

25. Frederick C. Adams, *Economic Diplomacy: The Export-Import Bank and American Foreign Policy, 1934–1939* (Columbia: University of Missouri Press, 1976), 32–33.

26. Lewis, *America's Stake in International Investments,* 619–29.

27. Adams, *Economic Diplomacy,* 32; Lewis, *America's Stake in International Investments,* 605.

28. Lewis, *America's Stake in International Investments,* 606.

29. Bureau of the Census, *Historical Statistics,* Series U 213-24.

30. Ibid.

31. Calculated by author from Bureau of the Census, *Historical Statistics,* Series U 213-24, U 274-94.

32. Calculated by author from Bureau of the Census, *Historical Statistics,* Series U 274-94.

33. David A. Lake, *Power, Protection, and Free Trade: International Sources of U.S. Commercial Strategy, 1887–1939* (Ithaca: University of Cornell Press, 1988), 77.

34. At each census from 1899 to 1929, wage jobs, expressed as a percentage of the total for the United States, exceeded the corresponding percentage of population only in the New England, the Middle Atlantic, and the Great Lakes regions. Bureau of the Census, *Location of Manufactures, 1899–1929* (Washington, D.C., 1933), 9.

35. On the rise and maturation of America's urban-industrial metropolises see David R. Meyer, "Emergence of the American Manufacturing Belt: An Interpretation," *Journal of Historical Geography* 9 (1983): 145–74; Michael P. Conzen, "The Maturing Urban System in the United States, 1840–1910," *Annals of the Association of American Geographers* 67 (March 1977): 88–108; Allan R. Pred, *The Spatial Dynamics of U.S. Urban-Industrial Growth, 1800–1914: Interpretive and Theoretical Essays* (Cambridge: MIT Press, 1966).

36. Calculated by author from Bureau of the Census, *Location of Manufacturers,* 50, 54–55. Data on value-added by manufacturing for Philadelphia and Pittsburgh are from Bureau of the Census, *Biennial Census of Manufactures, 1931* (Washington, D.C., 1935), 34–35.

37. The average for all the country's most export-dependent industrial sectors was one-third. Only in the area of rubber did the big eight's share of the industrial workforce drop below one-third, and even here 35 percent of the jobs

were located in Cleveland's "satellite" city, Akron. All figures calculated by author from Bureau of the Census, *Fifteenth Census of the U.S. Manufactures: 1929. State Series* (Washington, D.C., 1932), table 13. Data for Philadelphia and Pittsburgh from Bureau of the Census, *Biennial Census of Manufactures, 1927* (Washington, D.C., 1932), table 4.

38. In 1929, the leading foreign investors (foreign direct investment divided by book value of fixed capital, by sector) were in machinery (23.3 percent), mining and petroleum (17.7 percent), motor vehicles (14.9), and rubber products (13.8). Jeffry A. Frieden, "Sectoral Conflict and U.S. Foreign Economic Policy, 1914–1940," *International Organization* 42 (winter 1988): 59–60, 65, table 2.

39. See, for example, G. William Domhoff, *The Power Elite and the State: How Policy Is Made in America* (New York: Aldine de Gruyter, 1990), 107–51; Gabriel Kolko, *The Roots of American Foreign Policy* (Boston: Beacon, 1969); Lawrence H. Shoup and William Minter, *Imperial Brain Trust* (New York: Monthly Review, 1977).

40. The analysis here is based on final House votes. Eighteen roll call votes were used to measure support for free trade. The following pieces of legislation were included: Mongrel Tariff (1883); McKinley Tariff (1890); Wilson-Gorman Tariff (1894); Dingley Tariff (1897); Payne-Aldrich Tariff (1909); Underwood Tariff (1913); Fordney-McCumber Tariff (1922); Smoot-Hawley (1930); and the Reciprocal Trade Agreements Act (1934) and its extensions in 1937, 1940, 1943, and 1945. Paired votes and announced positions were treated as formal votes.

41. In the 1890s, 38 percent of all congressmen from the urban Northeast supported freer trade on average. In the 1930s the average share was 70 percent. In the rural Northeast the percent of congressmen favoring freer trade in the 1890s and 1930s was 27 percent and 36 percent, respectively.

42. On the changing partisan composition of the urban Northeast see David Burner, *The Politics of Provincialism: The Democratic Party in Transition, 1918–1932* (New York: W. W. Norton, 1967); Gerald H. Gamm, *The Making of New Deal Democrats: Voting Behavior and Realignment in Boston, 1920–1940* (Chicago: University of Chicago Press, 1986); Carl N. Degler, "American Political Parties and the Rise of the City: An Interpretation," *Journal of American History* 51 (June 1964): 41–59.

43. See Samuel J. Eldersveld, "The Influence of Metropolitan Pluralities in Presidential Elections since 1920: A Study of Twelve Key Cities," *American Political Science Review* 63 (December 1949): 1189–1206; Jerome M. Clubb and Howard W. Allen, "The Cities and the Election of 1928: Partisan Realignment?" *American Historical Review* 74 (April 1969): 1205–20.

44. From 1883 to 1945 the Democrats' average share of House seats in the rural Northeast was 25 percent.

45. V. O. Key, Jr., "The Future of the Democratic Party," *Virginia Quarterly Review* 28 (Spring 1952): 161–75.

46. On the impact of immigration on the Democratic party see Samuel Lubell, *The Future of American Politics* (New York: Harper and Row, 1965), 43–68.

47. Patrick J. Hearden, *Roosevelt Confronts Hitler: America's Entry into World War II* (DeKalb: Northern Illinois University Press, 1987), 50–51.

48. Roosevelt acted cautiously at first, looking for ways to make the RTAA more palatable to the rural West and the "small town" Northeast. But these efforts amounted to little more than "information campaigns." In the end, western agrarian concerns were sacrificed by the administration in favor of policies that disproportionately benefited the urban Northeast and the agrarian South. For a discussion of the Democrats' campaign in the rural West see Author W. Schatz, "The Reciprocal Trade Agreements Program and the 'Farm Vote,' 1934–1940," *Agricultural History* 46 (October 1972): 508–11.

49. As Republican presidential hopefuls like Alfred Landon came to learn: attacking reciprocal trade might be good for winning the party's western wing, and thus the nomination, but it came at the cost of alienating the party's eastern wing. For a compelling account of this shift see Thomas Ferguson, "From Normalcy to New Deal: Industrial Structure, Party Competition, and American Public Policy in the Great Depression," *International Organization* 28 (winter 1984): 41–94. On Republican tariff politics during the 1936 campaign see Schatz, "Reciprocal Trade Agreements," 506–8.

50. On business attitudes toward the tariff see Hearden, *Roosevelt Confronts Hitler*, 48–51, 164–65, 223–31.

51. Ibid., 50.

52. For Stimson's views on the nation's foreign policy during the 1920s see Hodgson, *The Colonel*, 193–203.

53. Asher Isaacs, *International Trade: Tariff and Commercial Policies* (Chicago: Irwin, 1948), 244.

54. Calculated by author from Bureau of the Census, *Historical Statistics*, Series U 274-94.

55. *Cong. Rec.*, 73d Cong., 1st sess., 1941, 87, pt. 2:5274.

56. Representative Charles I. Faddis, *Cong. Rec.*, 73d Cong., 2d sess., 1934, 78, pt. 5:5357. Faddis, a Democrat, represented the 25th district in Pennsylvania, a district neighboring Pittsburgh.

57. Technically, the RTAA was an amendment to the Smoot-Hawley tariff. The idea of MFN was to negotiate with the country or countries producing the major portion of a commodity imported or potentially importable into the United States and extend those concessions to others exporting the same commodity to the United States. Countries without most-favored-nation status would, however, be subject to the higher Smoot-Hawley tariff duties.

58. To be sure, many of the RTAA's key provisions, such as most-favored-nation treatment, had been part of previous tariff laws. Congress also kept the president on a tight leash by limiting his negotiating authority to only three years at a time. This shift in tariff-making powers is described in Lake, *Power, Protection, and Free Trade*, 204–12. See also Judith Goldstein, *Ideas, Interests, and American Trade Policy* (Ithaca: Cornell University Press, 1993), 152–58; Stephan Haggard, "The Institutional Foundations of Hegemony: Explaining the Recip-

rocal Trade Agreements Act of 1934," *International Organization* 42 (winter 1988): 91–119.

59. Between 1934 and 1939, the Roosevelt administration negotiated twenty-two trade agreements and three supplementary ones. One or more agreements were signed with the following nations: Argentina, Belgium, Brazil, Canada, Colombia, Costa Rica, Cuba, Czechoslovakia, Ecuador, El Salvador, Finland, France, Guatemala, Haiti, Honduras, Netherlands, Nicaragua, Sweden, Switzerland, Turkey, United Kingdom, and Venezuela.

60. One analyst indicates that exports to reciprocity nations during this period had jumped 63 percent while exports to nonagreement countries grew by only 31.7 percent. See Asher, *International Trade,* 273.

61. Lake, *Power, Protection, and Free Trade,* 208.

62. Bureau of the Census, *Historical Statistics,* Series U 317-34.

63. On the evolution of U.S. strategy toward Germany during this period see Hearden, *Roosevelt Confronts Hitler;* C. A. MacDonald, *The United States, Britain, and Appeasement, 1936–1939 (New York: St. Martin's Press, 1981); Frederick W. Marks III, Wind over Sand: The Diplomacy of Franklin Roosevelt* (Athens: University of Georgia Press, 1988); Dallek, *Franklin D. Roosevelt and American Foreign Policy.*

64. The following discussion of neutrality draws heavily on Robert Divine's *The Illusion of Neutrality* (Chicago: University of Chicago Press, 1962).

65. It also authorized him to prohibit Americans from traveling on ships of belligerents—a provision designed to prevent incidents such as the sinking of the *Lusitania* in World War I.

66. Most of those countries were already ineligible for private loans under the Johnson Debt-Default Act of 1934. The Johnson Act prevented private loans to any country that had defaulted on their World War I debts to the United States. By June 1934, all the European nations except Finland had defaulted on those debts.

67. For a good discussion of the problems the neutrality laws posed for deterrence see Arthur Stein, "Domestic Constraints, Extended Deterrence, and the Incoherence of Grand Strategy: The United States, 1938–1950," in *The Domestic Bases of Grand Strategy,* ed. Richard Rosecrance and Arthur Stein (Ithaca: Cornell University Press, 1993), 96–123.

68. Cited in Thomas N. Guinsburg, *The Pursuit of Isolationism in the United States Senate from Versailles to Pearl Harbor* (New York: Garland, 1982), 232.

69. Foreign buyers still had to pay cash on the barrel-head and use non-American ships to transport the goods.

70. Hearden, *Roosevelt and Hitler,* 168.

71. Representative Charles S. Dewey, a Democrat from Chicago, *Cong. Rec.,* 77th Cong., 1st sess., 1941, 87, pt. 1:511.

72. On the divisions within the business community over neutrality see Ronald N. Stromberg, "American Business and the Approach of War, 1935–1941," *Journal of Economic History* 13 (winter 1953): 58–78.

73. See Hearden's discussion of big business and its fears of a closed world in *Roosevelt Confronts Hitler,* 155-88.

74. See Stein, "Domestic Constraints, Extended Deterrence," 108-10.

75. For many businessmen, World War I was also "a sour memory." While corporate advisers gained considerable influence over the War Industries Board, which was responsible for organizing industries to meet wartime needs, the Wilson government's conduct was far from businesslike. Firms faced numerous delays in receiving payment and some believed that they had been shortchanged by the government. Gerald T. White, *Billions for Defense: Government Financing by the Defense Plant Corporation during World War II* (University, Ala.: University of Alabama Press, 1980), 3.

76. For a stimulating account of the struggle between New Dealers and big business see Brian Waddell, "Economic Mobilization for World War II and the Transformation of the U.S. State," *Politics and Society* 22 (June 1994): 165-94.

77. Ibid., 174.

78. Ibid., 175.

79. Ibid., 173.

80. For a general overview of southern internationalism see George B. Tindall, *The Emergence of the New South, 1913-1945* (Baton Rouge: Louisiana State University Press, 1967), 687-731; Paul Seabury, *The Waning of Southern "Internationalism"* (Princeton, N.J.: Center of International Studies, 1957); Marian D. Irish, "Foreign Policy and the South," *Journal of Politics* 24 (May 1948): 306-26; Alexander DeConde, "The South and Isolationism," *Journal of Southern History* 24 (August 1958): 333-46; George C. Herring and Gary R. Hess, "Regionalism and Foreign Policy: The Dying Myth of Southern Internationalism," *Southern Studies* 20 (fall 1981): 247-77.

81. The irony of this was not lost on southerners. As Luther Patrick, a congressman from Alabama, observed: "[T]hey had to start selective service to keep our Southern boys from filling up the army." Alfred O. Hero, Jr., *The Southerner and World Affairs* (Baton Rouge: Louisiana State University Press, 1965), 85.

82. Seabury, *Waning of Southern "Internationalism,"* 2.

83. Others have made the same point. See, for example, ibid., 3-7; Cole, *Senator Gerald P. Nye and American Foreign Policy,* 5-6.

84. Hull was one of three southern appointments to Roosevelt's cabinet. The others were Daniel Roper of South Carolina as secretary of commerce and Senator Claude Swanson of Virginia as secretary of the navy. See Frank Freidel, *F.D.R. and the South* (Baton Rouge, Louisiana State University Press), 42-43.

85. For an excellent summary of Hull's views about trade and its relation to security matters see Arthur W. Schatz, "The Anglo-American Trade Agreement and Cordell Hull's Search for Peace, 1936-1938," *Journal of American History* 57 (June 1970): 85-103. See also William R. Allen, "Cordell Hull and the Defense of the Trade Agreements Program, 1934-1940," in *Isolation and Security,* ed. Alexander DeConde (Durham: Duke University Press, 1957), 107-32; Irwin F.

Gellman, *Secret Affairs: Franklin Roosevelt, Cordell Hull, and Sumner Welles* (Baltimore: Johns Hopkins University Press, 1995).

86. Allen, "Cordell Hull and the Defense of the Trade Agreements Program," 126.

87. Quoted in Robert M. Hathaway, "1933–1945: Economic Diplomacy in a Time of Crisis," in *Economics and World Power: An Assessment of American Diplomacy since 1789*, ed. William H. Becker and Samuel F. Wells, Jr. (New York: Columbia University Press, 1984), 281.

88. The consensus among historians is that Roosevelt, after emphasizing nationalism during his first year in office, moved increasingly toward internationalism. The best account of Roosevelt and internationalism is Dallek's *Franklin D. Roosevelt and American Foreign Policy*. Others that share this view include Frank Freidel, *Franklin D. Roosevelt: Launching the New Deal* (Boston: Little, Brown, 1973); William E. Leuchtenberg, *Franklin D. Roosevelt and the New Deal* (New York: Harper and Row, 1963); Arthur M. Schlesinger, Jr., *The Coming of the New Deal* (Boston: Houghton Mifflin, 1958).

89. Germany was not alone in resorting to discriminatory trade practices: America, England, France, and others had, to greater and lesser extents, done the same. The Nazis, however, exploited these practices most fully.

90. For a summary of American opinion toward the situation in Europe and, more generally, toward the Axis Powers see Hero, *Southerner and World Affairs*, 91–103.

91. Ibid., 95.

92. On the 1938 election see Richard Polenberg, "The Decline of the New Deal, 1937–1940," in *The New Deal: The National Level*, ed. John Braeman, Robert H. Bremner, and David Brody (Columbus: Ohio State University Press, 1975), 1:246–66.

93. Wayne S. Cole, "America First and the South, 1940–41," *Journal of Southern History* 22 (February 1956), 46. See also Virginius Dabney, "The South Looks Abroad," *Foreign Affairs* 19 (October 1940): 176.

94. Cole, "America First and the South," 45.

95. The rest consisting mostly of petroleum products, lumber and wood products, naval stores, and sulfur. On southern dependence on foreign markets see B. U. Ratchford, "The South's Stake in International Trade—Past, Present, and Prospective," *Southern Economic Journal* 14 (April 1948): 361–75. See also Hal B. Lary, *The United States in the World Economy* (Washington, D.C.: GPO, 1943), 58–62.

96. Average for 1925–29. Robert E. Lipsey, *Price and Quantity Trends in the Foreign Trade of the United States* (Princeton: Princeton University Press, 1963), app., table G-11.

97. Calvin B. Hoover and B. U. Ratchford, *Economic Resources and Policies of the South* (New York: Macmillan, 1951), 427.

98. Ratchford, "The South's Stake in International Trade," 364–68.

99. Not all of this was a result of the worldwide decline in international trade brought on by high tariffs, stringent quotas, and currency controls. Domestic sub-

sidies for agricultural goods in the United States, especially cotton, and the New Deal's acreage control program also played a role. So did increased production of cotton outside the United States, and rising world-wide consumption of synthetic fibers.

100. In an average year, the United States sold about 6.27 million bales of cotton abroad, providing jobs for some 1.3 million southerners, with approximately 5.3 million dependents. These estimates are for the 1930–39 period. Data on cotton exports are taken from Hoover and Ratchford, *Economic Resources and Policies of the South,* 308, table 128. The ratios used to calculate cotton export employment and dependency are derived from Dabney, "The South Looks Abroad," 175.

101. Arthur S. Link, *Wilson: The Struggle for Neutrality* (Princeton: Princeton University Press, 1960), 138. See also Link, "The Cotton Crisis, the South, and Anglo-American Diplomacy, 1914–1915," in *Studies in Southern History,* ed. J. Carlyle Sitterson (Chapel Hill: University of North Carolina Press, 1957), 39:122–38; Gilbert C. Fite, *Cotton Fields No More: Southern Agriculture, 1865–1980* (Lexington: University Press of Kentucky, 1984), 92–93.

102. Link, "The Cotton Crisis," 135.

103. On the southern response to World War I see Tindall, *The Emergence of the New South,* 33–69; Herring and Hess, "Regionalism and Foreign Policy," 248–53; Richard L. Watson, Jr., "A Testing Time for Southern Congressional Leadership: The War Crisis of 1917–1918," *Journal of Southern History* 44 (February 1978): 3–40.

104. In the House, four-fifths of the southerners supported all of Wilson's wartime policies. In the Senate, two-thirds of the South's members voted for the administration's wartime initiatives. See Timothy G. McDonald, "Southern Democratic Congressmen and the First World War, August 1914–April 1917: The Public Record of Their Support for or Opposition to Wilson's Policies" (Ph.D. diss., University of Washington, 1962).

105. Tindall, *The Emergence of the New South,* 38–39.

106. See Idus A. Newby, "States' Rights and Southern Congressmen during World War I," *Phylon* 24 (spring 1963): 34–50.

107. Calculated by author from data in John C. deWilde, "The AAA and Exports of the South," *Foreign Policy Reports* 11 (April 1935): 40–42.

108. Once relatively inconsequential, Japan was now one of the biggest consumers of American cotton; Britain and Germany were the others. The Japanese, along with Chinese, were also now steady consumers of southern tobacco. During the same period, Japan and China, the main importers of southern cotton in Asia, took 29 percent of the South's cotton trade. Japan and China also took 20 percent of the South's exports of tobacco.

109. Seabury, *Waning of Southern "Internationalism,"* 15.

110. Representative Malcom C. Tarver (D-GA), *Cong. Rec.,* 77th Cong., 1st sess., 1941, 87, pt. 1:550.

111. Secretary Hull shared these fears about New Deal reformers. "If they really get in the saddle," he warned several months before Pearl Harbor, "they

will adopt a closed economy." Quoted in Hearden, *Roosevelt Confronts Hitler,* 231.

112. On this point see James C. Cobb, *Industrialization and Southern Society, 1877–1984* (Louisville: University Press of Kentucky, 1984), 27–50.

113. In 1880 southern per capita income was 51 percent of the national average; by 1920 it had risen to 62 percent; by 1930 it had fallen back to 55 percent.

114. "The South," noted Howard W. Odum, was "essentially colonial in its economy," having entered the 1930s with "the general status of an agricultural country engaged in trade with industrial countries." See his seminal *Southern Regions of the United States* (Chapel Hill: University of North Carolina Press, 1936), 353. The notion that the South was still a colonial economy was shared by many others. See, for example, Rupert Vance, *Human Geography of the South* (Chapel Hill: University of North Carolina Press, 1936), 442–81; Walter Prescott Webb, *Divided We Stand: The Crisis of a Frontierless Democracy* (New York: Farrar and Rinehart, 1937). A discussion of this theme in southern writing can be found in Clarence H. Danhof, "Four Decades of Thought on the South's Economic Problems," in *Essays in Southern Economic Development,* ed. Melvin L. Greenhut and W. Tate Whitman (Chapel Hill: University of North Carolina Press, 1964), 7–68.

115. Cobb, *Industrialization and Southern Society,* 36.

116. Dewey W. Grantham, *The Life and Death of the Solid South: A Political History* (Louisville: University Press of Kentucky, 1988), 87. The best account of the one-party system remains V. O. Key, *Southern Politics in State and Nation* (New York: Alfred A. Knopf, 1949).

117. On the southern variant of progressivism see Tindall, *Emergence of the New South,* 219–53; Grantham, *The Life and Death of the Solid South,* 55–57. For a discussion of scholarly debate on the roots of southern progressivism see Howard N. Rabinowitz, *The First New South, 1865–1920* (Arlington Heights, Ill.: Harlan Davidson, 1992), 118–31, 205–10.

118. Cobb, *Industrialization and Southern Society,* 28.

119. Freidel, *F.D.R. and the South,* 35.

120. There is little question, writes Elizabeth Sanders, that had southern lawmakers been free to implement their own recovery program, "it would have looked very different from the welfare/regulatory state that is the New Deal legacy." There would have been less federal regulation of the domestic economy, a much smaller Washington bureaucracy, and an even greater commitment to world trade. Elizabeth Sanders, "The Regulatory Surge of the 1970s in Historical Perspective," in *Public Regulation: New Perspectives on Institutions and Policies,* ed. Elizabeth E. Bailey (Cambridge: MIT Press, 1986), 127.

121. Freidel summarizes the dilemma confronting southern elites this way: "The South was so painfully in need of succor that they desperately sought federal aid; yet the New Deal inevitably threatened to upset the status quo and alter some of the cherished institutions upon which they fervently believed the very existence of Southern civilization depended." *F.D.R. and the South,* 35. For an excellent overview of this issue and its impact on the development of the early New Deal see Bruce J. Schulman, *From Cotton Belt to Sunbelt: Federal Policy, Eco-*

nomic Development, and the Transformation of the South, 1938-1980 (New York: Oxford University Press, 1991), 3-38.

122. Schulman, *From Cotton Belt to Sunbelt,* 47. This opinion is shared by other historians. See, for example, Tindall, *Emergence of the New South,* 618.

123. The Agricultural Act of 1933 provided refinancing for thousands of farm mortgages being called by private lenders and, more significantly, established the Agricultural Assistance Administration (AAA). The AAA authorized a wide range of activities designed to raise farm prices and incomes by regulating production, but it was careful to avoid antagonizing the planter class. Like other New Deal agencies, it put Washington-appointed administrators in each state, but the real power was granted to county-level committees. In the case of the South, this effectively granted southern landlords control of the program. In the end, the interests of wealthy commercial planters were well represented while the needs of thousands of subsistence farmers were largely ignored. My interpretation follows Alan Brinkley, "The New Deal and Southern Politics," in *The New Deal and the South,* ed. James C. Cobb and Michael V. Namorato (Jackson: University Press of Mississippi, 1984), 97-116. For a brief history of the early AAA and related issues consult Murray R. Benedict, *Farm Policies of the United States, 1790-1950* (New York: Twentieth Century Fund, 1953), 276-315.

124. The phrase is from Key, *Southern Politics,* 645.

125. On southern responses to various New Deal reforms see Bensel, *Sectionalism and American Political Development,* 147-73; David M. Potter, *The South and the Concurrent Majority* (Baton Rouge: Louisiana State University, 1972), 66-74; James T. Patterson, *Congressional Conservatism and the New Deal: The Growth of the Conservative Coalition in Congress, 1933-1939* (Lexington: University of Kentucky Press, 1967), passim.

126. The 1930s witnessed the birth of the so-called conservative coalition. This coalition of southern Democrats and Republicans, which figured so prominently in American politics after World War II, initially arose in opposition to New Deal legislation. More than 70 percent of the House votes that produced "conservative coalition" voting in the 1930s involved issues of government regulation, civil liberties, and social welfare. This figure is calculated from Mack C. Shelley II, *The Permanent Majority: The Conservative Coalition in the United States Congress* (Mobile: University of Alabama Press, 1983), 47, table 3-3. On the formation of the conservative coalition see Patterson, *Congressional Conservativism and the New Deal.*

127. This was not true of all southern lawmakers. A few southern members of the House and Senate vehemently opposed Roosevelt's foreign policies, just as some had taken issue with Wilson's wartime policies. In the 1930s, these so-called southern radicals—figures such as Robert Rice Reynolds of North Carolina, Huey Long of Lousiana, and Martin Dies, Jr., of Texas—preached what political scientist Charles Lerche has called "a militant and obscurantist doctrine of total withdrawal and noninvolvement in international affairs." Like isolationists from the rural West, "they combined reformism with isolationism," fusing "a demand for economic justice at home with a disavowal of the outside world." Internationalism, for them,

was a symbol of everything that was wrong in American society—big government, Anglophilia, and Wall Street. More fundamentally, they saw it as an ideology that the southern aristocracy used to maintain its hold on southern society. Charles Lerche, *The Uncertain South: Its Changing Patterns of Politics in Foreign Policy* (Chicago: Quadrangle, 1964), 53–54.

128. Ironically, Secretary Hull initially opposed the Export-Import Bank. As the role of the banks changed, and their first president, Hull's arch rival, George Peek, was forced out of the administration, so did the secretary's view of it. On the changing role of the Export-Import Bank, see Adams, *Economic Diplomacy.*

129. Ninety-one percent of the southern delegation also voted for the 1940 extension of the RTAA. Southern support in the Senate was also very broad. Most newspapers in the region echoed these sentiments, as did the cotton traders. Survey data on the issue is spotty, but a 1938 Gallup Poll is probably indicative of southern attitudes. In that survey, more than 90 percent of the southerners surveyed favored the general principles embodied in reciprocal trade—free trade and equal access. To be sure, there were pockets of protectionism in the South. Sugar cane producers in southern Louisiana, having always opposed free trade, also attacked the RTAA, claiming that they could not compete against cheaper Cuban, Dominican, and other foreign sugar. Coal mine operators in southern West Virginia, eastern Kentucky, and southwestern Virginia expressed similar doubts about the benefits of lower tariffs and expanded imports, as did textile millers in the Piedmont of Virginia, North Carolina, South Carolina, and Georgia. Yet no matter how much these groups protested, they were able to move congressional opinion only at the margins—a vote here, a vote there. On southern attitudes toward trade see Hero, *Southerner and World Affairs,* 140–43; DeConde, "The South and Isolationism," 339. The position of the cotton traders and southern newspapers is summarized in Tindall, *Emergence of the New South,* 402.

130. Robert L. Doughton (D-NC), chairman of the House Ways and Means Committee, put it this way:

> Are we to continue standing idly by while the whole commercial structure of our country is being undermined as Nero did while Rome burned? Are we to emulate the ostrich, and bury our heads in the sand and refuse to see that practically every country of continental Europe, as well as England and her major dominions, and several of the countries of South America have vested authority in the executive branch of their respective governments to negotiate reciprocal trade agreements with other countries for the purpose of removing trade restrictions, so that their foreign trade can prosper? The United States alone, among the major commercial powers of the world, is without the authority in the hands of the Executive branch of our Government. It is an alarming thing at a time like this, that we are practically the only nation on earth that has not vested the same or similar power in the hands of our Executive. (*Cong. Rec.,* 73d Cong., 2d sess., 1934, 78, pt. 5:5258)

131. The Smoot-Hawley Act reenacted the flexibility provision of the 1922 Fordney-McCumber Tariff. Like Fordney-McCumber, Smoot-Hawley authorized the executive to impose retaliatory duties of up to 50 percent on the goods of nations that discriminated against U.S. products.

132. *Cong. Rec.,* 73d Cong., 2d sess., 78, pt. 5:5357. Representative Hamilton Fish (R-NY) was more direct: "Thomas Jefferson would turn in his grave at the thought of transferring such autocratic and despotic powers to the Chief Executive. Where are the constitutional and Jeffersonian Democrats in the contest against an economic dictatorship? If they vote for this bill, it must be in open violation of every principle of Jeffersonian Democracy." *Cong. Rec.,* 73d Cong., 2d sess., 1934, 78, pt. 5:5614.

133. Representative Colgate W. Darden, Jr. (D-VA), *Cong. Rec.,* 73d Cong., 2d sess., 1934, 78, pt. 5:5451.

134. Peter Molyneaux, *What Economic Nationalism Means to the South* (New York: Foreign Policy Association, 1934), 24, 28. For a review of this theme in southern writing at the time see Danhof, "Four Decades of thought on the South's Economic Problems," 35–37.

135. U.S. National Emergency Council (Washington, D.C., 1938), 60. On the reformist character of the report see Schulman, *From Cotton Belt to Sunbelt,* 49–54.

136. Molyneaux, *What Economic Nationalism Means,* 20.

137. Will Clayton, cotton exporter from Texas and member of Hull's staff, spoke for many in the South: "If experience teaches anything it is that nature's method of automatic regulation through price, arrived at by competitive trading in free markets, is the only system which ever works in world commodities like cotton." Quoted in Tindall, *Emergence of the New South,* 400.

138. *Cong. Rec.,* 73d Cong., 2d sess., 1934, 78, pt. 5:5610.

139. Hero, *Southerner in World Affairs,* 91–103.

140. Ralph H. Smuckler, "The Region of Isolationism," *American Political Science Review* 47 (June 1953): 386–401.

141. On Senator Nye and his prominence in the isolationist camp see Cole, *Gerald P. Nye and American Foreign Relations.*

142. Samuel Lubell, "Who Votes Isolationist and Why," *Harper's Magazine* (April 1951): 29–36. In the face of criticism, Lubell subsequently qualified his claims about the primacy of ethnicity. See his *The Revolt of the Moderates* (New York: Harper, 1956), 273–75.

143. See Manfred Jonas, *Isolationism in America, 1935–1941* (Ithaca: Cornell University Press, 1966), 19–21; Leroy N. Rieselbach, "The Basis of Isolationist Behavior," *Public Opinion Quarterly* 24 (winter 1960): 645–57; David H. Bennett, *Demagogues in the Depression: American Radicals and the Union Party, 1932–1936* (New Brunswick, N.J.: Rutgers University Press, 1969), 269–71; Guinsburg, *Pursuit of Isolationism,* 11–12; Robert P. Wilkins, "Middle Western Isolationism: A Re-Examination," *North Dakota Quarterly* (summer 1957): 69–76.

144. In this respect, their agenda differed from that of more conservative isolationists. Drawing on George Peek's correspondence with other isolationists

in the late 1930s, historian Gilbert C. Fite concluded that many conservatives attacked Roosevelt's foreign policy in hopes of weakening popular support for his domestic policies. "It was hard to convince farmers, laborers, and small businessmen that the New Deal had ruined the country. The Liberty League had found in 1936 that not many voters were scared by the charge of socialism. However, if the President could be pictured as a warmonger or some kind of evil internationalist, a large number of voters might desert him. Thus by making the international question the major issue, Roosevelt might be beaten and his domestic policies reversed or scrapped." Gilbert C. Fite, *George N. Peek and the Fight for Farm Parity* (Norman: University of Oklahoma Press, 1954), 294–95. For an instructive comparison of "conservative" and "progressive" isolationists see Wayne S. Cole's analysis of Arthur Vandenberg's and Gerald Nye's views in "And Then There Were None! How Arthur H. Vandenberg and Gerald P. Nye Separately Departed Isolationist Leadership Roles," in *Behind the Throne: Servants of Power to Imperial Presidents, 1898–1968,* ed. Thomas J. McCormick and Walter LaFeber (Madison: University of Wisconsin Press, 1993), 32–53.

145. On the difficulties facing western agrarians in the 1920s and 1930s see Theodore Saloutos and John D. Hicks, *Agricultural Discontent in the Middle West, 1900–1939* (Madison: University of Wisconsin Press, 1951), especially 87–110; Richard White, *"It's Your Misfortune and None of My Own": A History of the American West* (Norman: University of Oklahoma Press, 1991), 463–95; Gerald D. Nash, *The American West in the Twentieth Century: A Short History of an Urban Oasis* (Englewood Cliffs, N.J.: Prentice-Hall, 1973), 65–109, 139–59.

146. Estimates of agricultural dependency on foreign markets by crop may be found in Austin A. Dowell and Oscar B. Jesness, *The American Farmer and the Export Market* (Minneapolis: University of Minnesota Press, 1934), 66–86. On farm production by region and state consult Ladd Haystead and Gilbert C. Fite, *The Agricultural Regions of the United States* (Norman: University of Oklahoma Press, 1955).

147. In 1930, 50 percent of the country's corn was harvested in the West. Harvey S. Perloff et al., *Regions, Resources, and Economic Growth* (Baltimore: Johns Hopkins University Press, 1960), 198.

148. Of course, some percentage of these feed crops was exported indirectly, in the form of livestock and livestock products. One should not, however, make too much of this. Pork was the only meat product exported in significant quantity by the 1920s, and here exports averaged less than 10 percent of total production.

149. For a discussion see Dowell and Jesness, *American Farmer and the Export Market,* 161–83. See also Sidney Pollard, *Peaceful Conquest: The Industrialization of Europe, 1760–1970* (New York: Oxford University Press, 1981), 264–70.

150. On the secular decline of agricultural exports see Lary, *United States in the World Economy,* 54–62.

151. Benedict, *Farm Policies of the United States,* 233.

152. Computed by author from Bureau of the Census, *Historical Statistics,* Series U 213-24.

153. *Main Currents in Modern American History,* 2d ed. (New York: Pantheon Books, 1984), 197.

154. Cited in James R. Connor, "National Farm Organizations and United States Tariff Policy in the 1920s," *Agricultural History* 32 (January 1958): 35-37.

155. *New York Times Magazine,* 14 January 1940, 1-2.

156. Wayne S. Cole, *Roosevelt and the Isolationists, 1932-45* (Lincoln: University of Nebraska Press, 1983), 6.

157. Justus D. Doenecke, "Power, Markets, and Ideology: The Isolationist Response to Roosevelt Policy, 1940-1941," in *Watershed of Empire: Essays on New Deal Foreign Policy,* ed. Leonard P. Liggio and James J. Martin (Colorado Springs: Ralph Myles, 1976), 150-51.

158. *Cong. Rec.,* 76th Cong., 2d sess., 1939, 85, pt. 2:1167.

159. Edward C. Kirkland, *A History of American Economic Life,* 3d ed. (New York: Appleton-Century-Crofts, 1951), 84.

160. Saloutos and Hicks, *Agricultural Discontent,* 105.

161. Signs of recovery began to appear in 1926, only to be dashed by the economic collapse of 1929.

162. Cited in Fite, *George N. Peek,* 11.

163. The cotton South was also devastated, as cotton prices dropped from $35.34 in 1919 to $17.00 in 1921. However, the slump was less prolonged in the South than in the wheat and corn belts. Tindall, *The Emergence of the New South,* 112.

164. Bureau of the Census, *Historical Statistics,* Series K 502-16.

165. White, *It's Your Misfortune,* 464.

166. Saloutos and Hicks, *Agricultural Discontent,* 100.

167. The most extreme case was Montana, where more than half the farmers lost their farms to foreclosure between 1921 and 1925. White, *It's Your Misfortune,* 464.

168. Saloutos and Hicks describe the basic dilemma that faced those who survived the collapse of real estate prices: "Suppose, for example, a man had purchased a farm for $20,000 during the last year of the boom, with a mortgage of $10,000 on it. By 1928 his farm would have shrunk in value to about $14,000, while the mortgage would probably have remained the same. Thus the farmer's equity would have declined from $10,000 to $4,000. And how could a $4,000 investment support a $10,000 mortgage?" *Agricultural Discontent,* 104.

169. For a discussion of the origins and consequences of McNary-Haugenism, see Fite, *George N. Peek,* 38-58; Saloutos and Hicks, *Agricultural Discontent,* 372-403; Bensel, *Sectionalism and American Political Development,* 128-47; Benedict, *Farm Policies of the United States,* 207-38.

170. The South's heavy reliance on overseas markets and its long-standing opposition to tariffs made it hard for western progressives to mobilize southern legislative support for the plan. Most southern lawmakers initially saw McNary-

Haugenism as a scheme to benefit perishable crops with large domestic and relatively limited international markets. However, declining cotton prices led many in 1927 and 1928 to reconsider their position. For a discussion of southern attitudes toward McNary-Haugenism see Bensel, *Sectionalism and American Political Development,* 142–43.

171. "The farmers, instead of putting their emphasis on trust busting with the hope that this would either preserve or restore what they believed would be a healthy state of competition, tossed such thoughts out the window and proceeded to build restrictive devices patterned to a great degree after those of industry." Saloutos and Hicks, *Agricultural Discontent,* 562.

172. Bensel, *Sectionalism and American Political Development,* 141.

173. Paul Kleppner, "Politics without Parties: The Western States, 1900–1984," in *The Twentieth-Century West: Historical Interpretations,* ed. Gerald D. Nash and Richard W. Etulain (Albuquerque: University of New Mexico Press, 1989), 295–338. On the theme of western colonialism and anticolonialism see Patricia Nelson Limerick, *The Legacy of Conquest: The Unbroken Past of the American West* (New York: W. W. Norton, 1987), 78–96; Gerald D. Nash, *The American West Transformed: The Impact of the Second World War* (Bloomington: Indiana University Press, 1985), vii, 3–14. On the relationship between western anticolonialism and isolationism see Ray Allen Billington, "The Origins of Middle Western Isolationism," *Political Science Quarterly* 60 (March 1945): 44–64.

174. Kleppner, "Politics without Parties," 328.

175. As Richard White observes, "Many of them would still join crusades against railroads, banks, and large corporations not because they disapproved of either capitalism or large corporations in principle, but because these economic organizations symbolized eastern control, control by outsiders." *It's Your Misfortune,* 386.

176. Kleppner, "Politics without Parties," 329.

177. The Republicans' lock on the region was, of course, broken in the 1930s. In the 1932 election, the region swung sharply toward the Democrats, and the Republicans lost badly in the region in the 1936 election as well. Yet as impressive as Roosevelt's personal victories were, they did not translate into Democratic hegemony in the region. Roosevelt usually ran considerably ahead of Democratic congressional and state candidates, and generally speaking the Republicans remained competitive in the region. Eventually Roosevelt would begin to lose western support. On the party balance in the region during the 1930s see Kleppner, "Politics without Parties"; John M. Allswang, *The New Deal and American Politics: A Study in Political Change* (New York: John Wiley, 1978), 89–111.

178. Kleppner, "Politics without Parties," 328.

179. Ibid.

180. In time, of course, this changed. As the federal government's role in promoting regional economic development expanded, it became the object of western ire and resentment. "Washington began to supplant Wall Street as the focus of anticolonial sentiment and rhetoric." But that was much later—decades later. Ibid., 330.

181. White, *It's Your Misfortune,* 354.

182. As historian Thomas Guinsburg points out, western senators also defined the issue of neutrality in terms that had strong sectional overtones. Senators from the rural West

> gave greatest credence to the extreme revisionist interpretation of the First World War and its vilification of munitions-makers and financiers. Consistently they railed at the eastern interests that had pushed the nation into the last war and, unless checked, would push it into the next. Inevitably these senators and the people they spoke for felt great distrust for the cosmopolitan 'internationalized' world of finance and diplomacy which they believed influential in the White House, irrespective of the party occupying it. (*Pursuit of Isolationism,* 287)

183. *Cong. Rec.,* 76th Cong., 2d sess., 1939, 85, pt. 1:384.

184. Representative U. S. Guyer (R-MO), *Cong. Rec.,* 76th Cong., 2d sess., 1939, 85, pt. 2:1257.

185. Representative Henry C. Luckey (D-NE), *Cong. Rec.,* 75th Cong., 1st sess., 1937, 81, pt. 3:2382.

186. Anti-British rhetoric was regularly employed by western isolationists in debates over U.S. policy toward Europe. On isolationists' attitudes towards the British, see Cushing Strout, *The American Image of the Old World* (New York: Harper and Row, 1963), 196–219.

187. Representative Henry C. Luckey (D-NE), *Cong. Rec.,* 75th Cong., 1st sess., 1937, 85, pt. 2:2383.

188. Guinsburg, *Pursuit of Isolationism,* 267.

189. The more economically involved Americans became in the European crisis, argued Senator Nye, the more difficult it would become to avoid military involvement:

> That is the danger of economic involvement—never crass profits. When industry after industry is operating on war orders, expanding their debts and their plants to fill war orders, when millions of farmers are mortgaging themselves to the hilt to grow food and cotton at war prices, when the British Empire is permitted to assume the terrible risk of a war of conquest on the basis of our supplies—then we have created what I mean by economic involvement. Then each decision we have to make has to be made in that situation, not in indifferent calm. Then any attempt to prevent further and more dangerous involvement creates panic at home and catastrophe abroad. When the living of millions of our people becomes dependent upon war trade with England, and upon her military success, and when England becomes dependent, perhaps for her very life, upon an unbroken stream of supplies from us, then, indeed, we will have reached the place where it is more bloody to go back than to go forward. We reached that place in the fall of 1916 and the early months

of 1917. We arrived at a financial crisis inextricably involved in allied financing, and at the same time we arrived at a crisis with Germany over the issue of armed merchantmen—an issue that, in turn, gave rise to the submarine controversies. All three have been intertwined in the past and they remained intertwined inextricably. (*Cong. Rec.,* 76th Cong., 2d sess., 1939, 85, pt. 1:368)

190. On the impact of the Great Depression in the West see Nash, *The American West in the Twentieth Century,* 139–59; White, *It's Your Misfortune,* 465–72; Theodore Saloutos, *The American Farmer and the New Deal* (Ames: Iowa State University Press, 1982), 3–14. See also Jordan A. Schwarz, *The New Dealers: Power Politics in the Age of Roosevelt* (New York: Alfred A. Knopf, 1993), passim.

191. White, *It's Your Misfortune,* 463–64.

192. Leonard J. Arrington, "The Sagebrush Resurrection: New Deal Expenditures in the Western States, 1933–39," *Pacific Historical Review* 52 (February 1983): 3.

193. On the regional distribution of New Deal spending see Don C. Reading, "New Deal Activity and the States, 1933–39," *Journal of Economic History* 33 (December 1973): 792–810; Leonard J. Arrington, "The New Deal in the West: A Preliminary Statistical Inquiry," *Pacific Historical Review* 38 (August 1969): 311–16; Leonard J. Arrington, "Western Agriculture and the New Deal," *Agricultural History* (October 1970): 337–53.

194. Nash, *The American West in the Twentieth Century,* 172.

195. See, for example, Gavin Wright, "The Political Economy of New Deal Spending: An Econometric Analysis," *The Review of Economics and Statistics* 56 (February 1974): 30–38.

196. Representative Dewey Short (R-MO), *Cong. Rec.,* 76th Cong., 2d sess., 1939, 85, pt. 2:1167.

197. Wayne Cole, *Roosevelt and the Isolationists,* 140.

198. James T. Patterson, "The New Deal in the West," *Pacific Historical Review* 38 (August 1969): 319.

199. Ibid., 324.

200. Ibid.

201. Ibid., 325.

202. Wayne Cole, discussing Senator Nye's investigation of the munitions industry, explains:

Initially, the munitions investigation was at least as anti-business as it was anti-war. Later the investigation broadened its attack so that the executive branch of the government as well as big business came under fire. This development too was logical in terms of agrarian interests. The President was more dependent upon the growing urban constituency for his political sustenance than he was upon the shrinking rural voting population. In Congress, however, and in state legislatures farming areas were overrepresented. If Nye's efforts to restrict presidential powers and to increase congressional authority in foreign affairs had prevailed, the effect generally would have been more welcome to rural America than to its cities. (*Senator Gerald P. Nye and American Foreign Relations,* 9)

203. See Schatz, "Reciprocal Trade Agreements," 498–514; Saloutos, *American Farmer,* 137–49; David L. Porter, *Congress and the Waning of the New Deal* (New York: Kennikat, 1980), 45–58.

204. The phrase is Arthur Krock's, Washington correspondent of *The New York Times* (Guinsburg, *Pursuit of Isolationism,* 231).

205. Cited in Steven Robert Brenner, "Economic Interests and the Trade Agreements Program, 1937–1940: A Study of Institutions and Political Influence," (Ph.D. diss., Stanford University, 1977), 85–86.

206. Schatz, "Reciprocal Trade Agreements," 511.

207. Cole, *Roosevelt and the Isolationists,* 207.

208. *The Democratic Roosevelt* (Garden City, N.Y.: n.p., 1957) 449–50, 460, 478. Tugwell's views about Roosevelt's political calculus are shared by others. See, for example, Milton Plesur, "The Republican Congressional Comeback of 1938," *Review of Politics* 24 (October 1962): 525–62; Howard R. Smith, *Economic History of the United States* (New York: Ronald Press, 1956), 619.

209. There are several versions of this argument. See Charles S. Maier, "The Politics of Productivity: Foundations of American International Economic Policy after World War II," in *Between Power and Plenty: Foreign Economic Policies of Advanced Industrial States,* ed. Peter J. Katzenstein (Madison: University of Wisconsin Press, 1978), 23–49; Michael Hogan, "American Marshall Planners and the Search for a European Neocapitalism," *American Historical Review* 90 (February 1985): 44–72; John G. Ruggie, "International Regimes, Transactions, and Change: Embedded Liberalism in the Postwar Economic Order," in *International Regimes,* ed. Stephen D. Krasner (Ithaca: Cornell University Press, 1983), 195–231; Franz Schurmann, *The Logic of World Power: An Inquiry into the Origins, Currents, and Contradictions of World Politics* (New York: Pantheon Books, 1974), 3–113; Fred L. Block, *The Origins of International Economic Disorder: A Study of United States International Monetary Policy from World War II to the Present* (Berkeley and Los Angeles: University of California Press, 1977); William S. Borden, *The Pacific Alliance: United States Foreign Economic Policy and Japanese Trade Recovery, 1947–54* (Madison: University of Wisconsin Press, 1984); Joyce Kolko and Gabriel Kolko, *The Limits of Power: The World and United States Foreign Policy, 1945–1954* (New York: Harper and Row, 1972); Robert W. Cox, *Production, Power, and World Order* (New York: Columbia University Press, 1987).

210. This argument is most forcefully developed in Ferguson, "From Normalcy to New Deal." For related accounts see Bruce Cumings, *The Origins of the Korean War,* vol. 2, *The Roaring of the Cataract, 1947–1950* (Princeton: Princeton University Press, 1990); Frieden, "Sectoral Conflict and Foreign Economic Policy"; Peter Gourevitch, "Breaking with Orthodoxy: The Politics of Economic Policy Response to the Depression of the 1930s," *International Organiza-*

tion 38 (winter 1984): 95–129; Michael J. Hogan, *The Marshall Plan: America, Britain and the Reconstruction of Western Europe, 1947–1952* (New York: Oxford University Press, 1987).

211. James Kurth reaches much the same conclusion in his "Between Europe and America: The New York Foreign Policy Elite," in *Capital of the American Century: The National and International Influence of New York City,* ed. Martin Shefter (New York: Russell Sage Foundation, 1993), 71–94.

212. This view is perhaps most closely associated with E. H. Carr. See his classic *The Twenty Years' Crisis, 1919–1939: An Introduction to the Study of International Relations* (1939; reprint, London: Macmillan, 1962), 234.

213. Frieden, "Sectoral Conflict and Foreign Economic Policy," 68.

214. The argument is most closely associated with historian Paul Kennedy and his *The Rise and Fall of the Great Powers: Economic Change and Military Conflict from 1500 to 2000* (New York: Random House, 1987).

215. The arguments are summarized in Richard N. Gardner's *Sterling-Dollar Diplomacy in Current Perspective: The Origins and the Prospects of Out International Economic Order,* rev. ed. (New York: Columbia University Press, 1980), 1–4.

216. Charles Kindleberger, *The World in Depression 1929–1939* (Berkeley and Los Angeles: University of California Press, 1973), 299.

Chapter Four

1. Walter LaFeber, *America, Russia and the Cold War, 1945–1992,* 7th ed. (New York: McGraw-Hill, 1993), 303.

2. Donald Bruce Johnson, *National Party Platforms of 1980* (Urbana: University of Illinois Press, 1982), 204.

3. On the 1980 election see Walter Dean Burnham, "The 1980 Earthquake: Realignment, Reaction, or What?" in *The Hidden Election: Politics and Economics in the 1980 Presidential, Campaign,* ed. Thomas Ferguson and Joel Rogers (New York: Pantheon Books, 1981), 98–140.

4. Herbert Asher, *Presidential Elections and American Politics,* 3d ed. (Homewood, Ill.: Dorsey, 1984), 164.

5. Ronald Reagan, News Conference, 29 January 1981, reprinted in *Public Papers of the Presidents of the United States, Ronald Reagan* (Washington, D.C.: GPO, 1982–90), 1981:57.

6. Henry A. Kissinger, *Diplomacy* (New York: Simon and Schuster, 1994), 773.

7. Daniel Wirls, *Buildup: The Politics of Defense in the Reagan Era* (Ithaca: Cornell University Press, 1992), 36.

8. *America's New Beginning: A Program for Economic Recovery* (Washington, D.C.: GPO, 1981), 1.

9. See, for example, the contributions in Michael J. Hogan, ed., *The End of the Cold War: Its Meaning and Implications* (Cambridge: Cambridge University Press, 1992).

10. Peter Trubowitz, "Sectionalism and American Foreign Policy: The Politi-

cal Geography of Consensus and Conflict," *International Studies Quarterly* 36 (June 1992): 173-90.

11. Kevin P. Phillips, *The Emerging Republican Majority* (Garden City, N.Y.: Anchor Books, 1970).

12. The "rustbelt" refers here to states in the regions of New England, Middle Atlantic, and the Great Lakes—i.e., the traditional manufacturing belt. The "sunbelt" refers to states in the Southeast, Southwest, and Pacific Coast regions and the Mountain West states of New Mexico, Arizona, Colorado, Utah, and Nevada.

13. The administration's policy reversals also reflected stubborn international realities. For a good discussion of Reagan's reversals and the limits imposed by the international system see Kenneth A. Oye, "Constrained Confidence and the Evolution of Reagan Foreign Policy," in Kenneth A. Oye, Robert J. Lieber, and Donald Rothchild, *Eagle Resurgent? The Reagan Era in American Foreign Policy* (Boston: Little, Brown, 1987), 3-39.

14. Quote from *Congressional Quarterly Weekly Report,* 21 January 1989, 143.

15. Aaron Wildavsky, "The Two Presidencies," *Society* 4 (December 1966): 7-14.

16. "Bipartisan Objectives for American Foreign Policy," *Foreign Affairs* 66 (summer 1988), 899. For a similar view see David L. Boren and John C. Danforth, "Why This Country Can't Lead," *Washington Post,* December 1, 1987, op-ed; John Brademas et al., "Building a New Consensus: Congress and Foreign Policy," *SAIS Review* 9 (summer-fall 1989): 61-71.

17. See, for example, Oli R. Holsti and James N. Rosenau, *American Leadership in World Affairs: Vietnam and the Breakdown of Consensus* (Boston: Allen and Unwin, 1984); I. M. Destler, Leslie H. Gelb, and Anthony Lake, *Our Own Worst Enemy: The Unmaking of American Foreign Policy* (New York: Simon and Schuster, 1984); James M. McCormick and Eugene R. Wittkopf, "Bush and Bipartisanship: The Past as Prologue?" *Washington Quarterly* 13 (winter 1990): 5-16; Thomas E. Mann, "Making Foreign Policy: President and Congress," in *A Question of Balance: The President, the Congress, and Foreign Policy,* ed. Thomas E. Mann (Washington, D.C.: Brookings Institution, 1990), 1-34; Gerald F. Warburg, *Conflict and Consensus* (New York: Ballinger, 1989); Mark Danner, "How the Foreign Policy Machine Broke Down," *New York Times Magazine,* 7 March 1993, 32-34.

18. Melvyn P. Leffler, *A Preponderance of Power: National Security, the Truman Administration, and the Cold War* (Stanford: Stanford University Press, 1992), 2-3.

19. Nicholas John Spykman, *America's Strategy in World Politics: The United States and the Balance of Power* (New York: Harcourt, Brace, 1942). The quote is from James Kurth, "America's Grand Strategy: A Pattern of History," *The National Interest* (spring 1996): 6.

20. Policymakers "were altogether cognizant that their country's national security resided in its relative economic and technological superiority over any potential adversary." Leffler, *A Preponderance of Power,* 10-12.

21. Kurth, "America's Grand Strategy," 7.

22. Robert Gilpin, *U.S. Power and the Multinational Corporation: The Political Economy of Foreign Direct Investment* (New York: Basic Books, 1975), 103–11.

23. For different accounts of this development see Gabriel Kolko, *Confronting the Third World: United States Foreign Policy, 1945–1980* (New York: Pantheon Books, 1988); Thomas J. McCormick, *America's Half-Century: United States Foreign Policy in the Cold War*, 2d ed. (Baltimore: Johns Hopkins University Press, 1995); John Lewis Gaddis, *Strategies of Containment: A Critical Appraisal of Postwar American National Security Policy* (New York: Oxford University Press, 1982); Ronald Steel, *Pax Americana* (New York: Viking Press, 1967).

24. See Trubowitz, "Sectionalism and American Foreign Policy."

25. These policies had far less appeal in the Great Plains and Mountain West. In part, this was due to fears of competition from overseas producers of cheap agricultural goods and raw materials. No less important was frustration over the distributive costs of foreign economic aid, mutual defense arrangements, and defense spending—policies that would bestow disproportionate benefits on the Northeast and South. See Justus D. Doenecke, *Not to the Swift: The Old Isolationists in the Cold War Era* (Lewisburg, Pa.: Bucknell University Press, 1979).

26. McCormick, *America's Half-Century*, 155.

27. Thomas M. Frank and Edward Weisband, *Foreign Policy by Congress* (New York: Oxford University Press, 1979); James L. Sundquist, *The Decline and Resurgence of Congress* (Washington, D.C.: Brookings Institution, 1981); Richard Haas, "Congressional Power: Implications for American Security Policy," in *Adelphi Papers* (London: International Institute for Strategic Studies, 1979), 153.

28. Their strategic visions are summarized in Holsti and Rosenau, *American Leadership in World Affairs,* and McCormick, *America's Half-Century,* 156–61.

29. On debates over national security see Wirls, *Buildup.* On foreign economic policy see I. M. Destler, *American Trade Politics,* 2d ed. (Washington, D.C.: Institute for International Economics, 1992).

30. The data set consists of roll call votes defined as "key" votes by organizations that monitor political activity in Congress on a regular basis. These organizations include Americans for Democratic Action, Americans for Constitutional Action, and *Congressional Quarterly.* The Americans for Constitutional Action began publishing an annual list of key votes in 1960. For the 1947–59 period, the roll calls selected by the Americans for Democratic Action and *Congressional Quarterly* were supplemented by those chosen by *The New Republic.* Since the Americans for Democratic Action was created in 1947, votes for the 79th Congress (1945–46) were drawn from *Congressional Quarterly* and *The New Republic.* For the 99th Congress (1985–86) votes from *Congressional Quarterly* and the Americans for Democratic Action were supplemented by those used by the *National Journal* in rating legislators.

31. Votes for arms control were treated as a vote in favor of a less expansive definition of the national interest.

32. Following convention, paired votes and announced positions were treated as formal votes.

33. The measure of party conflict used here is average partisan difference.

34. The position of each member of Congress on these votes was identified. A state support score for Cold War internationalism was then formed by averaging the scores for all members of a congressional delegation for each of the postwar presidencies (Truman through Reagan). For a fuller discussion see Trubowitz, "Sectionalism and American Foreign Policy."

35. The first and second dimensions account for 73.9 percent of the variance. Of that total, 52.3 percent of the variance is attributable to the first dimension and 21.6 percent is attributable to the second. A third dimension accounts for only an additional 9.3 percent of the variance. With the exception of the Reagan years, every presidency has at least 60 percent of the variance accounted for by the factor analysis. During the Reagan presidency a substantial 58.4 percent of the variance is still explained.

36. An examination of the factor loadings indicates that the pattern of state support for Cold War internationalism changes in the Nixon years. The precise timing of the change in House voting cannot be determined from the data presented here because I have aggregated Houses by presidency. A similar analysis was conducted House by House for the study period. The results are consistent with those described here. With respect to the realignment, the pivotal House appears to be the 91st (1969–70).

37. The figures are based on the indices used in the factor analysis above.

38. On the changing regional composition of the Democratic party see Richard Franklin Bensel, *Sectionalism and American Political Development, 1880–1980* (Madison: University of Wisconsin Press, 1984), 368–402; James L. Sundquist, *Dynamics of the Party System: Alignment and Realignment of Political Parties in the United States* (Washington, D.C.: Brookings Institution, 1983); Earle Black and Merle Black, *Politics and Society in the South* (Cambridge: Harvard University Press, 1987); Nicol C. Rae, *Southern Democrats* (New York: Oxford University Press, 1994). The impact of liberal Democrats on the party's national agenda is examined in Steven M. Gillon, *Politics and Vision: The ADA and American Liberalism 1947–1985* (Oxford: Oxford University Press, 1987).

39. Bensel, *Sectionalism and American Political Development,* 383, fig. 8.3.

40. The Republican share of the congressional vote in the South increased from 25 percent in 1948 to nearly 45 percent in the 1980 election. This upward trend in Republican electoral strength was equally impressive in the presidential vote. Dewey W. Grantham, *The Life and Death of the Solid South: A Political History* (Lexington: University Press of Kentucky, 1988), 180.

41. For accounts about the changing regional composition of the Republican party see Jerome L. Himmelstein, *To the Right: The Transformation of American Conservatism* (Berkeley and Los Angeles: University of California Press, 1990); Nicol C. Rae, *The Decline of the Liberal Republicans from 1952 to the Present* (Oxford: Oxford University Press, 1989); David W. Reinhard, *The Republican Right since 1945* (Lexington: University Press of Kentucky, 1983).

42. Norman J. Ornstein, Thomas E. Mann, and Michael J. Malbin, *Vital Statistics on Congress, 1989–1990* (Washington, D.C.: American Enterprise Institute, 1990), 11–12.

43. Zbigniew Brzezinski, "The Three Requirements for a Bipartisan Foreign Policy," in *Forging Bipartisanship*, White Paper, *Washington Quarterly* (Washington, D.C.: CSIS, Georgetown University, 1984), 15–16.

44. Harry Truman had to cope with a Republican-controlled Congress—the famous "do nothing" 80th Congress that passed such landmark legislation as the Truman Doctrine, the Marshall Plan, and the 1947 National Security Act. At the beginning of his tenure in office, Dwight Eisenhower had a Republican Congress to work with. But for most of his presidency he had to deal with a Democratic Congress.

45. See, for instance, C. Fred Bergsten, "The Crisis in U.S. Trade Policy," *Foreign Affairs* 49 (July 1971): 619–35; Harald Malmgren, "Coming Trade Wars?" *Foreign Policy* 1 (winter 1970): 115–43.

46. John T. Rourke, Ralph G. Carter, and Mark A. Boyer, *Making American Foreign Policy* (Guilford, Conn: Dushkin, 1994), 439.

47. Martin Feldstein, ed., *The American Economy in Transition* (Chicago: University of Chicago Press, 1980), 191–96, cited in Helen Milner, "Trading Places: Industries for Free Trade," *World Politics* 40 (April 1988): 354.

48. Destler, *American Trade Politics*, 199.

49. See, for example, Helen V. Milner, *Resisting Protectionism: Global Industries and the Politics of International Trade* (Princeton: Princeton University Press, 1988).

50. See, for example, Destler, *American Trade Politics;* Robert Pastor, *Congress and the Politics of U.S. Foreign Economic Policy* (Berkeley and Los Angeles: University of California Press, 1980).

51. Judith Goldstein, *Ideas, Interests, and American Trade Policy* (Ithaca: Cornell University Press, 1993).

52. John Kenneth Galbraith, *The Affluent Society* (Boston: Houghton Mifflin, 1958).

53. Barry Bluestone and Bennett Harrison, *The Deindustrialization of America: Plant Closings, Community Abandonment, and the Dismantling of Basic Industry* (New York: Basic Books, 1982), 4–5.

54. This trend began well before the 1970s but it accelerated during the decade. On this trend see Advisory Commission on Intergovernmental Relations (ACIR), *Regional Growth: Historic Perspective* (Washington, D.C.: ACIR, 1980).

55. See, for example, Leonard F. Wheat, "The Determinants of 1963–77 Regional Manufacturing Growth: Why the South and West Grow," *Journal of Regional Science* 26 (November 1986): 635–59; R. D. Norton, "The Product Cycle and the Spatial Decentralization of American Manufacturing," *Regional Studies* 13 (1979); Neil Smith and Ward Dennis, "The Restructuring of Geographical Scale: Coalescence and Fragmentation of the Northern Core Region," *Economic Geography* 63 (April 1987): 160–82; Walt W. Rostow, "Regional Change in the Fifth Kondratieff Upswing," in *The Rise of the Sunbelt Cities,* ed. David C. Perry and Alfred

J. Watkins (Beverly Hills: Sage, 1977), 84-103; Bernard L. Weinstein and Robert E. Firestine, *Regional Growth and Decline in the United States* (New York: Praeger, 1978).

56. John Agnew, *The United States in the World Economy: A Regional Geography* (Cambridge: Cambridge University Press, 1987), 161-85.

57. Candace Howes and Ann R. Markusen, "Trade, Industry, and Economic Development," in *Trading Industries, Trading Regions: International Trade, American Industry, and Regional Economic Development,* ed. Helzi Noponen, Julie Graham, and Ann R. Markusen (New York: Guilford Press, 1993), 1-44.

58. See Ann R. Markusen and Virginia Carlson, "Deindustrialization in the American Midwest: Causes and Responses," in *Deindustrialization and Regional Economic Transformation: The Experience of the United States,* ed. Lloyd Rodwin and Hidehiko Sazanami (Boston: Unwin Hyman, 1989), 29-59.

59. On the South see Norman J. Glickman and Amy K. Glasmeier, "The International Economy and the American South," in Rodwin and Sazanami, *Deindustrialization and Regional Economic Transformation,* 60-80.

60. *Business America,* 19 November 1979.

61. The figure measures foreign penetration of American export markets. It is based on data measuring the dollar value of exports by manufacturing sector. The manufacturing employment data for measuring trade were obtained from the U.S. Department of Commerce, Bureau of Economic Analysis, *United States Industrial Outlook* (Washington, D.C.: GPO, 1986) and the COMPUSTAT Annual Industrial database. Firm level employment data from all industries reported in the COMPUSTAT database (four-digit Standard Industrial Classification codes: 2000-3999) were aggregated in total and by state. For a fuller discussion see Peter Trubowitz and Brian E. Roberts, "Regional Interests and the Reagan Military Buildup," *Regional Studies* 26 (October 1992): 555-67.

62. Timothy Josling, *Problems and Prospects for U.S. Agriculture in World Markets* (Washington, D.C.: NPA Committee on Changing International Realities, 1981), 6-13.

63. The analysis is based on House voting on trade issues in the 98th Congress. Factor analysis was used to construct an index of state support for free trade from the roll call votes on trade matters. Only votes that loaded on the first component (i.e., where the loading was greater than 0.60) were used to construct the voting support index. One vote—a vote *against* domestic content legislation—was selected to define support for free trade. The direction of every other roll call vote was determined by its sign of "correlation" with this roll call. The position of each representative on the votes in the analysis was then identified and a mean support score calculated for the lawmakers from each state. Paired votes and announced positions were treated as formal votes. Hawaii and Alaska are not included in the analysis.

64. See the stimulating account of this and other Republican tactics in Benjamin Ginsberg and Martin Shefter, *Politics by Other Means: The Declining Importance of Elections in America* (New York: Basic Books, 1990), 101-29.

65. Goldstein, *Ideas, Interests, and American Trade Policy,* 230.

66. Agnew, *The United States in the World Economy,* 190.

67. Candace Howes, "Constructing Comparative Disadvantage: Lessons from the U.S. Auto Industry," in Noponen, Graham, and Markusen, *Trading Industries,* 45.

68. Gilbert R. Winham and Ikuo Kabashima, "The Politics of U.S.-Japanese Auto Trade," in *Coping with U.S.-Japanese Economic Conflicts,* ed. I. M. Destler and Hideo Sato (Lexington, Mass.: Lexington Books, 1982), 76.

69. Winham and Kabashima, "The Politics of U.S.-Japanese Auto Trade," 73.

70. Howes, "Constructing Comparative Disadvantage," 70–71.

71. Agnew, *The United States in the World Economy,* 189–91. See also Dan Luria and Jack Russell, "Motor City Changeover," in *Sunbelt/Snowbelt: Urban Development and Regional Restructuring,* ed. Larry Sawers and William K. Tabb (New York: Oxford University Press, 1984), 271–312.

72. Calculated from Kent Trachte and Robert Ross, "The Crisis of Detroit and the Emergence of Global Capitalism," *International Journal of Urban and Regional Research* 9 (June 1985): 210.

73. Richard Child Hill, "Economic Crisis and Political Response in the Motor City," in Sawers and Tabb, *Sunbelt/Snowbelt,* 271–312.

74. Trachte and Ross, "The Crisis of Detroit," 187.

75. Winham and Kabashima, "The Politics of U.S.-Japanese Auto Trade," 75. Japanese manufacturers did not even begin exporting autos to the United States in large number until the mid-1960s. By 1969, about one-fifth of all imports came from Japan. By 1975, this figure had climbed to 50 percent.

76. "Detroit: Hitting the Skids," *Newsweek,* 28 April 1980, 58.

77. Howes, "Constructing Comparative Disadvantage," 69.

78. "Detroit: Hitting the Skids," *Newsweek,* 28 April 1980, 58.

79. Winham and Kabashima, "The Politics of U.S.-Japanese Auto Trade," 115.

80. Declaring the plan "an important step in the right direction," Danforth pulled his bill.

81. Howes, "Constructing Comparative Disadvantage," 58–59.

82. Judy Sarasohn, "UAW Wins Backing for Domestic Content Bill," *Congressional Quarterly Weekly,* 11 September 1982, 2243–41.

83. The comment was made by William E. Brock III, U.S. trade representative. Alan Murray, "House Passes Domestic Content Bill," *Congressional Quarterly Weekly,* 18 December 1982, 3072.

84. Among those debated and rejected was one offered by William E. Dannemeyer (R-CA) to change the name of the bill to "The Smoot-Hawley Trade Barriers Act of 1982." An amendment by Dan Coats (R-IN), which was adopted by voice vote, called for the Department of Agriculture to study the effect of the bill on agricultural exports. The adoption of the Fenwick amendment was unexpected and led opponents to drop other amendments and allow a final vote.

85. Murray, "House Passes Domestic Content Bill," 3072.

86. Fenwick's amendment (adopted by a narrow 195–194 vote) declared that the measure should not "supersede" any "treaty, international convention or

agreement on tariffs and trade." That provision would enable U.S. courts to invalidate the measure for violating the GATT.

87. Gramm was still a Democrat in 1982.

88. *Cong. Rec.,* 97th Cong., 2d sess., 1982, 128, pt. 22:30007.

89. Ibid., 30028.

90. Ibid., 29982.

91. Ibid., 29992.

92. For a very thorough treatment see James Shoch, "Party Competition and American Trade Policy during the Reagan-Bush Era" (paper presented at the annual meeting of the American Political Science Association, San Francisco, Calif., 31 August 1996).

93. Calculations by author from Glickman and Glasmeier, "The International Economy and the American South," 77.

94. George Cloos and Philip Cummins, "Economic Upheaval in the Midwest," *Economic Perspectives* 8 (January 1984), 3.

95. Ibid.

96. Ibid. 6–7.

97. *Cong. Rec.,* 97th Cong., 2d sess., 1982, 128, pt. 22:30977.

98. Howell Raines, "Move to Curb Competitiveness of Imports Rises as Focus at End of Campaign," *New York Times,* 25 October 1982, B6.

99. Ronald Brownstein, "Business Moves Out, Labor Moves In . . . And the Two Parties Switch Sides," *National Journal,* 19 September 1987, 2329.

100. *Cong. Rec.,* 97th Cong., 2d sess., 1982, 128, pt. 22:29995.

101. Ibid., 29991.

102. Ibid., 30982.

103. Rodney A. Erickson and David J. Hayward, "The International Flows of Industrial Exports from U.S. Regions," *Annals of the Association of American Geographers* 81 (September 1991): 388.

104. Josling, *Problems and Prospects for U.S. Agriculture,* vi.

105. Ibid., 6–13.

106. Judith E. Sommer and Fred K. Hines, *The U.S. Farm Sector: How Agricultural Exports Are Shaping Rural Economies in the 1980's* (Washington, D.C.: U.S. Department of Agriculture, 1988), 2.

107. Farm real estate debt more than tripled during the 1970s. Ibid.

108. *Cong. Rec.,* 97th Cong., 2d sess., 1982, 128, pt. 22:30001.

109. Ibid., 30004.

110. Ibid., 30954.

111. Bruce J. Schulman, *From Cotton Belt to Sunbelt: Federal Policy, Economic Development, and the Transformation of the South, 1938–1980* (New York: Oxford University Press, 1991), 152.

112. The only part of the country to lose more jobs due to imports between 1977 and 1982 than the low-wage Southeast was the Great Lakes region. Glickman and Glasmeier, "The International Economy and the American South," 76.

113. Destler, *American Trade Politics,* 14.

114. Ibid.

115. Raymond A. Bauer, Ithiel de Sola Pool, and Lewis Anthony Dexter, *American Business and Public Poicy: The Politics of Foreign Trade* (Chicago: Aldine-Atherton, 1972), 39. See also Pastor, *Congress and the Politics of U.S. Foreign Economic Policy.*

116. William R. Keech and Kyoungsan Pak, "Partisanship, Institutions, and Change in American Trade Politics," *Journal of Politics* 57 (November 1995): 1130–42.

117. On the connection between congressional power and the New Deal alliance see Bensel's masterful account in *Sectionalism and American Political Development*, 317–67.

118. The phrase is Destler's. *American Trade Politics,* 65.

119. Keech and Pak, "Partisanship, Institutions, and Change in American Trade Politics," 1132; Destler, *American Trade Politics,* 31.

120. Pietro S. Nivola, "The New Protectionism: U.S. Trade Policy in Historical Perspective," *Political Science Quarterly* 101 (fall 1986): 577–600. See also Destler, *American Trade Politics,* 65–103.

121. See the discussion in Gary Mucciaroni, *Reversals of Fortune: Public Policy and Private Interests* (Washington, D.C.: Brookings Institution, 1995), 67–106.

122. References to trade in the House and Senate increased by 70 percent between 1975 and 1980. Destler, *American Trade Politics,* 81.

123. Ibid., 66.

124. See Robert E. Baldwin, "The Changing Nature of U.S. Trade Policy since World War II," in *The Structure and Evolution of Recent U.S. Trade Policy,* ed. Robert E. Baldwin and Anne O. Krueger (Chicago: University of Chicago Press, 1984), 5–31. See also Keech and Pak, "Partisanship, Institutions, and Change in American Trade Politics."

125. Fred M. Shelley et al., *Political Geography of the United States* (New York: Guilford Press, 1996), 222–27.

126. Larry L. Wade and John B. Gates, "A New Tariff Map of the United States (House of Representatives)," *Political Geography* 9 (July 1990): 284–304.

127. *State Growth* measures the relative capacity of state economies to bear the social burden or costs of the Reagan administration's free trade policies. It is based on the growth rate in nonagricultural employment from 1970 through 1980. This time frame is long enough to capture real structural change and is not overly affected by cyclical swings, strikes, or random growth. Using a shorter period or one that ended closer to the recession of the early 1980s would be undesirable. The measure was calculated from data appearing in the U.S. Department of Labor, Bureau of Labor Statistics, *Employment and Earnings* (Washington, D.C.: GPO, 1982). *Trade Vulnerability* measures the relative sensitivity of state manufacturing sectors to the world economy. It is a composite index measuring a state's vulnerability to foreign penetration of the domestic market *and* American export markets. The logic is straightforward: politicians representing economies specializing in sectors vulnerable to foreign competition will be less supportive of free trade.

The index was also derived using data published by the Bureau of Economic Analysis and COMPUSTAT.

128. The Senate scores were used rather than the House scores in order to avoid having the effects of key House votes present on both sides of the estimated model. The average state delegation ADA scores for the House and Senate in the 98th Congress have a correlation coefficient of 0.63.

129. This account draws on Trubowitz and Roberts, "Regional Interests and the Reagan Military Buildup."

130. See, for example, James M. Lindsay, "Parochialism, Policy, and Constituency Constraints: Congressional Voting on Strategic Weapons Systems," *American Journal of Political Science* 34 (1990): 936–60; Kenneth R. Mayer, *The Political Economy of Defense Contracting* (New Haven: Yale University Press, 1991); Ralph G. Carter, "Senate Defense Budgeting, 1981–1988: The Impacts of Ideology, Party, and Constituency Benefit on the Decision to Support the President," *American Politics Quarterly* 17 (1989): 332–47; Richard Fleisher, "Economic Benefit, Ideology, and Senate Voting on the B-1 Bomber," *American Politics Quarterly* 13 (1985): 200–11. Some of the better-known studies carried out during the 1970s include Robert A. Bernstein and William A. Anthony, "The ABM Issue in the Senate, 1968–1970: The Importance of Ideology," *American Political Science Review* 68 (1974), 1198–1206; James Clotfelter, "Senate Voting and Constituency Stake in Defense Spending," *Journal of Politics* 32 (1970): 979–83; Wayne Moyer, "House Voting on Defense: An Ideological Explanation," in *Military Force and American Society,* ed. Bruce Russett and Alfred Stepan (New York: Harper and Row, 1973), 106–141; Bruce Russett, *What Price Vigilance?* (New Haven: Yale University Press, 1970); Barry S. Rundquist, "On Testing a Military Industrial Complex Theory," *American Politics Quarterly* 6 (1978): 29–53.

131. James Q. Wilson, *Political Organization* (New York: Basic Books, 1973).

132. Kirkpatrick Sale, *Power Shift: The Rise of the Southern Rim and Its Challenge to the Eastern Establishment* (New York: Random House, 1975).

133. Harvey S. Perloff et al., *Regions, Resources and Economic Growth* (Baltimore: Johns Hopkins University Press, 1960), 225, 252.

134. Edward Ullman, "Regional Development and the Geography of Concentration," *Papers and Proceedings of the Regional Science Association* 4 (1958): 179.

135. Perloff et al., *Regions, Resources and Economic Growth,* 225, 252.

136. Ullman, "Regional Development and the Geography of Concentration," 185.

137. For an excellent treatment of the changing geographical distribution of economic activity see Joseph H. Turek, "The Northeast in a National Context: Background Trends in Population, Income, and Employment," in *Economic Prospects for the Northeast,* ed. Harry W. Richardson and Joseph H. Turek (Philadelphia: Temple University Press, 1985), 28–84. See also Bernard L. Weinstein, Harold T. Gross, and John Rees, *Regional Growth and Decline in the United States,* 2d ed. (New York: Praeger, 1985).

138. By 1970 nine of the nation's ten slowest growing states were now based

in the region. By contrast, the nation's ten most rapidly growing states were now located in the South and West. See Turek, "The Northeast in a National Context," 33.

139. Ibid., 38.

140. Throughout the 1950s and 1960s, job growth in much of the Northeast lagged well behind the national average. The reverse was true in most of the South and West.

141. Turek, "The Northeast in a National Context," 46–54.

142. William H. Miernyk, "Energy Constraints and Economic Development in the Northeast," in Richardson and Turek, *Economic Prospects for the Northeast,* 106.

143. Robert Jay Dilger, *The Sunbelt/Snowbelt Controversy: The War over Federal Funds* (New York: New York University Press, 1982), 167.

144. Miernyk, "Energy Constraints and Economic Development in the Northeast," 107–9.

145. Perloff et al., *Regions, Resources, and Economic Growth,* 151.

146. Shelley et al., *Political Geography of the United States,* 256–57.

147. Ibid.

148. *Business Week,* 17 May 1976, 92–114.

149. Ann R. Markusen, *Regions: The Economics and Politics of Territory* (Totowa, N.J.: Rowman and Littlefield, 1987), 164.

150. James C. Cobb, *The Selling of the South: The Southern Crusade for Industrial Development, 1936–1980* (Baton Rouge: Louisiana State University Press, 1982), 197.

151. Ibid., 198.

152. Western states also organized. In August 1977, the Western Governors' Conference voted to merge a number of western state organizations into a regional group called Westpo (Western Policy Office). Western politicians generally concurred in the South's views but did not spend resources on the controversy. Markusen, *Regions,* 184.

153. Quoted in Cobb, *The Selling of the South,* 201.

154. Ibid.

155. Bensel provides the best discussion of these initiatives. See his *Sectionalism and American Political Development,* 256–316. See also Elizabeth Sanders, "The Regulatory Surge of the 1970s in Historical Perspective," in *Public Regulation: New Perspectives on Institutions and Policies,* ed. Elizabeth E. Bailey (Cambridge: MIT Press, 1986), 117–50; ACIR, *Regional Growth,* 1–8; Robert Rafuse, Jr., "The New Sectionalism Controversy: An Overview" (paper prepared for National Governors' Conference, Center for Policy Research and Analysis, 26 January 1977).

156. Robert Reinhold, "Sunbelt Region Leads Nation in Growth of Population: Section's Cities Top Urban Expansion," *New York Times,* 8 February 1976, 1, 42; Wayne King, "Federal Funds Pour into Sunbelt States," *New York Times,* 9 February 1976, 24; Roy Reed, "Sunbelt Still Stronghold of Conservatism in U.S.," *New York Times,* 11 February 1976, 1, 11; B. Drummond Ayres, Jr., "Developing

Sunbelt Hopes to Avoid North's Mistakes," *New York Times,* 12 February 1976, 1, 24.

157. "The Second War between the States," *Business Week,* 17 May 1977, 92–113.

158. Joel Havemann, Rochelle Stanfield, and Neil Pierce, "Federal Spending: The Northeast's Loss is the Sunbelt's Gain," *National Journal,* 26 June 1976, 878–91.

159. James R. Anderson, "The State and Regional Impact of the Military Budget," *Cong. Rec.,* 94th Cong., 2d sess., 1976, 122, pt. 19:24274–77. Not surprisingly, these estimates were quite controversial. Some members charged that the estimates were based on spurious assumptions about the impact of federal spending. Most members from the Northeast and Midwest believed that the regional imbalances were actually starker than this study indicated. See Bensel, *Sectionalism and American Political Development,* 467n. 30.

160. Asked about the regional biases in defense spending, the speaker of the House of Representatives, Thomas "Tip" O'Neill of Massachusetts, claimed that it was "a political vendetta by the Nixon Administration, no question about it. We lost all these shipyards because Nixon hated the Northeast, he hated Massachusetts. There's no question about that." Bensel, *Sectionalism and American Political Development,* 279.

161. For an account see Dilger, *The Sunbelt/Snowbelt Controversy.*

162. Wirls, *Buildup,* 45, table 5.

163. For a good summary of the change see ibid., especially 46–52. On the geographic implications of the shift in military strategy see Ann R. Markusen et al., *The Rise of the Gunbelt: The Military Remapping of Industrial America* (New York: Oxford University Press, 1991); Breandán Ó hUallacháin, "Regional and Technological Implications of the Recent Buildup in American Defense Spending," *Annals of the Association of American Geographers* 77 (spring 1987): 208–23.

164. By comparison, operating funds increased by only 60 percent.

165. This measure is based on employment data from Marion Anderson, Micahel Frisch, and Michael Oden, *The Empty Pork Barrel: The Employment Cost of the Military Build-up, 1981–1985* (Lansing, Mich.: Employment Research Associates, 1986). Their estimates compare the jobs gained through military expenditure to the jobs that would have been created by an equivalent expenditure in the civilian economy. Their results were based on simulations run on the Multiregional Forecast Simulation Model (FS-53) developed by Regional Economic Models Inc. (REMI) of Amherst, Massachusetts. Estimates pertaining to the production of military-oriented durable goods are used here. These include obvious defense-related industries such as aircraft, guided missiles, ordnance, and tanks but also include sectors such as electronic tubes, communication equipment, and scientific and optical instruments. The data was normalized using manufacturing employment figures to control for differences in the size of states' industrial base. For a fuller discussion see Trubowitz and Roberts, "Regional Interests and the Reagan Buildup."

166. "As late as World War II ten states dominated prime contracts. All of

them, with the exception of California, ranged in a row from Massachusetts to Illinois." Markusen et al., *Rise of the Gunbelt*, 231. See also Jeffrey R. Crump, "The Spatial Distribution of Military Spending in the United States, 1941–1985," *Growth and Change* 20 (summer 1989): 50–62.

167. Markusen et al., *Rise of the Gunbelt*, 11. Prime contracts make up the largest single chunk of defense spending and refer to the money that the federal government pays for privately produced supplies, services, and facilities that range from airframes and aircraft engines to clothing, housing, and food.

168. The remainder went to the Great Plains states.

169. Markusen et al., *Rise of the Gunbelt*, 13.

170. Shelley et al., *Political Geography of the United States*, 221.

171. Markusen et al., *Rise of the Gunbelt*, 35.

172. "The landscape of American military-industrial cities is not simply the outcome of competition among various centers of self-started and self-fueled innovative complexes. It is primarily the product of the rise of strategic warfare in the 1930s and the onset of the cold war in the 1950s. Without these developments, the industrial heartland centers of aircraft production would have had a better chance of surviving in a competitive environment governed by commercial rather than military concerns." Ibid., 243.

173. Shelley et al., *Political Geography of the United States*, 221.

174. The main exceptions were in New England, notably Massachusetts and Connecticut.

175. Trubowitz and Roberts, "Regional Interests and the Reagan Military Buildup."

176. Thomas L. Muller, "Regional Impacts," in *The Reagan Experiment: An Examination of Economic and Social Policies under the Reagan Administration*, ed. John L. Palmer and Isabel V. Sawhill (Washington, D.C.: Urban Institute Press, 1982), 441–57.

177. For a similar interpretation see Ginsberg and Shefter, *Politics by Other Means*, especially 20–22, 90–91, and 138–43.

178. The analysis is based on House voting over national defense issues for the 98th Congress (1983–84). A broad definition of national defense is employed. It covers basic "meat and potato" issues such as military procurement, research, and development, but it also includes decisions over broader, strategic issues such as arms control, military aid, foreign intervention, military sales, troop deployments, and military alliances. Factor analysis was used to construct an index of state support for Reagan's military strategy from the roll call votes. Only votes that loaded on the first component (i.e., where the loading was greater than 0.60) were used to construct the voting support index. One vote—a vote on the administration's antisatellite weapons program—was selected to define support for the Reagan administration's military policies. The direction of every other roll call vote was determined by its sign of "correlation" with this roll call. The position of each representative on the votes in the analysis was then identified and a mean support score calculated for the lawmakers from each state. Paired votes and announced

positions were treated as formal votes. Hawaii and Alaska are not included in the analysis.

179. See note 127.

180. This argument is developed in Peter Trubowitz, "The Second Face of Strategy: Presidential Politics and Foreign Policy" (manuscript in preparation).

Chapter Five

1. The paper, "The Significance of the Frontier in American History," was later published in Frederick Jackson Turner, *The Frontier in American History* (New York: Holt, 1920).

2. On the impact of Turner's writings on American foreign policy see Walter LaFeber, *The New Empire: An Interpretation of American Expansionism, 1860–1898* (Ithaca: Cornell University Press, 1963); William A. Williams, "The Frontier Thesis and American Foreign Policy," *Pacific Historical Review* 24 (November 1955): 379–95.

3. Turner himself recognized the trade-off and argued a few years later that the frontier's disappearance created "demands for a vigorous foreign policy" and "extension of American influence to outlying islands and adjoining countries." See Frederick Jackson Turner, "The Problem of the West," *Atlantic Monthly,* September 1896, 289–97.

4. *The American Century* (New York: Farrar and Rinehart, 1941), 5–40.

5. Paul Kennedy, *The Rise and Fall of Great Powers: Economic Change and Military Conflict from 1500 to 2000* (New York: Random House, 1987).

6. The term "declinism" was coined by Samuel P. Huntington in his widely read "The U.S.—Decline or Renewal?" *Foreign Affairs* 67 (winter 1988–89): 76–97.

7. On the "law of uneven development" see Robert Gilpin, *The Political Economy of International Relations* (Princeton: Princeton University Press, 1987).

8. Jack N. Rakove, "Making Foreign Policy—The View from 1787," in *Foreign Policy and the Constitution,* ed. Robert A. Goldwin and Robert A. Licht (Washington, D.C.: AEI Press, 1990), 19.

9. Peter Gourevitch makes a similar point in his *Politics in Hard Times: Comparative Responses to International Economic Crises* (Ithaca: Cornell University Press, 1986), 64–65.

10. Some scholars working in this tradition now attach far greater weight to conflict in explaining consensus. See, most notably, Walter LaFeber, *The American Search for Opportunity, 1865–1913* (New York: Cambridge University Press, 1993); Thomas J. McCormick, *America's Half-Century: United States Foreign Policy in the Cold War,* 2d ed. (Baltimore: Johns Hopkins University Press, 1995).

11. Agnew, *The United States in the World-Economy,* 94.

12. See Peter Trubowitz, "Déjà Vu: Political Struggles over American Defense Policy," in *Downsizing Defense,* ed. Ethan B. Kapstein (Washington, D.C.: Congressional Quarterly Press, 1993).

Bibliography

Adams, Frederick C. *Economic Diplomacy: The Export-Import Bank and American Foreign Policy, 1934-1939.* Columbia: University of Missouri Press, 1976.

Advisory Commission on Intergovernmental Relations (ACIR). *Regional Growth: Historic Perspective.* Washington, D.C.: ACIR, 1980.

Agnew, John. *The United States in the World-Economy: A Regional Geography.* Cambridge: Cambridge University Press, 1987.

Allen, William R. "Cordell Hull and the Defense of the Trade Agreements Program, 1934-1940." In *Isolation and Security,* ed. Alexander DeConde. Durham: Duke University Press, 1957.

Allswang, John M. *The New Deal and American Politics: A Study in Political Change.* New York: John Wiley, 1978.

Anderson, Marion, Michael Frisch, and Michael Oden. *The Empty Pork Barrel: The Employment Cost of the Military Build-up, 1981-1985.* Lansing, Mich.: Employment Research Associates, 1986.

Archer, J. Clark. "Macrogeographical versus Microgeographical Cleavages in American Presidential Elections: 1940-1984." *Political Geography Quarterly* 7 (1988): 111-25.

Archer, J. Clark, and Peter J. Taylor. *Section and Party: A Political Geography of American Presidential Elections.* New York: John Wiley, 1981.

Arrington, Leonard J. "The New Deal in the West: A Preliminary Statistical Inquiry." *Pacific Historical Review* 38 (August 1969): 311-6.

———. "Western Agriculture and the New Deal." *Agricultural History* (October 1970): 337-53.

———. "The Sagebrush Resurrection: New Deal Expenditures in the Western States, 1933-39." *Pacific Historical Review* 52 (February 1983): 1-16.

Asher, Herbert. *Presidential Elections and American Politics.* 3d ed. Homewood, Ill.: Dorsey, 1984.

Ayers, Edward L. *The Promise of the New South: Life after Reconstruction.* New York: Oxford University Press, 1992.

Ayres, B. Drummond, Jr. "Developing Sunbelt Hopes to Avoid North's Mistakes." *New York Times,* 12 February 1976, 1, 24.

Baack, Ben, and Edward Ray. "The Political Economy of the Origins of the Military-Industrial Complex in the United States." *Journal of Economic History* 45 (June 1985): 369-75.

————. "Special Interests and the Adoption of the Income Tax in the United States." *Journal of Economic History* 45 (September 1985): 607-25.

————. "Special Interests and the Nineteenth-Century Roots of the U.S. Military-Industrial Complex." In *Research in Economic History,* ed. Paul Uselding. Vol. 11. Greenwich, Conn.: JAI Press, 1988.

Baer, George W. *One Hundred Years of Sea Power: The U.S. Navy, 1890-1990.* Stanford: Stanford University Press, 1994.

Baldwin, Robert E. "The Changing Nature of U.S. Trade Policy since World War II." In *The Structure and Evolution of Recent U.S. Trade Policy,* ed. Robert E. Baldwin and Anne O. Krueger. Chicago: University of Chicago Press, 1984.

Bauer, Raymond A., Ithiel de Sola Pool, and Lewis Anthony Dexter. *American Business and Public Policy: The Politics of Foreign Trade.* Chicago: Aldine-Atherton, 1972.

Beard, Charles A. *An Economic Interpretation of the Constitution of the United States.* New York: Macmillan, 1941.

Beer, Samuel. "The Modernization of American Federalism." *Publius* 3 (1973): 49-95.

Beisner, Robert L. *Twelve against Empire: The Anti-Imperialists, 1898-1900.* Chicago: University of Chicago Press, 1968.

————. *From the Old Diplomacy to the New, 1865-1900.* 2d ed. Arlington Heights, Ill: Harlan Davidson, 1986.

Benedict, Murray R. *Farm Policies of the United States, 1790-1950: A Study of Their Origins and Development.* New York: Twentieth Century Fund, 1953.

Bennett, David H. *Demagogues in the Depression: American Radicals and the Union Party, 1932-1936.* New Brunswick, N.J.: Rutgers University Press, 1969.

Bensel, Richard Franklin. *Sectionalism and American Political Development: 1880-1980.* Madison: University of Wisconsin Press, 1984.

Bergsten, C. Fred. "The Crisis in U.S. Trade Policy." *Foreign Affairs* 49 (July 1971): 619-35.

Bernstein, Robert A., and William A. Anthony. "The ABM Issue in the Senate, 1968-1970: The Importance of Ideology." *American Political Science Review* 68 (1974): 1198-1206.

Billington, Ray Allen. "The Origins of Middle Western Isolationism." *Political Science Quarterly* 60 (March 1945): 44-64.

Binkley, Wilfred E. *President and Congress.* 3d ed. New York: Vintage Books, 1962.

Black, Earle, and Merle Black. *Politics and Society in the South.* Cambridge: Harvard University Press, 1987.

Block, Fred L. *The Origins of International Economic Disorder: A Study of United States International Monetary Policy from World War II to the Present.* Berkeley and Los Angeles: University of California Press, 1977.

Bluestone, Barry, and Bennett Harrison. *The Deindustrialization of America: Plant Closings, Community Abandonment, and the Dismantling of Basic Industry.* New York: Basic Books, 1982.

Borden, William S. *The Pacific Alliance: United States Foreign Economic Policy and Japanese Trade Recovery, 1947-54.* Madison: University of Wisconsin Press, 1984.

Boren, David L., and John C. Danforth. "Why This Country Can't Lead." *Washington Post,* 1 December 1987, op-ed.

Brademas, John, et al. "Building a New Consensus: Congress and Foreign Policy." *SAIS Review* 9 (summer-fall 1989): 61-71.

Brady, David W. *Critical Elections and Congressional Policy Making.* Stanford: Stanford University Press, 1988.

Braudel, Fernand. *The Mediterranean and the Mediterranean World in the Age of Philip II.* Trans. Sian Reynolds. 2 vols. New York: Harper and Row, 1972-73.

Brenner, Steven Robert. "Economic Interests and the Trade Agreements Program, 1937-1940: A Study of Institutions and Political Influence." Ph.D. Diss., Stanford University, 1977.

Brinkley, Alan. "The New Deal and Southern Politics." In *The New Deal and the South,* ed. James C. Cobb and Michael V. Namorato. Jackson: University Press of Mississippi, 1984.

Brownstein, Ronald. "Business Moves Out, Labor Moves In . . . And the Two Parties Switch Sides." *National Journal,* 19 September 1987, 2329.

Brunn, Stanley D. *Geography and Politics in America.* New York: Harper and Row, 1974.

Brustein, William. *The Social Origins of Political Regionalism: France, 1849-1981.* Berkeley and Los Angeles: University of California Press, 1988.

Bryce, James V. *The American Commonwealth.* 3d ed. 2 vols. New York: Macmillan, 1894.

Brzezinski, Zbigniew. "The Three Requirements for a Bipartisan Foreign Policy." In *Forging Bipartisanship,* 15-16. White Paper. *Washington Quarterly.* Washington, D.C.: CSIS, Georgetown University, 1984.

Buhl, Lance. "Maintaining 'An American Navy' 1865-1889." In *In Peace and War: Interpretations of American Naval History, 1775-1984,* ed. Kenneth J. Hagan. Westport, Conn.: Greenwood, 1984.

Burner, David. *The Politics of Provincialism: The Democratic Party in Transition, 1918-1932.* New York: W. W. Norton, 1967.

Burnette, O. Lawrence, Jr. "John Tyler Morgan and Expansionist Sentiment in the New South." *Alabama Review* 43 (1965): 163-82.

Burnham, Walter Dean. *Critical Elections and the Mainsprings of American Politics.* New York: W. W. Norton, 1970.

———. "The 1980 Earthquake: Realignment, Reaction, or What?" In *The Hidden Election: Politics and Economics in the 1980 Presidential Campaign,* ed. Thomas Ferguson and Joel Rogers. New York: Pantheon Books, 1981.

———. "The System of 1896: An Analysis." In *The Evolution of American Electoral Systems,* ed. Paul Kleppner. Westport, Conn.: Greenwood Press, 1981.

Business America, 19 November 1979.

Business Week. "The Second War between the States." 17 May 1977.

Carnegie, Andrew. "What Would I Do with the Tariff If I Were Czar." *Forum* 19 (March 1895): 18-28.

Carr, Edward H. *The Twenty Years' Crisis, 1919-1939: An Introduction to the Study of International Relations.* 1939. Reprint, London: Macmillan, 1962.

Carter, Ralph G. "Senate Defense Budgeting, 1981-1988: The Impacts of Ideology, Party, and Constituency Benefit on the Decision to Support the President." *American Politics Quarterly* 17 (1989): 332-47.

Chester, Edward W. *Sectionalism, Politics, and American Diplomacy.* Metuchen, N.J.: Scarecrow Press, 1975.

Chubb, John E., and Paul E. Peterson. "American Political Institutions and the Problem of Governance." In *Can the Government Govern?* ed. John E. Chubb and Paul E. Peterson. Washington, D.C.: Brookings Institution, 1989.

Clark, Champ. *Great Debates in American History.* Ed. Marion Mills Miller. Vol. 3. New York: Current Literature, 1913.

Clinton, W. David. *The Two Faces of National Interest.* Baton Rouge: Louisiana State University Press, 1994.

Cloos, George, and Philip Cummins. "Economic Upheaval in the Midwest." *Economic Perspectives* 8 (January 1984): 3-14.

Clotfelter, James. "Senate Voting and Constituency Stake in Defense Spending." *Journal of Politics* 32 (1970): 979-83.

Clubb, Jerome M., and Howard W. Allen. "The Cities and the Election of 1928: Partisan Realignment?" *American Historical Review* 74 (April 1969): 1205-20.

Cobb, James C. *Industrialization and Southern Society, 1877-1984.* Louisville: University Press of Kentucky, 1984.

Cole, Wayne S. *Senator Gerald P. Nye and American Foreign Relations.* Minneapolis: University of Minnesota Press, 1962.

———. *Roosevelt and the Isolationists, 1932-45.* Lincoln: University of Nebraska Press, 1983.

———. "America First and the South, 1940-41." *Journal of Southern History* 22 (February 1956): 36-47.

———. "And Then There Were None! How Arthur H. Vandenberg and Gerald P. Nye Separately Departed Isolationist Leadership Roles." In *Behind the Throne: Servants of Power to Imperial Presidents, 1898-1968,* ed. Thomas McCormick and Walter LaFeber. Madison: University of Wisconsin Press, 1993.

Congressional Quarterly Weekly Report, 21 January 1989, 143.

Congressional Record. Washington, D.C., 1890-1901.

Congressional Record. Washington, D.C., 1933-41.

Congressional Record. Washington, D.C., 1981-91.

Connor, James R. "National Farm Organizations and United States Tariff Policy in the 1920s." *Agricultural History* 32 (January 1958): 32-43.

Conzen, Michael P. "The Maturing Urban System in the United States, 1840-1910." *Annals of the Association of American Geographers* 67 (March 1977): 88-108.

Coode, Thomas. "Southern Congressmen and the American Naval Revolution, 1880-1889." *Alabama Historical Quarterly* 30 (fall-winter 1968): 89-110.

Cooling, Benjamin Franklin. *Benjamin Franklin Tracy: Father of the Modern American Fighting Navy.* Hamden, Conn.: Archon Books, 1973.

———. *Gray Steel and Blue Water Navy: The Formative Years of America's Military-Industrial Complex, 1881-1917.* Hamden, Conn.: Archon Books, 1979.

Cooper, William. *The Conservative Regime: South Carolina, 1877-1890.* Baltimore: Johns Hopkins University Press, 1968.

Corwin, Edwin. *The President's Control of Foreign Relations.* Princeton: Princeton University Press, 1917.

Cox, Henry Bartholomew. *War, Foreign Affairs, and Constitutional Power: 1829-1901.* Cambridge, Mass.: Ballinger, 1984.

Cox, Robert W. *Production, Power, and World Order.* New York: Columbia University Press, 1987.

Crapol, Edward P. *America for Americans: Economic Nationalism and Anglophobia in the Late Nineteenth Century.* Westport, Conn.: Greenwood Press, 1973.

Crowell, J. F. "Shipping Industry of the United States: Its Relation to the Foreign Trade." In *Monthly Summary of Commerce and Finance of the United States.* Washington, D.C.: GPO, 1901.

Crump, Jeffrey R. "The Spatial Distribution of Military Spending in the United States, 1941-1985." *Growth and Change* 20 (summer 1989): 50-62.

Cumings, Bruce. *The Origins of the Korean War.* Vol. 2, *The Roaring of the Cataract, 1947-1950.* Princeton: Princeton University Press, 1990.

Dabney, Virginius. "The South Looks Abroad." *Foreign Affairs* 19 (October 1940): 171-78.

Dallek, Robert. *Franklin D. Roosevelt and American Foreign Policy, 1932-1945.* New York: Oxford University Press, 1979.

Danhof, Clarence H. "Four Decades of Thought on the South's Economic Problems." In *Essays in Southern Economic Development,* ed. Melvin L. Greenhut and W. Tate Whitman. Chapel Hill: University of North Carolina Press, 1964.

Danner, Mark. "How the Foreign Policy Machine Broke Down." *New York Times Magazine,* 7 March 1993, 32-34.

Davis, Lance E., and John Legler. "The Government in the American Economy, 1815-1902." *Journal of Economic History* 26 (December 1966): 514-52.

DeConde, Alexander. "The South and Isolationism." *Journal of Southern History* 24 (August 1958): 333-46.

Degler, Carl N. "American Political Parties and the Rise of the City: An Interpretation." *Journal of American History* 51 (June 1964): 41-59.

Destler, I. M. *American Trade Politics.* 2d ed. Washington, D.C.: Institute for International Economics, 1992.

Destler, I. M., Leslie H. Gelb, and Anthony Lake. *Our Own Worst Enemy: The Unmaking of American Foreign Policy.* New York: Simon and Schuster, 1984.

deWilde, John C. "The AAA and Exports of the South." *Foreign Policy Reports* 11 (April 1935): 38-48.

Dilger, Robert Jay. *The Sunbelt/Snowbelt Controversy: The War over Federal Funds.* New York: New York University Press, 1982.

Divine, Robert. *The Illusion of Neutrality.* Chicago: University of Chicago Press, 1962.

Doenecke, Justus D. *Not to the Swift: The Old Isolationists in the Cold War Era.* Lewisburg, Pa.: Bucknell University Press, 1979.

————. "Power, Markets, and Ideology: The Isolationist Response to Roosevelt Policy, 1940-1941." In *Watershed of Empire: Essays on New Deal Foreign Policy,* ed. Leonard P. Liggio and James J. Martin. Colorado Springs: Ralph Myles, 1976.

Domhoff, William G. *The Power Elite and the State: How Policy Is Made in America.* New York: Aldine de Gruyter, 1990.

Dowell, Austin A., and Oscar B. Jesness. *The American Farmer and the Export Market.* Minneapolis: University of Minnesota Press, 1934.

Earle, Carville. *Geographical Inquiry and American Historical Problems.* Stanford: Stanford University Press, 1992.

Eden, Lynn. "Capitalist Conflict and the State: The Making of United States Military Policy in 1948." In *Statemaking and Social Movements: Essays in History and Theory,* ed. Charles Bright and Susan Harding. Ann Arbor: University of Michigan Press, 1984.

Edwards, George C., III, and Wallace Earl Walker, eds. *National Security and the U.S. Constitution: The Impact of the Political System.* Baltimore: Johns Hopkins University Press, 1988.

Eichengreen, Barry. "The Political Economy of the Smoot-Hawley Tariff." In *Research in Economic History,* ed. Roger L. Ransom, Peter H. Lindert, and Richard Sutch. Vol. 12. Greenwich, Conn.: JAI Press, 1989.

Elazar, Daniel J. *American Federalism: A View from the States.* New York: Thomas Y. Crowell, 1972.

Eldersveld, Samuel J. "The Influence of Metropolitan Pluralities in Presidential Elections since 1920: A Study of Twelve Key Cities." *American Political Science Review* 63 (December 1949): 1189-1206.

Ellis, Richard J. *American Political Cultures.* New York: Oxford University Press, 1993.

Erickson, Rodney A., and David J. Hayward. "The International Flows of Industrial Exports from U.S. Regions." *Annals of the Association of American Geographers* 81 (September 1991): 371-90.

Feis, Herbert. *The Diplomacy of the Dollar: First Era, 1919-1932.* Baltimore: Johns Hopkins University Press, 1950.

Feldstein, Martin, ed. *The American Economy in Transition.* Chicago: University of Chicago Press, 1980.

Ferguson, Thomas. "From Normalcy to New Deal: Industrial Structure, Party Competition, and American Public Policy in the Great Depression." *International Organization* 38 (winter 1984): 41-94.

Fishlow, Albert. "Antebellum Interregional Trade Reconsidered." In *New Views of American Economic Development,* ed. Ralph Andreano. Cambridge: Harvard University Press, 1965.

Fite, Gilbert C. *George N. Peek and the Fight for Farm Parity.* Norman: University of Oklahoma Press, 1954.

———. *Cotton Fields No More: Southern Agriculture, 1865-1980.* Lexington: University Press of Kentucky, 1984.

Fleisher, Richard. "Economic Benefit, Ideology, and Senate Voting on the B-1 Bomber." *American Politics Quarterly* 13 (1985): 200-11.

Frank, Thomas M., and Edward Weisband. *Foreign Policy by Congress.* New York: Oxford University Press, 1979.

Freidel, Frank. *F.D.R. and the South.* Baton Rouge: Louisiana State University Press, 1965.

———. *Franklin D. Roosevelt: Launching the New Deal.* Boston: Little, Brown, 1973.

Friedberg, Aaron. "Is the United States Capable of Acting Strategically?" *Washington Quarterly* 14 (winter 1991): 5-23.

Frieden, Jeffry A. "Sectoral Conflict and U.S. Foreign Economic Policy, 1914-1940." *International Organization* 42 (winter 1988): 59-90.

———. "The Economics of Intervention: American Overseas Investments and Relations with Underdeveloped Areas, 1890-1950." *Comparative Studies in Society and History* 31 (January 1989): 55-80.

Fry, Joseph. *John Tyler Morgan and the Search for Southern Autonomy.* Knoxville: University of Tennessee Press, 1992.

Gaddis, John Lewis. *Strategies of Containment: A Critical Appraisal of Postwar American National Security Policy.* New York: Oxford University Press, 1982.

Galbraith, John Kenneth. *The Affluent Society.* Boston: Houghton Mifflin, 1958.

Gamm, Gerald H. *The Making of New Deal Democrats: Voting Behavior and Realignment in Boston, 1920-1940.* Chicago: University of Chicago Press, 1986.

Gardner, Lloyd C. *Economic Aspects of New Deal Diplomacy.* Madison: University of Wisconsin Press, 1964.

Gardner, Richard N. *Sterling-Dollar Diplomacy in Current Perspective: The Origins and the Prospects of Our International Economic Order.* Rev. ed. New York: Columbia University Press, 1980.

Garland, Gregory Lawrence. "Southern Congressional Opposition to Hawaiian Reciprocity and Annexation, 1876-1898." Master's thesis, University of North Carolina, 1983.

Gelfand, Lawrence B., ed. "Diplomacy and War Plans in the United States, 1890-1917." In *Essays on the History of American Foreign Relations.* New York: Holt, Rinehart and Winston, 1972.

Gellman, Irwin F. *Secret Affairs: Franklin Roosevelt, Cordell Hull, and Sumner Wells.* Baltimore: Johns Hopkins University Press, 1995.

Genovese, Eugene D., and Leonard Hochberg, eds. *Geographic Perspectives in History.* New York: Basil Blackwell, 1989.

Gilbert, Felix. *To the Farewell Address: Ideas of Early American Foreign Policy.* Princeton: Princeton University Press, 1961.

Gillon, Steven M. *Politics and Vision: The ADA and American Liberalism 1947-1985.* Oxford: Oxford University Press, 1987.

Gilpin, Robert. *U.S. Power and the Multinational Corporation: The Political Economy of Foreign Direct Investment.* New York: Basic Books, 1975.

———. *The Political Economy of International Relations.* Princeton: Princeton University Press, 1987.

Ginsberg, Benjamin, and Martin Shefter. *Politics by Other Means: The Declining Importance of Elections in America.* New York: Basic Books, 1990.

Glickman, Norman J., and Amy K. Glasmeier. "The International Economy and the American South." In *Deindustrialization and Regional Economic Transformation: The Experience of the United States,* ed. Lloyd Rodwin and Hidehiko Sazanami. Boston: Unwin Hyman, 1989.

Glickman, Norman J. *The Urban Impacts of Federal Policies.* Baltimore: Johns Hopkins University Press, 1980.

Goldstein, Judith. *Ideas, Interests, and American Trade Policy.* Ithaca: Cornell University Press, 1993.

Good, David F. "Uneven Development in the Nineteenth Century: A Comparison of the Habsburg Empire and the United States." *Journal of Economic History* 96 (March 1986): 137-51.

Gould, Lewis L. "Diplomats in the Lobby: Franco-American Relations and the Dingley Tariff of 1897." *Historian* 39 (August 1977): 659-80.

Gourevitch, Peter. *Politics in Hard Times: Comparative Responses to International Economic Crises.* Ithaca: Cornell University Press, 1986.

———. "International Trade, Domestic Coalitions, and Liberty: Comparative Responses to the Crisis of 1873-1896." *Journal of Interdisciplinary History* 8 (autumn 1977): 281-313.

———. "Breaking with Orthodoxy: The Politics of Economic Policy Response to the Depression of the 1930s." *International Organization* 38 (winter 1984): 95-129.

Grantham, Dewey W. *The Life and Death of the Solid South: A Political History.* Louisville: University Press of Kentucky, 1988.

Grassmuck, George L. *Sectional Biases in Congress on Foreign Policy.* Baltimore: Johns Hopkins University Press, 1951.

Greenstone, J. David. "Political Culture and American Political Development: Liberty, Union, and the Liberal Bipolarity." In *Studies in American Political Development,* ed. Karren Orren and Stephen Skowronek. Vol. 1. New Haven: Yale University Press, 1986.

Grenville, John A. S., and George B. Young. *Politics, Strategy and American Diplomacy.* New Haven: Yale University Press, 1966.

Guinsburg, Thomas N. *The Pursuit of Isolationism in the United States Senate from Versailles to Pearl Harbor.* New York: Garland, 1982.

Gunderson, Gerald. *A New Economic History of America.* New York: McGraw-Hill, 1976.

Haas, Richard. "Congressional Power: Implications for American Security Policy." In *Adelphi Papers,* 153. London: International Institute for Strategic Studies, 1979.

Haggard, Stephan. "The Institutional Foundations of Hegemony: Explaining the Reciprocal Trade Agreements Act of 1934." *International Organization* 42 (winter 1988): 91-119.

Hamilton, Allen Lee. "Military Strategists and the Annexation of Hawaii." *Journal of the West* 15 (April 1976): 81-91.

Harris, Carl V. "Right Fork or Left Fork? The Section-Party Alignments of Southern Democrats in Congress, 1873-1897." *Journal of Southern History* 42 (November 1976): 471-506.

Hathaway, Robert M. "1933-1945: Economic Diplomacy in a Time of Crisis." In *Economics and World Power: An Assessment of American Diplomacy since 1789,* ed. William H. Becker and Samuel F. Wells, Jr. New York: Columbia University Press, 1984.

Havemann, Joel, Rochelle Stanfield, and Neil Pierce. "Federal Spending: The Northeast's Loss Is the Sunbelt's Gain." *National Journal,* 26 June 1976, 878-91.

Hawley, Ellis W. *The Great War and the Search for a Modern Order: A History of the American People and Their Institutions, 1917-1933.* New York: St. Martin's Press, 1979.

Hays, Samuel P. *The Response to Industrialism, 1885-1914.* 13th ed. Chicago: University of Chicago Press, 1971.

Haystead, Ladd, and Gilbert C. Fite. *The Agricultural Regions of the United States.* Norman: University of Oklahoma Press, 1955.

Healey, Michael J., and Brian W. Ilbery. *Location and Change: Perspectives on Economic Geography.* Oxford: Oxford University Press, 1990.

Healy, David. *U.S. Expansionism: The Imperialist Urge of the 1890s.* Madison: University of Wisconsin Press, 1970.

Hearden, Patrick J. *Independence and Empire: The New South's Cotton Mill Campaign, 1865-1901.* DeKalb: Northern Illinois University Press, 1982.

———. *Roosevelt Confronts Hitler: America's Entry into World War II.* DeKalb: Northern Illinois University Press, 1987.

Hechter, Michael. *The Microfoundations of Macrosociology.* Philadelphia: Temple University Press, 1983.

Henkin, Louis. *Foreign Affairs and the Constitution.* New York: Norton, 1972.

Hero, Alfred O., Jr. *The Southerner and World Affairs.* Baton Rouge: Lousiana State University Press, 1965.

Herrick, Walter R., Jr. *The American Naval Revolution.* Baton Rouge: Lousiana State University Press, 1966.

Herring, George C., and Gary R. Hess. "Regionalism and Foreign Policy: The Dying Myth of Southern Internationalism." *Southern Studies* 20 (fall 1981): 247-77.

Hill, Richard Child. "Economic Crisis and Political Response in the Motor City." In *Sunbelt/Snowbelt: Urban Development and Regional Restructuring,* ed. Larry Sawers and William K. Tabb. New York: Oxford University Press, 1984.

Himmelstein, Jerome L. *To the Right: The Transformation of American Conservatism.* Berkeley and Los Angeles: University of California Press, 1990.

Hirshson, Stanley P. *Farewell to the Bloody Shirt: Northern Republicans and the Southern Negro, 1877-1893.* Bloomington: Indiana University Press, 1962.

Hobsbawm, E. J. *The Age of Empire, 1875-1914.* New York: Pantheon Books, 1987.

Hobson, John A. *Imperialism; A Study.* 1902. Reprint, London: Allen and Unwin, 1938.

Hodgson, Godfrey. *The Colonel: The Life and Wars of Henry Stimson, 1867-1950.* New York: Alfred A. Knopf, 1990.

Hoffmann, Stanley. *Gulliver's Troubles; or, the Setting of American Foreign Policy.* New York: McGraw-Hill, 1968.

Hogan, Michael J. "American Marshall Planners and the Search for a European Neocapitalism." *American Historical Review* 90 (February 1985): 44-72.

———, ed. *The End of the Cold War: Its Meaning and Implications.* Cambridge: Cambridge University Press, 1992.

Holcombe, Arthur N. *The Political Parties of To-Day: A Study in Republican and Democratic Politics.* New York: Harper & Brothers, 1924.

Hollingsworth, J. Rogers. *The Whirligig of Politics: The Democracy of Cleveland and Bryan.* Chicago: University of Chicago Press, 1963.

Holsti, Oli R., and James N. Rosenau. *American Leadership in World Affairs: Vietnam and the Breakdown of Consensus.* Boston: Allen and Unwin, 1984.

Hoover, Calvin B., and B. U. Ratchford. *Economic Resources and Policies of the South.* New York: Macmillan, 1951.

House, John W., ed. *United States Public Policy: A Geographical View.* Oxford: Clarendon Press, 1983.

Howes, Candace. "Constructing Comparative Disadvantage: Lessons from the U.S. Auto Industry." In *Trading Industries, Trading Regions: International Trade, American Industry, and Regional Economic Development,* ed. Helzi Noponen, Julie Graham, and Ann R. Markusen. New York: Guilford Press, 1993.

Howes, Candace, and Ann R. Markusen. "Trade, Industry, and Economic Development." In *Trading Industries, Trading Regions: International Trade, American Industry, and Regional Economic Development,* ed. Helzi Noponen, Julie Graham, and Ann R. Markusen. New York: Guilford Press, 1993.

Hunt, Michael H. *Ideology and U.S. Foreign Policy.* New Haven: Yale University Press, 1987.

Huntington, Samuel P. *Political Order in Changing Societies.* New Haven: Yale University Press, 1968.

———. *American Politics: The Promise of Disharmony.* Cambridge: Harvard University Press, 1981.

———. "The U.S.—Decline or Renewal?" *Foreign Affairs* 67 (winter 1988-89): 76-97.

Hutchinson, William K., and Samuel Williamson. "The Self-Sufficiency of the Antebellum South: Estimates of the Food Supply." *Journal of Economic History* 31 (September 1971): 591-612.

———. "Regional Exports to Foreign Countries: United States, 1870-1914." In *Research in Economic History,* ed. Paul Uselding. Vol. 7. Greenwich, Conn.: JAI Press, 1982.

———. "Regional Exports of the United States to Foreign Countries: A Structural Analysis, 1870-1910." In *Research in Economic History,* ed. Paul Uselding. Vol. 10. Greenwich, Conn.: JAI Press, 1986.

Ikenberry, G. John, David A. Lake, and Michael Mastanduno. "Introduction: Approaches to Explaining American Foreign Economic Policy." *International Organization* 42 (winter 1988): 1-14.

Irish, Marian D. "Foreign Policy and the South." *Journal of Politics* 24 (May 1948): 306-26.

Iriye, Akira. *From Nationalism to Internationalism: US Foreign Policy to 1914.* London: Routledge and Kegan Paul, 1977.

Isaacs, Asher. *International Trade: Tariff and Commercial Policies.* Chicago: Irwin, 1948.

Johnson, Alvin S. "Protection and the Formation of Capital." *Political Science Quarterly* 23 (June 1908): 220-41.

Johnson, Donald Bruce. *National Party Platforms of 1980.* Urbana: University of Illinois Press, 1982.

Johnson, Emory R., et al. *History of Domestic and Foreign Commerce of the United States.* 2 vols. New York: Burt Franklin, 1915.

Johnston, Robert J. "The State, Political Geography, and Geography." In *New Models in Geography,* ed. Richard Peet and N. J. Thrift. Vol. 1. London: Unwin Hyman, 1989.

Jonas, Manfred. *Isolationism in America, 1935-1941.* Ithaca: Cornell University Press, 1966.

Josling, Timothy. *Problems and Prospects for U.S. Agriculture in World Markets.* Washington, D.C.: NPA Committee on Changing International Realities, 1981.

Kanter, Arnold. *Defense Politics: A Budgetary Perspective.* Chicago: University of Chicago Press, 1975.

Karp, Walter. *The Politics of War: The Story of Two Wars Which Altered Forever the Political Life of the American Republic (1890-1920).* New York: Harper and Row, 1979.

Katzenstein, Peter. "International Relations and Domestic Structures: Foreign Economic Policies of Advanced Industrial States." *International Organization* 30 (winter 1976): 1-45.

Keech, William R., and Kyoungsan Pak. "Partisanship, Institutions, and Change in American Trade Politics." *Journal of Politics* 57 (November 1995): 1130-42.

Kehr, Eckart. *Battleship Building and Party Politics in Germany, 1894-1901: A Cross Section of the Political, Social, and Ideological Preconditions of Germany Imperialism.* Trans. Pauline R. Anderson and Eugene N. Anderson. 1930. Reprint, Chicago: University of Chicago Press, 1973.

Kennan, George F. *American Diplomacy: 1900-1950*. Chicago: University of Chicago Press, 1950.

——. *The Cloud of Danger: Current Realities of American Foreign Policy*. Boston: Little, Brown, 1977.

Kennedy, Paul. *The Rise and Fall of the Great Powers: Economic Change and Military Conflict from 1500 to 2000*. New York: Random House, 1987.

Keohane, Robert O. *After Hegemony: Cooperation and Discord in the World Political Economy*. Princeton: Princeton University Press, 1984.

Key, V. O. *Southern Politics in State and Nation*. New York: Alfred A. Knopf, 1949.

——. *Politics, Parties, and Pressure Groups*. New York: Thomas Y. Crowell, 1964.

——. "The Future of the Democratic Party." *Virginia Quarterly Review* 28 (spring 1952): 161-75.

Kimball, Warren F. *The Most Unsordid Act: Lend-Lease, 1939-1941*. Baltimore: Johns Hopkins University Press, 1969.

Kindleberger, Charles. *The World in Depression 1929-1939*. Berkeley and Los Angeles: University of California Press, 1973.

——. "The Rise of Free Trade in Western Europe, 1820-75." *Journal of Economic History* 35 (1975): 20-55.

——. "Dominance and Leadership in the International Economy: Exploitation, Public Goods, and Free Rides." *International Studies Quarterly* 25 (1981): 242-54.

King, Wayne. "Federal Funds Pour into Sunbelt States." *New York Times,* 9 February 1976, 24.

Kirkland, Edward C. *A History of American Economic Life*. 3d ed. New York: Appleton-Century-Crofts, 1951.

Kissinger, Henry. *The Necessity for Choice: Prospects of American Foreign Policy*. New York: Harper and Row, 1960.

——. *Diplomacy*. New York: Simon and Schuster, 1994.

Kissinger, Henry, and Cyrus Vance. "Bipartisan Objectives for American Foreign Policy." *Foreign Affairs* 66 (summer 1988): 899-921.

Kleppner, Paul. *Continuity and Change in Electoral Politics, 1893-1928*. New York: Greenwood Press, 1987.

——. "Politics without Parties: The Western States, 1900-1984." In *The Twentieth-Century West: Historical Interpretations*, ed. Gerald D. Nash and Richard W. Etulain. Albuquerque: University of New Mexico Press, 1989.

Koenig, Louis William. *The Presidency and The Crisis: Powers of the Office from the Invasion of Poland to Pearl Harbor*. New York: King's Crown Press, 1945.

Koh, Harold Hongju. *The National Security Constitution: Sharing Power after the Iran-Contra Affair*. New Haven: Yale University Press, 1990.

Kolko, Gabriel. *The Roots of American Foreign Policy*. Boston: Beacon, 1969.

——. *Main Currents in Modern American History*. 2d ed. New York: Pantheon Books, 1984.

————. *Confronting the Third World: United States Foreign Policy, 1945-1980.* New York: Pantheon Books, 1988.

Kolko, Joyce, and Gabriel Kolko. *The Limits of Power: The World and United States Foreign Policy, 1945-1954.* New York: Harper and Row, 1972.

Krasner, Stephen D. *Defending the National Interest: Raw Materials Investments and U.S. Foreign Policy.* Princeton: Princeton University Press, 1978.

Krugman, Paul. *Geography and Trade.* Cambridge: MIT Press, 1991.

Kurth, James. "Between Europe and America: The New York Foreign Policy Elite." In *Capital of the American Century: The National and International Influence of New York City,* ed. Martin Shefter. New York: Russell Sage Foundation, 1993.

————. "America's Grand Strategy: A Pattern of History." *The National Interest,* Spring 1996, 3-19.

Ladd, Everet Carll, Jr. *American Political Parties: Social Change and Political Response.* New York: W. W. Norton, 1970.

LaFeber, Walter. *The New Empire: An Interpretation of American Expansion, 1860-1898.* Ithaca: Cornell University Press, 1963.

————. *The American Age: United States Foreign Policy at Home and Abroad since 1750.* New York: W. W. Norton, 1989.

————. *America, Russia and the Cold War, 1945-1992.* 7th ed. New York: McGraw-Hill, 1993.

————. *The American Search for Opportunity, 1865-1913.* New York: Cambridge University Press, 1993.

————. "The Constitution and U.S. Foreign Policy: An Interpretation." In *Alternative Perspectives on the U.S. Constitution,* ed. Jules Lobel. New York: Monthly Review Press, 1988.

Lake, David A. *Power, Protectionism, and Free Trade: International Sources of U.S. Commercial Strategy, 1887-1939.* Ithaca: Cornell University Press, 1988.

Lanier, Osmos, Jr. "Anti-Annexationists of the 1890s." Ph.D. diss., University of Georgia, 1965.

Lary, Hal B. *The United States in the World Economy.* Washington, D.C.: GPO, 1943.

Lasch, Christopher. "The Anti-Imperialists, the Philippines, and the Inequality of Man." *Journal of Southern History* 24 (August 1958): 319-31.

Leffler, Melvyn P. *The Elusive Quest: America's Pursuit of European Stability and French Security, 1919-1933.* Chapel Hill: University of North Carolina Press, 1979.

————. *A Preponderance of Power: National Security, the Truman Administration, and the Cold War.* Stanford: Stanford University Press, 1992.

Legler, John. *Regional Distribution of Federal Receipts and Expenditures in the Nineteenth Century: A Quantitative Study.* New York: Arno, 1977.

Lerche, Charles O., Jr. *The Uncertain South: Its Changing Patterns of Politics in Foreign Policy.* Chicago: Quadrangle Books, 1964.

Leuchtenberg, William E. *Franklin D. Roosevelt and the New Deal.* New York: Harper and Row, 1963.

Lewis, Cleona. *America's Stake in International Investments*. Washington, D.C.: Brookings Institution, 1938.

Limerick, Patricia Nelson. *The Legacy of Conquest: The Unbroken Past of the American West*. New York: W. W. Norton, 1987.

Lindsay, James M. "Parochialism, Policy, and Constituency Constraints: Congressional Voting on Strategic Weapons Systems." *American Journal of Political Science* 34 (1990): 936–60.

Lindstrom, Diane. "Southern Dependence upon Grain Supplies: A View of the Trade Flows, 1840–1860." In *The Structure of the Cotton Economy of the Antebellum South*, ed. William Parker. Washington, D.C.: Agricultural History Society, 1970.

Link, Arthur S. *Wilson: The Struggle for Neutrality*. Princeton: Princeton University Press, 1960.

———. "The Cotton Crisis, the South, and Anglo-American Diplomacy, 1914–1915." In *Studies in Southern History*, ed. J. Carlyle Sitterson. Chapel Hill: University of North Carolina Press, 1957.

Lippmann, Walter. *The Public Philosophy*. Boston: Little, Brown, 1955.

Lipsey, Robert E. *Price and Quantity Trends in the Foreign Trade of the United States*. Princeton: Princeton University Press, 1963.

Livingston, James. *Origins of the Federal Reserve System: Money, Class, and Corporate Capitalism, 1890–1913*. Ithaca: Cornell University Press, 1986.

Loewenheim, Francis L., Harold D. Langley, and Manfred Jonas, eds. *Roosevelt and Churchill: Their Secret Wartime Correspondence*. New York: Saturday Review Press, 1975.

Loomis, Burdett A. "Congressional Caucuses and the Politics of Representation." In *Congress Reconsidered*, 2d ed., edited by Lawrence C. Dodd and Bruce I. Oppenheimer. Washington, D.C.: Congressional Quarterly Press, 1981.

Lowi, Theodore J. *The End of Liberalism: The Second Republic of the United States*. New York: W. W. Norton, 1969.

Lubell, Samuel. *The Revolt of the Moderates*. New York: Harper and Row, 1956.

———. *The Future of American Politics*. New York: Harper and Row, 1965.

———. "Who Votes Isolationist and Why." *Harper's Magazine*, April 1951, 29–36.

Luce, Henry R. *The American Century*. New York: Farrar and Rinehart, 1941.

Luria, Dan, and Jack Russell. "Motor City Changeover." In *Sunbelt/Snowbelt: Urban Development and Regional Restructuring*, ed. Larry Sawers and William K. Tabb. New York: Oxford University Press, 1984.

MacDonald, C. A. *The United States, Britain, and Appeasement, 1936–1939*. New York: St. Martin's Press, 1981.

Mahan, Alfred T. "Hawaii and Our Future Sea Power." *Forum* 15 (March 1893): 1–11.

Maier, Charles S. "The Politics of Productivity: Foundations of American International Economic Policy after World War II." In *Between Power and Plenty: Foreign Economic Policies of Advanced Industrial States*, ed. Peter J. Katzenstein. Madison: University of Wisconsin Press, 1978.

Malmgren, Harald. "Coming Trade Wars?" *Foreign Policy* 1 (winter 1970): 115–43.

Mann, Thomas E. "Making Foreign Policy: President and Congress." In *A Question of Balance: The President, the Congress, and Foreign Policy,* ed. Thomas E. Mann. Washington, D.C.: Brookings Institution, 1990.

Marks, Frederick W., III. *Wind over Sand: The Diplomacy of Franklin Roosevelt.* Athens: University of Georgia Press, 1988.

Markusen, Ann R. *Profit Cycles, Oligopoly, and Regional Development.* Cambridge: MIT Press, 1985.

———. *Regions: The Economics and Politics of Territory.* Totowa, N.J.: Rowman and Littlefield, 1987.

Markusen, Ann R., et al. *The Rise of the Gunbelt: The Military Remapping of Industrial America.* New York: Oxford University Press, 1991.

Markusen, Ann R., and Virginia Carlson. "Deindustrialization in the American Midwest: Causes and Responses." In *Deindustrialization and Regional Economic Transformation: The Experience of the United States,* ed. Lloyd Rodwin and Hidehiko Sazanami. Boston: Unwin Hyman, 1989.

Massey, Doreen. *Spatial Divisions of Labor: Social Production and the Geography of Production.* New York: Methuen, 1984.

Mastanduno, Michael. "The United States Political System and International Leadership: A 'Decidedly Inferior' Form of Government." In *American Foreign Policy: Theoretical Essays,* 2d ed., edited by G. John Ikenberry. New York: HarperCollins, 1996.

May, Ernest. *Imperial Democracy: The Emergence of America as a Great Power.* New York: Harcourt Brace Jovanovich, 1961.

Mayer, Arno J. "Internal Causes and Purposes of War in Europe, 1870–1956: A Research Assignment." *Journal of Modern History* 41 (September 1969): 291–303.

Mayer, Kenneth R. *The Political Economy of Defense Contracting.* New Haven: Yale University Press, 1991.

Mayhew, David R. *Congress: The Electoral Connection.* New Haven: Yale University Press, 1974.

McCormick, James M., and Eugene R. Wittkopf. "Bush and Bipartisanship: The Past as Prologue?" *Washington Quarterly* 13 (winter 1990): 5–16.

McCormick, Thomas J. *China Market: America's Quest for Informal Empire, 1893–1901.* Chicago: Quadrangle Books, 1967.

———. *America's Half-Century: United States Foreign Policy in the Cold War.* 2d ed. Baltimore: Johns Hopkins University Press, 1995.

———. "World Systems." *Journal of American History* 77 (June 1990): 125–32.

McDonald, Timothy G. "Southern Democratic Congressmen and the First World War, August 1914–April 1917: The Public Record of Their Support for or Opposition to Wilson's Policies." Ph.D. diss., University of Washington, 1962.

McDougall, Walter A. *Promised Land, Crusader State: The American Encounter with the World since 1776.* Boston: Houghton Mifflin, 1997.

McKinley, William. *Speeches and Addresses of William McKinley From March 1, 1897 to May 30, 1900.* New York: Doubleday & McClure, 1900.

McSeveney, Samuel T. *The Politics of Depression: Political Behavior in the Northeast, 1893-1896.* New York: Oxford University Press, 1972.

McWilliams, Tennant S. *The New South Faces the World: Foreign Affairs and the Southern Sense of Self, 1877-1950.* Baton Rouge: Louisiana State University Press, 1988.

———. "The Lure of Empire: Southern Interest in the Caribbean, 1877-1900." *Mississippi Quarterly* 29 (winter 1975-76): 43-63.

Meinig, D. W. *The Shaping of America: A Geographical Perspective on 500 Years of History.* Vols. 1 and 2. New Haven: Yale University Press, 1986-93.

Meyer, David R. "Emergence of the American Manufacturing Belt: An Interpretation." *Journal of Historical Geography* 9 (1983): 145-74.

———. "The National Integration of Regional Economies, 1860-1920." In *North America: The Historical Geography of a Changing Continent,* ed. Robert D. Mitchell and Paul A. Groves. London: Hutchinson, 1987.

Miernyk, William H. "Energy Constraints and Economic Development in the Northeast." In *Economic Prospects for the Northeast,* ed. Harry W. Richardson and Joseph H. Turek. Philadelphia: Temple University Press, 1985.

Millett, Allen R., and Peter Maslowski. *For the Common Defense: A Military History of the United States.* New York: Free Press, 1984.

Mills, Roger Q. "Reciprocity—Why Southward Only?" *Forum* 11 (May 1891): 268-75.

Milner, Helen V. *Resisting Protectionism: Global Industries and the Politics of International Trade.* Princeton: Princeton University Press, 1988.

———. "Trading Places: Industries for Free Trade." *World Politics* 40 (April 1988): 350-76.

Molyneaux, Peter. *What Economic Nationalism Means to the South.* New York: Foreign Policy Association, 1934.

Moore, James Tice. "Redeemers Reconsidered: Change and Continuity in the Democratic South, 1870-1900." *Journal of Southern History* 44 (August 1978): 357-78.

Morgenthau, Hans J. *In Defense of the National Interest.* New York: Alfred Knopf, 1951.

———. *Politics among Nations: The Struggle for Power and Peace.* 5th ed. New York: Alfred Knopf, 1973.

Moyer, Wayne. "House Voting on Defense: An Ideological Explanation." In *Armed Forces in American Society,* ed. Bruce Russett and Alfred Stepan. New York: Harper and Row, 1973.

Mucciaroni, Gary. *Reversals of Fortune: Public Policy and Private Interests.* Washington D.C.: Brookings Institution, 1995.

Muller, Thomas L. "Regional Impacts." In *The Reagan Experiment: An Examination of Economic and Social Policies under the Reagan Administration,* ed. John L. Palmer and Isabel V. Sawhill. Washington, D.C.: Urban Institute Press, 1982.

Murray, Alan. "House Passes Domestic Content Bill." *Congressional Quarterly Weekly,* 18 December 1982, 3072.

Nash, Gerald D. *The American West in the Twentieth Century: A Short History of an Urban Oasis.* Englewood Cliffs, N.J.: Prentice-Hall, 1973.

———. *The American West Transformed: The Impact of the Second World War.* Bloomington: Indiana University Press, 1985.

Newby, Idus A. "States' Rights and Southern Congressmen during World War I." *Phylon* 24 (spring 1963): 34-50.

Nincic, Miroslav. *Democracy and Foreign Policy: The Fallacy of Political Realism.* New York: Columbia University Press, 1992.

Nivola, Pietro S. "The New Protectionism: U.S. Trade Policy in Historical Perspective." *Political Science Quarterly* 101 (fall 1986): 577-600.

North, Douglas C. *The Economic Growth of the United States, 1790-1860.* Englewood Cliffs, N.J.: Prentice-Hall, 1961.

Norton, R. D., and John Rees. "The Product Cycle and the Spatial Decentralization of American Manufacturing." *Regional Studies* 13 (1979): 141-51.

Novack, David E., and Matthew Simon. "Commercial Responses to the American Export Invasion, 1871-1914: An Essay in Attitudinal History." *Explorations in Entrepreneurial History* 3 (winter 1966): 121-47.

Nye, Joseph S., Jr. *Bound to Lead: The Changing Nature of American Politics.* New York: Basic Books, 1990.

O'Connell, Robert L. *The Cult of the Battleship and the Rise of the U.S. Navy.* Boulder: Westview Press, 1991.

Odum, Howard W. *Southern Regions of the United States.* Chapel Hill: University of North Carolina Press, 1936.

Ó hUallacháin, Breandán. "Regional and Technological Implications of the Recent Buildup in American Defense Spending." *Annals of the Association of American Geographers* 77 (spring 1987): 208-23.

Ornstein, Norman J., Thomas E. Mann, and Michael J. Malbin. *Vital Statistics on Congress, 1989-1990.* Washington, D.C.: American Enterprise Institute, 1990.

Osborne, Thomas J. *"Empire Can Wait": American Opposition to Hawaiian Annexation, 1893-1898.* Kent, Ohio: Kent State University Press, 1981.

Osgood, Robert. *Ideals and Self-Interest in America's Foreign Relations: The Great Transformation of the Twentieth Century.* Chicago: University of Chicago Press, 1953.

Oye, Kenneth A. "Constrained Confidence and the Evolution of Reagan Foreign Policy." In *Eagle Resurgent? The Reagan Era in American Foreign Policy,* ed. Kenneth A. Oye, Robert J. Lieber, and Donald Rothchild. Boston: Little, Brown, 1987.

Paddison, Ronan. *The Fragmented State: The Political Geography of Power.* New York: St. Martin's Press, 1983.

Pastor, Robert. *Congress and the Politics of U.S. Foreign Economic Policy.* Berkeley and Los Angeles: University of California Press, 1980.

Patterson, James T. *Congressional Conservatism and the New Deal: The Growth of the Conservative Coalition in Congress, 1933-1939.* Lexington: University of Kentucky Press, 1967.

————."The New Deal in the West." *Pacific Historical Review* 38 (August 1969): 317-27.

Peet, Richard. "The Geography of Class Struggle and the Relocation of United States Manufacturing Industry." In *International Capitalism and Industrial Restructuring,* ed. Richard Peet. Boston: Allen and Unwin, 1987.

Perloff, Harvey S., et al. *Regions, Resources, and Economic Growth.* Baltimore: Johns Hopkins University Press, 1960.

Phillips, Kevin P. *The Emerging Republican Majority.* Garden City, N.Y.: Anchor Books, 1970.

Phillips, M. Ogden. "The Tariff and the South." *South Atlantic Quarterly* 32 (October 1933): 375-86.

Plesur, Milton. "The Republican Congressional Comeback of 1938." *Review of Politics* 24 (October 1962): 525-62.

Pletcher, David M. "Reciprocity and Latin America in the Early 1890s: A Foretaste of Dollar Diplomacy." *Pacific Historical Review* 47 (February 1978): 53-89.

————. "1861-1898: Economic Growth and Diplomatic Adjustment." In *Economics and World Power: An Assessment of American Diplomacy since 1789,* ed. William H. Becker and Samuel F. Wells, Jr. New York: Columbia University Press, 1984.

Polenberg, Richard. "The Decline of the New Deal, 1937-1940." In *The New Deal: The National Level,* ed. John Braeman, Robert H. Bremner, and David Brody. Vol. 1. Columbus: Ohio State University Press, 1975.

Pollard, Sidney. *Peaceful Conquest: The Industrialization of Europe, 1760-1970.* New York: Oxford University Press, 1981.

Porter, David L. *Congress and the Waning of the New Deal.* New York: Kennikat, 1980.

Potter, David M. *The South and the Concurrent Majority.* Baton Rouge: Louisiana State University Press, 1972.

Pratt, Julius W. *Expansionists of 1898: The Acquisition of Hawaii and the Spanish Islands.* 2d ed. Chicago: Quadrangle Books, 1964.

Pred, Allan R. *The Spatial Dynamics of U.S. Urban-Industrial Growth, 1800-1914: Interpretive and Theoretical Essays.* Cambridge: MIT Press, 1966.

Prisco, Salvatore, III. *John Barrett, Progressive Era Diplomat: A Study of a Commercial Expansionist, 1987-1920.* Tuscaloosa: University of Alabama Press, 1973.

Rabinowitz, Howard N. *The First New South, 1865-1920.* Arlington Heights, Ill.: Harlan Davidson, 1992.

Rae, Nicol C. *The Decline of the Liberal Republicans from 1952 to the Present.* Oxford: Oxford University Press, 1989.

————. *Southern Democrats.* New York: Oxford University Press, 1994.

Rafuse, Robert, Jr. "The New Sectionalism Controversy: An Overview." Paper prepared for National Governors' Conference, Center for Policy Research and Analysis, 26 January 1977.

Rakove, Jack N. "Making Foreign Policy—The View from 1787." In *Foreign Policy and the Constitution,* ed. Robert A. Goldwin and Robert A. Licht. Washington, D.C.: AEI Press, 1990.

Raines, Howell. "Move to Curb Competitiveness of Imports Rises as Focus at End of Campaign." *New York Times,* 25 October 1982, B6.

Ratchford, B. U. "The South's Stake in International Trade—Past, Present, and Prospective." *Southern Economic Journal* 14 (April 1948): 361-75.

Reading, Don C. "New Deal Activity and the States, 1933-39." *Journal of Economic History* 33 (December 1973): 792-810.

Reagan, Ronald. *America's New Beginning: A Program for Economic Recovery.* Washington, D.C.: GPO, 1981.

———. *Public Papers of the Presidents of the United States: Ronald Reagan.* Washington, D.C.: GPO, 1982-90.

Reed, Roy. "Sunbelt Still Stronghold of Conservatism in U.S." *New York Times,* 11 February 1976, 1, 11.

Rees, John. "The Impact of Defense Spending on Regional Industrial Change in the United States." In *Federalism and Regional Development,* ed. George Hoffman. Austin: University of Texas Press, 1981.

Rees, John, and Stafford, Howard. "Theories of Regional Growth and Industrial Location: Their Relevance for Understanding High-Technology Complexes." In *Technology, Regions and Policy,* ed. John Rees and Howard Stafford. Totowa, N.J.: Rowan and Littlefield, 1986.

Reinhard, David W. *The Republican Right since 1945.* Lexington: University Press of Kentucky, 1983.

Reinhold, Robert. "Sunbelt Region Leads Nation in Growth of Population: Section's Cities Top Urban Expansion." *New York Times,* 8 February 1976, 1, 42.

Rhodes, Edward. "U.S. Strategic Adjustment in the 1890s." Paper presented at the Social Science Research Council Research Workshop, *The Politics of Strategic Adjustment: Ideas, Institutions, and Interests,* Austin, Tex., 23-24 April 1994.

Richardson, James D., comp. *A Compilation of the Messages and Papers of the Presidents, 1789-1902.* Vol. 10. New York: Bureau of National Literature, 1902.

Rieselbach, Leroy N. *The Roots of Isolationism.* Indianapolis: Bobbs-Merrill, 1966.

———. "The Basis of Isolationist Behavior." *Public Opinion Quarterly* 24 (winter 1960): 645-57.

Rogowski, Ronald. *Commerce and Coalitions: How Trade Affects Domestic Political Alignments.* Princeton: Princeton University Press, 1989.

Roosevelt, Franklin D. *The Public Papers and Addresses of Franklin D. Roosevelt.* New York: Russell and Russell, 1969.

Rosenberg, Emily S. *Spreading the American Dream: American Economic and Cultural Expansion: 1890-1945.* New York: Hill and Wang, 1982.

Rosenberg, Hans. "The Depression of 1873-1896 in Central Europe." *Journal of Economic History* 13 (1943): 58-73.

Rostow, Walt. *The World Economy: History and Prospect.* Austin: University of Texas, 1978.

———. "Regional Change in the Fifth Kondratieff Upswing." In *The Rise of the Sunbelt Cities,* ed. David C. Perry and Alfred J. Watkins. Beverly Hills: Sage, 1977.

Rothstein, Morton. "America in the International Rivalry for the British Wheat Market, 1860–1901." *Mississippi Valley Historical Review* 47 (December 1960): 401–18.

———. "The New South and the International Economy." *Agricultural History* 57 (October 1983): 385–402.

Rourke, John T., Ralph G. Carter, and Mark A. Boyer. *Making American Foreign Policy.* Guilford, Conn.: Dushkin, 1994.

Ruggie, John G. "International Regimes, Transactions, and Change: Embedded Liberalism in the Postwar Economic Order." In *International Regimes,* ed. Stephen D. Krasner. Ithaca: Cornell University Press, 1983.

Rundquist, Barry S. "On Testing a Military Industrial Complex Theory." *American Politics Quarterly* 6 (1978): 29–53.

Russett, Bruce. *What Price Vigilance?* New Haven: Yale University Press, 1970.

Sack, Robert. "Territorial Bases of Power." In *Political Studies from Spatial Perspectives,* ed. Alan Burnett and Peter Taylor. New York: John Wiley, 1981.

Sale, Kirkpatrick. *Power Shift: The Rise of the Southern Rim and its Challenge to the Eastern Establishment.* New York: Random House, 1975.

Saloutos, Theodore. *The American Farmer and the New Deal.* Ames: Iowa State University Press, 1982.

Saloutos, Theodore, and John D. Hicks. *Agricultural Discontent in the Middle West, 1900–1939.* Madison: University of Wisconsin Press, 1951.

Sanders, Elizabeth. "Industrial Concentration, Sectional Competition, and Antitrust Politics in America, 1880–1980." In *Studies in American Political Development,* ed. Karren Orren and Stephen Skowronek. Vol. 1. New Haven: Yale University Press, 1986.

———. "The Regulatory Surge of the 1970s in Historical Perspective." In *Public Regulation: New Perspectives on Institutions and Policies,* ed. Elizabeth E. Bailey. Cambridge: MIT Press, 1986.

Sarasohn, Judy. "UAW Wins Backing for Domestic Content Bill." *Congressional Quarterly Weekly,* 11 September 1982, 2243–41.

Schattschneider, E. E. *The Semisovereign People: A Realist's View of Democracy in America.* New York: Holt, Rinehart and Winston, 1960.

Schatz, Arthur W. "The Anglo-American Trade Agreement and Cordell Hull's Search for Peace, 1936–1938." *Journal of American History* 57 (June 1970): 85–103.

———. "The Reciprocal Trade Agreements Program and the 'Farm Vote,' 1934–1940." *Agricultural History* 46 (October 1972): 498–514.

Schlesinger, Arthur M., Jr. *The Coming of the New Deal.* Boston: Houghton Mifflin, 1958.

Schulman, Bruce J. *From Cotton Belt to Sunbelt: Federal Policy, Economic Development, and the Transformation of the South, 1938-1980.* New York: Oxford University Press, 1991.

Schumpeter, Joseph. "The Sociology of Imperialism." In *Imperialism and Social Classes,* trans. Heinz Norden. New York: Augustus M. Kelley, 1951.

Schurmann, Franz. *The Logic of World Power: An Inquiry into the Origins, Currents, and Contradictions of World Politics.* New York: Pantheon Books, 1974.

Schwarz, Jordan A. *The New Dealers: Power Politics in the Age of Roosevelt.* New York: Alfred A. Knopf, 1993.

Seabury, Paul. *The Waning of Southern "Internationalism."* Princeton: Center of International Studies, 1957.

———. *Power, Freedom, and Diplomacy: The Foreign Policy of the United States.* New York: Random House, 1963.

Shannon, Fred A. *The Farmer's Last Frontier: Agriculture, 1860-1897.* New York: Farrar and Rinehart, 1945.

Shelley, Fred M., et al. *Political Geography of the United States.* New York: Guilford Press, 1996.

Shelley, Mack C., II. *The Permanent Majority: The Conservative Coalition in the United States Congress.* Mobile: University of Alabama Press, 1983.

Sherman, John. *Recollections of Forty Years in the House, Senate and Cabinet.* Vol. 2. Chicago: Werner, 1895.

Shoch, James. "Party Competition and American Trade Policy during the Reagan-Bush Era." Paper presented at the annual meeting of the American Political Science Association, San Francisco, Calif., 31 August 1996.

Shoup, Lawrence H., and William Minter. *Imperial Brain Trust.* New York: Monthly Review, 1977.

Shulman, Mark. *Navalism and the Emergence of American Sea Power, 1882-1893.* Annapolis: Naval Institute Press, 1995.

Simon, Matthew, and David Novack. "Some Dimensions of the American Commercial Invasion of Europe, 1871-1914: An Introductory Essay." *Journal of Economic History* 24 (December 1964): 591-605.

Sklar, Martin J. "The N.A.M. and Foreign Markets on the Eve of the Spanish-American War." *Science and Society* 23 (1959): 133-62.

Smith, Edwina C. "Southerners on Empire: Southern Senators and Imperialism, 1898-99." *Mississippi Quarterly* 31 (winter 1977-78): 89-107.

Smith, Howard R. *Economic History of the United States.* New York: Ronald Press, 1956.

———. "The Farmer and the Tariff: A Reappraisal." *Southern Economic Journal* 21 (October 1954): 152-65.

Smith, Howard R., and John Fraser Hart. "The American Tariff Map." *The Geographical Review* 45 (July 1955): 327-46.

Smith, Neil. *Uneven Development: Nature, Capital and the Production of Space.* Oxford: Basil Blackwell, 1984.

Smith, Neil, and Dennis Ward. "The Restructuring of Geographical Scale: Coalescence and Fragmentation of the Northern Core Region." *Economic Geography* 63 (April 1987): 160–82.

Smith, Robert Freeman. "Reciprocity." In *Encyclopedia of American Foreign Policy,* ed. Alexander DeConde. Vol. 3. New York: Charles Scribner, 1978.

Smuckler, Ralph H. "The Region of Isolationism." *American Political Science Review* 47 (June 1953): 386–401.

Snyder, Jack. *Myths of Empire: Domestic Politics and International Ambition.* Ithaca: Cornell University Press, 1991.

Sommer, Judith E., and Fred K. Hines. *The U.S. Farm Sector: How Agricultural Exports Are Shaping Rural Economies in the 1980's.* Washington, D.C.: U.S. Department of Agriculture, 1988.

Sprout, Harold, and Margaret Sprout. *The Rise of American Naval Power, 1776–1918.* Princeton: Princeton University Press, 1939.

Spykman, Nicholas John. *America's Strategy in World Politics: The United States and the Balance of Power.* New York: Harcourt, Brace, 1942.

Stanwood, Edward. *American Tariff Controversies in the Nineteenth Century.* Boston: Houghton Mifflin, 1903.

Stein, Arthur. "Domestic Constraints, Extended Deterrence, and the Incoherence of Grand Strategy: The United States, 1938–1950." In *The Domestic Bases of Grand Strategy,* ed. Richard Rosecrance and Arthur Stein. Ithaca: Cornell University Press, 1993.

Steiner, Michael C. "The Significance of Turner's Sectional Thesis." *Western Historical Quarterly* 10 (October 1979): 437–66.

Storper, Michael, and Richard Walker. *The Capitalist Imperative: Territory, Technology, and Industrial Growth.* Oxford: Basil Blackwell, 1989.

Strausz-Hupé, Robert. *Democracy and American Foreign Policy: Reflections on the Legacy of Alexis de Tocqueville.* New Brunswick: Transaction, 1995.

Stromberg, Ronald N. "American Business and the Approach of War, 1935–1941." *Journal of Economic History* 13 (winter 1953): 58–78.

Strout, Cushing. *The American Image of the Old World.* New York: Harper and Row, 1963.

Sundquist, James L. *The Decline and Resurgence of Congress.* Washington, D.C.: Brookings Institution, 1983.

———. *Dynamics of the Party System: Alignment and Realignment of Political Parties in the United States.* Washington, D.C.: Brookings Institution, 1983.

Tarrow, Sidney. *Between Center and Periphery: Grassroots Politicians in Italy and France.* New Haven: Yale University Press, 1977.

Tate, Merze. *The United States and the Hawaiian Kingdom: A Political History.* New Haven: Yale University Press, 1967.

———. *Hawaii: Reciprocity or Annexation.* East Lansing, Mich: Michigan State University Press, 1968.

Taussig, Frank W. *The Tariff History of the United States.* 8th ed. New York: Putnam, 1931.

Terrill, Tom E. *The Tariff, Politics, and American Foreign Policy, 1874-1901.* Westport, Conn.: Greenwood Press, 1973.

Tindall, George B. *The Emergence of the New South, 1913-1945.* Baton Rouge: Louisiana State University Press, 1967.

Tompkins, E. Berkely. *Anti-Imperialism in the United States: The Great Debate, 1890-1920.* Philadelphia: University of Pennsylvania Press, 1970.

Tocqueville, Alexis de. *Democracy in America.* 2 vols. New York: Alfred A. Knopf, 1945.

Trachte, Kent, and Robert Ross. "The Crisis of Detroit and the Emergence of Global Capitalism." *International Journal of Urban and Regional Research* 9 (June 1985): 186-217.

Tracy, Benjamin Franklin. *Annual Report of the Secretary of the Navy.* 51st Cong., 1st sess., 1889.

Trubowitz, Peter. "Sectionalism and American Foreign Policy: The Political Geography of Consensus and Conflict." *International Studies Quarterly* 36 (June 1992): 173-90.

———. "Déjà Vu: Political Struggles over American Defense Policy." In *Downsizing Defense,* ed. Ethan B. Kapstein. Washington, D.C.: Congressional Quarterly Press, 1993.

———. "The Second Face of Strategy: Presidential Politics and Foreign Policy" (manuscript in preparation).

Trubowitz, Peter, and Brian E. Roberts. "Regional Interests and the Reagan Military Buildup." *Regional Studies* 26 (October 1992): 555-67.

Tugwell, Rexford G. *The Democratic Roosevelt.* Garden City, N.Y.: n.p., 1957.

Turner, Julius, and Edward V. Schneier Jr. *Party and Constituency: Pressures on Congress.* Rev. ed. Baltimore: Johns Hopkins University Press, 1970.

Turner, Frederick Jackson. *The Significance of Sections in American History.* New York: Holt, Rinehart and Winston, 1932.

———. "The Problem of the West." *Atlantic Monthly,* September 1896, 289-97.

———. "Is Sectionalism in America Dying Away?" *American Journal of Sociology* 13 (March 1908): 661-75.

———. "The Significance of the Frontier in American History." In *The Frontier in American History,* ed. Frederick Jackson Turner. New York: Holt, 1920.

Tyrrell, Ian. "American Exceptionalism in an Age of International History." *American Historical Review* 96 (October 1991): 1031-55.

Ullman, Edward. "Regional Development and the Geography of Concentration." *Papers and Proceedings of the Regional Science Association* 4 (1958): 179-98.

U.S. Bureau of the Census. *Biennial Census of Manufactures, 1927.* Washington, D.C., 1932.

———. *Fifteenth Census of the U.S. Manufactures: 1929. State Series.* Washington, D.C., 1932.

———. *Location of Manufactures, 1899-1929.* Washington, D.C., 1933.

———. *Biennial Census of Manufactures, 1931.* Washington, D.C., 1935.

———. *Historical Statistics of the United States, Colonial Times to 1970.* 2 vols. Washington, D.C., 1975.

U.S. Department of Commerce, Bureau of Economic Analysis. *United States Industrial Outlook.* Washington, D.C.: GPO, 1986.

U.S. Department of Labor, Bureau of Labor Statistics. *Employment and Earnings.* Washington, D.C.: GPO, 1982.

U.S. House of Representatives, Committee on Foreign Affairs. *Hearings on H.R. 1776: A Bill Further to Promote the Defense of the United States, and for Other Purposes.* Washington, D.C.: GPO, 1941.

Vance, Rupert. *Human Geography of the South.* Chapel Hill: University of North Carolina Press, 1936.

Vatter, Harold G. *The Drive to Industrial Maturity: The U.S. Economy, 1860–1914.* Westport, Conn.: Greenwood Press, 1975.

Waddell, Brian. "Economic Mobilization for World War II and the Transformation of the U.S. State." *Politics and Society* 22 (June 1994): 165–94.

Wade, Larry L., and John B. Gates. "A New Tariff Map of the United States House of Representatives." *Political Geography* 9 (July 1990): 284–304.

Wallace, Iain. *The Global Economic System.* London: Unwin Hyman, 1990.

Wallerstein, Immanuel. *The Capitalist World-Economy.* Cambridge: Cambridge University Press, 1979.

Waltz, Kenneth N. *Foreign Policy and Democratic Politics: The American and British Experience.* Boston: Little, Brown, 1967.

———. *Theory of International Politics.* New York: Random House, 1979.

———. "A Response to My Critics." In *Neorealism and Its Critics,* ed. Robert O. Keohane. New York: Columbia University Press, 1986.

Warburg, Gerald F. *Conflict and Consensus.* New York: Ballinger, 1989.

Watson, Jr., Richard L. "A Testing Time for Southern Congressional Leadership: The War Crisis of 1917–1918." *Journal of Southern History* 44 (February 1978): 3–40.

Webb, Walter Prescott. *Divided We Stand: The Crisis of a Frontierless Democracy.* New York: Farrar and Rinehart, 1937.

———. *Divided We Stand: The Crisis of a Frontierless Democracy.* Rev. ed. Austin: Acorn Press, 1944.

Weinstein, Bernard L., and Robert E. Firestine, *Regional Growth and Decline in the United States.* New York: Praeger, 1978.

Weinstein, Bernard L., Harold T. Gross, and John Rees. *Regional Growth and Decline in the United States.* 2d ed. New York: Praeger, 1985.

Wheat, Leonard F. "The Determinants of 1963–77 Regional Manufacturing Growth: Why the South and West Grow." *Journal of Regional Science* 26 (November 1986): 635–59.

White, Gerald T. *Billions for Defense: Government Financing by the Defense Plant Corporation during World War II.* University, Ala.: University of Alabama Press, 1980.

White, Richard. *"It's Your Misfortune and None of My Own": A History of the American West.* Norman: University of Oklahoma Press, 1991.

Wiebe, Robert. *The Search for Order, 1877-1920.* New York: Hill and Wang, 1967.

Wildavsky, Aaron. "The Two Presidencies." *Society* 4 (December 1966): 7-14.

Wilkins, Robert P. "Middle Western Isolationism: A Re-Examination." *North Dakota Quarterly* (summer 1957): 69-76.

Williams, R. Hal. *Years of Decision: American Politics in the 1890s.* New York: Alfred A. Knopf, 1978.

Williams, William Appleman. *The Roots of the Modern American Empire: A Study of the Growth and Shaping of Social Consciousness in a Marketplace Society.* New York: Random House, 1969.

———. "The Frontier Thesis and American Foreign Policy." *Pacific Historical Review* 24 (November 1955): 379-95.

Wilson, James Q. *Political Organization.* New York: Basic Books, 1973.

Wilson, Joan Hoff. *American Business and Foreign Policy, 1920-1933.* Lexington: University Press of Kentucky, 1971.

Winham, Gilbert R., and Ikuo Kabashima. "The Politics of U.S.-Japanese Auto Trade." In *Coping with U.S.-Japanese Economic Conflicts,* ed. I. M. Destler and Hideo Sato. Lexington, Mass.: Lexington Books, 1982.

Wirls, Daniel. *Buildup: The Politics of Defense in the Reagan Era.* Ithaca: Cornell University Press, 1992.

Wolfers, Arnold. *Discord and Collaboration: Essays on International Politics.* Baltimore: Johns Hopkins University Press, 1962.

Wolman, Paul. *Most Favored Nation: The Republican Revisionists and U.S. Tariff Policy, 1897-1912.* Chapel Hill: University of North Carolina Press, 1992.

Woodward, C. Vann. *Origins of the New South, 1877-1913.* Baton Rouge: Louisiana State University Press, 1951.

———. *The Burden of Southern History.* Baton Rouge: Louisiana State University Press, 1960.

Wright, Gavin. "The Political Economy of New Deal Spending: An Econometric Analysis." *Review of Economics and Statistics* 56 (February 1974): 30-38.

Index

*Page references to tables and figures
are set in italics.*